The Civil War Papers of Lt. Colonel
Newton T. Colby, New York Infantry

To the memory of my father,
William E Hughes, Jr.,
1911–2001

Dad, unknowingly, got me started on the project, and encouraged me to keep going to preserve this material for our family's history and for anyone else who may be interested.

The Civil War Papers of Lt. Colonel Newton T. Colby, New York Infantry

NEWTON T. COLBY

Edited by WILLIAM E. HUGHES

McFarland & Company, Inc., Publishers
Jefferson, North Carolina, and London

> The present work is a reprint of the library bound edition of The Civil War Papers of Lt. Colonel Newton T. Colby, New York Infantry, first published in 2003 by McFarland.

LIBRARY OF CONGRESS CATALOGUING-IN-PUBLICATION DATA

Colby, Newton T., 1832–1905.
　　The Civil War papers of Lt. Colonel Newton T. Colby, New York Infantry / William E. Hughes, editor.
　　　p.　　cm.
　　Includes bibliographical references and index.

　　ISBN 978-0-7864-7382-3
　　softcover : acid free paper ∞

　　1. Colby, Newton T., 1832–1905 — Correspondence　2. Colby, Newton T., 1832–1905 — Archives.　3. United States. Army. New York Infantry Regiment, 107th (1862–1865).　4. Soldiers — New York (State) — Correspondence.　5. Soldiers — New York (State) — Archives.　6. New York (State) — History — Civil War, 1861–1865 — Personal narratives.　7. New York (State) — History — Civil War, 1861–1865 — Sources.　8. United States — History — Civil War, 1861–1865 — Personal narratives.　9. United States — History — Civil War, 1861–1865 — Sources.　I. Hughes, William E., 1941-　II. Title.
E523.5107th.C65　2012
973.7'47'092 — dc21　　　　　　　　　　　　　　2003007618

BRITISH LIBRARY CATALOGUING DATA ARE AVAILABLE

© 2003 William E. Hughes. All rights reserved

No part of this book may be reproduced or transmitted in any form or by any means, electronic or mechanical, including photocopying or recording, or by any information storage and retrieval system, without permission in writing from the publisher.

On the cover: Lt. Colonel Newton T. Colby and Civil War sword (photograph courtesy of Paul Newton Colby, Jr.); background (iStockphoto/Thinkstock)

Manufactured in the United States of America

McFarland & Company, Inc., Publishers
　Box 611, Jefferson, North Carolina 28640
　　www.mcfarlandpub.com

Contents

Preface	1
1. The Development of the Militia in Corning	3
2. The 23rd New York Volunteer Regiment	17
3. The 23rd New York Regiment at Arlington Heights	39
4. Ball's Cross Roads Skirmish	54
5. Munson's Hill	67
6. Upton's Hill	79
7. Bailey's Cross Roads	100
8. The Occupation of Fredericksburg	113
9. The 107th New York Volunteer Regiment	128
10. The 107th New York Regiment at Antietam	142
11. The 107th New York Regiment at Harpers Ferry	175
12. Antietam Ford	192
13. Near Fairfax Station and On to Chancellorsville	208
14. The Chancellorsville Campaign	224
15. The Veteran Reserve Corps	241
16. Camp Morton: Prison at Indianapolis	246

17. Old Capitol and Carroll Prisons—Washington, D.C.	259
18. The Lincoln Assassination	291
19. Old Capitol Prison—After Lincoln's Death	296
20. The Postwar Years	316
21. Looking Back	330
Chapter Notes	337
Bibliography	347
Index	351

Preface

Unlike pure regimental histories, the purpose of this work is to bring together all of the available material on the military career of one man, Newton T. Colby, during the Civil War. Lt. Col. Colby was not a well known name, but he saw a lot of history being made and crossed paths with many well known figures during the war.

What I have done is to compile and edit the many letters between Newton T. Colby and his father Merrill Colby that describe for us the war atmosphere. I have also included letters that were written and published by others in newspapers where they apply, official reports and documents, as well as excerpts from other works. I do not claim to be original with much of the material; however, there is much contained herein that has not been available outside the immediate family. The Colby family is privileged to have many original letters and documents written during the mid 1800s. These letters were saved by my grandmother's sister, Sarah Tomlinson Gifford, who was the granddaughter of Newton Colby. She, fortunately for us, felt that the letters should be saved. Much is owed to her for her foresight as they provide a window into history, not just for the family, but for anyone who might read them. Thanks should also go to my father William E. Hughes, Jr., his sister Elizabeth Meyer and her daughter Ann Cavanaugh as well as cousins Paul Colby, Mary Lou Wilkins and Jamie Gifford-Modick for preserving these family treasures which I shall refer to as the Colby Collection. Since this work centers on Colby's military career, material of a personal nature has been edited from the letters.

I have done much research and added information as it has been found that sheds more light on the life and times of Lt.Col. Colby. Having lived and served in the Civil War, he was part of a particularly interesting period of American history. His letters prompted me to read about and become interested in this great conflict. His writings allow us to share his experiences as he described them for all to see just what life was like for the common soldier. The thoughts of home and loved ones, of the economy, of politics in and out of the army, prove very interesting even today. War and army life was not always military engagements and glory. Much of it was dull, day-to-day drilling and work chores; the everyday life of the average soldier was not very exciting and was often drudgery. It is my opinion that had Colby not become sick with typhoid when he did, he would have seen more action and would have been able to enlighten us even more. It is also apparent to me that in light of his rapid promotion and organizational skills, he would have risen even higher in rank.

If his words shed but a little light on history then they were worth saving for future generations of our family. I have found it intriguing to walk some of the same battlefields that Newton did and feel a sense of being there with him. Someday future generations may appreciate the collection of material that is contained herein. An honest attempt was made to give credit to all sources of information and any slight was accidental. Spelling and grammar is as it appeared in the actual letters. I have also made an attempt to be as accurate as possible; however, people who have done this type of research know that relying on other sources can sometimes be confusing. Records were not always kept in a very organized manner and are hard to find, and not everyone observes and describes things the same way. I hope that anyone who reads this work gets some enjoyment from it and learns something of times gone by.

A special word of thanks is in order for two Civil War historians that I became friends with through this work. Both Richard Buchanan and George Farr of Elimira, New York, have shared material with me and I with them. It has been a pleasure to know these two gentlemen.

Lastly, I must thank my sons Bill and Keith, and my wife Marty. They have given up many vacations to my search for information and have put up with this project for some time. Special thanks is given to my wife, Marty, for her constant support and encouragement throughout. Her help in researching, editing and proofreading has been invaluable.

CHAPTER 1

The Development of the Militia in Corning

The Colby name is quite widespread, beginning in America in 1640 when Anthony Colby moved here from England. Landing in Maine and giving birth to a long line of Colbys, all of whom seemed to have large families, the Colby name spread throughout New England and throughout the growing United States. The branch that Newton T. Colby came from moved down into New York state. The country was growing very rapidly and new towns were springing up everywhere. It was a time of expansion and many people were moving around and looking for ways to invest in land or find locations where business might prosper. The Colbys were no exception as they speculated in land in New York and the midwest and looked for good business ventures to become involved in.

Colby history also shows us that they were very involved in their communities and served in the military in numerous ways. Ephraim Colby served as a private in Captain Joshua Abbott's Company in Col. John Starks' New Hampshire Regiment during the Revolution, seeing action at Bunker Hill and Trenton.[1] Ephriam's sons, Dr. Zaccheus Colby, and Col. Eastman Colby served in the New York State Militia from 1812–15. Dr Zaccheus Colby's son Merrill Colby lived in the Rochester area and was involved in many land transactions. Merrill, Newton's father, also served in the New York State Militia as Lieutenant Colonel during the late 1820s.

Merrill Colby married Dolly Thomson on April 25, 1830. She gave birth to a son, Newton, on June 2, 1832, in Rochester, New York. About 1841, Merrill moved the family to the village of Nunda, New York, where brother Luke had a nursery business. It was here that Newton received his schooling at the Nunda Academy and met both of his future wives. Newton married Mary Chase in Nunda on November 11, 1851. In 1853, as Corning grew to a fairly large village, business opportunities called to Merrill Colby. He leased a store front and went into business there. By August 1854, Merrill had established himself in business.[2]

As the town of Corning grew, a unit of local militia was formed. The *Corning Journal* reported on August 18, 1854, that a company of light infantry had been organized and named the Washington Guards. It was later designated the National Guard, 4th Company, 60th Regiment N.Y.S.M. The officers were W.B. Hatch, captain; N.T.Colby, first lieutenant; J.S.Belknap, second lieutenant. Arms were ordered and everyone was measured for uniforms. The company expected to join the encampment at Bath on September 16, 1854.[3]

The financial condition of the country was not very good at this time and there were not many prospects for change. It was difficult to find decent employment, because wages were low and the value of real estate had gone down. It had become difficult in the south to collect for goods manufactured in the north. The feeling that war was inevitable caused much concern and deepened the depression. From 1856 to 1861, Newton Colby worked as a merchant with his father and as an agent for the Buffalo and Erie Railroad.

February 27, 1857 "The company of National Guards paraded, with Pier's Military Band in the lead. Following the parade, dinner was served at the Tremont House, kept by S.L.Hillick. There was considerable oratory."[4]

May 21, 1857 "The New York State Legislature passed, and the Governor signed a bill appropriating $14,000 for the erection of a state arsenal in the village of Corning."[5]

September 10, 1857 "Five companies of the 60th Regiment of the State Militia are in camp, for general training, on the river flats east of Knoxville. [outside of Corning] On Thursday night a military ball was held in a large tent. Colonel R.B.Van Valkenburg is in command."[6]

January 14, 1858 "The local company of National Guards has the following officers: Captain L.Todd; 1st Lieutenant, N.T.Colby; 2nd Lieutenant, F.G.Wynkoop; Orderly Sergeant, W.A.Spencer; 2nd Sergeant, William P. Miller; 3rd Sergeant, William B.Rouse; 4th Sergeant, Levi Rowley."[7]

The threat of war was evident in some parts of the country and New York State was no exception. The men of the local guards, the 60th Regiment of the State Militia, were interested in offering their services to the Federal government. Newton Colby wrote and inquired about the possibility.

Corning New York
March 24, 1858

Hon J.B.Floyd
Secy War
Sir

I take the liberty of addressing you upon the following subject. I wish to ascertain if any prescribed form is necessary on voluntiring [sic] the services of Troops to Government?

Also—What is the pay of infantry—Company officers and privates. In case of acceptance—are expenses paid by Government from starting point (or homes) and where are they furnished with arms and equipments. Does the Government advance any portion of the pay.

An answer to these queries will greatly oblige.

Very Respectfully Yours and c
N.T. Colby

P.S. Are volunteers entitled to any Bounty—under present laws?[8]

Rec. March 29, 1858

The following reply to Newton's letter was received.

Report recd April 3,1858

The Adjutant General respectfully submits the following remarks in answer to the inquiries presented in the note accompanying this communication:

1st No prescribed form is necessary in the tender of the services of volunteers to the general government.

2d The pay and allowances of a company are as follows:

per month	
Captain	$118.50
First Lieutenant	$108.50
Second Lieutenant	$103.50

First Sergeant	$ 20.00
Sergeant	$ 17.00
Corporal	$ 13.00
Musician	$ 12.00
Private	$ 11.00

The officers in command of a company is also allowed $10 per month for the responsibility of arms and c and one ration per day and clothing, or money in lieu thereof.

3d Volunteers called into the service of the U.S. under existing laws are entitled to one day's pay and allowances for every 20 miles travel from their places of residence to the place of general rendesvous. they are usually furnished with arms and equipment at the place of muster into service.

4th The government does not advance any portion of the pay of volunteers.

5th Volunteers are not entitled to any bounty under present laws.

A.G. Office S Cooper
April 3/58 Adj Genl[9]

May 18, 1860   The Republicans nominate Abraham Lincoln.[10]

November 6, 1860   Lincoln is elected president to succeed President James Buchanan.

December 20   South Carolina secedes.[11]

Dec 25, 1860   Newton's brother, Henry H Colby, marries Emma J. Barton in Corning, Steuben County, NY., by Rev. H.F. Hill.[12]

January 9   Mississippi secedes.
January 10   Florida secedes.
January 11   Alabama secedes.
January 19   Georgia secedes.
January 26   Louisiana secedes.
February 1   Texas secedes.
March 4   Lincoln is inaugurated.
March 6   The Confederacy calls for 100,000 volunteers.[13]

Newton went to Washington in search of a job with the government. It was a busy place, as many men from throughout the country had the same idea, each seeking favors of his homegrown politicians. The following letter tells of Newton's trials at job seeking.

1. The Development of the Militia

Washington D.C. Mch 29, 1861
Dear Father

After much delay and tiresome labor of running about I have set myself down to write you a line according to agreement. Such another place for office seeking the world can not produce — Everybody anxious — Enquiring urging — boring for something — and I was never more disgusted in my life — yet still I am trying all in my power — Last evening I had been promised an interview with Genl Cameron and went to his house and rung the bell — which was answered by an old wench — I asked if Cameron was in and she said "no Sir" "Come come old gal" said I "show me to his room" She stuck to the text and repeated that he was out — I threatened her (blast this pen) with her masters displeasure and said I had an appointment with him — no go — finally putting my hand in my pocket I threatened to make her rich for life if she did not show me up — and she only stuck to her story the more stoutly — I gave it up and beat an inglorious retreat — Today Cameron has left town and will not return till Monday morning and I must either wait his return or lose all I have already done — I have got the room in a boarding house which Cousin Salmon has just left — he having gone back to New York so that my expenses are $1.00 per day less then at a hotel. Bray Dickenson has the appointment of Minister to Nicaragua — having failed to get the Marshall's Office — I shall not return till Monday or Tuesday next — but what my chances are no one that I am acquainted with knows.

Tell Mary that I am trying against a fierce current to obtain a decent salary and a position for us — and a more difficult task never fell upon the subscriber and that if I am doomed to disappointment as I much fear — That I return to my home to find peaceful consolation from the kind and loving hearts of those who are faithful — unlike the miserable tricksters and wire-pullers here — who promise all you ask and perform the promises never.

I am very tired to night and heartily sick of the whole performance and wish myself at home — as instead of being refreshed by being relieved from work — I find that I am harder tasked than ever-

Well I must close — and bid you good night-
Yours affectionately
Newton[14]

As Reported in the *Corning Journal*, the war had begun:
April 12, 1861 "The Rebels have begun the war by attacking Fort

Newton T. Colby and his wife, Mary Chase Colby (standing), and her sisters, Sarah Chase Bell (left) and Elmire Chase Merrick (right).

Sumter. This overt act of treason has aroused the people of the Free States. The State Legislature [NY] has passed a bill providing for the enrollment of thirty thousand volunteers, in response to a message from the Governor. Captain L. Todd of this village, [Corning] is raising a company of volunteers." A meeting of the local National Guards was held and all that were present voted to volunteer to the governments needs. This Corning Company became only one of many that were raised and eventually sent to Elmira for training as a regiment.[15]

April 15   Lincoln calls for 75,000 volunteers.
April 18   Robert E. Lee is offered command of the Federal armies.
April 18   The Union garrison abandons Harpers Ferry.[16]

With the spirit of volunteering moving through the North, the Corning/Elmira area was no exception. From this date on, the local papers were constantly publishing articles to inform their readers as to what was needed and expected to raise an army. The following articles were typical of the day.

April 18, 1861   "Soldier's Rations.— From the proposals of the Assistant Quarter Master General, for the supplies of the troops at Elmira, we extract the following, as it will interest many to know the kind and quality of food allowed to each man. All food to be cooked, clean and of good quality, and to consist of the following as stated: For breakfast at 7 A.M. there will be furnished for each man provisions in the following quantities: 1¼ pints good coffee, 8 ounces of Wheat Bread, ⅜ lb. Beef. At 12 Noon, for dinner ⅜ lb. of beef, well cooked, with necessary potatoes; 6 ounces of wheat bread; 2 quarts of baked beans for every ten men. And every other day, in lieu of baked beans, rice, bean or vegtable soup will be furnished at the rate of one pint per man, with all the necessary salt, pepper, and vinager. At 5 P.M. for supper 6 ounces of wheat bread; 2½ pints coffee; ¼ lb. cold beef or mutton.The coffee to be supplied will be properly refined and milk in due proportions to be provided."[17]

April 19   The 6th Massachusetts Regiment, while passing through Baltimore, was attacked by a mob of secessionists. It was necessary to march a few blocks to change trains in this city. Four were killed, and many more injured. They did make it to Washington where they were quartered in the Capitol. They were the first regiment to start for Washington. As there were very few troops in the city, many feared for its safety.

April 20   Robert E. Lee resigns from the U.S. Army.[18]

From the *Corning Journal*:

April 25, 1861   "Brigadier-General R.B.VanValkenburg has been placed in charge of the rendezvous for troops at Elmira. Charles C.B. Walker has been appointed Assistant Quarter Master General, and upon him devolves the duty of making suitable provision for the volunteers who rendezvous at Elmira. Elmira became the mustering in center and training camp for New York.

"The volunteers of this village [Corning] have been drilling the past week. They are full of pluck and enthusiasm. Their officers are L.Todd, Captain; N.T.Colby, First Lieutenant; William H.Jones, Second Lieutenant. The officers are doubtless as well qualified for their positions as those of any company which will be raised in the State — and the men are hardy and resolute, and can be relied upon to do their duty. Every patriotic heart warms towards the gallant men who have so promptly offered their fortunes and lives to defend the Union, and there is general determination to 'stand by the volunteers and make all suitable provision for the families of those who peril all to defend the glourious flag of Freedom.'

"At a meeting held to make provision for providing for families of those who enlist, the following committee was appointed to solicit and dispurse funds: J.N.Hungerford, S.Hammond, A.Olcott, Alfred Jones, and E.W.Ross, to act in conjunction with the Supervisors of this Assembly District.

"A Soldiers Kit — At this time, when so many are preparing for the war, a memorandum of things necessary to take along as baggage, will not be unacceptable. An old soldier contributes the desired catalogue, as follows: 2 flannal shirts, red preferable; 2 stout hickory shirts; 2 fine shirts, if you can take them along; 4 pairs woolen socks; 2 pair drawers, white cotton or wool, indispensable; black silk neckerchief, very useful; pocket handkerchief, indispensable; 2 pair stout boots, if you can take a second pair, 2 towels, indespensible; 1 piece of soap; 1 fine and 1 coarse comb; 1 tooth brush; 1 butcher knife (a good place for this is the boot); 1 quart tin cup; 1 button stick; 1 vial of sweet oil; 1 piece of rotten stone; 1 piece chalk; 1 button brush (nail brush will do); 1 flannel housewife for and full of needles — throw in a few pins while you are at it; 1 pair small scissors; strong white and black thread in tidy skeins; 1 blacking brush, if you can take it; 1 box blacking. Learn to pack your knapsack tidily, closely and conveniently for use. To the above you may add all the grub you can stow away inside and out, and replenish when you can, without waiting for the stock on hand to be exhausted."[19]

The Military Depot at Elmira-
The Regulations
Head Quarters, Elmira Depot
N. Y. Volunteers, April 26,1861

The following orders are promulgated for the government of the Depot.

1. Captain _____ is assigned to the command of the barracks and will make his Head Quarters therein.

2. He will daily designate an officer of the day, as Adjutant of the day and an Officer of the Police Guard.

3. At or before 9 o'clock of each day, the officer in command of the barracks will cause the morning reports of the commandants of companies to be consolidated and returned under his hand, to these Head Quarters; such report may also be required at any other time.

4. The Inspecting Surgeon will each morning before 9 o'clock, make a thorough inspection of the barracks and report the condition thereof to these Head Quarters at 10 o'clock. He will look well to the hygiene of the men and make such suggestions in regard to health, cleanliness and comfort, as he deems proper.

5. The utmost attention will be paid by commanders of the companies, to the cleanliness of the men, as to their persons, clothing, arm, accoutrements and equipments, and also to their quarters.

6. Reveille at 6 o'clock A.M. when companies will fall in for roll call, without arms, under the First Sergeants, superintended by a company officer.

7. Immediately after reveille roll call, the barracks will be cleaned up. The bed ticks and clothing carefully put away.

8. Surgeon's Call will be beat at 5:30 A.M., when sick will be conducted to the Hospital by First Sergeants of companies, who will, at the same time, report to the Surgeon all the sick in the company, other than in the hospital. The patients who cannot attend dispensary, will be immediately after, if not before, visited by the Surgeon.

9. The Surgeon's morning report will be handed in to these quarters before 9 o'clock A.M. of each day.

10. The morning report of companies signed by the Captain and First Sergeants will be handed to the Adjutant at the barracks, before 8 o'clock A.M. of each day.

11. "Peas upon a trencher," the signal for breakfast is to sound or beat at 7 o'clock, A.M.

12. At 8:30 A.M., the "Troop" will sound or beat, for the purpose of assembling the men for duty and inspection at Guard Mounting.

13. Guard Mounting will take place daily at 9 o'clock A.M

14. From immediately after Guard Mounting until 12 o'clock, the commandants of companies will drill their troops by squads or companies as the commanding officer of the barracks may direct.

15. Roast Beef—The signal for dinner will sound or beat at 12 o'clock noon, when there will be a roll call of companies, by First Sergeants.

16. At 1:30 P.M., there will company drill, under direction of company officers, which will continue by squads or companies at the option of the commanding officer of the barracks, until 4 P.M.

17. At 5 P.M., supper.

18. At 6 P.M., Retreat with beat, at which time there will be a dress

parade, after which roll call by First Sergeants, superintended by a company officer.

19. Tattoo will beat at 9:30 P.M., when there will be a roll call of companies by First Sergeant, superintended by a company officer. No soldier will be out of barracks at this hour, unless on duty or by special leave.

20. At 10 o'clock P.M., three taps will beat on a drum, when all lights will be extinguished except in officers' quarters.

21. The Police Guard at present will consist of one Sergeant, two Corporals, one drummer and men enough to furnish the required sentinels and patrols, not exceeding 24.

22. Sentinels will carry their arms habitually at support, or on either shoulder, but never will quit them. In wet weather they will secure arms. No sentinel will quit his post or hold conversation not necessary to the proper discharge of his duty.

23. Arms will not be loaded by sentinels or others without special order of the commanding officer of the barracks.

24. All guards not immediately on duty will be in line at parades and company drills.

25. The commanding officer of the barracks, or the officer of the day, will immediately after "Guard Mounting," and before the old guard is dismissed, read and explain to them the duties of guards and sentinels; and will, as often as convenient, read and explain to the officers and men their duties and responsibilities.

26. The officer of the day will make frequent visits to the sentinels on duty, to see that they are properly instructed in their duties.

By order of
R.B. VanValkenburgh, Brig. General, Commanding Elmira Depot.
Wm. Rumsey, Aid de Camp.[20]

"It was expected that the defensive attitude of the U.S. Government would soon give away to aggressive movements which will speedily crush out rebellion. President Lincoln's request for 75,000 troops was at first thought to be sufficient to crush the uprising. He, in accordance with the law in regard to such cases, gave twenty days time for all persons combined to resist the laws, to disperse and retire peaceably to their homes. No one felt that this problem would last very long."[21]

May 2, 1861 "Captain Elliot, U.S.A., was here [Corning] yesterday, and inspected the Volunteers. They will leave for the Elmira Rendezvous sometime next week." [22]

May 2, 1861 Contract for feeding the troops: "The contract for rations was awarded to Wm T Post and H H Purdy, at forty-two cents per day. Contract for knives 3½ cts each; forks do; cups 10 cts each; plates 9 cts each; spoons 2½ cts each, bed ticks 75 cts each, to Watrous & Cook. Contract for blankets not yet let."[23]

May 3, 1861 Lincoln calls for 42,034 three-year volunteers and enlarges the army and navy.

May 6, 1861 Arkansas secedes from the Union.

May 7, 1861 Tennessee forms an alliance with the Confederacy.[24]

May 9, 1861 "Volunteer Fund — The Committee to raise funds for the families of the Volunteers are receiving liberal subscriptions. The signers pledge themselves to pay a certain amount, per month, for two years if necessary."[25]

"Captain Todd's Volunteer Company has been ordered to go into quarters to-morrow in this village, [Elmira] and will probably remain until ordered to proceed to the seat of war. Maj. A. Field has contracted to supply them with food while here and they will lodge in the Arsenal. The Major will furnish a table that we doubt not will be as well supplied as those at any rendezvous in the state."[26]

From the *Elmira Press* as printed in the *Corning Journal*: "There are now at least four thousand strangers in town, most of them soldiers. Forty-nine companies are quartered at the various Barracks, while many more are impatiently waiting for the construction of Barracks for their accommodation —"[27]

May 10, 1861 The Company, under Captain Todd, enter temporary quarters at the State Armory.[28]

May 12 Troops restore full Federal control in Baltimore.[29]

"A Testament and a sewing set with needles, pins, thread, etc., have been presented to each local volunteer by the ladies of the village."[30]

"Southern Tier Regiment — The following Companies have been organized as a Regiment under the above title, but it has been designated as No. 23, by the order of the State Military Board.

Southern Tier Regiment	H.C. Hoffman Colonel
Capt Loyden	Cuba
Capt Schick	Bath
Capt Todd	Corning
Capt Doty	Hornellsville
Capt Fowler	Elmira
Capt Dingledy	Elmira

Capt Powers	Waverly
Capt Barstow	Oswego
Capt Clark	Cortland
Capt Chapman	Watkins

"This regiment will we fully believe earn honorable distinction in the field; and will bear with it the best wishes of the people in the localities which furnish the Companies composing it. It is gratifying that the Regiment is made up of Companies raised in this vicinity. There will naturally be much more regard for the sick or wounded, and the band of friendship already existing, most become stronger as common dangers and suffering tend to bring them closer fellowship. The Officers are men highly competent to discharge their duties, and justify possess the confidence of the privates in their military skill and daring. Where they lead the Regiment will follow courageously, and doubtless perform deeds of valor which shall be hereafter treasured as we now linger over the recorded deeds of patriots of former days, whose heroism aided in securing the blessings of Liberty to the Land. The Field Officers are as follows, H.C. Hoffman, Colonel, (late Capt. of the Southern Tier Rifles, Elmira) N.M. Crane, of Hornellsville, Lieut. Colonel and W.H. Gregg, of Elmira, Major.

"Col. Hoffman has made the following appointments Adjutant — William W. Hayt, Albany, (late of Corning) Quarter Master, M.H. Manderville, Geneva; Chaplain, Rev. E.F.Crane, Elmira; Surgeon, Dr. Churchill, Oswego; Surgeon's Mate, Dr. Wm. X. Madill, Elmira; Sergeant Major, Lathrop Baldwin, Elmira.

"The office of Pay Master, Quarter Master's Sergeant, Drum Major, Fife Major, and Principal Musician, are yet to be appointed."[31]

Corning Volunteers No. 1

"On Monday afternoon, the Corning Volunteer Co. No. 1, commanded by Capt. Todd, left for the Elmira Recruiting Center to remain until ordered into active service. This may be within a few days or not for some time, yet the company, as such, has departed to return only when commanded. Previous to leaving this village, the Company marched through several of the principal streets, escorted by the entire Fire Department of Corning, and were accompanied to Elmira by Alliance Hook & Ladder Co., Alfred Jones, Foreman, and by Hose Co. No.1, John Wilson, Foreman, and by quite a number of prominent citizens. The occasion was one which can never be forgotten. Those in advanced age recalled the days of 1812, when our country was threatened by an invading force, and the people rallied to arms under the eye and inspiring words of Revolutionary heros. Now those heros sleep in honored graves, but their virtues have been transmitted to their descendants, and will shine with equal lustre in the deeds yet to be performed in the preservation of the blessings of Freedom, purchased at such a tearful cost. The 'sword of Bunker Hill' gleams with unwonted brightness. The glittering regiment flashes the fire of Liberty. The music of the drum and the rumble in city and village of the earth beginning to tremble under the heavy tread of armed men, the clash of arms and the roar of artillery have already echoed among the hills and even now may be gathering volume in the mountains of Virginia. It was a sad day for the village when its first gallant volunteers left home and all that was dear in obedience to the call of their country. It will undoubtedly be a sad day when the Company again returns. The casualties of the camp and field, the hardships that rack the frame and make disease a frequent visitor, the exposures and scanty supplies of food and clothing that render the pestilential air of the malarious regions deadly effective, the "leaden rain and iron hail" of the battle field, sweeping like a tempest, companies, regiments, and battalions into heaps of undistinguishable dead, these are the dangers that must cross the path of the gallant volunteers, before they can hope to return to their homes. A merciful Providence may graciously preserve most of them from the dangers incident to their service. It would be a miracle if all were to return unharmed, and then who shall greet them as they arrive, hushed in victory, rejoicing in their safety, or broken in health and bearing the scars, men in honorable strife or perhaps crippled and maimed in the conflict, will not be the same sympathizing crowd that on Monday backed the efforts. Death may pass by the darling soldier around whose head whistles a hundred bullets to strike with fatal dart the loved ones quietly reposing in the endeared home of peace.

"As the train bore the patriotic Volunteers eastward another train started westward bearing a coffin in which rested a beautiful lady, dead to all the tumult and sadness around her. Consumption had thus early cut short her life, and mourning friends, a sister and mother, were bearing her to rest near the home of her childhood. We were reminded of the words of the prophet, which for nearly three thousand years have echoed in the hearts of the descendants. 'Weep ye not for the dead, neither bemoan him, but weep more for him who goeth away, for he shall return no more nor see his native country.'

"Around us were scores of friends of early and later years, friends who at the call of duty had rallied to defend their country and now obedient to orders, prepared to march forth to death or victory. The dark uncertain future never seemed darker to many than when the hand of a brother, husband, son or friend was grasped and the silent tears flowed. Patriotism rendered the sacrifice easy and none were heard to murmur at the stern call of duty. Those who thus laid themselves upon the alter of their country went forth as did the patriots of the other time...."[31]

CHAPTER 2

The 23rd New York Volunteer Regiment

Washington Pickett Duty

"The Twenty-Third N.Y. Regiment called the 'Southern Tier Rifles' began to be formed during April at Elmira, New York. The men were crowded into halls and churches and had many hardships. They drilled in the streets and fields until their feet were sore. There were sword and flag presentations, along with many speeches. Finally organized, they moved to the barracks at Elmira. There they drilled in battalions with dress parades and many spectators."[1]

While the 23rd regiment was being trained at Elmira, many other troops were arriving in and around Washington. After sufficient troops were in place around Washington it was time to move into Virginia. President Lincoln had decided to have the troops seize the heights from Arlington south to Alexandria. "The Confederate flag flying from a staff at Alexandria had been a constant eyesore to him. Again and again he was seen standing with a gloomy face before one of the south windows of the White House looking through a glass at this flag."[2]

"On May 24, 1861, 10,000 Federal troops entered Alexanderia, Virginia to put and end to the demonstrations in favor of Virginia's secession that were disturbing authorities in Washington. Colonel Elmer Ellsworth, a good friend and former law partner of Abraham Lincolns back in Springfield, was shot and killed at the Marshall House in Alexandria, Va. after hauling down a Confederate flag."[3]

"Ellsworth, a native of Saratoga, N.Y., had won fame before the Civil

War as the founder of the National Guard Cadets, later renamed the U.S. Zouave Cadets of Chicago, an organization that he patterned after France's colonial troops, down to the baggy pants, sashes, short jackets and fezzes worn by French Zouaves in Algeria. The Zouave Cadets toured the East the summer before the war, performing crack drill maneuvers before rapt audiences from New York City to Washington. Their complete drill took four and a half hours and comprised more than 500 movements and figures. When the war began, Ellsworth traveled to New York to raise a regiment of Union volunteers. Recruiting heavily among the city's fire departments, he clothed the volunteers in his favored exotic regalia and dubbed the colorful regiment the 1st New York Fire Zouaves in honor of their origin."[4] The Regiment consisted of about 1,100 firemen.

"Upon entering Virginia and seeing a Confederate flag atop the Marshall House, Col. Ellsworth set out to take it down. He and several men entered the building where he and a lieutenant went to the roof of the three story house and Col. Ellsworth tore it down. On his way out of the building a man shot Ellsworth on the second floor with a shot gun. Lincoln cried when he heard of his death and ordered a White House funeral in the East Room that was attended by generals and diplomats. A description of the funeral was written later by Clara Barton."[5]

"Early in the war, just after Col. Ellsworth had been killed, President Lincoln was beset with all kinds of problems. Not the least of which was that of men seeking favor with positions in the government that swarmed about the White House. 'The grounds, halls, stairways, closets, are filled with applicants, who render ingress and egress difficult,' wrote Secretary Seward. The President and his staff were beseiged by those who wanted only to see the President for five minutes and Republican politicians pulled 'wires' for offices or positions."[6]

Finally the time came for the 23rd Regiment to move on towards Washington where troops were gathering from everywhere. They boarded a train for the slow journey south, stopping at Williamsport and Sunbury, Pennsylvania, where they were greeted, cheered and refreshed by the locals.

"The 23rd Regiment Infantry—(Southern Tier Regiment) was formally organized at Elmira, N.Y., May 10, 1861 and mustered in July 2, 1861. There was a grand Fourth of July parade followed by many speeches. The regiment left the state for Washington, D.C. on July 5, and on July 9th the Regiment was located at 'Camp Diven' Washington, D.C. attached to Hunter's, then Sedgwick's, then Keye's Brigade, Division of the Potomac to October, 1861. From Oct 15, 1861 in Wadsworth's Brigade, McDowell's Division, Army of the Potomac; from March 13, 1862 in 2d, Patrick's Brigade, 3rd Kings's Division, 1st Corp, Army of the Potomac."[7]

2. The 23rd New York Volunteer Regiment 19

Newton T. Colby first enrolled May 6, 1861, in Co. D, 23d Regt NY Vols for a period of two years at Corning. Co. D was principally recruited at Corning. He mustered in as first lieutenant May 16, 1861, but only served until May 15, 1862, with this regiment. He was commissioned first lieutenant, July 4, 1861, with rank from May 6, 1861.[8]

Head Quarters Co. D 23 Regt
Elmira June 23, 1861

My Darling

Since I left home I have not heard from you and was beginning to believe that you had made up your mind not to write — This morning I have just come off gaurd duty — having been on all yesterday and last night — so I am feeling rather stupid — but I wished to write to you and I am at it. Well we were duly mustered into the U.S. service — yesterday — and may be called away before long and think we had better get ready to go to Nunda this week say on Saturday and I send you by the bearer ten dollars — We were paid for ten days service $36.00 which is all the money I have and must pay my board bill out of that — so you see how short I am. The first of July however we are to have more and I will send you enough for your wants.

Dear little wife if I yearn so to see you after we leave here — I hardly know what I shall do — You little dream (I guess) how much I wish to see you to day I love you as I shall or can never love woman again — and there is no power in mortal hands which shall lead me ever to be false to you — Dearest can you too say this? I believe I obey the call of duty when I go as I do and I mean faithfully and honorably to discharge it — and may God help me to keep from vice of any kind — and if his will to protect my safe return to you.

Use the money I send in getting the children and yourself such things as are needful — I only wish it was tripled in amount. Tell Father to be sure and fix my trunk and have the wood put in the shed. Tell him to get a canvass cover for the trunk.

Now good bye dear wife till we meet
Yours ever Newton[9]

From the *Corning Journal*:
"The departure of the Southern Tier, or 23rd Regiment of N.Y. State Volunteers will long be remembered by the immense crowd assembled at

Elmira, to bid farewell to the gallant Volunteers. This Regiment is composed of Companies from contiguous Counties in this section, and comprises as resolute, hardy and well disciplined men as any which has left the Elmira rendevous. The volunteers left in the best of spirits, and the prayers and blessings of the thousands to whom they were endeared by the ties of kindred or friendship, accompany them to the seat of war. The regiment left Elmira at 11 A.M., Friday, and reached Williamsport before three o'clock where a bountiful dinner was provided by the patriotic ladies of that village. After the soldiers had done justice to the tables, the Ladies insisted upon filling their knapsacks with enough food to serve as rations for three days. All honor to the noble ladies of Williamsport, who have thus fed, gratuitously, seven Regiments from this state, passing through that village."[10]

"About ten miles out of Baltimore they stopped and were told by Colonel Hoffman to 'load at will.' They all wondered if they would experience the same fate as did the Massachusetts troops, who had to get off the train and march several blocks to get on another train. The troops had to get off the train and march several blocks to get on another. They drew up in line before that great town, fixed bayonets and loaded their guns and they passed through Baltimore without incident except for vocal harassment."[11]

"During a rainy, stormy night they stopped over at Annapolis Junction. In the morning they observed many troops moving towards Hagerstown and Harper's Ferry."[12]

"While the troops were waiting there, a party of four strayed away from the cars, and at a distance of about a mile from the Junction encountered an old farmer standing on the veranda of a farm house. Some fine black cherries near the house were very tempting, and one of the party quite civily called out:

'Hilloo, stranger! will you sell us some of those cherries?'

'No!' snarled the old man addressed as 'stranger.'

'Will you then give us a few to eat?' asked the soldier.

'No! I've no cherries for Union soldiers,' he replied.

"The four men then consulted. This sounded like secesh. They had volunteered to fight that species of animal, and now that they had found him should they back down, and like cowards go back without the cherries? That would never do. This philosophy prevailed, and placing a rail against the tree, the most daring of the party made ready to climb. The son of the farmer now came out, gun in hand, and cried out:

'Climb that tree, sir, and you're a dead man!'

"Turning to his comrades, the foremost said: 'See to your revolvers!'

"Then, addressing the son, he added: 'You have refused us the small gift of a few cherries simply because we are Union soldiers. From this we conclude that you are a d — d rampant secesh, and were you not a coward you would now be in the rebel army. So we know that you dare not harm us. And should you attempt to shoot me (pointing to his comrades), you have seen your last sunrise. So, then if my life is worth more to you than your own, shoot me.'

"Saying this, he vaulted into the tree, and the boys loading themselves with cherries, returned. The story soon got wind, and before the train left, not a cherry remained to the old fellow who would not give a cherry to Union soldiers."[13]

From the *Corning Journal*:
"The 23rd reached Washington safely on Saturday evening, where it will probably occupy the entrenchments of some Regiment ordered to advance. After a brief period devoted to drill, it will, doubtless, be led into active service, and give a glorious account of itself."[14]

They actually arrived in Washington sometime after midnight on Sunday, July 7, 1861. The rain had stopped and it was very warm and steamy. Troops had been gathering in the city for about two weeks and the accommodations were not much.

"The Twenty-Third then moved about two miles north of the city and set up camp at Meridian Hill. The weather was oppressive during the day but it was made easier by the good supply of cool water from a cold spring and brook at the camp. The regiment now learned all about camp life; how to spread their blanket on the ground; to cook salt junk, beans, coffee; wash dirty clothes; and to complain about everything.

"Guard duty was very important as they expected an attack at any moment. This seemed to be true of all 'new' regiments."[15]

Head Quarters "Camp Diven"
Washington D.C. July 9, 1861
Dear Father —

Although I promised to write as soon as I arrived I have been so busy and so tired and so hot and so up side down — that I could hardly find time till now — We had a long tedious ride from Elmira and was delayed on the R.R. from Baltimore to Washington by the passage of troops that were moving from Washington to Harpers ferry to reinforce Genl Patterson — so that we did not arrive in Washington till saturday night at midnight (about 2 oclock) — We were quartered by companies in buildings on

Louisiana Avenue—and on Monday morning left for our camp about 2 miles out of the City on Meridan Heights—We were not troubled in Baltimore—but for 50 miles before we reached there we were reminded that we were approaching the enemys country by seeing the R.R. track and bridges held by picket guards—At Annapolis junction we were delayed as I said above—by the passage of troops and we found encamped and visited a part of the Massachuets 6th—You will recollect they were attacked by the mob in Baltimore—They are noble fellows—hospitable and kind—We had a dress parade on ~~Washington~~ Pennsylvania Avenue and the crowd who were looking on applauded it by clapping hands very handsomely—We have got a good location for our camp the ground being high and dry with plenty of shade and good spring water handy—I have been quite well since leaving Elmira up to this time—I see that the N.Y. daily papers say that our Regiment is ordered into Virginia—but up to this time it is not so—Undoubtedly we shall be though before long—though no one can tell with certainty.

Yesterday (sunday) Capt Todd—Ensign Jones and myself went up to the White House and I prevailed upon the old janitor to admit us—While in the House his Excellency the President drove up to the front door and alighted and came in—We stood in the anti room and when he entered we saluted him by raising our caps—and in return he bowed and touched his hat!! Dont ever speak to me again! We have been envied by all the officers in the Regt—

This after noon the Regt to which the Nunda Company belongs came in from Elmira—and I saw and talked with the officers—To night I am to attend the Presidents Levee and will talk to him —"Who wouldn't be a soldier" I have not got a cent and feel the need of money badly—but expect to get our pay in a few days—You have no idea of the number of troops in and about the City—Their camps are on every side—I slept under a tent last eve on the ground—upon a rubber blanket and never woke up once during the night—and never enjoyed a mattress better-

The 3rd Maine Regt were encamped within a short distance of us when I retired to sleep and when I woke in the morning they were gone to Virginia—having received orders and departed at 2 o clock in the night!!

We have just had a fine shower and it is cool and comfortable—We have made no arrangements yet about feeding and I just buy a loaf of bread and a pint of milk and live on bread and milk—being both cheap and wholesome—The weather here is said to have been very hot for this place for the past few days—but it does not seem to be any warmer than it is in Corning—Tell mother for me that I feel under great obligation for all the love and kindness she has always shown me and I will try and show her if

I live how much I appreciate it and will at least never forget — and you too dear father — have been more kind than I ever deserved — May God bless you both — Tell Henry — my only brother — to remember that I have always thought more of him than was always apparant and if I return I shall be happy to meet him prosperous and happy and respected — But I am rather "going it" for you all knew this before.

Not having a pen and ink handy I have written this with pencil — I send you a Washington Paper — announcing our arrival — I wrote to Mary yesterday and once while at Corning the last time — but have not heard a word from her — Please say to her to write immediately as I wish to hear from her very much. Direct to me — 23 Regt NY Vol — care Col Hoffman.

I will write to Mary again tomorrow and to you in a day or two — Genl Van Valkenburg and A S Diven franked and gave me 50 envelopes so I save the postage — Please write soon —

Give my best respects to Mr Austin and all enquiring friends —
Tell Henry and Mother to write
Affectionately Yours Newton[16]

"Franking of letters by Congressmen was one of the perquisites of the boys, and there are cases of their going to the President with letters to be franked when they failed to find, or were refused by, their Congressman. One noticeable feature of Mr. Lincoln's life, at this time, was his relation to the common soldier. Officers he respected, even deferred to, but from the first arrival of troops in Washington it was the man on foot, with a gun on his shoulder, that had Mr. Lincoln's heart. Even at this early period the men found it out, and went to him confidently for favors refused elsewhere."[17]

Gen. VanValkenburgh and Col A.S. Diven were both members of Congress and thus had the franking rights.

For the *Corning Journal* from a member of the 23rd:

Camp Diven, Meridan Heights,
Washington, D.C., July 12th, 1861.
Friend Pratt:

Not knowing whether you have a regular correspondent from the seat of War or not and feeling that we could make no better return for the many kindnesses received as soldiers, at the hands of Corning friends, I have concluded to address to you a few lines, giving such account of our whereabouts and occupations as a feeble pen will furnish. Omitting any mention of our pleasant departure from Elmira, with which you are perfectly familiar, I shall simply describe what proved to be a very pleasant journey: Arriving at Williamsport at about three o'clock, P.M., we halted, and forming line, paraded the principal streets of that beautiful village; after which we partook of a bountiful collation; provided by the ladies of the place; which refreshed the inner man, while approving smiles and sympathizing words cheered our hearts.

After a rest of a couple hours, we jumped aboard, and with our train of 21 long cars started on our journey down the beautiful valley of the West Branch, noting our passage southward by the advanced state of vegetation.

On every hand, from cottage and field, we received the welcome cheer. At every stoppage, the depots were crowded with cheering friends, anxious to express their own love for the Union, by manifesting their interest in us. And this has been the experience of all those who have preceded us. One can hardly realize the depth and earnestness of the Union feeling of the country, until he dons the soldier coat and marches towards the battle field.

We passed many pleasant villages and much fine scenery. Keeping the direct route, by the Northern Central Railway, we passed opposite Harrisburg about mid-night, and entered Maryland soon after sun-rise. From this point the Railroads are guarded, and here we first find the soldier on duty. The sight of the little army tents at distances of perhaps 60 rods, and the soldiers engaged in preparing breakfast, washing clothes, and other duties of camp life, elicited repeated and hearty cheers from our boys—they had met their brothers.—I think it was Pennsylvania 12th stationed there. Before we came to the relay house we halted, and getting out of the cars, loaded our guns, so as to be ready for any emergency which might occur at Baltimore. We reached that place at about 10 o'clock Saturday morning, when we formed regiment line and in presence of a few spectators, primed our muskets; then forming close column in mass with music playing at the head of the columns we marched through streets crowded with every size, age, and I had almost said color—certain it is that the colored element predominated.—From open windows the ladies greeted us, and on every side the national Flag was waved.—Thanks to Gen's Butler and Banks, Baltimore seems now to be a safe high-way, even for Northern soldiery. The appearance and conduct of the Regiment was very creditable, eliciting many compliments from the citizens, and the Baltimore Press (a seccession sheet) gives us great praise for neatness and soldierly bearing, ranking us next to the New York Seventh among the Regiments that had passed through the city—forgive the egotism, soldiers are properly vain. Taking cars again at the Baltimore and Ohio Railroad depot, we arrived at one o'clock, P.M., at Annapolis Junction, half way between Baltimore and Washington, where we were detained eight mortal long hours, by trains bearing troops from Washington to Harper's Ferry, some three regiments. Here we found an encampment of parts of two regiments, one of which being the immortal Massachusetts 6th, with whom we had a pleasant chat, learning a little of camp life, and something of what we are to expect. At nine o'clock in the evening we started onward, and were soon in Washington, having completed the trip without accident, or any unpleasant incident. About midnight, we arrived at temporary barracks, and were provided with supper, some at the Assembly rooms in Louisiana Avenue and some at a neighboring church. Sunday we were allowed to roam at will, through the city, and the boys took the opportunity to look at the Capitol, White House, and other places of interest, some of them took a bath in the broad Potomac, that Rubicon (to the Rebels) which we are so anxious to pass.

In the evening we gave our usual dress parade in the presence of many citizens, and we think it was quite a success, since we received many cheers and encomiums, but I will not thrust them upon you, as you may see them yourself, in the city papers. Monday morning, at an early hour, we formed line and marched through Pennsylvania Avenue, passing many of the public buildings. A march four and a half miles northward, brought us to the place of encampment-a large open field, skirted by woods, and applied with abundance of water. After a rest of an hour or so, we turned to and pitched our tents, and our village was ready for use. The boys take kindly to camp life, and submit cheerfully to the evils incident thereto. Cooking and washing are new occupations for many, but they prove ready scholars. As a general rule, we enjoy good health, though the change of climate and the free indulgence in cold water cause slight sickness which a few days will remedy. The camp is very orderly—no drunkeness or quarreling—in fact, harmony has ever been the distinguishing trait of the Southern Tier Regiment. Our Corning boys are quite well, only one or two cases of measles; and our officers, the same we had when we left, are the pride of the company. We mean to render a good account of ourselves, when the chance offers. There are many rumors of marching orders every day, and they cannot be long delayed—but whither, we know not, and care not. Washington is full of troops—on every hill side the white tents of the soldier glisten in the sun. The other Corning company arrived yesterday. You will hear from some of us from time to time, as anything of interest occurs.

Respectfully Yours,
C.K.[18] [thought to be Cyrus Kellog, Co.D. appointed Sgt. August 1, 1862, 2nd Lt. May 15, 1862]

Historian Bell I. Wiley, writing in the photo-history *The Image of War: Shadows of the Storm*, described the typical routine of infantry regiments this way:

> The following is the typical routine of infantry regiments during quiet periods.
> Recruits had to learn to adjust to the regimented routine of army life. Their day was directed by bugle or drum from sun up to lights out at night. First came reveille, sounded about dawn, to wake the soldiers and summon them to roll call. After lining up and responding to their names, they were dismissed until a second call a half-hour later called them to breakfast. The third call sent the ailing to the regimental surgeon and the well to duties such as cleaning quarters, tidying company grounds, and cutting wood. At about 8 o'clock the first sergeant of each company turned out his guard detail for the next twenty-four hours' duty, inspected them, and marched them to the regimental parade ground. The guards were formed into line, inspected by the adjutant, and sent to their posts. Details were so ranged that each member stood guard only two hours out of every six.
> Next came the call for drill until lunch which was followed by a brief post-luncheon period of relaxation. They were then called to another drill that normally lasted one or two hours. The men then returned to their quarters, brushed their uniforms, blacked their leather, polished buckles and buttons, and cleaned their weapons in preparation for retreat, which consisted of roll call, inspection, and dress parade. Dress parades were the occasion for reading orders and making official announcements.
> Supper call came shortly after retreat, followed not long after dark by tattoo, which brought another roll call, after which the men returned to their quarters. The final call of the day required the cessation of noise and the extinguishing of lights.
> The Sunday routine differed from that of the other days. The major event of the Sabbath was a general inspection of quarters, grounds, personnal, and equipment. The inspector, usually the brigade commander or one of his staff, carefully observed clothing, weapons, and other equipment. The usual outfit of a Federal infantry was a long woolen dress coat of dark blue with a high stiff collar; a dark blue jacket or blouse which for field service was much preferred to the dress coat; light blue trousers; black brogan shoes; a flannel shirt; long flannel drawers; socks; blue cap with a black visor; and a long blue overcoat with a cape.
> The soldiers were then required to stack arms, unsling their knapsacks, and lay them on the ground for inspection. The inspector checked the contents of the knapsack, and if he found a dirty garment he rebuked the offender. The soldier's prescribed equipment included a haversack for his food, a canteen, a knapsack for extra items of clothing, stationery, toilet

2. The 23rd New York Volunteer Regiment 27

articles, and other personal items, a leather cartridge box, and a small leather pouch for percussion caps. He concluded the inspection shortly before noon by going through the company quarters.

For comfort and convenience they often shed some of their equipment. Knapsacks were frequently discarded and the contents rolled in a blanket which the soldier threw over his left shoulder and tied at the ends above his right hip. Many carried small skillets and tin cups hung off of their belts.

Soldiers usually spent Sunday afternoons writing letters, playing games, reading, or gambling. Those of religious inclination might attend prayer meetings or listen to sermons delivered by the regimental chaplain.

Every other month soldiers were mustered for pay. Standing in company formation, each soldier certified his presence by responding "here" when his name was called. After the mustering officer had accounted for every man listed on the roster, he forwarded a copy of the muster roll to the adjutant general in Washington.[19]

"The Regimental Colors, procured by the generous contributions of the citizens of Elmira for the gallant Southern Tiers, arrived in the town yesterday morning. [July 17] We had the pleasure of examining them, and pronounce them to be elegant. They are made in all respects by the regulation standard. The Regimental Banner has upon one side the National and upon the reverse the State Coat of Arms, and the words 'Twenty-third Regiment New York Volunteers.' These words are also upon the National Emblem, the Stars and Stripes. A neat golden scroll upon the staff of each banner contains the following: 'Presented by the citizens of Elmira to the 23rd Regiment N.Y.S.V., Col. Hoffman commanding.'

"The colors were taken to Washington last evening by Geo. M. Diven, Esq., and will be presented to the Regiment on Saturday (tomorrow) afternoon, on which occasion Hon. A.S. Diven is expected to make the address."[20]

"President Lincoln and his Cabinet officers drove daily to camps. Very often his outing for the day was attending some ceremony incident to camp life: a military funeral, a camp wedding, a review, a flag-raising. He did not often make speeches."[21]

July 18, 1861
Dear Father

I am most welcome and kind letter came to hand last evening and I intend to reply altho I have no special news to tell. We are still situated on Meridian Hill which we first encamped and we are in some respects favorably located. We have our drills early in the morning and late in the afternoon — thusly avoiding the excessive heat of the noon day — My health is pretty good with a little touch of bowel complaint which is rather annoying — Nothing serious however. Up to this time I have not failed to appear always at parade and at drills and to perform my whole duty. The weather is pleasant with showers rather frequently which cools the air and makes it more pleasant — Yesterday we had a big day being received by his Excellence the President of the U.S. and also having stand of Colors presented through Hon A.S. Diven by the ladies of Elmira — The President and Secretary Seward were on the ground in the Presidents open carriage and soon after came Diven in another carriage with the Colors — Diven made a speech and presented the Color and then we marched in review before the old Abe — Saluting him with our swords as we passed — After passing before him twice — once at common time and once at quick time — we formed line and he passed slowly down the front on foot and once again in the carriage — He was dressed in a plain gray suit and looked common enough — Secretary Seward who followed him — bobbed about "like a Duck in a gale of wind" in trying to keep up and keep step with Old Abes long slim legs. Old Abraham strode along paying no attention to Seward and seemed to care little whether he kept up or stayed behind. I have attended two levees at the White House and been presented and shook the presidential digits on both occasions.

The last time Genl. Scott was there and as soon as people were appraised of it (+ it was rapidly buzzed about) You ought to have seen how quick every one started to get a sight at the old Hero — Such was the rush that he could get no farther than the secondary hall (you pass across two halls and entrance rooms) and the other rooms were almost entirely deserted — Even the President being No 2 in the list of big folks — He wore his uniform with big Epauleths and no small amount of gold embroidery on it — Gov. Sprague of Rhode Island and the Presidents wife prominaded the Parlor or East Room — Sprague is a very small sized fellow and wears glasses and does not look over and above smart — Secretary Chase (of the Treasury) Genl. John A Dix and lots of great folks were there. Not much ceremony was observed — Every one walking about and talking freely.

The other day I took my autograph book and started on a trip to get the signatures of big men — I got the name of every Senator and all the notable members of the house and when coming home I met Genl. John A Dix on the street and asked for and obtained his name! I shall get Old Abe's — Genl. Scott's and the Vice Presidents yet — as well as the cabinet ministers — I went over to Virginia the other day and visited Alexandria where Col. Ellsworth was shot. The house is still standing and a guard is placed there — I went in and stood where the gallant Zouave fell. The floor and staircase have been entirely cut and hacked by the curious who all get pieces to send away — The bed tick on which his body was laid (it was a hair mattress) lies on the floor (or rather the small remnant of it) and the hair of the bed scattered all over the floor — The stairway being down I had to climb up a slanting board to get up to the flag staff-from which once flowed the secession flag which cost Ellsworth's life — but which now bears the stars and stripes. I climbed up the flag staff and with my knife worked off a piece — part of which I enclose — together with a piece of the bed tick above mentioned as curiosities. The house was an old one and is now about used up. Alexandria has suffered the entire loss of trade and everything is at a stand still — I stepped into a Drug store — enquired for a paper of Tobacco — but the proprietor informed me that he had none and could get none as the federal troops were using all the transportation routes and they would not carry his goods. The place had about 12000 inhabitants but there are now only about 3 or 4000. It is pleasantly situated on the Virginia side of the Potomac about 9 miles below Washington — The fare is ten cents each way — from Washington-We are in daily expectation of orders to move into Virginia and shall do so doubtless within a week — The Union Regt. to which the Lima Company belong arrived here and stayed only a day or two and were ordered over there.

Your kind and generous offer to send me money is only the continuation of that fatherly kindness and love and for which accept my best wish and kindest thanks — I will not however avail myself of it — as I can shift for myself but if Mary is *in need* and you can assist her I will remit it within a very short time — as our pay rolls have been handed on and it can't be long before we are paid. Please write and ask if she is short as I only left her $400 — Give my best love and respect to Mother and Henry and Emma — Remember me to all the friends — Mr Austin — Hungerford — Thompson — Foster and all

Yours Ever Newton[22]

"The special correspondent of the *Elmira Press* has the following in relation to the Southern Tier Regiment, encamped at Meridian Heights, two miles from Washington:

'I am happy to be able to state that Hurlburt from Addison, the young man who thought to be dying yesterday, is much better to-day, and will probably now soon recover. The sanitary department is in excellent condition and Drs. Churchill and Madill are doing all they can to improve it — Major Gregg is rapidly recovering from the wound received from the kick of a horse while at Elmira and will probably be entirely well in the course of a week or ten days at the farthest. Adjutant Hayt has been severly indisposed but is now rapidly convalescing — Col. Hoffman, and the other officers of his staff are enjoying the very best health, and the climate evidently agrees with them. They remain in the camp with the men nights, a much better course then that adopted by the officers of the regiments who spend their time at Willard's and other popular resorts.'"[23]

July 16 McDowell's Union army advances upon Manassas Junction, Va.[24]

"We hear very gratifying reports from the Southern Tier Regiment at Washington. Col. Hoffman is not a graduate of West Point, but he has made military science the study of his lifetime, and there are few West Pointers who can teach him what to do. The friends of the Southern Tier Regiment will have daily cause to congratulate themselves on the efficiency and ability of its commander. The men will never undergo any unnecessary hardships while Col. Hoffman is the commander, and they will be nerved, with the assurance, to bear with unfaltering courage such as are unavoidable."[25]

Camp Diven July 19
Dear Father

I forgot to enclose these relicts in the last letter I wrote to you and I send them by private Woodward — who is discharged as being disabled by sickness — the ticking I cut from the bed on which Ellsworth was laid after being shot and a piece of the flag staff on which the session flag hung-They may be interesting to you and please send the one directed to Mary — to her — as I forgot to do so in a letter I wrote her — I will write you again soon — Wrote you yesterday. We are to be reviewed again to day by Gov Morgan of our state. I am feeling pretty well — I send much love to Mother Henry and wife — Please write often —

Affectionately Your Son
Newton[26]

Washington DC
National Hotel July 22
Tuesday
Dear Father

I take advantage of one of our's being discharged and going home to send you a line — I have come down from camp this morning to look about a little — You have doubtless heard of the battle of yesterday (Monday) and it was a big thing I assure you. It appears that our troops were largely outnumbered and in attacking Bulls Run — attacked a position very strongly entrenched — so much so that when we took a battery — we could not hold it as there were other batteries in its rear completely commanding it. There is much fault found with General Officers — who would order up a Regiment to attack a position and then after the Regt had taken it — they were left without support entirely and had to fall back of course and lose all they had gained by perhaps loss of life.

The Ellsworth Zouaves distinguished themselves and suffered a terrible loss — Our troops had to fall back and they even retreated as far as Washington and fears were even felt that they would attack the place — Regiments came straggling into the city in every shape — Showing that there was almost a rout — I talked with many officers who were in the fight and they all say that while our men fought splendidly — they were poorly commanded — Some regiments came in without their guns — looking worn and miserable — and many wounded are being brought in — Considering the disparity in numbers we made a grand fight and the loss of the enemy must be larger than ours.

I talked with a private — just from the battle field and he said that as he was at a spring for a drink — he found a rebel lying by its side — shot through the body — who told him before he died that our fire was terribly effective and that their men fell by scores — and were only kept on the ground by the constant arrival of reinforcements — Davis was there himself as I have been reliably told many times by officers who saw him — on a white horse-

The rebels had probably 80 000 men — while our entire attacking force was only 32 000 all told-

Sunday evening about 6 P.M. our regiment received orders to hold ourselves in readiness to march at 4 o clock in the morning — with rations for two days — We were to protect the retreat (as is supposed) and check pursuit and were to take no baggage at all — The greatest bustle prevailed and we were up most all night — Early the next morning we were supplied with Enfield Rifles — but the orders to move did not come and here we are still.

I think there must have been some blunder in the attack at the time — as I think the design was to have Genl Patterson attack on the other side at the same time — We could distinctly hear the connonading in our camp-

Washington City is greatly excited and crowds are gathered on almost every corner — discussing the battle — Our Camp Sutler went over to the field of battle and he says the road between here and there is strewed with guns—accoutrements—coats and c and c left by the troops in their retreat—

There is no danger but what our columns will retrieve this repulse soon—as the eye of old Scott is upon them and they will pay for it heavily—

Our loss is said to be 700 killed and about a 1000 wounded—while the most reliable account of rebel killed puts their loss in killed alone at 2500.

I am feeling well and have written you before several times—and received but one from you—Please write often—Have not got our pay yet and are short—but will get it soon they say—*You must not* try to send me any—but if you can send Mary $5 please do so and I will refund it soon—as she must be entirely out of money-

We expect to go into Virginia soon—but when—or where no one can tell.

Give my love to Mother—Henry—Emma and all friends—Mr Austin—Thompson—Hungerford and Foster—

Affectionately Yours Newton

P.S. I have written so fast that there may be some error which please excuse—I will write again soon—Write to Mary and tell her I am all right—Our boys are eager for a fight and I think will give a good account of themselves—and as for me I shall do my duty straight out—

I saw Genl Scott this morning—He got out of his carriage and a large crowd had collected to see the old hero and when he slipped from his conveyance their cheers broke spontaneously from them—He raised his cocked hat—and shook many by the hand and passed into the building—He looks like a hero—

But I must close—I send you much love and affection-

Yours ever Newton

P.S. I have just seen a member of the Lima Company (they belong to the Union Regt) and they were in the fight—they lost about 20 men—and Hall and Phillips—Ensign and 1st Luit are missing though he says they will probably come around yet—They had to travel 15 miles—the last five on a run and then without resting—shoved into the fight-Capt Perkins is all right and here with his company.[27]

"The Bull Run Races"

Written by a lady immediately after the first battle of Manassas or Bull Run, July 21, 1861. Her home being very near the turnpike over which the panic-stricken Federals made their flight back to Washington, she was an eye-witness of the famous retreat. From an unknown newspaper.

> Yankee Doodles started off,
> To march upon Manassas,
> But long before they reached that place
> They ran like frightened asses.
>
> Yankee Doodle, mend your paces,
> Yankee Doodle Dandy,
> Homeward from Virginia races,
> Yankee Doodle Dandy.
>
> 'Tis hard to tell who first did turn
> His back upon Manassas,
> But whoever did the race begin
> Was followed by the masses.
>
> Yankee Doodle etc.
>
> They thought they'd get us in a fix,
> 'Twixt Fairfax and Manassas,
> But found Confederate watch dogs there,
> Full bent upon harrasses.
>
> Yankee Doodle etc.
>
> Yankee Doodles took champagne
> To drink while at Manassas,
> But, sad to tell, 'twas left behind,
> And drunk from rebel glasses.
>
> Yankee Doodle etc.
>
> Poor Yankee Doodles, I have sung
> Of some of the harrasses
> That did befall them as they went
> A marching on Manassas.
>
> Yankee Doodle, mend your paces,
> Yankee Doodle Dandy;
> Homeward from the Bull Run races,
> Yankee Doodle Dandy.[28]

The 23rd Regiment moved their camp across the Potomac to Fort Runyan in Virginia on July 23.

For the *Journal*
Camp Diven, 23rd Regiment, N.Y.S.V.
Washington, D.C., July 26th, 1861

Dear Sir: I thought I would keep you somewhat informed of the whereabouts and condition of the Corning Volunteers, although I presume you keep pretty well so, from people from that vicinity, that visit us, for I find that even off here, we receive some calls from old friends, whom we are always glad to see. We are now in the State of Old Virginia, at Arlington, very pleasantly encamped; but feeling a little uncomfortable over the retreat of our forces on Sunday last, but at the same time, proud of our volunteer soldiers, and if they are only well officered, or officered by men that will be the last to run, and at the same time keep them cool as possible, they will be ready to do whatever is asked of them. Confidence in their officers is all that is required.

Gen. McClellan is to take command of our department, an officer that we can place confidence in. The soldiers here, about Washington, are anxious to wipe out what few stains were made a week ago, and I have confidence enough in them to think they can do it, and will do it.

The men are all doing first rate, with the exception of Thrall of Little Flats and he is improving. We are none of us as fleshy as when we left Corning, but it is of a tougher quality, and a browner color.

We carry on three kinds of business in camp: Cooking and Washing, as well as the exercise of drill, and I think our regiment is now ready for any kind of business that may be required of them. We have Enfield Rifles, and I think we pretty well know how to use them, by the looks of our target, each day as we practice. My men I am proud of; was when I left Corning; and am more so, the longer I have command of them. A little before one this morning, there was a discharge of musketry about one and a half miles from us; of course the long roll was played, and every regiment in line; our regiment was alarmed for the first time, and every man was at his post in double quick time; but the alarm proved to be false. After the engagement we called the roll, and every man was present, particularly at breakfast.

But I will not weary you with a long letter.

Yours, & c.,
L. Todd, Captain[29]

July 27, 1861 McClellan replaces McDowell as commander of Federal troops in the Washington area.[30]

July 27, 1861
Saturday

2. The 23rd New York Volunteer Regiment

Dear Brother —

I have just completed a tour of duty as officer of the Guard — and am seated on the bank of the Potomac — on Arlington Heights — opposite Washington City — to answer your very welcome letter which came to hand safely last evening — In plain sight of where I sit — and across the river I can see the Capitol — The Smithsonian Institute — The White House — The Treasury Building — the Patent Office — and the Washington Monument — all of them objects of no small interest to Americans — Up the river I can see Georgetown and on the water vessels of all kind from the war steamers with its port holes and big guns to the little sail boat — Below the bank on which I sit — the ground is low and level for ½ mile before you reach the Potomac — being in fact almost entirely a marsh — across which to the long bridge is the road to Washington — This road is crowded all the time with long trains of Army wagons ambulances carts and officers on horseback and At the end of the bridge on this (The Virginia) side of the river — are earthworks with guns mounted and palisades fixed in the ground — and after you cross the level marsh and mount the hill you come to more extensive fortifications — called Fort Runyon — where we have some very heavy artillery and 3 regiments of troops — passing through this fort you come to another level plateau and on the right of the road as you approach we are encamped in company with the Jersey 1st and passing our camp and distant about ½ mile you ascend another small hill on the top of which are other entrenchments and called Fort Albany — and in this fort was stationed the troops from Albany — and among them Capt Stafford of Corning — now a private — I saw him the other day and he has since gone home — his term having expired. I have described our situation and c — thinking it might interest you — We are about 4 miles from the lines of Rebel Pickets — and a private from the fort close by us — was killed yesterday by going out a little to far in search of berries — by two gents accompanied by two ladies on horseback (the ladies were probably men in womens cloths) who came riding by. Our man managed to crawl home to our lines — but died yesterday — after describing how he was shot —

I shall ask for a furlough in three or four weeks — if we are not to move into active service and come home and see you all again — I saw some Ohio troops on their way home the other day — their time being up — and I fairly envied them — for they were going home — Home sounds good I tell you — not that I am homesick — but I would like to see the nearest and dearest once more — But it may be long before I do. Write often and give me all the news — Father must write often as I look eagerly for his letters— Give him and mother my love and regards and remember me to all friends—

Love to yourself and wife— Be a good kind boy to your father and believe me-

Your Brother affectionately Newton[31]

Aug 1st 1861
Thursday
Dear Father

Your very kind and welcome letter came to hand about ten minutes since and having some leisure time — I hasten to reply. We are encamped where we were when I wrote you last and have fought no battles yet— though how soon we may — is not certain —for Genl McClellans orders are that no officer be absent from there quarters and other things look as if work was anticipated — We have heard some considerable heavy firing— to day on our right — apparently distant six or eight miles— but what it is we are all unable to say — Last night it was awful hot and we had a severe thunder storm and it rained very hard — Most of the night. Our tents however kept off the water finely— as we have a good board floor laid so we were none the worse for it — but all the regiment were not as well provided for and they got up rather damp in the morning. I have been all day waiting patiently the arrival of our Paymaster who was to have been on the ground this morning but it is about six o'clock P M and he has not made his appearance — Blast him — there is no excuse either for the pay rolls are all signed and all he has to do is come and take them and pay the money— which has been ready for him more than a week— Such infernal work makes everyone in the Regt discontented and dissatisfied and is perfectly and outrageously mean and I hope the infernal ass will get some idea of the way we resent such lousy treatment — when he does come.

as I am informed that all the reason of delay in paying is because the Paymaster can not get small change enough — it being all in 20 dollar pieces— Please write often as you can — and tell mother and Henry to write and give them my kindest regards— I will write by *mail* and send money by *express-*

Yours Affectionately
Newton[32]

The Regiment moved to Arlington Heights from camp near Ft. Runyon on August 5, about one half mile from Gen. Robert E. Lee's house. About mid August, a very hot month, the 23rd was formed into a brigade with the 21st and 35th N.Y. Volunteers, and placed under Brig. Gen. James S. Wadsworth. They remained at Arlington Heights to Sept. 28.[33]

National Hotel
Washington D.C. Augt 8, 1861
Dear Father

I have at last succeeded in getting away from camp to send you some small part of my pay and I have but very few minutes to write in — as I came down in an ambulance with some sick soldiers of our Regt (among them was chub Howell) who were to get discharge.

I enclose herewith a Draft on New York for $170 — Which distribute among the men and women whose names I send you on a list enclosed — and if possible — have them notified immediately that it has been sent to them — as they mostly are very much in need of it — Their friends have written them that it has been sent. I send you $40 — which please use to pay off as far as it goes my little debts— like the hired girl and c I had to send Uncle Luke $60 to pay Walls note and $20 to Mary and their months board bill and some little necessaries used up my $160 — hard dollars pretty quick — but I have over $200 — due me in about 3 weeks and then will pay up both Foster and Hungerford.

Be sure and take receipts and forward to me each one as you pay them — and do so as early as possible.

Pay Fuller (the shoemaker) and Pritchard and such — other little matters as are most pressing — W W Curtiss my old neighbor too-

I will write more at length soon. We have changed our camp again and now are one of the frontier Regts— I send love to Mother and Henry and all friends.

In haste affectionately Yours
Newton

    Please pay these sums to the following persons:
    John B Sherwood from his son Delos $20.00
    W.J. Palmer (of Knoxville) from his brother $10.00
    C.J. Chatfield (P.Post) from A.J. Jaynes $15.00
    Mrs. Kate Heath from her husband John Heath $50.00
    Mrs. Margaret Decker from her husband T.J.Decker $10.00
    F Calkins from his son F Calkins $10.00

Mrs. Henry Witt from her husband $15.00
Sent by myself to you — $40.00
$\overline{\$170.00}$
F Calkins lives up back of Reese's in Gibson
Mrs. Decker lives in Knoxville
Mrs Kate Heath is daughter in law of the owner of "Heath's Block"-
Please pay promptly and let no one have the money but the ones named above — unless they direct it themselves —[34]

CHAPTER 3

The 23rd New York Regiment at Arlington Heights

During August, the 23rd Regiment took its turn doing picket duty and reconnaissance in the areas of Falls Church and Ball's Cross Roads. These duties were much preferred to chopping wood.

Regimental Return

For the month of August, 1861 shows Field and Staff and Companies stationed at Arlington Heights except as follows:

Record of Events

Aug 5/61 Co A moved with Regt from near Ft Runyan to camp on Arlington Heights—14th on grand guard at Balls X roads—Sept 26, 27 and 28 on grand guard at Hall's House west of Balls X Roads 27t part of Co under Lt Mowers [1st Lieutenant Cornelius F. Mowers, Co. A] had a skirmish with enemy. The enemy attacked with small arms at long range 28t Sept the Co with portions of 25 and 35 Regts were attacked by the enemy with small arms and the artillary shot and shell. Frank M Vanwarners [Van Wormer] ankle sprained. Corpl Luke N Beagle a strain across the bowels the latter thought to be permanent. Co D while on Picket duty 27th Aug was attacked by a sup force of Rebels one slightly wounded by a ball grazing the side. Lt Coulby [Colby] with seven men from my Co, Two from Capt. Dingleday Co while scouting by order of Lt. Col Comdg were fired on by Rebels, one of Capt Dingledays men wounded on neck, one killed while on retreat. Co E on picket duty Co F while on picket duty one mile west of Balls X Roads attacked by a sup force. Thos Carrol killed [bullit passed through his body], Elias Algnon [Algair—wounded Ball's Cross Roads-8/27/61-wounded neck flesh wound & finger—served as teamster at Brigade, Division, or Corps headquarters], W L Crescade slightly wounded in knee.

copyist Patterson[1]

The following letter talks of money matters and shows how Newton cared for the men of his company. He sent home money for them and saw to it that their families received it safely through his father Merrill.

Arlington Heights
August 9 1861
Dear Father

Yesterday I went to the city [Washington] where I have been trying to get for some days without success—and send you a small amount of money to pay some of the most pressing of my small debts.
We are encamped just back of Genl Lee's house on Arlington heights and are one of the most advanced Regiments and stationed too I am reliably informed at the weakest point of our line—Just in front of us is 30 or 40 acres of cleared ground—planted to corn and c with an ordinary farm house and barn on it—and our folks are erecting a redout and are to mount a battery there—This cleared space of cultivated ground is surrounded on all sides by a dense wood—part of which is being rapidly felled for two purposes—both to obstruct the ground and to give better range to our artillery—and it seems awful to see how war devastates and destroys—Even in private parks and yards—monumental trees and shrubs of beautiful growth are hacked down and handsome shade evergreens planted along the road and adding greatly to the pleasant appearance are laid low—Such trees too—as I never saw before—Some species of cedar I think—most beautiful in their regular pyramidal form—While I have been writing this—Shermans Battery has moved past our camp and taken position about ½ mile in front of us—they have 8 brass 9 pounders and 3 splended rifled cannon—with 6 horses on each piece and each powder wagon—We had an alarm—or rather—we were turned out by orders from Genl McClellan at about 2 o clock, the night of the 7th,—I was officer of the guard and situated as we now are the guard are required to be vigilant and on hand and accordingly I heard the sentinal at the camp entrance—challange—and I went out to see who it was and found a

Dragoon — bearing (he said) important orders to our Colonel — Pretty soon the lights began to flash about Camp and with no noise — still and quietly — our boys "fell in" and marched out into Regiment line — and stood to our arms for an hour or so and then were dismissed to quarters — The Colonel got orders from McCellan to be ready to resist an attack — and probably some move of the enemy was the cause — We expect an attack and it is believed on all hands here that it will come soon — The Rebels have 6000 men at Falls Church as I was informed by a man who saw them yesterday — My health is good and I wish to hear from you — I want you to take enough from the amt I sent you to repay the $2 — you so kindly sent Mary and any other sums you have paid for me — Tell mother to write — and I will answer Henrys kind letter soon — and I will try and write to Frank Brown — say nothing about it however — Old Pratt thinks he spites me terribly by sending his little abortion of a paper to Todd [Capt. Luzern Todd] and Jones [2nd Lt. William H. Jones] and one or two others and not to me — Awful aint it? Yet I still live —

Yours affectionately
Newton[2]

Lieutenant Colby at Arlington Heights, August 1861. Photographs originally made by a Brady photographer. Courtesy of Richard S. Buchanan, Elmira, New York.

August 12 from Capt. Dingleday: "Monday last, (12th) in the

Captain Luzern Todd at Arlington Heights, August 1861. Photograph originally made by a Brady photographer. Courtesy of Richard S. Buchanan, Elmira, New York.

evening, two wagons heavily loaded with boxes and barrels, filled with provisions, found their way into our camp — Of course it produced a lively and interesting scene. All packages and parcels, where the directions were not obliterated, were speedily delivered to their respective owners. Night approached however, before half the store were disposed of. In the morning Captains Todd, Barstow, and your humble servant [Capt. Dingleday], (by order of the Colonel) formed a committee, who finished the job. All articles that had no particular direction, were collected, and after liberally supplying the hospitals, the balance was divided into ten parts and equally distributed among all the companies in the regiment. How grateful everything was received, and how well relished, I will not attempt to describe, but to the gratification of all the generous donors I would say, that most all the goods and provisions arrived in good order."[3]

Aug. 13   From Capt. Dingleday: "On the evening of the 13th, while the boys were gathered around their respective officer's quarters, exhibiting the many goods received, from their friends and offering to the captains and Lieutenants a piece of each, and making out a bill of fare for to-morrow, our Adjutant with his usual good nature, forced himself between us and informed, or rather ordered me [Capt. Dingleday] to get my company in marching and fighting order as soon as possible. Away went cream and jelly cake, and farewell doughnuts for a while. I could hardly tell, which news the boys received with the greatest enthusiasm, and came to the conclusion the news for a 'muss' pleased them more than that of the arrival of provender. In a short space of time three companies, A, F, and D were tramping in a roundabout way, and over awful roads, towards Ball's Cross Roads. News had been received at Head-quarters that our pickets apprehended an attack, and our business was to check and protect our lines.— Half of companies F and D were thrown along the lines, while the rest were held in reserve, to rally to any point of attack. Company A was detailed for scouts. Everything however, remained quiet during the night and towards morning, when no more danger was apprehended, the boys went to a creek close by and washed the mud off their pants and shoes, after which operation they laid both pants and shoes along the road to dry, suffering their extremities however, to remain in the pants. In less time than is required to pull trigger, all who were relieved were fast asleep, slumbering apparently as sweetly as though they were reposing upon the latest of Hobble's Spring Beds. The air was very cold, and it was laughable to see how the boys rolled themselves into the smallest bundle possible, in order that their short blanket might cover them all over. Some of them came without blankets, and were seen to crowd themselves between two rails in the fence, believing in the doctrine that a fellow feels warm when he gets squeezed. About noon on the 14th, we returned to camp, where to our delight we met a number of distinguished lady visitors of Elmira. Their visit to our camp is considered a great honor and will long be remembered. They returned to the City of Washington yesterday, and embark for home to-day."[4]

Arlington Aug. 14, 1861
Dear Father

Though I do not owe you a letter yet I will write again—for I suppose you are at all times willing to be troubled with my letters— We have been having very wet weather very cool— The health of my camp is remarkably good— and the men appear to be generally healthy— Our duties are severe—as our turn comes about twice a week for—either— wood chopping— Gaurd duty— Outpost duty— or detailed on special service— Yesterday I came off from 24 hours duty on our outposts— which are about 1½ miles on our front— in the direction of Fairfax Courthouse— We detail about 35 men and they are strung along a road—just in the edge of a woods— two men on each post—for the space of about a mile— and they stop and examine all passengers— There is generally a Captain and Lieutenant sent with the men and they have the charge of the line— Guard duty here is about the same it is every where— and one has to keep up all night and exercise vigilance and caution— but the special duty is rasher— as you will see when I attempt to describe— a trip which I participated in— since last evening—

We had just been dismissed from dress parade and were lazily filling our pipes for a smoke — when Adjutant Hoyt came in haste to our quarters to communicate the Col's orders — that our company — be instantly got under arms and provided with 30 rounds of ammunition each and to report ourselves for orders — at the head quarters of the 35th which is quartered near us — It was just growing dark — and a drizzling rain was falling — but the prospect of seeing some fun — and the excitement — Kept us all in good humor — and away we went. I was equipped — with heavy boots — in the tops of which I stuck my breeches — a thin jacket coat — Sword and revolver — liquor flask — haversack filled with crackers and cheese — and over all a rubber blanket — By the time we had started it was dark — and the roads were muddy — and added to all — not one of us knowing anything of our destination or the object of the expedition — only that our picket gaurd had been driven in *somewhere* — Our force comprised the 3 right companies of our regiment — being Capt Schlicks Co A — of Bath [Capt.Theodore Schlick] Capt Dinglida's [William W Dingleday's] Co. F.- of Elmira and ours — making in all a force of about 150 men — and we were strengthened by two more companies from the 35th upon our arrival at their camp — giving us a total of about 250 strong — We were led by a U.S. officer mounted on horseback — and off into the dark and rain we went — now passing through a dark silent woods and then emerging into a chopping where trees lay every which way and around, over and among these we had to pick our way up hill and then down again — sometimes wading thro brooks and puddles of large dimensions and nearly always wading in mud — Nor was this all for wherever it was *possible* we went at double quick — At length we entered a deep dark woods and the word passed from each officer down the line — "Silence men-not a word" — and we silently closed up and tramped on — passing the house of Lieut Hunter (now a rebel officer) which is partially destroyed — and then through a wide field or two — and finally came out on a highway and were ordered to halt and load — It must have been about 9 o clock at night when we paused here and we confidently expected that we should soon face the enemy — but not a man failed us in the expected trial on the contrary — they were eager to be led on and in ten minutes we were again moving on — down the road on a run — towards the extreme lines of our army — Arriving at a place called Balls Cross Roads — we halted and each company was deployed along each of the three different roads that come in here — and ordered to defend them from attack — and at the same time scouts were sent off in the direction of the enemy — We were drenched with rain and sweat when we took our position — but standing on post a short time set us to shivering — with the cold — for the weather had changed and the night was decidedly cold — Well — wet — tired and shivering we stayed all night — but were not attacked — and daylight brot some comfort — as we could at least see the country — and there was no danger of our killing each other by mistake — In the morning in company with two other officers I took a tramp of about two miles — towards Falls Church — and went out beyond our picket lines — and on gaining the summit of a hill close to Falls Church (which place is held by the rebels) we saw about 40 rebel Cavalry — in orchard — on our right — and distant about ½ mile from us — They were mounted and drawn up in line and though we could have reached them with our Enfield rifles — we decided not to molest them — as orders to the contrary were in force — After surveying the place to our satisfaction — we turned about and went back to our troops —

While out here — we got any quantity of large ripe peaches — and they were fine and luscious — about noon we were relieved and returned to camp — and found things just about as we left them there. Col Hoffman [Col. Henry C. Hoffman] and Lt Col Cranes — wives are in camp — they having come on a visit and just as I went to sleep last night they were getting a serenade from some of our fellows — It is next to impossible to get a furlough and I dont know when I can make you a visit — but will try for one sometime in Sept — We had another awful cold night — last night — but I was in my quarters — well wrapped up in blankets and felt rather better than I did at Balls Cross Roads — the previous evening-

I have not heard from you in some time — but please let me hear soon — Tell Mother — that Mary wrote me that she heard that she (mother) was going to send me some cake and c — but tell mother that it will be labor lost and money wasted — for we have enough to eat and the cake generally spoils — before we get it — I got one that Mrs Gillett kindly sent me — but it was all mashed up and there was nothing but crumbles left. Please give my best thanks — to Mrs G however — for the present — Do not forget it — for the people in Corning who have in the smallest way tried to act friendly and show me favors — are a devilish sight too scarce to allow me to neglect any one who has thought of me — I am getting to be a famous horse back rider — and scarcely a day passes — but that I ride more or less — I will send you a photograph of myself on horse — before our quarters at Arlington-

Remember me to all *friends* and that wont take you long — tell my enemies I care not a farthing for any man among them — and ask no odds — I send much love to my brother and hope to hear soon from him

Affectionately yours
Newton[5]

"'A Story of Gen. McClellan'

"The Washington correspondent of the *Philadelphia Inquirer* tells this story of Gen. McClellan — It may be true:

"General McClellan is in the habit of riding around occasionally in citizen's dress so accompanied by a few of his staff. A few days ago he was walking through one of the encampments across the Potomac, and passing the rear of the tents he saw a bucket of coffee standing near a fire. He ask what it was, and one of the soldiers said, 'coffee.'

"It looks more like slops, he replied. 'Oh,' said the soldier, 'it is not fit to drink, but we have to put up with it, and our food is not a bit better.' 'Well whose fault is it?' he asked — 'Oh, our Quartermaster is drunk most of the time, and, when not he is studying how to cheat.' McClellan passed on, and seeing more evidence of the dirty and slovenly manner in which the Quartermaster conducted his operations in his tent, he accosted him with the remark that the men were complaining of bad treatment from him, The Quartermaster flew into a passion and swore it was none of his business, and he had not better come sneaking around trying to make mischief. McClellan answered him, telling him he had better be cautious how he talked. Quartermaster replied, 'Who are you, that you assume so much apparent authority?' 'I am George B. McClellan, and you can pack up your traps and leave!' The Quartermaster was struck dumb, and McClellan turned and left him."[6]

Letter from Fred Burritt to *Elmira Weekly Advertiser* and *Chemung County Republican*:

Camp 23d N.Y.V. Arlington Heights
Thursday, Aug. 20th, 1861
Mr. Editor:

You may have heard of a scouting adventure of Lieut. Wilkie, near Falls Church, a week ago Saturday, in which a command of 25 men taken from our pickets and a straggling party of the Mass. 9th, he ventured two or three miles in advance, to Taylor's tavern, close by the Church, where the enemy are posted in force — routing a few Rebel cavalry and killing three, though narrowly escaping a bullit which passed through his own hair. Private Beck of Co. F. also being saved from death by the failure of a rebel's pistol. The traitor band probably thought a large force was upon them, their camp being aroused and they bringing out two pieces of their artillery in preparation for attack. The skirmishers then made a judicious retreat, keeping in the bushes and timber when possible, until some "secesh" dragoons were heard approaching by the road to the right, when the lieut. ordered his men into the brush by the wayside to cut them off.

The supposed "Black Horse Cavalry" came along at headlong gallop; every Enfield was cocked and "at a ready," and every man's finger on the trigger in exultant expectation, when a closer view revealed the features of our Sergeant Major DeVoe and Surgeon Madill, who will be more careful in future, I trust, in venturing so near the enemy unarmed as they were.

Several of our men have enjoyed opportunities of smelling powder, Ensign Andrews and Sergeant Baily of our Co., H, were out on picket duty, last Thursday, and tried their hands at private scouting and exploring far in advance, when they were suddenly reminded of their whereabouts—being apprised of the locality by a bullit hole through the coat of one and the clipping of an inch or so from the Zouave cap tassel of the other.

Our line of pickets are quite reckless in their sports and freaks when on duty. Firing frequently contrary to orders, and venturing away from their posts in which case they are liable to shoot each other, and be shot at by friends of other regiments.

Ours are stationed about two miles in advance — their right extending to those of the Mich. 4th, on the road to Fairfax, and the left resting on the picket lines of the N.Y. 35th, perhaps three-forths of a mile, to the left, in the woods. In front is a belt of felled timber and bushes, averaging about 40 rods in width. Beyond are the silent woods of the beautifully picturesque, but now desolated and soul-saddening landscape.

On the right of the road is a roughly, comfortably built dwelling, whitewashed as usual hereabouts, tenanted by an honest farmer from New York, whose family consist of an aged sire, himself, wife and handsome daughter. The hospitable house is consequently a place of resort to the gallant officers and men who can afford to discard their rations and buy a meal.

The surrounding country is beautiful at this season, but an unnatural stillness seems to prevade the very atmosphere, only broken by the occasional report of a gun or two, and the galloping of scouts and couriers; or perhaps, in the night time, the suspicious tinkling of the mysterious and ominous cow bell in the thickets, with now and then the music of those "winged warblers" of the night called mosquitoes, who sound their bugles to the charge, and rush upon the weary sentinel with the lances poised and poisoned.

Our Regiment still remains in the position occupied for the last 15 days, with little transpiring round about that we can observe, except the erection of earth works in a field to our front and left, which are rapidly

Merrill Colby, father of Newton T. Colby. Colby family collection.

approaching completion. Seventy of this regiment have been out to-day to labor in the trenches under the direction of Capt. Alexander of the U.S. Engineer Corps.

Besides these we have 150 men detailed as choppers, 90 men for guard and 30 odd for picket duty; besides companies B, G and C, who went out as scouts in a body with 24 hours rations, probably as skirmishers in anticipation of an attack.

Hence you will naturally infer that every other private is on some especial duty every other day, his leisure occupied with gun cleaning, bringing water, cooking, drying his clothes or some other pastime equally profitable.

Health is generally good and all in good spirits, and the most of us anxious to discharge our duties as active participants in the great battle which we all know to be imminent—yes, all are anxious I think.

We have a belligerant member of Co. H., aged 15 years and 18 days—a precocious warrier who volunteered with the written consent of his parents in May last, who can keep his arms in order, endure fatigue, illustrate the theory of self denial, use expletives, adjectives, and interjections in conversations and chew tobacco as well as "any other man."

Yours truly,
F. Burritt

P.S.—9 A.M.—Capt. Dingledy has just returned from beyond the Orange & Alexander R.R. whither his inclinations led him with Doc. Madill, to see how our skirmishers and scouts were doing. But he reports contrary to rumor, that although shots were exchanged no engagement was had and none of our three companies were killed.[7] Frederick Burritt, Captain Co. H., was appointed Corporal Aug. 1, 1861, Promoted Serg-Major, May 7, 1862.

3. The 23rd New York Regiment at Arlington Heights

Arlington Heights Wednesday
Aug 21, 1861
Dear Father

    Your very welcome and kind letter came to hand in good time — and I found much encouragement and pleasure in reading it — Since I wrote you last — there has been but little doing and I can therefore give you but little news that will interest you — though we are detailed nearly every day for working or fatigue duty — which duty is of many different kinds — One day I command a party for wood chopping (clearing away woods) — the next for outpost duty — and another to work on the forts — and c and c. Yesterday I was ordered to take 64 men — 1 sergeant — 2 corporals and report at the Arlington House for orders — and had liberty to detail the men from the Regiment as I saw fit — Well — the order was read to the Regiment when on dress parade (as all orders are) and as soon as we came off from parade — I was beseiged and begged of — by more than 5 times the number — I was ordered to take — to allow them to go — They thought that we would go on a scout and perhaps get a chance at the rebels — I decided to take 6 men from each of the 9 companies and 14 from our own which made the 64 men — Our men were so eager to go — that I hardly knew who to take — and two of our men who I could not take actually went away from our quarters with tears running down their cheeks!! No one knew where we were to go — not even the Colonel — I started off with the men and went to the Arlington House — and halted them in line and went myself into the house to report for orders to Capt Alexander of the U.S. Engineers — Well after a while the noble Captain A. ordered one of his orderlies to guide us to our destination and away we went again and after about 4 miles marching we came to the ground — and stacked our arms —

    Just try and immagine the blank looks of the men — when they were informed for the first time that they were to dig in the mud and assist in building a fort which is being erected here !! I think it was most decidedly — "a big thing on Snyder" — but of course there was no help for it and they stripped their coats and went at it — There has been so much rain that the mud was deep — Especially when the dirt had been moved and it was heavy and sticky — so much so that it was hard work to move it — By Jove we worked hard all day — (that is the men did) and then went home — and it is a standing joke in camp about our *scouting* — We have a line of forts — nearly all completed — reaching from Alexandria to the Chain Bridge — a distance of 10 miles — along the Virginia side of the Potomac — mounting in each — from 10 to 25 heavy guns — so that we are nearly all ready to receive company. Even as distinguished as that of Beauregard or Davis— The forts are of different shape and sizes but are generally large — and on the outside are surrounded with a ditch — about 20 feet wide and 10 feet deep — and on the outside of the ditch (of some of them) are large trees laying — with the butts toward the fort and spiked together and the limbs sharpened so that any one would have a tough job to even get to the ditch — Even were there no one in the fort firing on them.

I am greatly obliged for the promptness with which you paid the money entrusted to me by the men and by your sending me the receipts…

God Bless you both — I send much love to Henry and wife and hope they will be both happy and prospered — Tell Henry not to think of enlisting — under any circumstances — Write often —

Yours Affectionately
Newton

P.S. We were ordered to get the cooks to work and have 3 days ration cooked and be ready to march at daylight. It is morning and raining and we are still here — but may start at any time The cooks worked all night[8]

Private
Arlington Heights
Aug 24, 1861
Dear Henry

I enclose a letter which you may hand to Brown and he may publish it if he sees fit — We have but little here in the way of news— Tell Father that Jim Wadsworth of Genisco has been appointed our Brigadier General and I think some of trying to get a place on his staff— *Now don't you make this public or say one word to any one but Father*— Remember now —for I have but little idea that I can succeed — Write me soon and tell me all the news. I got a letter from Mother too and was very glad to hear from both — Tell Mother I intend to write her very soon and that she may always be sure that her letters are warmly welcome — I send love to you all — In haste affectionately yours

Newton[9]

"The first death has at last occurred in the Southern Tier Regiment. James Peas [Pease], a member of Capt. Barstow's Company, living at Tioga Centre, was injured while chopping, by the falling tree, and has since died."[10]

3. The 23rd New York Regiment at Arlington Heights

For the *Journal*:

Camp 23rd Reg't N.Y.V.
Arlington Heights, Va., Aug. 24th, 1861

Friend Pratt — Our camp, now upon the extreme elevation of Arlington Heights, about a mile-and-a half south of the Georgetown ferry, is both pleasant and healthy. We are but a short distance from Arlington House the late residence of the rebel General Lee, now occupied as the Head-quarters of our army officers. Many pleasant memories cluster around it, — among others, I am told that it was the place of Gen. Washington's marriage. We are in the woods, and our camp is well supplied with water from two springs and a small creek furnishes a fine opportunity for bathing and washing. I remark a better attention, by our whole regiment, to cleanliness in respect to clothing and person, than I expected. We are obliged to be our own laundresses, and I suppose with all the appliances of hot water, soft soap, wash boards, and hands skilled to the labor, washing is hard work; much more so when performed by the side of a creek, with cold water, hard soap, and hands all unused to it. But in spite of all, our regiment is the neatest I have seen. Our boys are generally well, — only slight colds and a few rheumatic pains, the result of recent wet weather, of which for the last two weeks we have had an undue share, and these vanish when any call looking to service is given. The business of the Regiment is now rather fatigue than military duty; daily details are made of wood chopping, throwing up entrenchments, &c. We also send out a picket guard, which duty is rather sought than avoided by the boys, as giving the best opportunity for adventure. Some of the more venturesome of the regiment occasionally pass beyond our picket lines, and take a look at the confederate troops, performing, if we are to believe the reports which come to us from home, but which find little credit here, deeds of startling valor.

The government is building near us a number of forts or redoubts upon which detachments from the neighboring regiments are employed — they are constructed by digging a ditch 18 or 20 feet wide and 10 feet deep, throwing the dirt into an embankment which being thoroughly pounded and sodded on the inside furnishes a good protection. They are generally built facing four ways the rear being protected by a close fence of oak posts, loop-holed and sharpened at the top. Within the enclosures are magazines for powder and when mounted will require a large force to take one. Chopping out roads and falling trees to obstruct the passage of an army occupy some of our time. Aside from these matters we are not a very laborious set. No very striking incidents have occured lately — our pickets occasionally take a stray secesh and send him to Washington to report; sometimes ladies meet with their kind attentions; a day or two a lady residing near here passed our lines by means of a pass duly authenticated, but when beyond the lines she met a scout which she supposed was a rebel picket and presented a rebel pass; but the gentleman happened to be a Federal soldier and furnished her an escort to headquarters.

A week today we buried a young man out of Capt. Summer Barstow's Co.C, who died from injuries received from a falling tree while chopping. His name was Pease. It was the first death in the Regiment and the measured cadences of the funeral march and reversed arms were sad sights and sounds to us. Our own company propose forming a league in which by contributions from each member monthly a fund will be formed for sending home bodies of any member who may die while in service. We hear that our friends at home are bringing forward the second guard for the defense of our government; we shall welcome to the field all who may come and trust that honor and success may attend them. It seems to me as I look at it advantageous, for those who can, to place themselves in regiments already in active service, since then they can have all the benefit of the experience of officers who have learned the way of providing for a regiment. We are fortunate in being in a regiment where the officers give their personal attention to the comfort of their men and we are much better provided for than many other regiments. Our food is excellent in quality and abundant in quanity; much better than I anticipated and no just cause for complaint exists. The regiment is very orderly — no drunkeness — no quarreling, and good attention to duties gives promise that it will reflect honor upon the counties from which it has been gathered.

Elder Crane, our chaplain, holds frequent prayer meetings which are well attended and interesting; he is assidous in his attention to the spiritual welfare of the men and his care for their temporal comfort was clearly demonstrated upon his recent visit at Elmira. A man in Co.H was accidently wounded yesterday while on picket, but not seriously.

Respectfully yours,
C.K.[11]

Captain Summer Barstow, mentioned in the previous letter, was wounded in the head by the ball of a musket accidentally discharged while on march on August 27, 1862. He resigned February 16, 1863.[12]

Fred Burritt of Co. H writes:

3. The 23rd New York Regiment at Arlington Heights

August 26th

About ten A.M., of Monday, we marched down to the Virginia terminous of Long bridge, passing our late camping ground, now deserted, and through Fort Runyon after we passed into a spacious field, where we were received with seven other Regiments by General McCellan's appearance.

It was the first time most of [us] had seen so large a body of infantry in motion at once, and reminded one of an old fashioned "General Training" of school boy days, long passed, on a grand scale minus the civilians, truant urchins, children, and venders of ginger-bread and fruit, who used to be present on those occasions.

We arrived at our camp again about five p.m., dusty, hungry and tired—though well satisfied with our excursion. Our new colors were out on the occasion, and of course they by far excelled everything on the ground, thanks to the patriotism and generosity of our ladies.[13]

CHAPTER 4

Ball's Cross Roads Skirmish

"Col. Hoffman and the quartermaster of the regiment, hearing that a large force of secessionists were in the vicinity of the Falls Church, took a circuitous route and got on top of a house about a mile from the church to reconnoiter. They had a good glass, but were unable to detect the presence of troops in any force in the vicinity."[1]

For the *Journal*
Camp 23rd Reg't N.Y.S.V.
Arlington Heights, Va., Aug. 31st, 1861

Friend Pratt — Our boys have at length been permitted to try their mettle with the enemy. Last Tuesday our company and company "F," Capt. Dingleday, (one of the Elmira companies) received orders to get one day's rations and their blankets and march. As we passed out under command of Lieut. Col. Crane, we were joined by three companies from the 14th N.Y.S.M., of which our friend, Dave Compton is a member, and marched to Ball's Cross Roads. Leaving a detachment from the 14th as a reserve and guard for other roads, we marched forward about a mile and halted on the brow of a hill overlooking the railroad, which here passes through a narrow valley or gorge. Here company F, was deployed along the road, and our company upon a cross road at their right. We found there part of a company from the 12th N.Y.S.V., which had been on duty through the night. Our pickets, who had been stationed on the other side of the railroad, had, during the previous night been compelled to retire to this point. Soon after we arrived, Lieut. Colby took a squad of men with him and

4. Ball's Cross Roads Skirmish

crossed the railroad to reconnoitre, passing up the opposite hill and getting a view of the rebels, they were fired upon but escaped unharmed. Sergeant Sherwood also went out with two or three to get an introduction, and from the sounds which reached our ears, we concluded that he had succeeded for the firing became rapid. At every fire the rebels yelled like so many hyenas. One of them bit the dust from the sure aim of the Orderly, he was seen to make three efforts to rise, but had to give it up. Considerable bodies of the enemy were seen moving about and now and then full companies in uniform and well drilled. At short intervals the firing was rapid, sometimes assuming the character of vollies, as it slackened in one place our men would stir up a nest in another, and the leaden bees would again buzz around their ears. Getting behind trees they waited their opportunity and taking sure aim made every bullet tell. One man in company F, was about this time wounded in the neck and one finger but made out to get back to his company. The skirmishing continued some two or three hours, but at last the rebels, tired of the fun and perhaps thinking to outflank our men, made a rush in a body up the hill and the Lieut. and Orderly with their men made some tall "double quick," with a body guard of some 500 or 600 rebels at their heels, howling like maniacs. They fired a volley at our men, the balls of which passed over our heads, another volley, and at the command of our Captain we laid down avoiding them. About this time young Carroll, of Capt. Dingleday's company received a ball through the bowels and fell and another man was wounded in the leg, but not dangerously. Our men were told to deploy through the woods, which was done and a fair return made of the fire. The rebels finding that they had something to meet turned and seeking shelter in the woods kept up a rapid fire which our men returned, sheltering themselves partly under a rise of ground at the roadside, taking sure aim and making our bonny Enfields tell a deadly tale every time. After a sharp fire for an hour the rebels thought best to retire, and our men gathered up their traps and ralling to one point, formed line to find no one from our company injured. A Sergeant who had ventured to near had been taken prisoner, and had delivered up his rifle, when one of our men drew up his piece and shot his captor, compelling him to resign his prize and victim, upon which the Sergeant grabbed his rifle and sought better neighbors. Another attempted to strip of Carroll's watch and gun but was shot by one of our Painted Post boys (Cobb) [William H. Cobb], and concluded not to take the booty. The boys seemed to enjoy the fun and were sorry when it was through with and will pitch in again at the first opportunity. Our Captain was right among us all the time — cool and collected, giving his commands as calmly as in camp, he passed through a cross fire when the balls flew like hail, but they did not seem to discompose him a bit. How he escaped is a wonder — in fact, how the whole company managed to get through and no one be hurt is very strange — they will not often be required to stand a more direct or severe fire. The rebels must have been armed with the same or as serviceable pieces as we, for we picked up balls similar to our own after the skirmish and must have numbered at least 600, as they were seen during the early part of the day going through battalion movements. I have tho't best to give you this imperfect sketch since some of our friends might perhaps like to know when the boys met fire, and how they stood it. The whiz of the ball is very distinct and heard before the ball reaches one — it seems that one could mark the track, and, if but one came, dodge it. The day after, one of our men scouting around, picked up a gun near a spot where blood was found. A lady living on the road the rebels were obliged to pass — reports that she saw them carry by her house 32 bodies, and they were seen till a late hour with lanterns, looking for their dead and wounded — so we think we must have done some work — and made a fair exchange 1 for 32. Last evening the rebels made an attempt to bring down Prof. Lowe and his balloon, which is at times elevated near here for purposes of observation, by firing rifled cannon and throwing shells at it, but were unsuccessful, though they came pretty near. We were gratified by a sight of our esteemed townsman, Mr. Alex Olcott, day before yesterday, who favored our camp with a visit — he will probably give you a more graphic account of our little skirmish. We are in usual health, and matters move along about the old way — but the mail is closing, and I must make my adios.

Respectfully yours, CK.[2]

Written by Sgt. Cyrus Kellog, Co. D., who was promoted 2nd Lt. on May 15, 1862, the day Lt. Colby resigned from the regiment.

The following is part of a letter by Captain William W. Dingleday of Co. F.:

Arlington Heights
September 1st, 1861
Friend Dumars:

Sufficient has transpired of late to furnish an item for the letter I promised you. You have no doubt heard, ere this, of the skirmish which took place a few days ago, one mile west of Ball's Cross Roads and about three miles from our camp.

On the 27th inst., Companies A, F, and D, of our regiment, in connection with three companies of the Fourteenth New York State Militia, were ordered out to form a reserve for our picketts, under command of our gallant Lieutenant-Colonel Crane. Company A was stationed one mile and a half to the right, on Hall's Hill, Companies D and F nearly opposite each other — the former near a fence at the edge of a piece of woods, the latter in the road, partly concealed in a ditch.

Scouts were sent out beyond the line of pickets, as information had been received on our arrival that things looked rather suspicious in front. Between the hours of two and four P.M. the scouts and pickets came in double quick, with the intelligence that a large body of rebels were about to attack us. Shots had already been freely exchanged.

Colonel Crane, having positive orders not to bring on an engagement west of the cross-roads, but to retire and hold the latter at all hazards, ordered us to retreat. The order was reluctantly obeyed, not however, without causing some of the "gray backs," who were too indiscreet, to repent of their folly. We fell back a few rods to the next fence, when it was discovered that the rebels were trying to outflank us. The firing then commenced in good earnst. The entertainment was brief but exceedingly interesting, and after a short time, it was evident that the rebels were more anxious to retreat than our own men.

We have to lament the loss, in this engagement, of one who was very dear to and a great favorite with us all. Thomas Carroll was shot through the heart. He enlisted as a private, but through his worth and exemplary conduct was promoted to corporal. Elias Algair received a bad wound in the neck, and also had a part of the middle finger of his left hand shot off. Several others were slightly wounded. Company D, being protected by the woods, sustained no injury.

In the evening, a section of a rifled battery was placed in position in the road, to give the rebs a warm reception should they pay us a visit after dark. All remained quiet until morning, when they commenced throwing shot and shell in the direction of Hall's Hill, where Company A was stationed. That company was also ordered to fall back. Occasionally, they would send a shell at us, without, however, doing any damage.

The occasion brought Generals McDowell, Keyes, and Wadsworth promptly to the spot, who, after learning the details of the affair, complimented Colonel Crane and his command very flatteringly. We learn today from a lady whose residence is near where the conflict took place, that the rebels acknowledge a loss of eleven killed and many wounded. From her statement, they outnumbered us two to one, but were all under the influence of liquor, which proved a serious disadvantage to them. All is quiet now, however, and peace reigns again in Israel.[3]

A widow lady residing in that section who has since retired within our lines for protection states that thirty-two rebels were carried past her house on that evening, who were shot in the skirmish, twenty-five of whom were dead, she thinks.

The enemy's loss may be ascribed to the efficacy of the scouts and skirmishers who were enabled to pick off many of them from behind trees, and firing from general cover.[4]

As reported by the *Elmira Daily Advertiser*, letter from Fred Burritt of Co. H:

Full particulars of the Skirmish with the Rebels.
Picket Station No. 10, 23d. N.Y.V.
Alexandria Co. Va., Wednesday, Aug. 28, 1861
Editor Advertiser:

Yesterday morning Companies A. F. & D. and five men from each remaining Company, with about one hundred men of the Thirty-fifth, and detachments of each the Twenty-fifth and Fourteenth N.Y. Regiments, all under the command of our Lieut. Colonel, went as advance pickets and skirmishers, to watch the movements of the enemy, and are still unrelieved, perhaps nearly a mile from us, judging from occasional discharge of small arms and cannon in the direction of Ball's Cross Roads and the Orange and Alexandria Railroad [Alexandria, Loudon and Hampshire Railroad] to the left.

At four P.M. yesterday, Col. Hoffman entered the lines of our encampment from this direction, and the order was given for every man to fall in with thirty rounds, and canteen filled. Every man of the guard not on immediate duty, being included in the order, and those sentinels on their posts, being relieved at their earnest solicitation, by invalids unfit for active field service when practical, that they might have a chance in.

Rumors and conjectures abounded through-out our community. Then private Allgair of Co, F came in on foot, his shoulders drenched in blood from a bullit shot through the back of his neck. Next our pickets from this line at double quick under Ensign Durland came in and fell into ranks of their respective companies having been ordered back by their officer, Capt. Dingleday, who immediately joined his command in the advance post.

About five o'clock an ambulance entered the lines with the remains of Thomas Carroll, of Co. F., he having been shot through the heart and instantly killed.

He will be much regretted not only by the officers and men of his own company, but by his acquaintances through-out the Regiment. I first knew him as an employee of Mr. Rutter in the Elmira Car Shops, and his former character for industry and correct deportment has been well sustained in his short career as a soldier.

Sergeant Boker [Bowker] of the same company was shot in the foot, and there have been various reports of others being wounded, taken prisoners and killed on our side, but I am unable to give you any further facts, with certainty.—Quite a number were killed and wounded of the Union troops, and they retaliated with effect.

Our boys were driven from their position on the other side of the railroad, by a superior force of the enemy, and last night a battery of two pieces. Firing in that direction has been frequent for the past fifteen minutes, and of course I am anxious to know what's up as a party of infantry are said to have recently gone in that direction, by a road to our left. You may be aware that Co's A.F. and D. are commanded repectively by Captains Scalick, Dingleday and Todd—of Bath, Elmira and Corning.—It is now raining hard, and the firing continues.[5]

Letter from Lt. Newton Colby:

Arlington Heights
Thursday Aug 29 [1861]
Dear Father

Having been very busy for a few days past—I have been prevented from answering your very interesting and kind letter—but having a little leisure I will try and write you to day. First in order allow me to inform you to that I have been under fire for the first time on Tuesday—The 27th last—and in all probability I shall never again be where I shall see bullits fly thicker—But let me begin at the beginning—Tuesday morning—orders came from head quarters to our Colonel—to detail two companies and a Field Officer—who would be joined by three companies from other Regiments—and proceed to Balls Cross Roads—Well—an Elmira Company and ours was selected and having been joined by the others we went there and by orders of the Lt Col Crane—took position just on the brow of the hill on our side of the Rail Road—being about 1 or 1½ miles beyond Balls Cross Roads—The road from the cross roads to the place we occupied is straight and quite level—and runs through an open country until reaching us—We were on the brow of a rather steep long hill—covered on both sides of the road with woods—until you get to the bottom and there the road crosses the Rail Road—and asends the hill on the other side of the valley — Down the hill on our side and up the other side too — the road had been cut down so that there were high banks on each side — The road on the opposite side of the R Road went through the cut above mentioned and was pretty steep until — you get up the hill and there is a level spot with woods only on one side. In the valley and on each side of the Rail Road there was no woods for 3 or 4 rods — it having probably been cleared for the Rail Road — After arriving to the edge of the woods and on the brow of the hill we halted and our company was detailed to occupy one side of the road in the edge of the woods and the other company was drawn up along the road — By order of the Lieut Col — I was to take 4 men and proceed down the hill and find out how things were — and he says — he ordered me not to cross the R Road — but I did not hear that part of the order — if he gave it. Well I took a rifle from one of the men and with the men I went down the hill and just in the edge of the woods and a few rods from the RR I came upon our outside line of Pickett gaurds — who cautioned me not to go into the open ground as the Rebels were in the woods and would fire on us — I reconnoitered the other side thoroughly and sent one of my men to the Lt Col — to get his field glass and got into a place on the hill side where I could see the road on the opposite hill and I saw the Rebels to the number of 4 or 500 — with one piece of artillery — commanding the road — They had grey uniforms and were commanded by an officer on horseback — Well all I could discover made me believe that there were none of the enemy below the artillary station and I accordingly determined to cross the Rail Road and go up the hill and look about — and did so — and when I got up there I found our Orderly Sergeant — Sherwood [1st Sgt Delos C. Sherwood] and two or three of our men — We got behind some trees — when all of a sudden some of devils fired at us. The shots came from just in front of us and apparently were about 15 or 20 rods off — Just then I saw one of the grey whelps behind a tree — partly and fired at him — with what effect I could not tell — Well it was pop-pop till at length one of my fellows undertook to run across the road to another tree and as he got into the middle of the road and about 10 feet distant from me — he tumbled into the road and called out that he was shot twice! As he fell — the cowardly cus set up the most infernal yell I ever heard and as for me I was completely carried away with rage and excitement — Sergt Sherwood just then got a fair shot at one and knocked him head over heels and now it was our turn to hurra and we did I tell you and I gave the word to charge and drive the "sons of bitches" out of the wood — and we all jumped from behind our trees and rushed forward — most imprudently too — for they received us with a volley — which although they did not hit us — convinced me at once that they had more than 40 men right before us — Oh Lord how the balls whistled around us—and by gracious just quess my surprise on looking to my left into the open field—to see 30 or 40 of them going round to cut us off—I hastily order the men to fall back and that as quick as it could be done and away we went down the hill—When we got across the Rail Road—we halted and were thinking of trying to make a stand—when whiz whiz—came another volley all around us—Again we took to trees and on looking back saw them in large numbers crossing the Rail Road—I made a shot from my tree that I think cost them a man—for he stood perfectly exposed and not more than 20 rods off—No sooner had I fired than a Ball struck the tree that I was behind and the bark flew into my neck in a fine shower—Lieut Bradley of "ours" who was behind a tree close by sung out—" By G_d Lieutenant you have got to look out-" and I thought so too and made a run through the balls which constantly swept the hill side to another tree—and then to another till I reached the open fields and here I had about 50 rods to go over and the edge of the woods behind me lined with rebels firing like the very devil at us—But there was no other course except to be taken and I preferred taking the chances through the field. Just ahead of me was Sergt Sherwood and just behind me Corpl Crandall—[Corp Albert R. Crandall] (of Alfred) [N.Y.] and every time they fired the balls whistled pretty close I ask you—and we fell to the ground and then up and away—In this way we managed to reach our company—so tired that I could hardly stand—I found Capt Todd ready to give them a warm reception—I told him how they were coming and we both decided that we would deploy into the woods and meet them—and he gave the order to do so. I leaned against the fence to rest a minute and the company had got 8 or ten rods off where the Lieut Col came riding up and ordered us all to fall back as they were out flanking us—I repeated his order to Capt Todd and then fell back—and such a storm of bullets as swept the road from each side as I "ske daddled" down the road—I never saw—Jupiter—how they did whistle and hiss—striking the bushes—rails and in the dirt on every side—Capt Todd had his men—about ½ the company—full down behind the fence and briskly returned the fire—while the others were ahead of me falling back—The Captain did not hear the Cols order—and consequently stayed behind and he behaved cool and well and so did all our men—We were the last to retire—the other company having left the ground before I came up the hill and the Captain could not rally them—We retired in good order—with at least 4 or 500 men before us—in all I came awful close to being cut off and surrounded in the woods—Now I tell you and just think—their men and us came out of the woods at the same time and if we had been a few minutes later we might have landed in Richmond—Well we all got back to the Cross Roads and found we had one man killed dead and several (6 or 8) wounded — while the loss of the enemy must have been 20 or 30. Indeed a woman who lived the other side of the R Road said she counted 32 men carried by on litters the evening after the fight — I fired 4 or 5 shots and I think I hit my man twice out of the 5 shots, once in the valley by the RR and once above the RR on the hill — I fired into a group of ½ dozen huddled together — I can say and fully feel to thank God that I am alive today — and though it was a skirmish only — still all are of the opinion that balls will never come thicker or faster than they did there — I send you a map which I tried to make — showing the situation of our troops and where the rebels attacked us and other locations — After we got back to Balls Cross roads — a part of Shermans Battery came dashing up to support us in case they made an attack — but all was quiet through the night — but the next day the Rebels came out about 2 miles on our right with artillery (see map) and commenced throwing shells and rifled cannon shot at Halls House — their aim was very bad — the shells bursting high in the air and after firing 10 or a dozen times they desisted — Genl McDowell — who came up ordered Genl Wadsworth to go to Halls House and withdraw our pickets and it was done — After our fight a company of U.S. Cavalry came dashing up to Balls Cross Roads — stayed a few minutes and then put back again — McDowell and his staff were all there and Wadsworth too. About 4 P.M. we were relieved by companies from other Regiments and returned to camp and I was glad to find a place under cover to lay my tired legs — the night before being passed lying in the road — with my rubber blanket under me in company with Capt Baldwin of the Brooklyn 14th where our picket lines joined each other — Taken all together we had an exciting time-

With regard to my appreciation to Genl Wadsworth — I hardly know how to get at it — for I would hardly like to have him know that I wanted such a place — I would like it if I could only get it in the right way — or would like a place in the commisary department — which could be had by application to the war department — If Wadsworth would only offer me a place — or I could get it without compromising myself — I would like it much — If Judge Johnson would write to him and recomend me incidentally it would help — Do not let any one hear about it — I hardly know how to do what I ought to do — Col Hoffman would not help me I know — for he had much rather I would stay in the Regiment. Advise me how to do it — Do not write to Mary — the particulars of our skirmish as I have written to you — for it would alarm her and she already is much disatisfied — I am a little surprised that you too wish me out of it and home again for I thought you deemed it my duty to go — I know I owe you *all* and ought to *now* try and repay you some of the care and anxiety I have caused you and if God spares my life I will do so.

You will see by the above that I run off the lines—it was rather too dark to write and I could not see well—I have then only to add a few words this morning before the mail comes. Remember me to all our friends and give much love to mother and Henry and wife I intend to come home as soon as I can obtain a furlough—The Captain will come home first and after his return I will come—We buried the poor fellow who was killed in the fight yesterday at the Soldiers home in Washington. He was a Corporal and I knew him well—as a smart good boy—He was shot in going from the edge of the woods across the open field—and fell instantly and a Seargant fell by his side wounded—and a rebel ran out to where they lay and began to rifle them of their plunder—The Sergt who was only slightly wounded—said " I suppose I am a prisoner"—Yes G_d D_m you—have you any more arms? asked secesh—No said our man and the cowardly cus began to take the dead mans watch out of his pocket—Just then our fellows saw him and fired so close that he run and left everything behind and just as he mounted the fence a ball struck him and killed him dead. Our men then went and got our dead man and brot him in—his watch being found by his side on the ground—Alex Olcott was here yesterday and can tell you how we all are. Write soon. Affectionately yours

Newton[6]

From the *Elmira Journal*:

The following letter, from C.J. Chatfield, Jr. (Charles J Chatfield was appointed Corp. August 4, 1861—and wounded battle of Bull Run August 31, 1862), a member of Capt. Todd's company, was not intended for publication, but as it is an interesting sketch of the first skirmish, we have been permitted to publish it.

Camp 23rd Reg't N.Y.S.V.
Arlington Heights, Va., Aug. 31st, 1861

Dear Friends at home-We have heard the whistling of bullets for the first time.—Tuesday morning, Co. F, Capt. Dingleday, (Elmira second) and Co. D, were ordered to Ball's Cross Roads, where we were when I wrote Frank about wading the mud. We advanced about one mile beyond our former position, to the top of a hill over looking the Alexandria and Leesburgh Railroad. By order of Lieut. Col. Crane, Capt. Todd sent four men who were afterwards joined by several others, who left us when the firing commenced. We then lay there awaiting further orders until three o'clock, when the scattering fire, which had been kept up all day, to our right and left (as this was our picket line) became more central, and as the fire became general, each volley was followed by shouts and yells which led us to believe that our men had been cut off, but shots continued to be fired at intervals and the yelling drew nearer and still nearer until a few of our men came running up the road and assured us of their safety. They were closely pursued, however, by the enemy who fired a volley which passed just over our heads cutting off twigs and leaves in abundance. All this time, no enemy was to be seen, and Col. Crane ordered a retreat. Co F, then retreated, down the road, thus leaving our left unprotected. "Down, men, lie close," called Capt. Todd, hurriedly; and, indeed, there was need of it, for the departure of Co. F, so emboldened the enemy that they leaped the rail fence at the edge of the woods, and deployed as skirmishers, in the field, just across the road to the left of us. We were somewhat surprised at this movement, as we were looking for them directly in front, and more to the right. The first intimation that we received of this approach in this direction, someone who had crossed the road to gain the shelter of the bank which probably saved many of us, called out "See our boys coming over the fence." Looking in the direction indicated, we saw the pickets of the New York 21st (Buffalo reg't) [by the way, they lost ten men prisoners in the morning] some on and others just over the fence. Before they had fairly left the fence, the rebels rushed from the woods and poured a heavy volley out after them. Here it was that Carroll of Co. F, fell shot through the bowels, as he turned to have one more shot. Sergeant Boker [3d Sgt. James B Bowker], of the same company was wounded in the leg and fell to the ground. A seccesh sprang over the fence and ran out to the dead man and picked up his rifle, and was taking his watch from his neck, when Wm. Cobb, who behaved with the utmost coolness throughout the whole affair fired at him from behind a haystack in the field. He let go of the watch, dropped the gun, and staggered to the fence. He fell from the top rail, headlong and was dragged into the woods by his comrades, into the bushes. Another rebel who had taken Boker's gun, seeing his comrade's fate threw the gun and sprang over the fence. Our men continued to fire from behind the trees, and the high bank of the road. Couriers now began to arrive from Col. Crane, ordering Capt. Todd to fall back. Not until the

Opposite: Map of the skirmish at Ball's Cross Roads, from letter of August 29, 1861. Colby Family Collection.

4. Ball's Cross Roads Skirmish

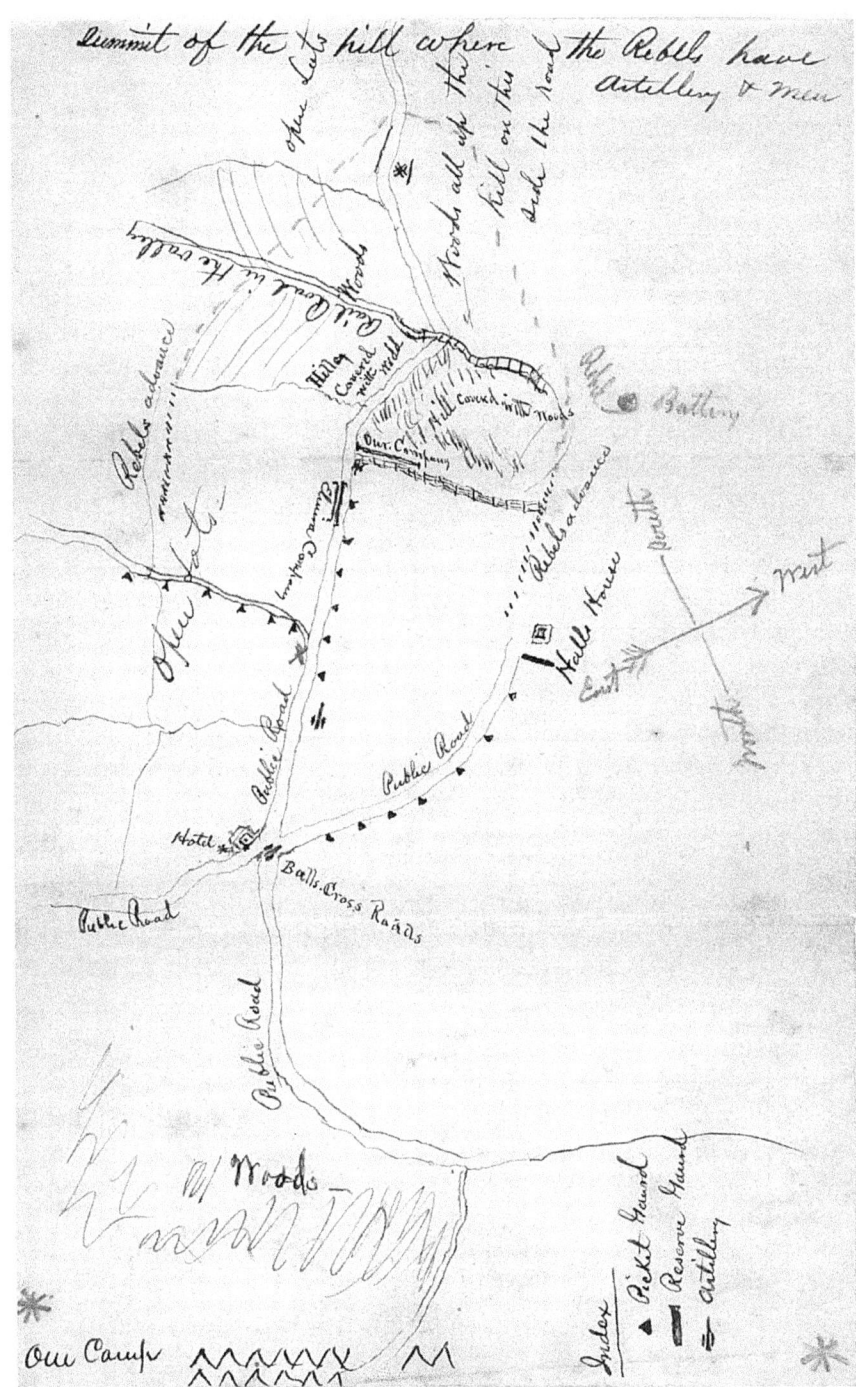

third order did he comply, and then he seemed very reluctant. He behaved with the utmost coolness, and Orderly Sherwood raged like a lion. His shouts of defiance rose above the cracking of the rifles, and the yells and howls of the rebels. I presume you have read of their practicing a peculiar cries, in the letters of various escaped prisoners and others. Their accounts scarcely come up to the truth, for of all the noises under the sun, this capped the climax. When the rebels found that they had a heavy fire to meet, they fell back to the cover of the woods, and soon their firing ceased entirely. We then fell back to Cross Roads, with the dead and wounded, and were posted for the night, in a field on the left of a field piece that had been brought up in the evening in case the enemy should endeavor to occupy the Cross Roads. No alarm occurred during the night, and the next morning some boiled pork and bread were sent down to us, and we had liberty to walk about and see what we could see for a short time. A road runs off to the right of the Cross Roads, winding up the hill to a house which stands in a clearing nearly on the summit. This house was used as headquarters for that division of the picket. The Orderly and myself and two or three others went up to this house in the afternoon and found two companies of some Irish and Dutch regiment, and Co. A, of our own, who were sent out the day before we were. Just as we reached the house the pickets came running in with the intelligence that the rebels were advancing down the valley with two pieces of artillary and sure enough before they had fairly come in, a shell whizzed over the house and exploded in the woods a short distance below. We went back to the Cross Roads, and found Gen. McDowell and staff there, and two companies of cavalry as a reinforcement.

I am detailed for picket to-day, and must close this letter.

Good bye Charles[7]

The railroad involved in this skirmish was at that time the Alexandria, Loudon and Hampshire Railroad Company. After a name change to the Washington & Old Dominion Railroad, it remained an active railroad until 1968. The right of way was turned into a 44 mile long recreation park in 1982. The exact location of the skirmish is where Wilson Boulevard crosses the Washington & Old Dominion Park. Today the town of Ballston, Virginia, is located at what was then Ball's Cross roads.

CHAPTER 5

Munson's Hill

"The regiment continued to drill and take up a defensive position as part of the Washington defense. There were numerous incidents throughout the area, but nothing of a major nature.

"It was during August 1861, that a civilian, Prof. Thaddeus Lowe and his gas aerial balloon made 23 flights over 34 days from Ft. Corcoran and Ball's Cross Roads. He observed and mapped enemy positions and movements in the Falls Church area, including Upton's and Munson's Hills."[1]

Also from the *Ledger*:

The Surprise of a Union Picket Guard at Munson's Hill

Narrow and Probable Escape of Daniel Munson, &c.
ALEXANDRIA COUNTY, VA. (near Bailey's Cross Roads) August 28 Yesterday, shortly after noon, our picket guard, twelve men strong, at Munson's Red Hill, a mile above Bailey's Cross Roads, was surrounded suddenly by a force of about 300 secessionists, who opened fire upon them, killing one man. Another was killed by being shot in the back by one of his own comrades. Six of the twelve were captured by the enemy, and the other four escaped back to our guard (of a company) at Bailey's Cross Roads.

Mr. Daniel Munson, hearing the firing so near his residence, mounted his horse to ride toward our lines. As he emerged from his gate on the turnpike a volley was fired from the hill, two hundred yards up the road, one shot bringing the horse to the ground. The horse fell and he extricated himself and ran across Bailey's field, in the direction of B's house. Nothing of his whereabouts has since been heard of here. He probably got of safely, however.

The secessionists pursued the four retreating men to a point near Bailey's Cross Roads, when the appearance of a company of regular cavalry coming to the reinforcement of the guard there, caused the enemy to face about and make again for Munson's Hill.

Heretofore that guard has been but a single company. I do not believe that it will soon again be set upon in any fashion, unless a general attack be designed by the enemy.—Washington Star[2]

"Professor Lowe could see from his balloon that the rebels had fortified Munson's Hill which was directly behind Upton's Hill. Cannon and rifle pit could be seen and it was supposed that they meant to keep possession of this area."[3]

Fred Burritt writes:

Aug. 31st: "Saturday morning last, every man able to stand under the weight of his gun and accoutrements, was in ranks at nine o'clock, with knapsack on his back, packed in approved style, and every species of property which we hold and use bailees of Uncle Sam for at least two hours as the regiment was inspected and mustered preparatory to the disbursement of two months wages among us—An officer of the regular service officiated, first inspecting arms and dress of each man while in colmn, and calling the roll, after which each company retired to its own ground, where its rifles were stacked in lines and every knapsack opened for inspection of contents, in front of the tent of its owner, and tents and grounds were subjected to close scrutiny."[4]

Seven P.M.—"We have just returned from three hours battalion drill and review by the General of our Brigade, about a mile and a half to the southwest on the premises of that ex. U.S. officer and now rebel Col. Hunter. The grounds were by no means Macadamised, but very uneven, and kept in the style of a gentleman's country seat in this section, overgrown with every species of vegatation indigenous to the soil of the old Dominion, abounding in hornet's nests and fences and buildings in the usual state of dilapidation."[5]

"Orders have just been received for the cooking of two days rations in preparation for a march, or a fight if one should be ordered which is hourly more probable, and the enemy are reported in threatening attitude before chain bridge, and in fact seem to be extending and strengthening their whole advance line. Prof. Lowe has made reconnoisances, daily for the past week, a mile or two north and west of this camp. It is not true as the papers have it that shot or shell have been fired at him, his balloon never having been within reach of artillery belonging to the enemy.

"Our men would feel ill disposed to exchange this for any other camping ground, after the labor expended in clearing up the brush and making the wilderness comfortable as a residence."[6]

A typical report about Prof. Lowe:

"Narrow Escape of Prof. Lowe's Ballon"

"Saturday afternoon, Professor Lowe made an ascension with his ballon from Ball's Cross Roads. As he neared the earth in descending, two shots were fired at the ballon by the enemy, from a rifled gun, which fell four or five rods only short of it."[7]

The *Philadelphia Ledger* reports:

"The Firing Across the River Only Gun Practice"

"The firing across the river this morning of heavier guns than have heretofore been heard at this point, was occasioned simply by the exercise of the men at the guns stationed in some of the U.S. fortifications in the vicinity of the Chain Bridge, and near Alexandria. The enemy also fired several shots this forenoon from rifled guns on Munson's Hill, at the Union pickets without however killing or wounding a man."[8]

"The Rebel's on Munson's Hill"

"The Confederates on Munson's Hill can be distinctly seen with a good glass, and their movements rendered perfectly visible. Most of each morning is devoted to drill, and small bodies of troops can be distinctly seen performing their various evolutions."[9]

Arlington Sept 6 1861
Dear Father

Your kind and welcome letter came safely to hand this P.M. and I hasten to reply though I have little to communicate that will interest you— Since our skirmish at Balls Cross Roads— we have been laying about camp— with little to do— Yesterday however we went (the whole Regiment) out about two miles and were reviewed by Genl Wadsworth and had rather a fatiguing time — On our return to camp we found orders from Headquarters for us to have on hand and keep always— two days rations and be ready to march at short notice — Having had such orders— several times before — we do not apprehend that we are *certain* to move — by any means—The Rebels are entrenching on Munsons Hill just across the Rail Road—where we had our little fight—and their infernal rag floats in sight of our picket guards—They have a brass cannon—covered with bushes—just exactly on the first level—on the hill above the rail road—where the man under my command was shot and wounded—Rather a curious incident occurred on the R R track a few days since—It was this Capt Loyden [Capt Marshall M Loydon] (of Cuba, NY) was out there on outpost duty and taking 20 men went down the hill to the edge of the woods—by the R Road to see what he might discover—His men and himself were all behind trees and imagine his surprise to see a Rebel Captain step out from behind a tree on the opposite side of the track and call to him to meet him on the track! Nothing daunted—out stepped Loyden (first telling his men to cock there guns and keep their "eyes skinned") and they met on the track and talked about half an hour! Mr Rebel asked Loyden if he could give him a copy of the New York Herald—but Loyden had none with him—Poor devil—he doubtless had not seen a northern paper for months and asking first thing for the Herald is rather significant—Rebel Captain then went on to speak of shooting at picket guards and said it was mere murder—Loyden agreed with him—but reminded him that it was begun by them—Rebel replied that if one of his men were catched at it—"he would shoot him like a damned dog"—Just then a shot was fired from the hill on the rebel side and the Rebel Captain turned sharply round and asked his men "Who in hell did that?" but it proved to be an accidental shot from some of them back on the hill side—Rebel Captain asked if the report of the victory of Genl Butler and Commodore Stringham was true? Of course it is said Loyden—but rebel said he guessed there was some mistake but Loyden told him he knew it was true—for Genl Butler was in Washington and Loyden says Rebel Captains face grew long and looked sad—"Well" said Mr Rebel "this is a cursed unholy war and I heartily wish it ended"—Finally bidding each other "good morning" they each returned to their respective sides of the Rail Road to their men and were ready to kill each other at first opportunity—My experience—in those woods the other day would have led me by irresistable impulse to have put a ball through Mr Rebel—before he could have called me once—The very instant he showed himself—in doing which I shall have lost the pleasure of his conversation which I should have regretted much—They were so dis-courtious when I was last there—that they had no respect whatever for my shoulder straps—but whenever I fired from behind a tree—they would fire a dozen shots right at me guided by the smoke of my gun—and in the excitement—they forgot civility entirely-Blast their infernal rebellious heads—We at least gave them a pretty good idea of how we could shoot—for it cost them rather dearly—for the latest estimate of their killed and wounded is 20 men—and then they gained not an inch of ground—

We are about done working on forts and cutting wood and I think before long you will hear big news—for I think big things are being cooked up—with regard to the staff of Genl Wadsworth—the appointments are all made and with the exception of his son—are all regular army men—So many appointments have been made in the comissary department that I fear it would be impossible to get in there—so I am floored all around—Just my usual luck. Well I suppose I must stand it—but I would like to have had one of the situations very much—I have become a great rider on horseback and have a horse whenever I choose—having made friends with the stable Boss—of the Regular Army stables near our camp—and I like to ride vastly—Probably Capt Todd will be in Corning next week—and I shall try hard for a furlough on his return—We have not yet received our pay—but will get it very soon—as the rolls are all made and been handed to the paymaster—I want to come home very much just as soon as we are paid off and mean it too—if it is possible. Tell mother I often think of her and would greatly like to see her—I intended writing to her long before this—and will do so soon—for she need not fear that I shall ever forget what I owe to her care and love—Remember me to my only brother—and tell him I wish to hear from him very often and his wife too—Give my regards to all friends—I received Curtis's letter last eve and was greatly pleased with it—and will try and answer it soon—Tell Chas Thompson I have a letter to him ready and will mail it soon. Write again very soon dear Father and believe me

Affectionately Your Son Newton[10]

From Corp. Charles J. Chatfield, Co. D

For the *Journal*
Camp 23rd Reg't N.Y.S.V.
Arlington Heights, Va., Sept. 6th, 1861

"I presume we shall remain for some time in our present position, unless some unexpected movement is made by Beauregard. General Wadsworth was in camp to-day, and ordered all the trees cut out from inside the lines of sentries and Col. Hoffman is having a log guard-house built, which does not look much like a speedy removal. Our squad have built us a cabin and hoisted the tent over it for a roof. We have bunks up one side, like a steamboat cabin, three deep, and on the other side a double bunk, hoisted so that there is room under it for the table, on which I am now writing. We have a stationary seat in front of it something like a desk at school minus the back to the seat, so that five can live pretty comfortably, as we are all very accommodating. I wish you could look in on us to-night as we gather in quarters to escape the heavy dews of this climate. Jaynes [Alexander J. Jaynes—died Dec. 15, 1861 at Falls Church of fever] and Sergeant Witt [2nd Sgt. Henry Witt] are asleep, one over our heads and the other on the top shelf on the other side on the cabin. Sergeant Kellogg and myself are writing to friends, and Corporal Crandall is practicing phonography, or short-hand, (in which he is quite proficient) as he intends to prepare himself for a newspaper reporter at the close of the war.

Things look nearly ready for a forward movement as the forts and roads are about completed, and the men have an opportunity of resting from their labors, which have been rather ardous. Captain Todd has not been very well for several days and we don't want to take the field without him as no one could exercise such an influence over the men as he. We hope to see him among us soon. There are quite a number of cases of intermittent fever in camp. Two men cut themselves quite badly while chopping today, one will probably prove crippled for life."

Sept. 8: "Gen. McClellan, however, will undoubtedly make it straight, as he is never caught napping, and is over to look at us nearly every day. He is always accompanied by his escort (The Sturgis Rifles) as his life might, otherwise, be endangered by some stray inhabitant of the "sacred soil," who (indignant at the intrusion of one so actively engaged in subverting the liberties which the F.F.V.'s formerly enjoyed of hanging and flogging Northern citizens) might end his career of usefulness by rifle ball or pistol shot from the bushes with which these Virginia roads are, in many places, lined for considerable distances. Our orders were renewed last night in regards to two days extra rations and our guns are inspected twice daily, in order that no one's carelessness shall place any obstacle, however slight, in the way of our complete success should we be attacked. All is quiet today as befits the occasion. Elder Crane is slightly indisposed, so that we have no service, and no passes can be obtained to cross the river on account of the uncertainty of events for the next few days. We sleep with our guns at our sides and cartridge boxes serve as pillows.

We have considerable time now that is unemployed, and could read much if we had books or papers. Men come to see me daily and often many times a day for something to read."

Sept. 10: "There was quite a little skirmish on the lines yesterday, and the rebels were driven back. The rebels have built a fortification about three quarters of a mile from Ball's Cross Roads, and throw shells at our pickets occasionaly. The men are making themselves generally comfortable, building log cabins, & c. The grounds are being cleared of trees and bushes and the space in front of the tents is swept daily. We drill a short time morning evening.

We had an inspection by a United States Officer the other day, and we were pronounced the banner company of the regiment. I saw James yesterday. He is well, but as I was in command of a chopping squad of fifty men, I had no time for conversation.

The weather is comfortable, and we enjoy ourselves much. Elder Crane sends his kindest wishes for your prosperity, & c. They are awaiting an attack with all patience, and no passes are given to the city, and a Colonel's pass is necessary to pass the field guard. Mounted patrols scour the country to return all straggling soldiers to their camps. Gen. McCellen's order for the strict observance of the Holy Sabboth, was read to us on parade last evening."

C.J.C.
[Charles J. Chatfield][11]

Arlington Heights Sept 11th
Wednesday 1861
Dear Father

As Capt Todd leaves for Corning this morning I thought I would drop you a line — though there is little to tell in the way of news. The rebels are in front of us and are plainly to be seen from our outposts but opinions are divided as to what they will do — Some say they will withdraw and abandon their position and others that they intend to advance and attack our lines. Every evening we see their signal lights and they — as well as us — make ballon assensions — By the way — there have been so many false reports about our skirmish at Balls Cross roads — printed in the Elmira papers — some of them malicious as well as false — that I hope Capt Todd will set some of the lies at rest — The report in the *Corning Journal* is not entirely accurate — though Kellog stated all he knew — but he was not with my reconoitering party and tells that part of it only by heresay — All the men over there were under my command and we all stayed and fought them until we were nearly cut off by a flank movement and then of course retreated — or run — just as any one but a fool would have done — No good could have possibly have resulted in one staying longer — But not withstanding our rapid retreat — we were not so *entirely frightened* — but that we stopped and fired back on them whenever opportunity offered — and I am quite certain that I rid the country of one rebel there — for you know I am not accustomed to missing as large a mark as a man — with a rifle — when he no farther off than 20 rods! and I resting against a tree — I had 7 or 8 men and they almost as many hundred! Could I do different? Capt Todd was cool and acted first rate and so did nearly every man we had —

I do not know how long he will stay with you — but suppose it will be about two weeks — and when he returns I intend to make a hard push for a furlough — We are not paid yet but expect it daily —

I send my comission by the Capt and wish you would take care of it for me till I return —

I was down to Washington yesterday but it is very quiet and there are no news — I see Genl Wadsworth quite often and we all think him a fine man every way — Give my love to Mother and Henry and tell them I hope to see them before many weeks — Respects to all enquiring friends — and say to them that we do not fear anything the Rebels can do — for we are ready for them — and I think their day has gone by forever — Ensign Jones — was not in our skirmish at all — he having gone to the city just before we were ordered off — How he gets along — I refer you to Capt Todd to say — But breakfast is nearly ready and the Capt leaves camp very soon — for home — home! how I would like to come and see you all in the old home —

I have become so used to sleeping in the open air — that it seems to me that it would choke me to sleep in a house and I cant tell how a bed would feel! It is very difficult to get a furlough and I cant tell when I can get it — if at all — If Todd comes back without getting all the men needed — I may possibly take his place as recruiting officer. Write often and believe me

Affectionately Your Son
Newton[12]

"Item of News" [from *Corning Journal*]:

"Gen. McCellan on Saturday made a ballon ascension with Prof. Lowe, and spent two hours in making reconnoisances of the enemy's position.

"It has recently been discovered that the rebels, in addition to their fortifications on Munson's Hill, have recently erected a formidable battery, commanding the Leesburgh Turnpike, about seven miles from the Chain Bridge. There does not appear, however, to be any considerable body of troops in the vicinity. It also appears that on Wednesday last week the rebels actually made an attempt to effect a crossing of the Potomac at Great Falls, about sixteen miles above Washington, but were repulsed with considerable loss."[13]

September 19, 1861—"Captain Todd, of Company D, Twenty-Third Regiment, New York Volunteers, has arrived [in Corning] from the front, on special service as a recruiting officer. Two hundred and fifty men are wanted to bring the Regiment up to full strength. Captain Todd says: "I want 25 good men to fill up my own Company."[14]

Washington Sept. 19, 1861
Dr Father

Enclosed I hand you the following amount—which please distribute immediately as directed.

For myself to pay note to Thompson	$ 50.00
1 Pckg to Mrs E M Lacey	$ 30.00
1 Pckg to Mrs Charlotte Messinger	$ 20.00
1 Pckg to Henry Witt	$ 20.00
1 Pckg to Margaret Decker	$ 16.00
1 Pckg to Mr Joseph Whitford	$ 15.00
1 Pckg to W.B. Thomas	$ 15.00
1 Pckg to Capt Todd	$ 10.00
1 Pckg to Mrs Anna Mott	$ 20.00
	$196.00

List of men that money was sent home for:
Henry C Lacey—mounted orderly for Gens. Wadsworth, Patrick and Paul
William H. Messinger—3rd Sgt—discharged 12/10/'61 for disability
Henry Witt-2nd Sgt
George E Lacey
Thomas J Decker
William Whitford
Oliver J Thomas
William H Mott

The money to Mrs E.M. Lacey is to be given to the carpenter Lacey's wife and the next is Bill Messingers wife—and you know Witts wife and that to Decker same as before and Joseph Whitford lives at Beaver Dams and his son has written to his father to call on you for it and the next one is to Thomas the butcher—and the last one you probably know...

Please have the money distributed promptly as you will know it is needed badly — and write me enclosing receipts as before I know it is much trouble — but I can not refuse to do it for our fellows very well-

I will write before long again — Henrys very welcome letter was received yesterday enclosing one from you — We do not *really* apprehend a battle — though there may be one any hour-

Give my love to Mother Henry and all our friends

In haste Yours affectionately
Newton

P.S. Open the envelopes when you deliver them and know that there is the correct amount in each — as marked.[15]

Arlington Va. Sept 25, 1861
Dear Father

Perhaps you were a little surprised to get a note from me to the effect that I wanted Mary to come out here — but I do wish it as I think it would be of good service and would afford me great pleasure. She can stay here two or three days and return with me — Do not fail to have her come — if she can do so safely — I fear however that the letter I wrote to her to come will not reach her in time to come with Todd — Luit Wilkinsons wife (of Elmira) is coming and I intend to have Mary come with her — Have her come if possible for her to come safely and in company with some reliable people — but she must not think of setting out alone — I think Redfield would give her a pass but if he does not — still I wish her to come — If Todd comes before she reaches Corning — and there is no one coming tell her not to come — Have her start all right if she does come and go to Elmira with her if you can — or if you could come out here with her — it would be very pleasant — What do you say? I will give you $10 towards expenses of your trip if you will come — You could stay here two or three days and see all worth seeing — board at a private boarding house which I shall have all ready for you — Come and write me so that I can meet you at the depot or if Mary comes without you — telegraph and I will meet her at Baltimore.

In haste Yours Newton[16]

"The Confederates had an outpost at Munson's Hill, a spot about 7 miles outside of Washington from which they could see the city. Septem-

5. Munson's Hill   77

Military pass for Colby and his wife. Colby family collection.

ber 28, 1861 Southern soldiers evacuate Munson's Hill, Va. after a minor skirmish. The Federals thought it was fortified and when they finally 'took' it, they found that one log, painted to look like a cannon had been left behind."[17] Another source said that the rebels used stovepipes mounted on wheels for the trick.[18]

Brigade Head Quarters
Uptons Hill
Oct 4th 1861
Guards and Patrols
Pass M. Colby, E. Colby and Mrs. N.T. Colby to
Washington and return
Good until Oct 6th 1861
By order of Gen Wadsworth
Lieut S.N. Benedict A.D.C.[19]

Corning Oct 4, 1861
My Dear Son

   Your very kind letter came to hand yesterday. Nothing would give me more pleasure than to be able to contribute to your advancement to some situation that would please you — The elections in Bailey's Regt. have taken place I have heard — but have not been informed further than to learn that Scott was defeated for Maj.— I am of the opinion that you are a little too modest — I can see no impropriety in boldly making known to those who have positions to bestow that you wish for a situation. If the Col. is your friend consult with him as to the best course to persue — and get him to help you — Ask Wadsworth for the appointment and tell him that you can present him testimonials of character and ability from Van Volkenburg-Ervin-Johnson and others — that your friends here have advised you to get a situation in the Genl Staff as they felt as the Old Steuben was entitled to it [Steuben county men] — Make friends with the Maj. so far as necessary at least to prevent his opposing you — For all their wraving [sic] if they do not win — they at least will do no harm — Never be dispondant if you cannot obtain the situation you wish — The question thus is — whether it is but to hold on to the one you now have and run the chances — Altho the pay is fair I for one do not wish to have you continue against your will — or expose your health by the inclimines of the season. Charley Thompson Esq will I heard him say be in Washington next week — and if you can make any capital out of him be prepared to take advantage of it — While you remain I hope you would be respectful and obedient to the those that circumstances have placed above you — and altho those under may not be companionable that it is greatly for your interest to keep the good will of the men — which you can do by kind words and actions that cost nothing — Should you want a petition to Wadsworth or Pres let me know — I think Bailey's Regt will be down soon and probably Thomson will come with them — Keep up good courage and if you deem it advisable on the whole to resign I think no one will charge you with having done so through fear or lack of courage — whether you participate in any more battles or not — I have just heard a report that you have advanced to Fairfax — If so write me as soon as possible and let me know how you are situated there — Todd was intending to leave today but I hear that he has a letter from the Col. directing him to wait until further orders — I think there is a shaddow of a prospect that something will be done with the defenses at home on our frontiers — it may be done by State Militia and there may be a call for volunteers for that purpose — Nothing has been done yet farther than a recommendation to have this subject attended too by states authorities — These thoughts presented to you are for considerations have passed through my mind and have been written about as fast as you will read them — If they are of the least use in guiding you in the accomplishment of your wishes I shall be well paid for writing — Hoping you will make yourself as happy as circumstances will permit — I am as ever devotedly yours —

Father

    (Written on edge of letter: "I had a letter from Mary day before yesterday *all well*)[20]

CHAPTER 6

Upton's Hill

"On Tuesday Oct. 8, 1861 the 23rd Regiment had been busy most of the day digging and building a fort nearby. They had recently had some very hot weather but on this day it had cooled down comfortably. Last night when the cool front came through the guards were pelted by heavy rain and hail with high winds. At about 2 o'clock the rains knocked down the tent of Chaplain Crane drenching everything in it. The tent was shared by Lieutenant-Colonel Crane, our adjutant and Seargant-Major William Robinson."[1]

Uptons Hill Oct 16, 1861
Dear Father

Sergt Witt having obtained a furlough and being about to leave for Corning I avail myself of the chance to write you a few words — There is little news here — and no fighting yet — I have not heard a word from you since you left — I suppose from what I hear however that the application to Col B-was unsuccessful-as I hear he has orders to come this way on the 17th and if so of course his appointments are all made — I saw Capt Norwood last Sunday (he was made a Captain in the comissary department — from being a private in the next company on our left) and he says I can get a place like his very easily (in his opinion) He says that there is a demand for comissaries and that the War Department no longer appoints them — leaving it to the Brigd General to recommend any one he likes and *they* then grant the comission — and that if I can find a General — who has not got a comissary on his staff I can win — He has promised to assist me in any way he can — and said he would send me the names of Genl Officers who needed comissaries and would recommend me to them — He is a fine fellow and may assist me greatly — I have had a letter from Mary since she left — dated at Corning — If I find a place such as I want — I will write and have you get me some documents — recomendatory and c. Capt Woodards pay is about $300 per month — and nothing to do!! I may get a furlough after next pay day — but it is very uncertain — We had orders to advance again the other night — but did not start — We may fight any time — within an hour and may not for a week or two-It will not be long however before we sail down upon them with our whole line and then we will have a big fight indeed-I am anxiously waiting to hear from you — please write soon — Give my love to Mother-Henry and wife and baby-Austin and all friends.

In haste affectionately Yours Newton[2]

Uptons Hill Oct 19 1861
Saturday Evening
Dear Father

Your long looked for letter came to hand this P.M. and I hasten to reply — With reference to my matters I am not disappointed in learning that the old Colonel holds out no prospect of my obtaining the place we talked of — as I had made up my mind that it would turn out so — such being my usual luck — Well — I have other plans in my head — and I intend to follow them too — though the prospect is that they will terminate as heretofore — Of course it is unnecessary for me to *tell you* that I desire to change my position very much — for you already know it — but how to accomplish it — without being accused of putting myself forward too much I have studied long and hard — All I have been able to do thus far — is to ascertain that there are two Brigades that are not supplied with comissions viz — Wadsworth and Pecks — Genl Wadsworth — of course — I know but with my enemy the Major to assail me to the General — I probably could do but little — and Genl Peck I know nothing of except that he has the reputation of being a fine man — and lives in Syracuse — Letters of *just the right kind* from Judge Johnson and Hon Wm Irvine to Wadsworth might be of great benefit — but they would have to be of such a nature as to appear to come from them — altogether — and without any prompting of mine — I would cheerfully pay $50 if I could secure the appointment of comission — or if I could get either Major or Liut Col — in Bailys Regiment — If Chas Thompson could be interested enough to work as he well knows how — he could do it for me if it could be done — and I would pay him a plump

$50 — What do you think? I tried hard to secure Jake Lansing a place on Hoffmans staff and he might perhaps return the compliment now — Judge Johnson too could influence Baily to favor me in the Election-I shall not remain where I am very long — be the consequences what they may — and I must confess — they will be serious enough — I am disatisfied and can not make up my mind to associate with either officers or privates in the present company for the officers are of a stamp that are not agreeable — and the men of a class with whom I have no sympathy or sociability — So now if in your opinion there is any prospect of success in Bailys Regt — have Thompson get to work and work earnestly — and get Johnson and Irvine to fix up some way to move old Waddy and thereby have two irons in the fire at once — I will try — and if I fail why so be it — I am accustomed to it and it will only be one added disappointment.

Well I have bored you enough with my own matters — not but that I know you would willingly aid me in any way in your power — however — for I know full well your love and kindness all my life — *If* I once could get a place where I could — I would try and make some small return for the liberality you have always shown me in money matters and I know that I have always paid in full (in my heart) the affection I have received and been the unworthy object of —

Monday Evening Oct 21, 1861

I wrote the above yesterday and having been busy all day in command of a detail of men who are working on a fort towards Falls Church — I have been able to finish it — We daily expect orders to advance again — There has been a prisoner at Head Quarters today — who reports that the rebels have abandoned Manassas and Bull run and gone into Western Virginia and Kentucky with the exception of a few Regiments — I do not believe the report however — Every day I remain serves but to make my decision to resign — only the surerer and more certain — The nights are very cold and provisions of a decent kind are not to be had and I have eaten two bushels of clear dirt within the past two weeks — It is nearly three weeks since I have been out of Camp to go any where only on duty — I look anxiously for your letter and therefore please write often — I have heard from Mary twice since you left her and have written her twice — Liut Sullivan [Lt. Florence Sullivan] applied for a furlough to day — and it was granted by the Colonel and approved by the Brig General — and then McDowell refused to approve it and he had to give up going — They are very strict about furloughs — so much so that I well know I can not get one if I try — If I could I would not resign at present for I would like to try and get some other situation before leaving this one — I shall probably take the chances in our next fight before I resign — and will certainly if it comes off soon for I know we will whip them — and I would dearly like to participate in a victory — and there too no man would ever insinuate that I feared to take the risks of battle — I *know* that I have too much pride to ever turn back on a fight and will not-Do what you are able for me without allowing my matters to annoy you in any way — Tell Henry to write me and every body else who cares enough for me and it will keep me from the blue devils — I send love to Mother and hope to see her dear old face again before long.

Affectionately Yours Newton[3]

Oct 21, 1861 Federal troops are defeated at Ball's Bluff, Va.
Nov. 1, 1861 Winfield Scott resigns as general in chief, to be replaced by McClellan.

Head Quarters 23 N.Y. Vols.
Upton's Hill Va Nov 1st 1861

I hereby concent that Lieut N T Colby of Company D 23 NY Vols be granted leave of absence for 20 days from Nov 10th to December 1st 1861 for the purpose of arranging unsettled business and removing his family from Nunda to Corning NY.

H.C. Hoffman
Col 23d NY Vol.

approved Col S Wadsworth

We have but one Officer absent from this Regt with leave of absence and his leave expires before this takes effect.

Liut N.T.Colby[4]

Uptons Hill Nov 7, 1861
Dear father

Though I received your letter enclosing one from mother too — several days since I thought I would delay answering them till I could write something new and interesting but having waited thus long and there having occurred nothing worthy relation — I hasten to write lest you suffer me sick. We are still where you found us — and are doing nothing at all — only drilling and freezing and starving — which perhaps may seem to you — to be occupation enough — The weather is quite cold — Especially the nights and there has been no end to the high winds lately — and the sleep one can get with the tent snapping and cracking over his head — does not amount to more than half a ration — To make the most of it. The recent severe rains have so swollen the Potomac that foot passages hardly cross it and teams and wagons are entirely stopped — in consequence of which we do not get full allowances of bread and c It will be remedied tomorrow I hear however — Todd came here a few days since and I have applied for a furlough and got the Col's consent and also Genl Wadsworth but have yet to get McDowell's and McClellan's and the consent of the last two is where I shall find any chief difficulty — They must either consent to a furlough or a resignation —*for I am coming* home if life and health are spared —

We are to be paid sometime the coming week and I intend to start for home (if I get my leave) just as soon as I am paid so that I can pay a few more debts when I do come — I am owing for board here considerable and the cold weather has obliged me to wear and purchase an overcoat — but I hope to be able to ride home free and if so will have enough left to do something with in the way of debt paying — Todd brot me a damming letter from Hungerford and I immediately answered it — he spoke of the debt as a "confidential" one and c. I expect to be laid in wait for — and badgered and annoyed by every pup in the corporation — but if my experience in the service is worth anything to me I will show some of the abusive cus the benefit of the tactics — I fully intend to pay *all my debts* and I fully intend to be my own judge of which I shall pay first and the man who interferes with my business must take harsher consequences than they have heretofore suffered from so doing — Dont think that I shall be to meek and patient — for there is not the least danger of it...

The high water in the Potomac is bringing down daily — bodies of the poor fellows who fell in the fight at Edwards Ferry above us — What a piece of wretched management was that — where blundering authorities managed to expose a mere handful — of our brave fellows — to more than triple their number and that too with all means of retreat cut off! And more than that —*for there were 10000 men under arms and awaiting orders — on this side of the river within two miles of* the battle field — and they not only were *not* ordered forward —*but were ordered back to camp!!* A few more examples of this nature and the confidence so necessary to success will be entirely wanting — between our troops and their General Officers — We are daily looking for some news from our fleet — hoping to hear of brave deeds and glorious results from them — if we are prevented from accomplishing anything here — Wadsworth staff is full so that there can be no chance with him — for me — I went over there in company with Capts Chapman [Capt. James H Chapman], Todd and Adj Hoyt [1st Lt. William W Hayt] to try and accomplish something for Seymour Denton towards getting him a Pay Masters situation — but there is but little hope of doing anything — I regret very much that it is so — for he is one whom I would cheerfully oblige in any possible manner — and should be happy if I could be of service to him — for I consider him among the "few" who live in Corning who posess souls — and who have true generosity and unselfish dispositions — or in other words — are Gentleman. Give my love to Henry and mother and Emma —

write often and believe me
Very Affectionately Yours
Newton[5]

The following was reported in Frank Leslie's newspaper of December 14, 1861.

"Grand Review of the National Army at Washington: Seventy Thousand Men on the Field"

The review held by Gen. McClellan on Wednesday, the 20th of November, presented a spectacle never witnessed on this side of the Atlantic, for on that day nearly 70,000 patriot soldiers stood in arms ready to meet the enemies of their country, who combine the twofold characters of rebels and brothers.

The spot chosen for the review was the open plain adjoining Bailey's Cross Roads, and the adjacent hills, Mason's and Munson's. We have described and illustrated these localities so often that we shall content ourselves by adding that Bailey's Cross Roads are situated eight miles from Washington, in the direction of Fairfax Court House, at the junction of the Columbia turnpike and the Alexandria and Leesburg turnpike. Between the Cross Roads and Munson's Hill, a mile and a half distant towards Falls Church, is a plain two miles in length, which was prepared by clearing off the fences, filling up the ditches, etc., for this grand display.

At half-past nine o'clock the General commanding, attended by all his staff officers, left his headquarters, escorted by a column of 1,000 regular cavalry. The array was most imposing as this splended cortege moved through the streets, the cavalry marching by platoons until it reached the bridge, where it was compelled to march by columns of four, and afterwards defiled along the road leading by Arlington Heights to the review ground. Gen. McClellan was plainly attired. As he rode in advance of his numerous retinue he was loudly cheered.

In the upper and lower divisions, Gen. McCall's and Gen. Heintzelman's from which a march of some eight or ten miles had to be made, the troops were astir at from two to three o'clock in the morning, and were on the march long before daylight. All of the seven divisions on the Virginia side of the Potomac were represented in the review, but enough were left in each to supply double the usual picket force to guard the camps, and a reserve in addition strong enough to repel any attack in force the enemy could make.

As early as nine o'clock the head column of Gen. Blenker's division, the headquarters of which are nearest Bailey's, began to arrive at the grounds from the Washington road. Soon after McDowell's advance guard appeared on a road entering the grounds from the same direction, but farther to the west. Next came the head of Gen. Franklin's column, approaching from the Alexandria road, and soon after the division of Gen. Smith began to enter the grounds from the direction of Falls Church. Gen. Fitz John Porter was next on the ground, bringing his forces by still another road. The troops now poured in from all directions, those under Gen. Heintzelman following Gen. Franklin's division, and the column of Gen. McCall succeeding that of Gen. Smith, and continued without cessation until half-past eleven o'clock.

The scene now was most exhilarating — more than 20 Generals, with their staffs, numbering above 150 horsemen, were dashing hither and thither arranging their divisions— which presented a total of above 70,000 men, including seven regiments of cavalry, numbering nearly 8,000 men.

At a quarter past 11 o'clock the President of the United States entered the grounds in his carriage, followed by the Secretary of State, also in his carriage, and by the Secretary of War and Post-master general, accompanied by Mrs. General McDowell and by two daughters of General Taylor on horseback. The party were escorted to a slight elevation near the center of the area, marked by a white flag, where they were soon joined by General McClellan and his staff. The cavalry escort was formed in line on the left. The seven regiments of volunteer cavalry, and the entire artillery present, were placed on the outer margin of the grounds. The infantry was formed into columns by divisions in mass. Everything being now in readiness, a salvo to the President and General-in-Chief was fired by four batteries of artillery designated for that purpose.

In the meantime the president and secretary of State, Secretary of War and Assistant Secretary of War, alighted from their carriages, mounted horses and prepared to accompany General McClellan in his review of the lines. This occupied about an hour and a half. Then commenced the march of the troops past in review. The honor of leading the column was assigned to the First Rifle Regiment of Pennsylvania Reserve, or the Bucktails, which was with General McClellan in Western Virginia. The divisions then passed in the following order:

First — General McCall's division, composed of the brigades of Generals Meade, Reynolds, and Ord.

Second — General Heintzelman's division, composed of the brigades of Generals Sedgwick, Jamison, and Richardson.

Third — General Smith's division, composed of the brigades of Generals Hancock, Brooks, and Benham.

Fourth — General Franklin's division, composed of the brigades of Generals Slocum, Newton, and Kearney.

Fifth — The division of General Blenker, composed of the brigade of General Stahl and the two brigades commanded by senior Colonels.

Sixth — The division of General Fitz John Porter, composed of the brigades of Generals Morell, Martindale and Butterfield.

Seventh — The division of General McDowell, composed of the brigades of Generals King and Wadsworth, and a brigade now commanded by Colonel Frisbie.

Upon the right of the General commanding during the review were the President, the Secretary of State, the Secretary and Assistant Secretary of War, Quartermaster General Meigs, and the Prince de Joinville. Mingled with his staff were general Sumner, and from time to time a number of division and brigade Generals whose forces were in review. Upon the ground were also all the rest of the Cabinet officers, and a number of Foreign Ministers and their families, grouped in carriages and on horseback around the carriage of the president, which containing Mrs. Lincoln and some friends, was immediately opposite to the position of the Commanding General. Among these were Governor Andrew and lady, of Massachusetts; the Misses Stewart, nieces to Colonel Scott, Assistant Secretary of War; Frederick A. Seward, Assistant Secretary of State, and lady; Hon. Montgomery Blair, Postmaster General, and lady, and two daughters of General Taylor; Mrs. General McDowell, Mrs. General Smith; Francis P. Blair, senior, Esq.; W. Russell, of the Times; Frank Leslie's Artist, etc.

One of the most interesting features of the day to many was the martial music, played by more than 50 bands, most of which were of the first order. In two or three instances the bands of the whole brigades were consolidated. The consolidated band in General Butterfield's brigade numbered 120 pieces, and played with excellent effect, while the brigade was passing in review, a quickstep, entitled "The Standard Bearer Quickstep," composed for and dedicated to General Butterfield.

The whole review was most admirably conducted. Infinite credit is due to General McDowell, who was the commander of the review, for the promptness with which his vast column moved."6

December 12, 1861 "Ladies of Hornby [Corning] have sent fifty pairs of socks to Captain Todd's Company and have forwarded a box of supplies for hospital use. Several shipments of food, including relishes, have been sent from Corning also."7

December 23, 1861 "Snowing, sleeting, raining, freezing — high wind — low temperature."8

Upton's Hill, Va, Dec 26
Dear Father

Though I have written you a letter since I received one — yet here am I.

No particular news here — but all sorts of rumors about our advancing — and I suppose that the infernal fools at the north are trying to bring a heavy influence to bear through congressmen and otherwise — to induce another onward — to Richmond — Bull Run affair — I wish I had a dozen of the wise heads of *Corning*— to take out *only* on *Pickett duty* and post them on the advance post — and if they dont lose their inclinations to brawl about —"why dont they do something and forward to Richmond +c +c" How easy it is to sit by the fire and swear and fume because we dont fight twice a week — Genl Averell said to me the other day — that the fight was to be — in this locality — between the Quartermaster's — or in other words will be decided by plenty or scarcity of food and forage.

Tomorrow morning at 5 A.M. (pretty early eh?) we leave camp with one days rations on reconoisance and we may see some fire and may not. I shall probably be in command — as Todd is sick — and I know not — or how much force we take — but I presume we go towards Fairfax and take at least one Brigade — perhaps more. Doubtless you will see some mention of it in the papers-

Henry wrote that he would start for here on Wednesday — and if he started — is now in Washington — but I have not been able to go down and shall not be tomorrow either — as we have to go out in the morning — If I get back all right — I will try and go down Saturday —

Irvine has left Elmira I see but only went to Gettysburg with their Calvary Regt — Big thing — aint it — As to staying here long I do not intend to — not that I have to leave — as some lying fools wish to have it — but because I am sick of going without decant food and having no decant rest or anything else — and associating with an idiot ("idiot" applies to either of the other officers!) I continue to discover signs of "dissatisfaction in the Company"—but unfortunately—I am not the object of their dissatisfaction—The best men in the company are my friends—and I firmly believe that I have no real enimies here—I may remain two weeks longer but I think not more than that—though events may necessitate a longer stay—If I come home I shall need some employment of course and if you think of anything in the mean time—you can say so when I return—I want to try Averill for a place and mean to as soon as I can get a chance—Give my love to Mother—how I would like to see you both—and tell her I am well and hearty and am looking out for the box of Goodies—she so kindly sent me—Well I must to bed—for I have to march probably 15 miles tomorrow—but by the time your eye rests on this sheet I shall probably have done it and got over the fatigue too—if I have good luck—so good night.

affectionately your son
Newton

    Note written over the top of the previous letter:

    I guess Todd will go out tomorrow with us—as he is not seriously sick—only a little under the weather—but at any rate do not tell that your son "commands" a company in the Army of the Potomac—"a la Jones"!![9]

Uptons Hill, Va Dec Jan 1st, 1862
Dear Father

    Your very welcome letter was received about ten minutes since and I hasten to reply.

    Let me first most heartily wish you a happy new year—and many of them too—when I may be at home and share its comforts with you. You say Irvine told you that he had written to me—and if so he told you a point blank lie—for he *never did* confound him—he is a pettyfoging sneak—So you have had another fire eh? Well it is characteristic of the "hole" we live in—There is but little good in it—not enough to save it from fire—and barely enough to save it from the ancient accompaniement of brimstone—and now that "I and Todd" are absent from it I wonder that Sodoms fate does not befall it.

    The trunk of "plunder" came to hand all right—on New Years Eve and I have eaten so much to day that I have the belly ache to night—and I need hardly say how much I am obliged to the friends who so kindly contributed to my comfort.

    I have just been called out of my tent to exercise rather an unpleasant authority as Officer of the Gaurd — viz — to arrest a soldier in Co. E charged with stealing a watch off from the dead body of Jayne — one of our boys who died in the hospital — I went and found the fellow and brought him before his accuser and they began to blow each other and finally I had to jerk them apart by main strength to keep them from punching each others heads — Fine — is it not? With regard to Henry — I cant say how well he will do — I went to the City and got him boarded at Mrs Andersons for $4½ per week and went part way over to Bailys Regt with him with his sack full of envelops and am anxiously waiting to hear how he does — for he agreed to write me immediately — Write soon. Give my love to mother and believe me very truly

Yours Very Affectionately
Newton[10]

For the *Corning Journal*:

Head Quarters 23 Reg't N.Y.V.
Camp McDowell, Jan. 6, 1862

Friend Pratt: I noticed in your last issue a communication from W.J. Gilbert, Esq., relative to the sanitary condition of our hospital. We recognize on the part of the author an anxiety to do good and to ameliorate if possible the condition of our sick soldiers. A simple statement of the facts as to the condition of our regiment, at the time of Mr. Gilbert's visit, will I trust throw a different light upon our Hospital arrangements, and show our friends in the "Southern Tier," that we do care for, and as far as possible do all in our power to relieve the sufferings of those stricken down by disease. From the 28th of Sept., the time of our advance to Upton's Hill, to the 6th of Dec. we occupied a medium sized two story house containing seven rooms, four of which were appropriated to the sick, the balance were required for the use of the Surgeons and attaches. True it was not such a building as we wished for, but considered ourselves exceedingly fortunate in obtaining so good a place, while neighboring Regiments were compelled to use tents and suffer much from the cold. Our camp during this time was situated in a ravine, where we were continually exposed to the changeable winds from the north and west which are very injurious at this time of year, in this climate, to almost all who are not throughly acclimated. Add to this the vegetable and animal decomposition that must necessary take place in a camp where eight hundred men are congregated for a long time, their surroundings, manner of living &c., and we wonder not that disease shows itself in some form. Other Regiments were suffering much from epidemic fevers, and in fact the whole army of the Potomac was more or less afflicted. About the middle of November the first serious case made its appearance in our midst, gradually it increased in severity as well as in the number of its victims, until our small hospital could hold no more. Search was immediately commenced for a larger building, which was found at Fall's Church about one mile in advance of our regiment. Both Camp and Hospital were now moved. Just at this Mr. Gilbert arrived. Our hospital was not yet in order, because of delay in transportation. And here I wish to correct an error that Mr. G. labors under. The present Hospital is a large Church divided into two wards — the sick and convalescent. Each ward is about 30 by 45 ft. with four doors and four large windows that let down from the top, so that ventilation can be controlled at will. Each ward contains about twenty bunks, six feet in length by two and one half in width. Upon these are placed — first a straw bed, next a blanket, then the sheets and quilts in number sufficient to keep the patient warm and comfortable. The pillows are made of hay or feathers. All of these articles we are abundantly supplied with, and have been since our occupation of Upton's Hill. At the time Mr. Gilbert was here, few, if any of these things were on the beds, because we were having new bunks made, with a view of thoroughly renovating every thing that came from the old hospital. Every bed was filled with clean fresh straw, the pillows well aired, in fact, every precaution was taken by the officers and men to rid ourselves of the fearful epidemic which was prevailing so extensively at the time. At no time could a more unfavorable impression be made. In the midst of an epidemic of Typhoid and Typhus fever, the hurry and bustle of moving camp and hospital equipage, a casual observer might come to the conclusion that the sanitary arrangements of our Regiment were very imperfect. But not so. Up to the time when these maligant fevers first made their appearances — which was about the middle of November we had lost, by disease in Regimental hospital, but one. The whole number of deaths being seven; three of these died in General Hospital, one was killed in a picket skirmish, one was killed by the falling tree, and one was poisioned by eating wild fruit. These are the numbers of deaths in our regiment up to that time, thus making our loss but one third of that in the Gen. Hospital. When Mr. G. was here we had on the sick list one hundred and forty names, sixty-three of which were typoid and tiphus fevers. At the writing of this I am informed by one of the surgeons that there are but two cases of acute disease under treatment in the Regiment, all fevers having entirely disappeared. We feel happy to be able to congratulate ourselves that we are again restored to our former healthy condition and trust that Divine Providence may so continue it, so that we may be able to render a good account to our country, in assisting to crush out the most despicable and damnable rebellion that devils in the guise of God's image were ever engaged in.

Truly yours, Wm. W. Hayt,
Adj't 23rd Reg't N.Y.V.[11]

Camp McDowell
Upton Hill Jany 19, 1862
Dear Father

Your very kind and welcome letter has just been received and I hasten to reply.

I am just as undecided as ever — about leaving my present situation — and the hesitation is due to the fact that I hardly feel as though I ought to leave before one heavy blow is struck at treason and because I have no certainty of employment elsewhere — I am in formed that Todd has threatened to resign in the spring and I have heard him say that he should ask for a furlough next month — I have nothing whatever to do with him or to say about him —

You wrote me that Scott — of Lansing Company had the appointment of Signal Officer and so he had — but he failed to pass the examination and has returned to his old position in his regiment — If there is one taken from our Regt — I think my chance will be as good as any ones — I have not been idle and should they ask us for an officer I have pretty good reasons for believing I will get it —

It rained hard all night and is raining very hard now and the roads are nearly impassable and there is nothing but mud on all sides — We have just finished another tour of picket duty — and though it was rather cold we had a very pleasant time — There being a full moon the night was clear and beautiful — and so still was it that a footstep could be heard nearly a mile — as it crashed through the crust of the snow and ice — Of course we were not molested by the Rebs — Todd and Jones were both absent in the city and I had things all my own way — I send you a portrait of old Waddy our Brig Genl and I call it a pretty correct likeness — dont you?

So Henry had to stay in Harrisburg eh? Did he relate his impressions of the swamp where our camp is? Or the pleasant walk he took through the woods one night in search of our camp — where he lost the way? or does he ever mention my kindness in dividing my bed with him thereby giving him a comfortable nights rest-? for which kindness — by the way — he never appeared very thankful!! Ask him if he is not sorry now that he did not go for a soldier — as he wanted to last spring? Tell him that the mud is two feet deeper now—than when he was here—Give my love to mother and tell her that if she was here I would *as usual* give her a job of mending my breeches—There is a hole in the seat of them a foot square—and the worst of it is—I have no others. I must go to bed and sew this up—as the weather is too cool to wear them as they are—I hope I may be at home again in the spring—permanently—but of course can not tell how I may be situated. Write as often as your cares will permit—Above all take good care of your health—if business goes to the devil.

Believe me Affectionately and truly Your son
Newton[12]

Corning Jany 3 [23] 1862
Dear Son

Your fine and affectionate letter of the 19th came to hand the evening that Luther left for Washington and having written you by him is my excuse for not answering it sooner—The kindness and interest you manifest in my welfare is very gratifying and in a great measure rewards me for any trouble or anxiety I may have taken or felt on your account—You tell me not to let you or your matters disturb me in the least—But I presume in mature reflections you would hardly wish me to feel thus—At least it would be very difficult to comply with such a request—I have always felt a just interest for your welfare and success and at no time more than at the present—I can but feel—anxious that your life and health may be preserved—that your career as a military officer—be it long or short—may be a credit to you—and not the least—that you may the demoralizing influences of Camp Life—A strictly moral and even a christian character always will command respect in court or camp—At the same time I have the most entire confidence in your judgement and ability to meet all the difficulties that are inevitable attendance on the life you are leading with great firmness and discipline I feel at times a great anxiety to have you return home—But I am confidant that your anxiety on that subject is fully equal to mine—And am willing to leave it to your judgement to decide when that time shall be—Mother since sending your letter—has manifested a good deal of anxiety about you—She thinks the wide breach you complain of in your rear should be repaired without delay and regrets her inability to assist you in restoring it to its former safe conditions—Luther returned this morning—I have seen him but a few minutes. He speaks highly of your kindness in showing them the Elephant and c He says you have had a sword presented you by some of the men belonging to your company — I am very much gratified in your receiving it as a token of the respect and attachment of those doing duty under you — and hope it has not be done in such a manner as to increase or produce any unkind feelings between you and any of the officers or men in your company — If there are any that have not contributed to the purchase from any motives — treat them as well if not a little better than before to let them know that you mean to be impartial. This will prevent any dificulty and increase the number of your friends in the company. On this subject it is probably unecessary that I should advise you as your own good judgement will prevent you so far as you can continully retain the good will of all the men in the co.

[end of letter missing][13]

"After a week of snow and rain the streets and parade grounds were nothing but endless mud. The only cheery point was that the enemy suffered more for want of supplies.

"Chaplain Elder Crane left on Tuesday Jan. 27 for home and dearly missed by all. He was expected to be replaced by Mr. Dubois." [James DuBois was appointed Chaplain in place of E.F. Crane.][14]

Camp McDowell
January 29, 1862
Dear Father —

Having a chance by the hands of Dr Terbell I have decided to write you a few lines and to request your very earnest attention to some things I have to say. So — "front face and attention" First to tell you the news and the situation I am in just at present — Mud — mud — mud — "et nihil sed mud" (there's latin for you!) on every side. except over head — and even there it would be if a little dirt was mixed with the rain that comes so plentifully every day or two — and as a natural consequence of the mud we are "cabined-cribbed" confined — in camp — cant even obey the calls of nature without wading through the tenacious sticky compound — and even the sacred character of the soil affords no relief — Were it not for the awful state of the roads I think beyond doubt we should set out for Centerville and Manassas — and will do so just as soon as the going will permit — I anticipate the roughest time we have seen by far if we do go — for we shall not take our tents and in fact nothing except the veriest necessaries — simply what we can carry on our backs — and at this season the weather is very unreliable here and we may lie a week without covering — But then if we only give the rebels a nice thrashing — one that they will not soon forget — why we are entirely willing to go —

I presume you have heard of the very accessable and handsome present — which our company made me the other day — It was really a surprise to me and affords a satisfactory answer to the falsehoods — circulated by certain persons — Nothing could have been better timed — and Col Hoffman who presented it on behalf the Company — made a neat little speech — and his connection with it. The affairs added much to the pleasure of it — The presentation took place just in front of my tent and the company — with many from other companies — with quite a number of my fellow officers — The Colonels wife — the staff and c were present — I attempted to make suitable acknowledgement — of course — We had a nice little time and I think with a couple of exceptions — that all were much pleased — The sword and belt cost $25 — as I am told — and is a beautiful one and bears the following inscription on a small silver plate "presented to Liut N.T. Colby by Co D 23 Regt N.Y. Vols — Jany 25, 1862" I hope to live and treasure it up to show my children —

Well — do not say too much about it for I have adopted the silent style and quietly await whatever may come — and I fear nothing that may be said about me for I am entirely innocent of any chicanery or low trickery against any one — and the truth and right must (it seems to me) be apparant some time — Now then I wish you to write and say what you think about my coming home — I am tired of this life and long for the quiet of my own fireside — say to me just what you think and keep back nothing — Were I out of it I would not go into the service again for a Colonels comission — Can I quit honorably? Can I obtain employment? Give my best love to mother — and tell her that I will come home just as soon as I may do so honorably — and that I often think of her and wish to see her — Remember me to Henry and wife with much love — Write me just as soon as you get this — Elder Crane has resigned and gone home — and I presume you will see him — He was one of my best friends and I shall miss him much — tell him so for me-

Affectionately your son Newton

Note written on the top of the page: "Bill Hoyt has gone home on leave and I am acting as adjutant in his stead by order from headquarters and am also a 'Judge Advocate' on a regimental court martial. Big thing, eh? I am of vast importance just now dont you see?"[15]

6. Upton's Hill

The following letter is from Newton's cousin George G. Colby, who served with the 23rd Missouri Regiment, to Merrill Colby, Newton's father:

Chilicothe Mo.
Co K 23rd Regt Mo Vols.
Camp Tindall Feb. 5th /62
My Dear Uncle

Upon my arrival in Mo. I wrote you, but received no answer and at the risk of being thought — obtrusive, I write once again. If this meet with neglect, I shall feel no resentment; only melancholy, I am indeed a stranger in a strange land; my principal enjoyment, is the memory of old associations, old friendships, and endearments. I am not insensible to the charmer of novelty, but the impressions of the past are too deeply engraved on my heart, to yield to the impressions of the present. I will not fatique you with a tiresome narrative of my nursery labors, nor of my capture and detention by the rebels. My life in the distant west has not lacked eventfulness; but until lately it has been rather unpleasant. I am now in the Army, and in a position to enjoy life. I enlisted as a private, and was soon promoted to a lieutenancy. In which office I hope to do good service for my country. I am cheerful; even happy with a tinge of melancholy arising from my absence from home, from the scenes of my youth and the more rational enjoyments of mature age.

If this war continues and I have oportunities to do so, I will endevor to win for myself a name. And at its close shall revisit the paternal roof to receive a *Mothers* kiss, and a *fathers blessing. I have now considerable time* for *study* and reflections; and *shall use it to advantage.*

I now more than ever appreciate the kindness of maternal admonition and have carefully abstained from every species of dissipation. I understand Cousin Newton is in the Army; but in what Regt, I know not. Please give my respects to *Cousin Mary*, and ask her why she has not answered my letter. And now dear uncle except [sic] for yourself and my excellent Aunt, my sincere *love* and *esteem*. Give my regards to Henry and wife. As I am not conscious of having done any thing to forfeit your esteem, I hope you will favor me with an early reply; containing such information as your judgement shall dictate as most likely to interest me. In conclusion I subscribe myself

Your Nephew
George G Colby

P.S. Tis reported that the rebels have crossed Mo. River in large numbers and threaten an attack soon.

G.G.C.[16]

Cousin George G Colby was never able to fulfill his dreams of making a name in the Army. George was born at Greece, Monroe Co., N.Y., May 1, 1840, and was mustered into the Army December 12, 1861, as a private at Chillicothe, Mo., for three years. He was promoted to 2nd Lieutenant on January 7, 1862, and served at Chillicothe until March. His regiment, the 23rd Missouri Infantry, Co. K., moved to St. Louis until April. During the battle of Shiloh, Tenn. (Pittsburg), on April 6, 1862, the whole regiment was captured. He was held at several locations and suffered from exposure and starvation. He was held at Montgomery, Al., and then Madison, Ga., until Oct 4, 1862, then was moved to Richmond until Oct 11, 1862. His name appears on a list of Lieutenants, C.S.A. delivered at Aiken's Landing, Va., and exchanged for Lieutenants of the Federal Army. He was listed as age 24, 5'9" and a nurseryman.

Nov. 25, 1862 A hand-written letter of resignation was written at New Brunswick, N.J., by George Colby. By special order of the Adjutant General's Office, Washington, D.C., dated Nov. 11, 1862, he was honorably discharged as physically unable to perform duties.

George was later employed as a clerk in the office of 2nd Auditor of the Treasury in Washington from July 1864 to Oct 1886 and from Oct 1893 to May 1905. He often suffered and or missed work because of chronic rheumatism and liver trouble that he got while in rebel prisons. He married Lillie K. Boothby at her home in Limerick, Maine, on Aug. 12, 1875, by Rev Albert Cole. She was born about 1854. Their children were: Guy B. Colby b 9/3/1876; Wilmer Colby b 12/26/1880; Wm. G. Colby and Geo. G. Colby Jr b 7/4/1883 (twins). George went on pension about 1890 until his death Sept. 13, 1915, at Limerick, Maine. Lillie died Aug. 27, 1926.[17]

Camp McDowell
Uptons Hill Feby 11, 1862
Dear Mother

I received your very kind and welcome letter last evening and I need not assure you dear mother — that I was real glad to hear directly from you and very greatful for the expressions of affection and interest towards me — I have long intended to write to you — but my time has been occupied to a great extent and then I knew you always heard from me by Father and Mary's letters — but I will try hereafter to remember how you have often done for me and imitate your good example —

We are still at our old camp — at Uptons Hill — and are doing next to

6. Upton's Hill

nothing as a Regiment — though I have been quite busy in several different capacities — having been detailed on a Board of Court Martial and acting Adjutant — Hoyt-(our adjutant) went home and since his return has been sick and I act still in his place. I presume you get the news just as soon as we do here and perhaps sooner — so there is little to tell of — except personal matters I am well and quite hearty — now — though I had a slight attack of billions cholic a day or two since — With regard to Coming home — I hardly know what to say — for things so mixed up here that I hardly can decide what is for the best — I suppose If I leave that the immense Todd will blow long and loud and many at home will think I am afraid to stay — I am all right — as far as our men are concerned — and could send Mr Todd into trouble quick — had I the inclination — but I quietly wait and pay no attention to him whatever — he feels terribly about my sword presentation — and has told a dozen lies about it — but he has very bad luck — somehow — among the officers of the regiment — for — with one or two exceptions they laugh at him —

Another reason that makes it bad about coming home is the want of business to live on — If I pay my debts I can have nothing left of what is due me — and would come pretty close to starving — and that is not pleasant — you know — I am now making a large and persevering effort — to obtain another place and if I fail I may come home — I wish nothing said about my intention however — or rather *say that* I intend to stay *5 years* if necessary. I suppose that Corning is pretty well filled with lies about me from the manufactory here — but there is one consolation and that is that I must be in somebodys way or I would not be noticed so much!! Somebody must be a little hurt — and somebody must fear something from me — Todd even went to the Colonel about my presentation and complained and told the Col that there were only 6 or 8 men concerned in the present to me — but one of our men who asked the Col to present the sword for the company — told me — that the Colonel asked and they informed him the exact number of men who contributed towards it — and consequently he knows Todds lying!! One of our field officers who heard him tell the Col — told me that he got mighty little consolation from Col Hoffman —

I am quietly watching events — and if I fail to get another place will probably come home this month — not because I fear anything that anyone here cant do — but because I am tired of camp life and of being absent from my family and friends — I wish to be again where I can live among civilised people and enjoy home comforts — Write as often as your time will permit — Tell father that I have signed an allotment roll and made $50 per month payable to him — and it will be sent to his care every two months—Remember me to Henry and all friends Tell Mary I expect a letter from her and will write to her tomorrow if possible—

Give her my love
Newton[18]

Camp McDowell
Upton Hill Feby 20 1862
Dear Father

I have waited a long time for you to write—but getting no answer to my letter I wrote again—I have invented every reason I could think of to account for your continued silence—and I now formally protest—and "by these presents do protest" against a farther continuance of the blockade—You will therefore please take notice and govern yourself accordingly—

We are still mud bound—and comparatively inactive—Col Hoffman left here for home this morning—on leave—for 8 or 10 days—so I suppose we will be idle for that length of time—at least—though we have rumors that Manassas and Centerville rebels intend to make a concentrated attack on us here very soon—and to give some coloring to the report—we have had two batteries ordered to go out to our front—with a strong force of cavalry—to strengthen our picketts. With regard to myself—I intend to stay this month out any how—but probably not much longer—Todd—This morning made his regular morning speech to the company—in which he said he would transfer any of his men who were dissatisfied with him to any other company in the regiment—and that now he should consider peace restored to the company and should say no more—When you recollect that I have never answered any of his boyish—silly—folly—or noticed it in any way—I think you will agree with me that it amounts to an acknowledgement of defeat—in his attempt to get me out of the company—He has said that there were but 10 men concerned in the presentation of my sword—but I am now to show the names of 22 who contributed towards it—and have been assured by many others—that they would cheerfully have done so—had they known of it—A few days since—an order was read to the regiment—calling for volunteers to—go west and man the gun boats on the Western rivers—Two thirds of our company offered themselves—I guess—and among them Sherwood—our orderly Sergt—The Colonel accepted the orderly as one of the volunteers (only five were to be taken from our regiment) and no sooner was he accepted—than the brave felow attempted to back out!! He induced a man to go to the Colonel and offer to take his place — but the Col said *No sir* and the fellow was fast — Every man he went to — to take his place — but one — refused!! They all thought we were to be rid of him at last — but alas — I fear that he will yet succeed in backing out —

The eloquent and accomplished Jones — and the ponderous skillful thief taker — Van Ellen arrived in camp not long since — They are the honored guests of Todd — and therefore look for an inventory of short comings and slanders respecting your son — as soon as they reach Corning — Do not be disturbed with any charge less than murder in the first degree as I am in shape to prove myself clean of any thing else — Do not permit them to say anything disrespectful of either our Captain or Ensign — as they are universally beloved and respected and esteemed by their fellow Officers in the Regiment! — They are really immense — and in my opinion they were the original inventors of Gas and many other valuable discoveries — My health is very good — but I am getting seedy as to clothes — having bought nothing since I was in Corning — Of course if I come home — I shall not need any more military clothing — I told Col Hoffman the other day that I thought of resigning — and the reason why — and he said he would like to have me stay — and said that we ought to settle our troubles — that he thought Todd acted very foolishly — *For him* that was saying much I assure you — Col Crane — (always my firm friend) says I ought not to allow such an ass as Todd to influence me at all — and that if I only keep cool I am all right-

Write soon-and tell me the news — if there is any in your splended city — Are you satisfied with the taking of Donelson and Roanoake Island? Dont you think they are glorious victories?

Remember me kindly to Mr Austin and any other inquiring friends —
Give my best love to Mother and Henry

Affectionately Your Son
Newton[19]

CHAPTER 7

Bailey's Cross Roads

"The first week of March found the 23rd involved in drilling morning and afternoon by squads, companies and battalions. Thursday March 6, 1862 General Wadsworth marched all hands with full packs out to Lewisville Road. There they pitched their tents, they picked them up again and marched back."[1]

March 9, 1862   "At eleven P.M., the cooks were told to prepare rations for three days and all expected to march before morning."[2]

"At about 3 o'clock on March 10th, to the tune of 'Yankee Doodle' the regiment moved out towards Centerville in the rain. They found no enemy at Centerville, Fairfax or Manassas. The regiment camped about two miles north of Centerville for five days. On the 11th, Generals McClellan and McDowell rode up to a cheering crowd. They stopped to shake hands with our General Wadsworth."[3]

March 11, 1862   McClellan is removed as Federal general in chief but retains command of the Army of the Potomac.[4]

Near Centerville
Mch 12, 1862
Dear Father

   I enclose some letters and secesh provisions returns picked up at Manassas by Col Hoffman and given by him to me — I thought they might interest you and other Corning friends — Col H says that the works at Manassas amount to but very little and are of no great extent — In fact — I suppose that the famous stronghold of Manassas was made dangerous and notorious only and solely by the "blowing" and brag of Rebels— Show the letters to Mary — and to any who would be interested — I have seen Sabre's, Guns, Bowie knives and lots of plunder obtained at Manassas— The rebels left behind their tents— supplies—clothing and c — I will write again soon I suppose we are to go on to Richmond

Take care of my dear ones till I come and believe me

Very Affectionately Your Son
Newton[5]

"On March 15th the regiment moved to Alexandria in the pouring rain to board transports. They had to march twenty miles in the storm without food or rest. With the wet clothing adding much weight and discomfort to the trip, it is noted that Major Gregg [Maj. William M Gregg] and Colonel Crane relieved many of their burdens to allow them to rest and keep up. Due to the rains, a stream called Four Mile Run had turned into a lake and was impassable. When it did not recede the next day, the regiment returned to Upton Hill to their rude cabins. After two days there they moved their camp about a mile to Bailey's Cross Roads where they stayed until the 4th of April."[6]

Baily's Cross Roads
Mch 20, 1862
Dr Father

I wrote the enclosed leter — while staying here and if you think proper you may give it to Pratt or to Brown if you choose and rub Pratts name out. We are still here and no one knows how long we may stay The informalist works here you ever saw and I think most of the officers condemn McClellan as the cause — Many do so most emphatically. I am well — The mail is waiting and I must close —

In haste yours ever
Newton[7]

Letter from Lieut. Colby
For the *Journal*:
On the march near Alexandria

Provision Return for capt Graves' Company, 11th Reg; N.C. Vols. commencing Nov. 16th and ending Nov. 1st 1861

No. of Men	14
No. of Days	4
No. of Rations	56

(Oh Lord what a large Company!)
N. T. Colby

Fresh Beef	42
Bacon	14
Flour	56
Corn Meal	
Rice	
Coffee	
Sugar	
Molasses	
Whisky	
Vinegar	56
Candles	14
Soap	56
Salt	56
Lard	5

Explanation: Sugar is 35 cents per pound!!!
N. T. C.

B. Y. Graves Capt
Commanding Company

Commanding Post

This page and opposite: Provision returns from 11th North Carolina Regiment, March 12, 1862. It was given to Colby by Col. Hoffman from Manassass, and includes comments written by Colby in pencil. Colby family collection.

7. Bailey's Cross Roads

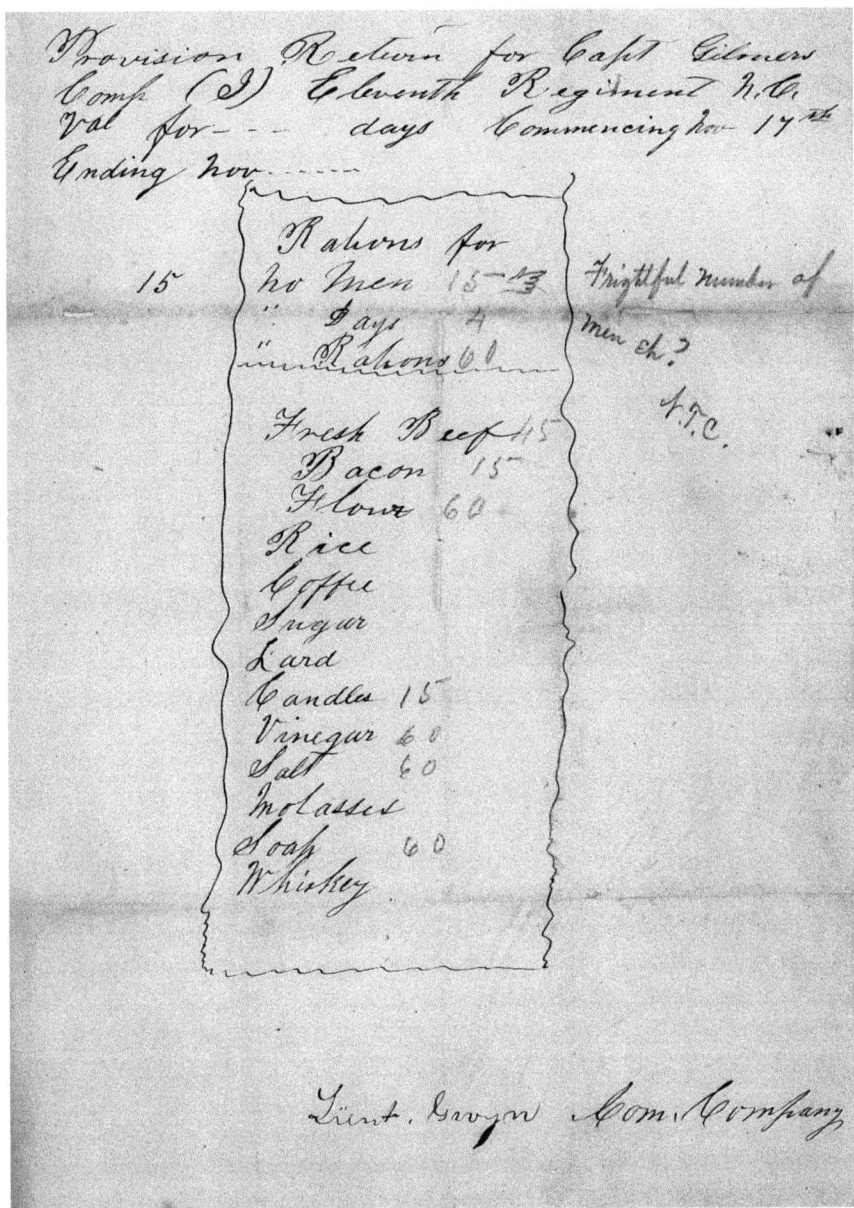

March 18, 1862

    Friend Pratt: In the hope that I can succeed in interesting your readers in attempting a description of some of the incidents which have befallen the 23rd, I sit by our bivouac fire and recall to mind the events of the last week. An order to advance Sunday night brought the Regiment into line at 5 o'clock in the morning of Monday and away we tramped to attack the famous works of Centerville and Manassas (the last named place is pronounced Manassa not Manassas, by all the inhabitants of the vicinity)

Carrying pack loads on our backs that would draw tears from our friends to look at, slipping and wading through the mud slightly moistened by a fine sifting cool rain, we about 3 P.M. bivouacked for the night in a pine woods, distant about 2½ miles from Centerville and remained there till Saturday morning.

While staying here we were agreeably surprised by the appearance of a couple of our Corning friends, Messrs. Stearns and Way, and in their company I visited Centerville, Bull Run and Manassas, and in doing so we walked a distance of at least 30 or 40 miles; visitors were there already and memorials and mementos of these plains were eagerly sought after by all, and I presume that ten tons of relics were thus carried away. So many more competent than myself have described these places that I will not attempt to do so more than to say, that all agree in saying, that the stronghold of Manassas differed in all respects from what they had previously imagined it to be. We slept at night in a house on the battlefield of Bull Run — visited the spot where the fighting was most severe — saw the still unburied bodies of our gallant fellows — a hideous sight, lying mostly near the spring where raging thirst had driven them thro' the storm of bullets — the stone house used by our surgeon as a hospital, — a round marble pillar marking the spot where a rebel Colonel fell, and bearing the inscription thus "Col. Henry Bartow" "they have killed me boys but never give up the fight," and many other objects of interest. At one place where we stopped to get a drink, a young lady of the colored persuasion informed us that the rebel officers and even their wives, took a fancy to use the bones of our men to manufacture pipestems, tooth-picks, finger rings & c & c, thereby I suppose illustrating their chivalrous christian humanity. At another house I found a young lady of about twenty years of age, busily engaged in spinning, affecting ignorance of what her employment was, I asked what she was doing, she replied shortly, "spinning air," taking up a roll of wool that lay across the machine, I asked what it was, she replied "wool air," "ah" said I "is this the tail of the animal?" "La, no sir, them ere is made with cards," "then you play cards here do you?" said I trying to get funny, and as long as I love I shall never forget the look of horror assumed by the whole household, (consisting of eleven children, with their parents) as she indignantly replied, "I reckon we don't sir, we's Baptists!" Being so sound theologically, it is with regret I add, that there was not a person of the whole family who could read or write. We saw much that was novel and interesting, enough to fill a volume and in fact I am not sure but I am under a half promise to the two gentlemen who accompanied me to issue a work and even agree with them upon the title, but my present labors will prevent its early appearance.

Regiment after regiment of Calvary, long black masses of Infantry and batteries of Artillary, passed on through Manassas, evidently following up the retreating foe. Towards night of the same day, tired and weary we entered our camp again and prone on mother earth slept sweetly and forgot our toil, and under the little apology for tents, which we carry with us, when on the march. Saturday morning brought a change in the programme and we took the back track, being ordered to go to Alexandria and there embark on transports, for some "terra lucognito" or other, and started about 11 A.M. That day's march will linger long in the minds of every poor devil whose fate to endure a share of it damps miseries, for it poured furously all day, and not a man escaped being wet entirely through. In addition to tramping 20 miles through mud and fording streams swollen by the rains to treble their usual depth, and finally our Regiment was stopped and obliged to bivouac by the road side, by a stream that had swept away the bridge. Only a portion of our Brigade got across, and it was reported that the 35th lost a man by being drowned while attempting to cross. The subscriber suffered some, got wet, boots full of water, back of neck ditto, and I rather surmise that considerable of the water in my boots found its way there via my shirt collar, thence down my back. Had my rations, (consisting of ten cents worth of sugar cakes) in my overcoat pocket, and when dinner time came, to my great disgust I found that the water had reduced them to their original elements, namely, dough, and had incorporated with them a 3 cent paper of tobacco. Began to regret being a soldier, and my cup of misery overrun when Adj't Hayt imparted the pleasing intelligence that a bottle of Porter, which I had intrusted to his saddle bags had jolted out and was lost! Cold, hungry and wet, the regiment pitched their tents and tried to sleep, and generally succeeded. In the morning came another change, and we were ordered to return to our old camp at Upton's Hill; Alexandria being so full that we could not get quarters there, and there being no probability of our transports being coaled, and otherwise ready for several days. Well we arrived at camp again about 2 P.M. of Sunday the 16th inst., and felt as though we were at home once more. Tuesday afternoon however we again were ordered to go to Alexandria, and packed up and started and had got only about 1½ miles on the way, when orders arrived for us to stop and bivouac, and thus we are here by the roadside, trying to be patient and believe everything is all right, and are finding it uphill work. Why we are stopped here, instead of returning to our comfortable camp which is so near, passes my comprehension. The boys say that the authorities are waiting for a rain storm, and if so they will not have wait long, as the weather is threatening now.

Hoping for the best but feeling dubious,
I am very respectfully yours,
N.T.C.[8]

"The Washington correspondent of the Tribune tells the following sickening story of Rebel atrocities at Centerville and Manassas:

"Some of the residents at Centerville say that members of the Sanitary Commission and other soldier visitors to Manassas assert positively that there is evidence so strong as to force the belief that the Mississippi soldiers have been digging up the bodies of National soldiers buried at Bull Run, boiling off the flesh and making the bones into trophies. The skulls were frequent tent ornaments, and were also used for soap dishes. Knives and forks, rings and even spurs, were constructed from the bones, Soldiers of the Brooklyn 14th recognized on the field of Bull Run, by their red trowsers, comrades who had fallen there, lying unburied and headless."[9]

This poem was found, hand-written, among the Colby papers, author unknown.

> Old Jeff's Litany
> Good devils and all ye infernal spirits!
> Save me from the "Rail Splitter"
> and his vengful Legions.[10]

"On the 24th of March, 1862, General McClellan issued a general order prescribing the kinds of flags that should designate corps, division, and brigade headquarters. He directed that the First Division flag be red, the Second blue and the Third red and blue. All were to be 6 feet by 5 feet."[11]

Washington March 25, 1862
Dear Father

I am quite unsettled as to what I shall do—I had the good luck to get my pay without being obliged to *bleed*—as most of our fellows do—I know of one of our officers who paid 20 per cent to get his pay roll cashed. We are not yet embarked—but are daily expecting orders to go—My pay did not amount to quite as much as usual from the fact that there was February which is a short month — My expenses too — have been larger this month — and I have been obliged to refit to some extent — You know I have never had a new coat — since we have been in the service — and I have had to get one — as I feared if we went farther south — I could not get them from for any price — and my boots too— were worn entirely through by our long marches — and boots cost eight dollars in this wooders country — So I am not able to remit as much as usual.

Give my love to Mother and Henry and wife-
In Haste Affectionately Your Son
Newton[12]   _____

Washington March 26, 1862
Dear Father

We have a new Brig General — a man by the name of M B Patrick — formerly at the head of the Peoples Agriculturial College at Ovid NY — and also a graduate of the West Point and been in the service during the war with Mexico — and till now a member of McCellans staff — He is said to be a fine man — I return to our mud hole to day — having to walk about six miles — I wrote — while waiting for breakfast — in the same room where you and Cousin Eastman and I and Mary discussed the future together at Mrs Andersons — and I can almost see you now — would that I could quite — I have not heard from you in some time and hope to hear often — Tell mother that I don't believe she would know me — if she were to see me — for I look more like a brigand [robber and bandit] than a white man — I have not worn a white shirt — in two months and have six clean and nice here at Mrs Andersons where I mean to leave them — My two trunks are at Mr Louis Bailys — at Baily's Cross Roads — where I leave them at present — I have bought a carpet bag to take with me and all my wordly goods that I carry are stored in that — My Epaleths-my sword, shirts and c are here — No one knows certain where we are to go — I rather guess that quite a large force will be sent to Texas or New Orleans — There has been 60,000 men already sent down the river — and it does not seem to reduce the number of Troops perceptibly —

Tell Charley Thompson — I will send him a copy of Hardee's Tactics — which I picked up at Manassas and would like to send him more — but could not carry but little away — as we were on foot — I will not forget to send him something of the kind however for he has been very obliging and I hope I never forget a good turn done me —

Give my best love to Mother and Henry and Mary — and write often-
Very Affectionately Yours
Newton[13]

Major Gregg of the Twenty-Third writes a letter to Judge Thurston in which he notices meeting some "contrabands" on the march of Manassas. He said: "We saw many able bodied chattels on their way to freedom. I inquired of many of them if they were leaving their masters. They generally replied, 'Our masters have left us.' I inquired of such as had started if they knew the North Star, to which they replied 'yes'; I advised them to travel toward it if they preferred freedom to slavery. It does me a great deal of good to see eight to fifteen hundred dollars' worth of property walking away from our enemies, without the trouble of loading and unloading our Government wagons.'[14]

"We are gratified to learn that Lieut. N.T. Colby, of Co. D. 23rd Regiment N.Y.S. Volunteers, has been appointed by Brig. Gen. Patrick, as an Aid-de-Camp. Gen. Patrick has the command of the Brigade, of which the 23rd is a part, since the retirement of Gen. Wadsworth, recently appointed military Governor of the District of Columbia."[15]

Baileys Cross Roads
Mch 28, 1862
Dear Father

I have been appointed an Aid de Camp on Genl Patricks staff and that so much betters my position — that I trust you will be willing I should remain here — at least till after this expedition is done. You of course are aware how much more comfortable it allows me to be and how much safer I am and asks much less exposer. I sleep in a nice comfortable bed and even on the march — will be allowed to carry a bed and blankets plenty. Do not go away from Corning yet — for I will come home within six weeks — I think my appointment is to last — at least during this expedition.

I will write again and longer soon but believe you owe me several letters yet —

Give my love to Mother and Henry and
believe me faithfully and
Affectionately Your Son
Newton[16]

Bailys Cross Roads
March 31st 1862
Dear Father

Your very welcome letter — announcing the arrival of the funds sent you — came to hand to night —

While on the march — my expenses are more than double — but I suppose that I now draw about $20 per month more — than while in the line — I desire to come home — dear father — quite as much as you wish to have me — but situated as I now am — it would be a dishonorable thing — and I feel that I owe it to my children — not to do it — now — at least —

After the present Expedition — I will come home — Genl Patrick — says that I shall act as his aid — during the Expedition at least — I have asked of Van Volkenburg to use his influence to make it a *permanent* thing — (by writing him) — but have not heard from him — Van V — knows Genl P — quite well and voluntarily gave me a letter — asking for an appointment as signal officer — and I presume I can get it — after the Expedition — My present duties are light — having only to ride with The General where ever he goes — and having an orderly who takes care of my horse — I like the position very much — Todd has been very friendly and evidently thinks he has been defeated utterly — in his attempt and trys to make it all right now by being over kind — He is considerably chagrined I think to see me where I am — though — Direct your letters precisily as you have done and I will get them — even if we do move down the river — Where we are going I know not — but report says that we go first to fortress Monroe — and thence to Richmond — I shall never stay — in the South till warm weather — so you need not fear it — I will write you again as soon as we reach Alexandria to ship — so you may know all I can tell you — I have been there several times and seen troops leaving on the steamers — the steamers are the old familiar boats from the Hudson river — Those large river steamers — and they go off crowded, cavalry, Artillery and infantry — seemingly without end — Genl Patricks a queer sort of a man and very strict in discipline and makes the ducks in his brigade fly around some. I tell you this morning he reprimanded our orderly privately for swearing and said he would discharge him from service if he heard it again. He never drinks anything like liquor — and keeps the Sabboth as far as possible — He is quite hasty in temper though and is a savage — when provoked — Well I must close as I have been in the saddle all afternoon and am quite tired and sleepy — Thank God — I have a good bed to sleep in and a roof to keep me dry and warm. Tell mother her idea that she will not see me again is moonshine — for a bad penny is sure to return and I feel certain — I have a presentment that I shall kiss her within six weeks —

Give her my best love and regards and remember me kindly and affectionately to my brother Henry and his wife. Help Mary with the money I send you if she needs it — believe me dear father

Very Affectionately Your Son
Newton[17]

    April 4, 1862   McClellan's Union Army on the Peninsula starts its advance.
    April 5, 1862   McClellan besieges the Confederate defenses at Yorktown, Va.[18]
    April 8, 1862   The 23rd leaves camp near Alexandria.
    April 9, 1862   The 23rd camps near Brentsville in very wet conditions.[19]

On April 12, near Bristo, [Bristow, Va. is on the railroad between Mannassas and Richmond] "Joseph M. UpDeGraff of Co. K, was shot by a pickett patrol. He offered no serious resistance but banter with the patrol. He was buried with military honors in a private cemetery nearby, but later removed to Elmira By former Chaplain Crane."[20]

Head Quaters 2d Brigade
Camp Near Bristoe, Va. Sunday
April 13th 1862
Dear Father

    Yours of the 7th inst came to hand last evening and I need not tell you how much I was pleased to hear from you — I had been a long time without hearing a single word from home and your very kind letter was doubly welcome — though I was very sorry to learn that you were ill and that you had to submit to the sale of your goods — Believe me Father — I sympathise fully with you — but do not allow yourself to be dispirited or uneasy about the future —
    yet I know we are never destined to any real suffering from want or poverty — Give up the fight and pass over the weapons to me — whenever you choose and while you counsil — let me execute and I snap my fingers in the face of want and poverty — I can *I am sure* — always so manage — as to have enough of everything for Mother and you — The money I receive for my services in this war — I intend shall be the smallest part of the real compensation or I hope to so arrange matters — as to secure a situation permanently in some Governmental department or business — and I pledge

you my sacred honor that while *I have you also have and shall have of anything* I possess— Mary wrote — sometime however that you talked some of staying with her while you were alone — during mothers trip to the east — I really wish it may be so— and hope you will go there and stay as I shall feel much less anxiety for Mary and the children —

Well we are encamped for the present near a little place called Bristoe — on the R Road running from Manassas to Richmond — Discipline is being fully carried out under Genl Patrick and very strict orders prohibit any plundering or jayhawking in our vicinity — Patrols and gaurds are everywhere — Only yesterday a private by the name of Updegraff of our Regiment — a resident of Elmira — was shot and instantly killed by the seargent of a patrol — for refusing to halt when ordered to — The Seargent ordered him to halt several times and told him that he was in command of the Provost Gaurd but Updegraff paid not the slightest attention to the order — but began to cap his gun! Updegraffs companion — a private by the name of Packard (by the way he is the same fellow who painted my house in Corning) stopped and gave up *his* gun to the sergeant and Updegraff was shot with the very gun given up by Packard — There is not much news with us— and I suppose that you get much sooner than we do— There will be a tremendous heavy battle fought at Yorktown within ten days— or two weeks— beyond doubt — McClellan is there and has been back to Washington and asked for reinforcements and Gen Franklins Division — which was out here with us— has gone to Alexandria and then embark to go down there — with McCellan — We do not know here — whether we are going on or if we are to go back and go down the river I think however that we shall go on — McCellan is rather playing out — with the Army — though there are still some who believe in him — He has never — yet commanded in a battle and with the disasterous exception of Balls Bluff — has had no connection with a fight — so far as the public are aware — Still he may have planned everything and left other's to execute — Mother's fears — that my horse would throw me — caused me to *smile* pretty *strong* — To be sure — I may be thrown and injured — but I do not fear it — I pride myself upon being — a *good* rider and have done no small amont of riding for the last year — I have a fine large — powerful bay — young and a *little* awkward but he is of great endurance and will learn very easy and is *kind* — *very kind* disposition — He is moreover a splended jumper — taking a fence or ditch beautifully — I wish I could ride him up to your door this very Sunday afternoon — and I *think* I could rather enjoy the visit — I shall come home in May — if I am well — and perhaps will conclude to stay at home — It will however depend much on events here. What could I make a living at? Give my warmest love to Mother and Henry and tell Henry to write —

watch over my family too—advising and counseling Mary—give my respects to Dr Pratt Mr Austin—Chas Thompson—Rogers—Cardwell Newell—Judge Johnson and any inquiring friends Write often—directing to Lt Colby A.D.C. Genl Patricks Brigade—Kings Division—Washington D.C.

Very Affectionately Your Son
Newton[21]

"April 16th the 23rd Regiment moved toward Catlett Station and then on to Falmouth on the 18th. They marched twenty-three miles the first day, most of which was during a severe rain storm. When they finally bivouaced, the men were so tired that many just laid down in the rain without tents or supper. The Rebels had fled to Falmouth the night before and in their haste to escape had destroyed everything they could not take with them. Many steamers and merchant vessels were destroyed as were bridges and much cotton at Fredericksburg."[22]

Regimental records reported

April 19 The 23rd was opposite Fredericksburg—camped on the old Washington boyhood farm on the Rappahanock. Rebs burnt 3 bridges including railroad bridge, on Fri. and Sat. 18th and 19th.[23]

CHAPTER 8

The Occupation of Fredericksburg

From Company Muster Roll of Co D 23d Regt N.Y. Infantry: "1st Lt Newton T Colby is entitled to extra pay for extra duty as aid de camp to Gen Patrick from Mch 26 to April 23d."[1]

Letters from the Army

We are permitted to publish the following extracts from a letter from Adjutant Hayt 23rd Reg. N.Y. Volunteers, dated opposite Fredericksburg, Va., April 23rd:

Here we have been since Saturday evening encamped in one of the most beautiful spots I ever saw, on the opposite side of the Rappahannock river from Fredericksburg, and in plain sight of it. The city has a population of about 8,000, and is yet decidedly "secesh." The rebels left the city on Friday and Saturday, but not until they had burned the bridge, or about half of it, and also a quantity of stores. They had a small steamboat and two or three sloops loaded with 70,000 bushels of corn. Steamboat, sloops, and corn were all destroyed on Friday evening. But I will go back. I wrote you at Cattel's Station about a mile and a half from there. We remained there until Friday morning, when at six o'clock we took up our line of march, retraced our steps as far as Cattel's, crossed the railroad and left its line. When we left Bristoe our destination was Gordonsville. You will find in Harper's Weekly of the 19th inst., a map of the seat of war in Va. We are as near Richmond (about 60 miles) as we would have been as Gordonsville. We marched on Friday, eighteen or twenty miles, almost a two

113

days march. The day was fine, but too hot for the men, until 5 o'clock, when it began to rain, and it fairly poured until we turned in for the night, about 8 o'clock. It was as dark as tar — no guides could be found — not a lantern — and to make the matter worse, all the teams were stuck fast in the mud about two miles in the rear, and we had not a mouthful to eat. When we started in the morning I put into my saddle-bags a piece of ham and some hard crackers, just for lunch. About twelve o'clock we halted but the teams were so far in the rear that we could not get our rations, and the ham was so bad I could not eat it, so was obligated to get along with the crackers and water. When we halted for the night I was used up, had been without food for so long, and completely wet through. Our march had been a fatiguing one — a good part of the way through the woods and fields — sometimes in hard ground, and then in sand up to the horses knees, riding hither and yon, doing by best to encourage the poor fellows who were constantly leaving the ranks, expecting every minute that our horses might get stuck in some mud hole, and then trying in the dark to find a good camp ground, and you may imagine that we were not in the very best of spirits. However a few of us fortunately found a house, or what was called a house occupied by an old man and his wife. All they had to refresh us was corn meal and coffee. The old woman made us a hoe cake and after eating a little of that and drinking a good lot of coffee, began to feel somewhat revived. We sat by the fire about an hour and then spread our blankets on the floor and went to sleep and slept soundly until reveille, half-past four o'clock. The old couple, the husband seventy-five, the wife seventy years of age, belong to that class known as "poor whites." They own the house they live in and about fifty acres of good land, with a few cattle, hogs, and chickens, and yet I don't believe you could find in the whole north a mechanic's family, if the husband was sober and industrious, so devoid of comforts as this family seemed to be. And so ignorant too. But they are all about alike in that respect. The negroes, although you can scarcely find one who can read or write, are much superior in their knowledge of the world to the "poor whites."

Well about nine o'clock we started again, our regiment as the rear guard — all the "train" between us and the balance of the brigade. This position, on the march through an enemy's country is one of labor and responsibility. We learned that there were numerous parties of the Texas Rangers scouring the country, waiting for an opportunity to make a dash on the rear, and cut off any stray baggage wagon or small squad of men. So you see that we had our hands full. If a wagon broke down we had to wait until it was repaired, if a soldier gave out we waited until he could be put in an ambulance. However, after a march of eleven miles we reached

8. The Occupation of Fredericksburg

our present position, and found the other three regiments had arrived about two hours in advance of us. Of course it would rain, and rain it did all night long, and all day Sunday and part of Monday. Monday night the weather cleared up, and yesterday and to-day have been two beautiful days, but somewhat windy. The last storm was a cold one, and a great many of the men during the march had thrown away their overcoats, the weather being warm, and every one was mistaken — so Sunday and Monday there was a good deal of suffering. But the wind now is fair and square in the northwest and we all hope for a long spell of good weather. The season here is very backward, but on Friday, for the first time, we were gladdened with the sight of peach trees loaded with blossoms, and broad fields of wheat and grass a foot high...."[2]

"The rebels are making use of their negroes in a variety of ways. At Lee's Mills, when they found the fire from the telescopic rifle too sharp for them, they compelled the negroes to load their gun, and several of them were shot while attempting this dangerous work. Oh! Chivalry! Chivalry! Chivalry!"[3]

"PONTOON BRIDGES-Portable boats are flat bottomed, thirty feet long, two and a half feet wide at the bow, and five feet wide at stern, swelling out at the sides to the width of six feet. Each is on a running gear of four wheels and is used as a baggage wagon for the positioners, carrying its proportion of string pieces and of plank. On reaching a river the boats are unloaded, floated across by a cable made fast up the stream, then the string pieces are laid across from one boat to the next, and on these are placed the planks, each twenty-one feet long, which form the gangway of that width. It is a fine sight to see a regiment come to a river bank with a pontoon train, unload and launch their boats, moor them in a line, and in less than five minutes from the time when the word "halt" was given, have a bridge say six hundred feet in length, over which an army can safely pass with artillary and baggage."[4]

Opposite Fredericksburg
May 1st 1862
Dear Father

The 1st of May 1862 — finds me on the banks of the Rappahannock — a simple Lieutenant in the 23rd NY Vol — just exactly what I was one year ago to day — I had the distingushed honor of acting as Aid De Camp to his Royal Highness — Genl Patrick for the space of about one calander month and was there relieved from duty and ordered to join my Regiment — The same fate befel Lieut Wheeler of the 21st and Adjutant Steven-

Drawing of Fredericksburg, Virginia. *Harper's Weekly*, April 26, 1862.

berg also of the 21st who were detached on staff duty at the same time I was—so you will observe that I was not disgraced in any way by being relieved—I—in fact—cared but very little about it—as the position was not a pleasant one—owing to the unpopularity of Patrick—Every body—both officers and men dislike him exceedingly—I only regret the loss of the horse—but aside from that I am better off in the line—but I do not intend to remain there—for after serving a year without bettering myself at all—I think I shall ask to be excused from further service. Todd has said for a month past that he should resign this month but—if I do—I presume he will not—though there is no general between us now—Col Lord—of the 35th came to me the other day and voluntarily offered to obtain me a staff position on Genl Kings Staff—Genl King is a fine man and commands our (McDowell) old division and of course is a Major General—I much wish I could obtain the place—but I have no expectations of it whatever—as the preference for me of our Col—out of some twelve or fifteen in the Division—can effect but little—no—I shall without doubt come home about the middle of this month if I can get my resignation accepted—What shall I do for a living? Have you any plan? This country—is the finest by far of any I was ever in—and I think money could be made here in time of peace—faster then any place I know of—There is a man at Falmouth (a little place this side of the river) who came here 3 or 4 years ago from Elmira—He had not a spare dollar when he came and has accumulated (so he told me himself) $3000 ahead—in the time he has lived here and he is not a very shrewd smart man either—When our Brigade came here he started a little 7 by 9 grocery store—getting his few articles of sale—across the river at Fredericksburg—he takes from two to 400 dollars per day from our troops! and at prices that are perfectly appalling—For instance—flour in Fredericksburg is 6 to 7 dollars per barrell and he retails it at 6c per pound! and sells a dozen barrells a day! Of

8. The Occupation of Fredericksburg

course this trade is only good while our forces are here and we may leave tomorrow. No soldier is allowed to cross to the city from this side and the secesh will not come from the other — What do you say to coming here to live when the war is done? The country is perfectly beautiful — and they raise nearly all kinds of fruit in perfection especially peaches and grapes — The river abounds in fine varities of fish — Wild turkeys — quail and other game are found and the climate is good. The Typhus fever is the prevailing type of disease and that is generally severe — which is a drawback of course — I have not had a letter from you in a long time and begins to think you have forgotten that you have a son in the Army — This is the 3rd letter I have written without hearing a word from you in reply — but I hope to be home all safe and sound before there is time to write many more — You need not write to me after the 13th — unless I write for you to continue-I enclose some curiosities — in the shape of some very ancient Virginia currancy which was current during the revolution — and has doubtless been in the hands of our heros of the struggle for independance — I have also enclosed some to Judge Johnson — thinking it might be of interest to him — I procured it of a Dr Morrison a wealthy slave holder — living 3 or 4 miles from our camp — He said his Father left him $15,000 of it — all — of course — a total loss — I enclose a letter to Dr Pratt — and you may give it to him — or burn it as you see fit — I hardly think it fit for publication but to him. Give my love to mother — and Henry and remember me to my *numerous* friends and *admirers* in the City —

Keep the money you have unless it is necessary to pay it and for Mary or yourself and believe me

Affectionately Your Son
Newton[5]

From the *Journal*: "The following extracts from a letter from Lieut. N. T. Colby, 23d, Reg. N.Y. Volunteers will be found interesting. Want of space compels us to omit the remainder:

"We learn by a subsiquent letter from Lieut. Colby dated May 1st, that one of the bridges had been finished, and that Co. D. had been just ordered to march across the Rappahannock river and guard the bridge. The first Company to make the advance."

Opposite Fredericksburg, Va., May 1st, 1862.

Friend Pratt: Seated in the cabin of an old slave — familiarly known as "Uncle Billy" — permit me to renew my attempts at "correspondence," and to record some of the impressions I have acquired — of men and things on the banks of the Rappahannock. We made our appearance here on the 19th of April — and I confess That I have greatly enjoyed the experience of Virginian customs and habits during the time we have been here. Our camp is on a hill, overlooking the city of Fredericksburg, from which we are separated by the Rappahannock. Our long deadly rifle cannon surmount the heights, completely commanding the town, and it only needs the word of command and Fredericksburg is in ruins, will add one more to the list of cities sacrificed by this wanton rebellion. The rebels in their retreat burned the bridges, (three in number — including the R.R. bridge) and thus cut off immediate pursuit as well as occupation of the place, and we have at the time I write no troops on that side, though we have a bridge of canal boats nearly across, as well as a pontoon bridge, and I am informed that a portion, or all of Gen. Augur's Brigade are to occupy the town tomorrow.

Several days since I went over to town — but with the exception of three ladies and the colored population I received nothing but cold looks and scowls. It was Sunday, and a service was just over. I, or rather we, (for there were two friends with me) encountered quite a number of ladies returning from church, but with two exceptions, not a single one took any notice of us, despite our rows of bright brass buttons, and our boots blacked brilliantly, and our forage caps jauntily stuck on our loyal American heads. The exceptions were two young ladies, Misses Clark, and I record the name in honor, for they not only politely saluted us — as we passed them, but afterward, having had the pleasure of an introduction by their father, with whom I had become acquainted, and by one of the first citizens of the city, and a sound Union man too-they assured me they always had, and always would recognise and welcome Union soldiers.

The "inevitable nigger," is not concealed "in the fence" here, but is omnipresent and in such numbers, as to really lead one to think it a necessary sanitary regulation to forbid their further increase. They absolutely swarm in the city, varing in complexion from the "ponderous depth of pitchy" blackness, to the mellowest tint of tropical climes, and there is no question of the sincerity of their welcome. They are universally struck with surprise at being treated like men, instead of chattels, though evincing by their abject slavish actions that they feel more like chattels then men. The presence of our troops here has placed the slave owners of the vicinity in an awkward dilemma. A gentleman by the name of Dr. Morrison who lives near here, and who owns a large number of slaves, informed me to-day that he couldn't get any work out of any of his niggers whatever, as they tell him that now they are free, and that they will hire themselves to him

8. The Occupation of Fredericksburg

for wages, but will no longer work "for nothing." The result, the Dr. predicts will be a famine, as the corn planting time is fast going by, and there are no servents to do the work. I asked him why not tie them up and give them a sound thrashing, and he answered that he dared not, for there were so many in the vicinity (meaning our forces) who probably were unaccustomed to such measures, and would become predjucial against him, that they might interfere and perhaps injure him or his property.[6]

A letter by an unknown writer, printed May 2 in the *Philadelphia Ledger* and *Daily Transcript*, provides a view of affairs at Falmouth, VA.:

Here we are, encamped opposite Fredericksburg, a perfect hot-bed of seccession. Every day the inhabitants come over, visit our camps, take mental notes, and return to dispatch couriers to the rebel army. This very day a lawyer of Fredericksburg, who has notoriously held the position of Adjutant in the rebel army, was within our lines, boasting his disloyalty. He made a perfect tour of inspection, conversed with the men uninteruptedly, and gathered more news in a day to send to Richmond than your correspondent would be allowed to convey to you in a month. I do not wish to envince a complaining spirit, but the absurdity and stupidity of some of these army arrangements offend my sense of the beautiful to such a degree that I cannot forbear an occasional remonstrance. Heretofore Fredericksburg has not been occupied. Though the rebels had large quantities of flour, grain and other stores secreted there, no action has been taken to secure them, and night after night they have been carted away. Had we placed a few pieces of cannon upon the heights commanding the town, and sent over a flag of truce to bring back the Mayor and Common Council, then informing these gentlemen that if a single thing were removed an experiment would be made upon the city with shell, I fancy that nothing would have been disturbed. We might also have informed them that for every Union man pressed into the rebel service, we would force ten secession sympathizers into our army, and place them in the front ranks in the first engagement that for every Union man's farm laid waste, we would destroy the property of a dozen rebels, I fancy that a different condition of things would have been inaugurated. But this would be establishing a reign of terror, says one. Establishing a reign of terror! Great God! It already exists. When Union are obliged to flee from their homes, and secret themselves in the woods for their lives, the reign of terror cannot much further go, and common sense suggests that here it should be ended. One thing is certain, we must either make war or make peace. It is impossible to have both these luxuries at once — to fight and shake hands at the same time. We must either treat these people as enemies or friends. Until they avow themselves loyal, would it not be well to make them them feel the pains and penalties of disloyalty?

You have already learned by telegraph that some gunboats, a fleet of canal-boats for bridging purposes, and a ferry boat have arrived here fron Alexandria. The ferry boat of course had to be supplied with coal, and a good joke was played on the Mayor by Captain Robinson, who seized all the coal at the gas works for the purpose, thus shutting off light from dwellings and countenances of the natives, at a time, too, when the town was destitute of candles. The Mayor remonstrated, but our peremptory Quartermaster demonstrated very clearly that we ourselves were short of candles, and that their condition would be no worse than ours. This is practical. The idea of standing out in the cold ourselves that our enemies may have shelter, is being rapidly "played out." I think it very probable that we shall have a battle in this vicinity very soon after crossing the Rappahannock. Rebel cavalry were seen to day within two miles of Fredericksburg, and I have it from a very authenic source, in fact by several confirmatory stories coming from different sources, that the enemy have a force of 10,000 to 15,000 men within ten miles of the town. Great apprehension is entertained of a dash into Fredericksburg by the rebel cavalry to-night. The company of which I made mention in a former part of this letter, has not been thrown over, for the reason that the bridge is not yet built, and we would have no means of supporting them should the enemy swoop down. At the same time our General is excessively averse to leaving the Union men of the burg unprotected, the more especially as it is feared the rebels will seize the present opportunity to descend and carry off the few Union men that remain. The morning will show whether these fears are well grounded or not.

author unknown[7]

An April 21 letter, originally printed by the *Richmond Enquirer* but reprinted on May 6 in the *Philadelphia Ledger* and *Daily Transcript*, described the occupation of Fredericksburg:

The report of the advance of the Union forces reached Fredericksburg Thursday afternoon. As late as midnight Thursday night General Field, who was in command of the Confederate troops, assured citizens that he did not believe, from the reports brought in by his pickets, that the Yankee force was suficient to threaten an attack which involved the occupa-

8. The Occupation of Fredericksburg

tion of the town. The citizens and the "civil authorities" rested, therefore, hopefully on the belief that Gen. Field's troops would defend and save the town from Yankee occupation. This hope was sadly crushed, for at seven o'clock on Friday morning it was discovered by the citizens that the bridges across the river were in flames, and that the Confederate troops were retreating from Falmouth and making their way through Fredericksburg into the country in back of it.

I have no desire to criticise our General or his troops, but it is due to the citizens and "civil authorities" to say that they were sorely distressed when they found the Yankees were not resisted and beaten back. Nor was this sorrow lessened when they found that the Yankees forces consisted of a single brigade; for it was not until 3 o'clock on Saturday afternoon that an accession of force was added to one brigade, before which our troops retired. I trust it may appear that our officers did not know that the Yankee force was so small, or that they were erroneously informed as to its strength.

By nine o'clock on Friday morning the Yankees had planted their cannon so as to command the town; and a regiment of their cavalry appeared near the river, which was fordable at several points not much over knee deep. General Field's entire force had evacuated the town, and Fredericksburg lay at the feet of the Yankees.[8]

Partial Letter from Newton Colby to his wife Mary:

People here — hire a few slaves — and the niggers work and support both themselves and their employees — so that White — has nothing to do! This is actually true too — The land here is fine — and the country beautiful — The rappahanock river abounds in fine fish — Shad-(they are plenty here for 5 cents each) herring — Bullheads — suckers and c and c. Sweet potatoes — peaches — plums — grapes — and all the vegetables that flourish at the north — beside some that we do not grow — are very particularly plentiful — Peaches especially do well — and even grow wild in the woods! I have actually seen peach trees in the woods in full blossom — perhaps the result of accident — but there the tree's were in a thick piece of woods —

By the way you have never acknowledged the receipt of the things I sent you by Stearns — A book of Poems — some secesh letters — some cotton bolls and c and c — Did you get them? So you have decided upon a regular attendance at the P-Church eh? I am very much pleased to hear it — and I would give almost anything if I could accompany you — for you well know that I prefer attending that church to any other and when I come home — I hardly think you will ever find fault with non attendance on my part — Does this please you — darling? It seems as if I could not hardly wait for two long weeks to roll away—and then too I really regret to leave our fellows and go home—I shall actually feel sad at leaving those brave hearts with whom for a long year I have shared all kinds of fortune—I could wish to bide my time and return with the Regiment but I yield to your wishes—and my own too darling and come to our home—I have been a full year in the service and am no better off—in fact—I think I am ten years older in appearances and have unavoidably acquired habits that will unfit me for some time for business there too—the Officers have decided to employ a foass [sic] fund—and my proportion of the expense will amount to $20—each pay day and that reduces my pay very materially—and of course I must pay it—as I would not like to be the only Officer in the line who refused to pay his portion—Col Hoffman pays $50 each pay day—and it is regularly proportioned down to 2d Liuts—but they nearly all growl at the expense but have to stand it—

I am going out to pick some May flowers if I can find them to send you in this letter—Please accept them with the warm full love of your husband—who prefers to clasp you in his arms ere long—I must close here darling—I send love to all our little ones—watch over them dear wife for me a short time longer-

Ever your own
Newton

P.S. I reopen this to say that our Co with 3 others (one from each Regiment are going somewhere to be gone for several days. I have just returned from Brigade Headquarters and learn that we are going across the river to Fredericksburg—to gaurd the bridge—Ours will be the very first company that side of the river—We shall have better quarters probably—

Write often
Newton

Tell Father to add this to Pratts letter if he publishes it-

P.S.—Co. D are under orders to cross the river and gaurd the new bridge—just completed—They will be the first company across the Rappahanock and first to escape the City—[9]

Pontoon bridges were constructed and on May 2nd General King and General Patrick along with Company D, and Captain Todd, of the 23rd New York Volunteers passed over the bridge. They stationed pickets at important points and occupied a large warehouse near the river.

It wasn't until May 7th that the entire 23rd [the other 9 companies] crossed the river and placed Fredericksburg under the stars and bars for the first time. General Patrick was made military governor of the city and the 23rd had the guard duty.[10]

From the Fredericksburg *Christian Banner*:

"Pursuant to orders of Brigadier-General Patrick, on Wednesday, the 7th of May, 1862, the Southern Tier Rifles, Twenty-third New York State Volunteers, Colonel H.C. Hoffman commanding, took up its line of march from camp near Falmouth for the occupation of Fredericksburg, arriving in the city at nine o'clock A.M. Such respectful regard was paid to the sensitiveness of the inhabitants of our town as to dispense with the martial music usual upon such occasions, the regiment marching to its quarters with fine and soldierly bearing. Companies were immediately detailed and dispatched to outposts guarding the various approaches of our town.

"The officers of this regiment—field, staff and line—are gentlemen of the highest respectability and of dignified and courteous demeanor, and such has been the respectful deportment of this entire command as to elicit the most unbounded admiration and confidence of all the inhabitants of our town.

"By order of Colonel Hoffman, Sergeant-Major Devoe and Color-Corporal Crocker flung the time-honored flag—the good old "stars and stripes"—to the breeze, at headquarters, opposite the railroad depot, immediately upon their occupation. This regiment, we learn, has been chosen for occupation of the town on account of its high character and respect, ability, and rigid discipline; and from what we have seen, we are confident a more judicious selection could not be made. Witnessing, as we do, the preservation of all personal rights and privilages, the protection of private property, and the unrestricted conduct and continuance of the accustomed business pursuits of our citizens, we can not but conclude that this war is waged by the general Government upon principles infinitely transcending in mercy all others which the world has ever known, and of which history affords no precedent or parallel."[11]

It is possible that Lt. Colby, having been aide de camp to General Patrick, and feeling strongly about showing respect towards southern people and their property, was the reason why the 23rd, Co D., was selected for this mission. McClellan's advance on Richmond forced the Rebels to abandon Norfolk.[12]

Letter from Captain Todd
For the *Journal*:
Fredericksburg, Va., May 11th, 1862

Friend Pratt: Feeling that you would have no objection to hear of the where-abouts of the Old Corning Company, and what they are doing. I have concluded (contrary to old habits,) to write a short letter We left our winter-quarters about the first of March, and that was the first time my men really knew what soldiering was; but they have endured what could not be avoided, with very little murmuring, all things considered. We left our camp near Alexandria on the 8th of April, and on the 9th encamped near Brentsville; had a fine wet time never to be forgotten, remained there one week, long enough to get dry, from there we marched to the Rappahannock and encamped on the the old Washington farm, the place where Washington passed his boyish days; it is a place that throws a man's thoughts far back to what the Colonies then were, what they afterwards became under his leadership, and then the thought comes, what is his old State doing now; fighting for the aristocracy and trying to put down the interests of the people; and after that comes the reflection what Virginia might be with a fair share of enterprise unfettered by slavery. The country about the Rappahannock is very fertile, surface rolling and the climate healthy and salubrious, and all considered excepting slavery, a very fine section to live in; and the Virginians I believe generally think so, for they can take a farm of 100 acres and raise as much on it as our New York farmers can on three hundred. My company was ordered to cross the river on the 2d day of May, and were quartered in a whare-house near the river, it being the first time we have been quartered in a building since we left Elmira, and I assure you that we felt ourselves "highly honored" in being allowed to remain so near some of the first families of Virginia. We did not expect much attention, but we received more than we expected, by being asked the questions, why we were here, and why we did not stay at home and let them alone? and the next morning we found that some of the ladies gave us the wide side of the walk, and that the gentlemen as we met them, kept their eyes square to the front; but this feeling has in part passed away, and they find that private property is respected, and the ladies find that their houses are not troubled by even a ring or a rap at the front door; and contrary to their expectations we are partially civilized since we have taken off the suit of the "greasy mechanic!" Some of the ladies throw tracts and sermons on the rebellion, upon the side walks, feeling the importance of converting as many as possible of the mis-guided soldiers from the error of coercion. Fredericksburg is a city about 200 years old and contains about 9000 inhabitants, or would if there had been no rebellion, and (as the ladies said to me) the people had remained at home where they ought to be; and from the number of stores here it must done a good business. The water power is very good, and with the right kind of business men it might be considerable of a manufacturing town, but the inhabitants here generally like to live an easy life and not be too much troubled with new ways and new improvements. As for the negro population I would like to see them free; and know that Virginia would be more prosperous as a free state, but yet I believe that those I have seen are better off here than they would be to go north; and they are as well dressed on the Sabboth as a majority of the citizens in Corning, but they of course want their freedom, and look upon the Union army as the men that are here for that purpose instead of being here as we are to put down the rebellion. The rebels destroyed a large amount of property, some of it belonging to private individuals to prevent its falling into our hands, but there was an amount left in different places that could not very well be destroyed as they left in great haste. We have already found about 25,000 bushels of corn.

Last Tuesday the other nine companies of our regiment came over and are quartered in different parts of the city; last evening the remainder of the Brigade came over and encamped just out of the city. The health of my men that remain with me is good, I have eight men in the Washington and Alexandria hospitals, not very sick but unfit for duty, I had just (as I Thought) finished my letter as the long roll beat, our cavalry had taken 13 rebel prisoners, and were chased in by the rebel infantry.

Of course our Brigade immediately fell into line of companies in light marching orders, and ordered to take the Bowling Green Road. Our companies are quartered some squares apart in the city; Company D was in line in a few minutes, and at the word double quick, march, were off at the jump; double-quick is a fine exercise, if it is not too long, we marched about three miles, formed line, and threw out skirmishers, but the rebels fell back too fast for us; one of the cavalry horses was shot, the ball passing not very far from Gen. Patrick's head; by the bye, our new General is a man of discipline, and so long as every officer toes the mark all goes right. The weather is very pleasant here and quite warm, and vegetation is pretty well advanced, and I suppose about four weeks earlier than in the State of New York. Yours truley,

L. Todd, Capt., Co. D. 23d Reg.[13]

Lieut. Colby, having served in the regiment for a year and been aide de camp for a month, saw no real future advancement in staying. He thus requested and received a discharge.

Fredericksburg May 13th 1862
Col H C Hoffman
Comdg 23 NY Vols

The undersigned — a first lieutenant in Co D 23d N.Y. Vols respectfully tenders herewith his resignation of said office and asks permission to be discharged from the service — The resignation to take effect from May 16th 1862 — on account of unsettled business and family at home — I would furthur say I am not at present in arrest or under charges and know of no reason why any might be prepared against me.

Very Respt. N.T. Colby
1st Liut Co D 23d N.Y.V.

Head Quarters 23d NYV
Fredericksburg May 11th 1862
Respectfully Forwarded
H C Hoffman
Col Comg
Respecfully forwarded
*recommended M R Patrick Brig Gen Comg[14]

Fredericksburg, Va. May 13, 1862
Brig Genl Patrick
Comdg 2nd Brigade
Sir

The undersigned having tendered his resignation would respectfully submit the following reasons for its acceptance

That his father — a hardware merchant — has been obliged to close his business — in which the undersigned has been concerned — and whose enforced absence will be a great injury — to both. That the family of the undersigned need his care and assistance — and he further believes his presence necessary to their welfare and comfort, and having been a year in the service — he may not unreasonably — in the view of the foregoing reasons — now ask a discharge from service.

Very Respectfully
N.T. Colby 1st Liut.[15]

Co D 23d N.Y.V.
Headquarters, Depot
Rappahanock
May 15, 1862

"EXTRACT"

The following named officer having tendered his resignation is hereby discharged from the military service of the United States: is to take effect from this date —

1st Luit N T Colby 23 N Y Vols
By command of Maj General McDowell
(signed) Samuel Breck
Assistant Adjutant General[16]

I certify that the above is a true copy, and that I have this day paid N T Colby $277.75 in full from Feby 28, 1862 to May 15, 1862, both days inclusive.

W M Crumback
Paymaster U.S. Army
Washington, May 19, 1862[17]

The 23rd N.Y. Regiment remained on duty at Fredericksburg until May 25.

CHAPTER 9

The 107th New York Volunteer Regiment

Lieutenant Colby returned home to Corning after resigning from the 23rd N.Y.V. He had been very dissatisfied with the politics in the regiment and the lack of opportunity for advancement. Newton had no immediate means of supporting a family but went home anyway. When he heard that a new regiment was to be raised, he immediately became involved. He was given the rank of Captain but had to raise his own company of men. To accomplish this task, he opened a store front office in Corning as a recruiting office. His advertisement in the *Corning Journal* brought in many eager recruits. The following notice was printed to attract attention to the new regiment: "We understand that another Southern Tier Regiment is to be raised under the recent call for more troops by our government."

War Meeting

On Thursday evening last, [July 24, 1862] [The] Concert Hall was early filled by an eager and enthusiastic audience of both sexes, in response to a call for a meeting to encourage enlistments.

S. T. Hayt called the meeting to order and nominated for President, Hon. T. A. Johnson, who was unanimously chosen. Hon. A. C. Morgan, Lindley; A. H. Erwin, W. C. Bronson, Samuel Adams, Erwin, Col. N. B. Stanton, Hon. Asem Endy, Daniel Rogers, Hornby; Dr. J. B. Graves, Alex Olcott, Capt. Colby and Capt. Creamer were chosen Vice Presidents; Geo. B. Bradley and C. H. Thompson secretaries.

Judge Johnson stated the object of the meeting and introduced Hon.

A. S. Diven, who made an earnest appeal for the immediate enlistment of an army to save the Government, which was threatened not only by rebels, but by foreign power, who were waiting for a reasonable excuse to interfere. He was followed by Hon. R. B. Van Valkenburgh who asked the young men of Steuben [County] to follow him! And give aid to the government and the brave volunteers who enlisted last year, but were now in danger unless timely succor went forward. Rev. T. K. Beecher, Hon. Tracy Beadle and H. M. Hyde, each made earnest and effective speeches.

At the conclusion of each address, Miss Kate Dean, the American Prima Donna, sang a national or a patriotic song, unequalled in manner and effect.

Soon after the organization of the meeting, Patterson's Cornet Band and a large delegation of citizens from Painted Post [N.Y.] arrived; the former aiding by their fine music, much in the enthusiasm of the occasion.

Not more than one half of the people could gain admittance to the Hall, and a meeting was organized in front of the Dickinson House, at which Col. Bostwick presided, and speeches were made by Maj. Smith, Messrs. Diven and Beecher. Sometime before the hour of the meeting several rounds were fired from the cannon, and the Martial Band played a number of stirring airs.

The results of the meeting have been measurably satisfactory. Enlisting received a fresh impetus, and a fund of $2,000 has been secured to pay bounties and further enlistments in the company now forming here."[1]

"Lieut. N.T. Colby, recently of the 23rd Regiment, N.Y.V., has opened a Recruiting Office in this place, under authority from Col. Seafard, for the purpose of forming a Company for the Young Southern Tier Regiment. Lieut. C. is a good officer, and we hope he will meet with success. See advertisement in another column."[2]

July 1862 "Change was so scarce that postage stamps were in common use in Corning."[3]

"The New Regiment — The appointment of Gen. Van Valkenburgh as Colonel of the new Regiment and Hon. A.S. Diven as Lieut. Colonel, gives general satisfaction.— Both gentlemen left their seats in Congress a few days before adjournment to come home and arouse the people to the necessity of immediately responding to the call for troops.

"Gen. Van Valkenburgh is one of the most competent Militia officers in the state, and will prove an eminently cabable officer in active service.

"Lt. Col. Diven has no especial military experience we believe, but his

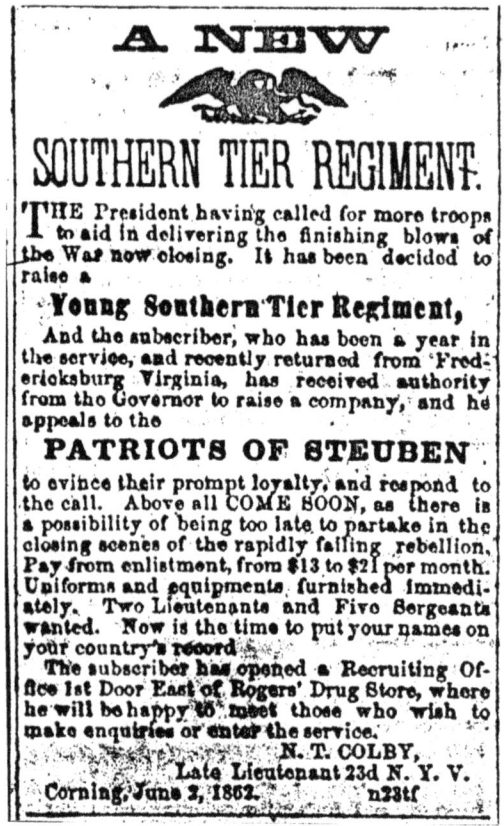

Advertisement placed by Colby in the *Corning Journal*, June 5, 1862, to raise a new regiment.

ability, enthusiasm amd patriotism are unquestioned, and we believe he will acquit himself handsomely in his new position. Dr. P.H. Flood, of Elmira, has been appointed Surgeon of the new Regiment from this Senatorial District."[4]

"There was a large and enthusiastic War Meeting at Caton Centre on Tuesday evening. [August 5] The speakers were Capt. N.T. Colby, Dr. Ingersoll and Geo. R. Graves of this village [Corning], and Rev. Allen B. Woodworth of Newfield. Dr. Ingersoll and C. Minier, Esq. of Caton, gave each $10 bounty, & others gave smaller sums to those who volunteered. Eight or ten good able bodied citizens volunteered, and as many more promised to do so this week. The Baptist Church was crowded to overflowing, and the meeting did not break up until nearly midnight."[5]

"Capt. Colby has now more volunteers than are requisite for a Co. at the minimum standard, and will doubtless have 101 men this week. Those who wish to get into a good company will do well to 'hurry up'."[6]

August 7, 1862   "The new Regiment to be commanded by Col. Van Valkenburg has been recruited up to full strength."[7]

August 11, 1862   Newton Colby — Mustered in as Capt. Co I 107th NY Vols.[8] "The 107th Regiment — The new Regiment for this Senatorial District reached the minimum standard last week and its full number on Monday. In reply to a dispatch announcing the former pact, Col. Van Valkenburgh was notified that his Regiment would be known as the "107th N.Y. Volun-

9. The 107th New York Volunteer Regiment

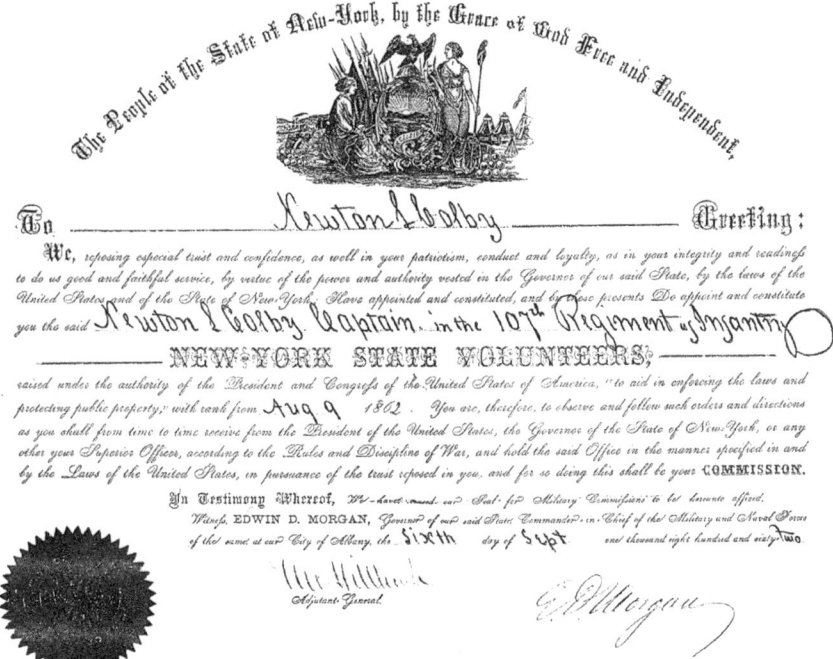

Certificate presented to Newton T. Colby on September 6, 1862, proclaiming him Captain of the 107th Regiment Infantry. Courtesy Mary Lou Wilkins.

teer Regiment" the first recruited in the state under the recent call. It is not three weeks since the work began and the speedy success which has been attained is eminently creditable to the patriotism of the Counties of Steuben, Chemung, and Schuyler. The fact that it was the first organized is a source of pride. Gov. Morgan, in compliment, has forwarded to the Colonel a beautiful Banner for the Regiment. The Volunteers are superior in intelligence and character to preceeding Regiments. It is as a whole a noble body of men — with officers worthy of their high position, and the good wishes and prayers of the people who attend them."[9]

Field Officers of the 107th — The following is a list of the Field Officers of the One Hundred and Seventh Regiment:

Colonel-R.B. Van Valkenburgh, Bath
Lieut. Col.-A.S. Diven, Elmira
Major-G.L. Smith, Elmira
Adjutant-Hull Fenton, Havana
Surgeon-Dr. P.H. Flood, Elmira

Assist. Surgeon-Dr. J.D. Hewitt, N.Y.
Chaplain-Rev. E.F. Crane, Elmira
Quarter Master-E.P. Graves, Corning
Quarter Master Sergeant-L.B. Chidsey, Hornellsville
Commissary Sergeant-Henry Inscho
Sutler-Isaac H. Reynolds, Elmira
Company A (Elmira)
  Capt.-M.C. Wilkinson
  First Lieut.-John M. Losie
  Second Lieut.-Thomas K. Middleton
Company B (Elmira)
  Capt.-L. Baldwin
  First Lieut.-M.V.B. Buchman
  Second Lieut.-George Swain
Company C (Painted Post)
  Capt.-Wm. F. Fox
  First Lieut.-Charles Fox
  Second Lieut.-Irving Bronson
Company D (Elmira)
  Capt.-H. M. Stocum
  First Lieut.-S. A. Bennett
  Second Lieut.-O. D. Reynolds
Company E (Elmira)
  Capt.-Wm. L. Morgan
  First Lieut.-Wm. L. Morgan, Jr.
  Second Lieut.-Harlow Atwood
Company F (Addison)
  Capt.-James H. Moles
  First Lieut.-J. Milton Roq
  Second Lieut.-John F. Knox
Company G (Bath)
  Capt.-John J. Lamon
  First Lieut.-H. G. Bingham
  Second Lieut.-Ezra Gleason
Company H (Havana)
  Capt.-E.C. Clark
  First Lieut.-H. Delos Donnelly
  Second Lieut.-Lewis O. Sayler
Company I (Corning)
  Capt.-N.T. Colby
  First Lieut.-B. Carr Wilson

Second Lieut.-Natheniel E. Rutter
Company K (Hornellsville)
Capt.-Allen S. Sill
First Lieut.-John M. Goodrich
Second Lieut.-Alonzo Howard[10]

Capt. N.T. Colby listed the following positions on his morning reports for Co. I:

1 Capt	4 Sgts	1 Drummer
1 1st Lt	8 Corp	1 Fifer
1 2nd Lt	1 Bugler	75-82 recruits[11]

"By late 1862 both sides had adopted similar systems of organization for their land forces: an ARMY was composed of two or more CORPS; each CORPS was composed of two or more DIVISIONS; each DIVISION was composed of two or more BRIGADES; each BRIGADE was composed of two or more REGIMENTS; each REGIMENT was composed of ten COMPANIES, which on paper usually contained 100 men, but often were only half that."[12]

August 13, 1862 107th Regiment was formerly organized at Elmira, N.Y., and referred to as the Campbell Guards.[13]
August 14, 1862 1 o'clock A.M. Regiment moved towards Washington from Elmira.
August 16, 1862 11 o'clock A.M. Regiment arrived Washington. 5 o'clock P.M. moved from Washington to Camp Seward near Fort Albany, Va.
August 18, 1862 Distributed arms to the Regiment.
August 20, 1862 Distributed accouterments.[14]
August 22, 1862 Rainstorm blew in at night.[15]
August 23, 1862 6 o'clock A.M. moved from Camp Seward to Fort Lyon, about 8 miles.[16]

"Movement of the 107th — We learn that Col. Van Valkenburgh received orders to move from 'Camp Seward' on Saturday morning last, and proceed to Fort Lyon, three miles from Alexandria, to take the place of an old regiment, which had been garrisoning that point. Fort Lyon is said to be one of the strongest fortifications in the country, and in case of a reverse to our arms near Fredricksburgh would prove a point of great importance. The location is said to be eminently healthy and pleasant."[17]

Camp Seward, Va
Aug 24th 1862 [Sun]
Dear Father

    Though I have not had a letter from you since leaving home and though I have once before written you a short hasty note — yet I will write you to day for I prefer to have you owe me one or two letters — We have changed our position and are at present encamped at Fort Lyons — a large fort — about a mile and one half below Alexandria on the high bank of the Potomac. Direct your letters (and tell Mary too — for I forgot it) just the same as before — to Washington — We have a very fine place for camp and expect to stay here for some time — for four of our companies are to take charge of the fort and learn the heavy artillery drill — Four of the least experienced Captains have been selected to go into the fort — but no one can say with any certainty that we shall remain here a week — Van Valkenburg says we will not see any fighting unless we see it within twelve days but *why* he says so I can not tell. At least — the 86th — Col Bailey have really started out of Washington and will probably go to reinforce Pope who doubtless will fall back no farther after Bailey joins him — They (the 86th) were in Alexandria last night and are now on their way towards the Rappanhannock — Rumors of changes in our field officers prevail — but no one seems to know when or how they will be made — Smith — our Major is at home in Elmira now but will probably be back soon. As I write — the valley below us is fairly choked up with troops for miles each way — going out to reinforce Pope — McClellans forces or rather a portion of them arrived in Alexandria a few days since by transports and went right off towards Pope — Hookers division came last night and they too go to day — They look as though they had seen hard times I tell you — but look like veterans and real soldiers — Officers of high rank are seen with privates clothes on and ragged straw hats and rusty swords and yet they are as ready to face the foe as if they glittered in fresh equipment. It is the general opinion here that McClellan has played out — His failure to take Richmond — after taking his army through the battles and swamps of the Peninsula — is fatal to him — He very narrowly escaped with his army — and in fact — but for Popes advance — thereby compelling the rebels to concentrate before him (Pope) He would have faired badly — However he is safe now — a part of his army having landed at Acquia Creek and gone across to Fredericksburg and the remainder came here — Pope has been fighting more or less for several days — but the news for the present is not divulged — He has fallen back 16 miles this side of Culpepper — which would seem to indicate that the Rebels are too numerous for him — I saw Col Hoffman the other day — He is *sick* at Baileys House — Baileys Cross roads and the regiment is under Lt Col Crane — My vest has not yet come to hand and a pair of pants I ordered at Elmira have not been received — I need them very much — Have you written for those pills yet? My men are all well and I think are satisfied — I need a coat pretty bad — but cant afford one yet. I find my second Liut — to be quite a fine fellow and Wilson is doing very well — but is rather airy —

Now then write soon and tell me what the particular lie is — that the Corning pups are telling about me just now — and invite them to kiss my — foot — Of course by this time they have arranged some lie or other and are busy circulating it — Tell Henry *not to be fooled into volunteering for if he does he ought to be hung and will be sorry when its too late* — Give my love to Mother and tell her that I have just finished the cake she put in my Haversack — to day and was mighty glad to get it-

If their are any decent folks in the hole you at present reside in who ask after me — give them my respects. Tell me all the news when you write and believe me dear father

Affectionately Your Son
Newton[18]

August 28, 1862 "A Georgian under Longstreet said, 'one of the hottest days I ever experienced.'"[19]

August 30, 1862 A clean, lovely day. Ten o'clock A.M., Regiment moved from Fort Lyon to Camp Seward near Camp Craig about 8 miles. Rain fell during the night.

August 31, 1862 "Soggy, nasty morning."[20]

From the Field and Staff Muster Roll Report August 31st, Camp Seward, near Fort Albany, Va. "In consequence of the changes of camp the Regiment has had very little time for drill and being entirely composed of raw recruits they are not as yet proficient as soldiers but are doing all they can to learn."[21]

The daily schedule for the regiment as ordered by Col. Van Valkenburgh:

Reveille	Daybreak
Sick call	½ after revellie
Squad Drills	6 o'clock A.M.
Breakfast	7 o'clock A.M.

Captain's morning report	7 o'clock A.M.
Guard mounting	8 o'clock A.M.
Squad drills	9 o'clock A.M.
Dinner	12 M
Company & squad drills	5 o'clock P.M.
Supper	6 o'clock P.M.
Dress parade, retreat	Sundown
Tattoo	9½ P.M.
Taps	10 o'clock P.M.[22]

September 1, 1862 Thunderstorms in the afternoon.

"McClellan was instructed that he had nothing to do with the troops engaged in active operations under Pope, but to command the limited garrison in front of Washington."

Sept 2, 1862 "Gen. McClellan was ordered to again take command of the Army of the Potomac that had been under Pope, as well as the defense of Washington. In a matter of very few days he had strengthened the defenses around the capital and prepared to pursue Lee into Maryland."[23]

September 3, 1862 The 107th moved camp from Fort Craig to near Fort Albany.

September 6, 1862 Saturday they left Camp Seward, Fort Albany at evening to join McClellan's Army in Maryland; marched 13 miles and bivouacked near Rockville.[24]

"The Second and Twelfth Corps, under Generals Sumner and Williams, moved to Rockville; thence on Frederick, the Twelfth Corps moving by a laterial road between Urbana and New Market, thus maintaining the communication between the center and right wing, as well as covering the direct route from Frederick to Washington."[25]

Sept 6, 1862 The first campaign of the 107th regiment was to begin.

"The marching orders— the hurried perparations— the filling of the haversacks and canteens, the rolling and slinging of blankets (knapsacks and tents were left behind), the falling in, the standing in line ready for the 'forward' that came just as night fell — off at last, one thousand men-boys we would call them —fresh from home, marching in columns of four, guns at a right shoulder, the long column winding out and away up hill and down dale, with a steady tramp, tramp, the cadence broken only by 'the laugh, the shout, the witticsm arch.' The night air grows cool and crisp — the pace quickens — the moon shines down upon the dark mass of men, horses, wagons and artillery. It glistens upon the bayonets and gun-barrels, and the line becomes a rippling, tossing stream of shimmering steel. Ah! who can forget it? As they cross the Potomac along the old acqueduct [sic] bridge, some one begins to chant the 'Battle Hymn of the Republic'; one by one the marching men catch up until it passes from company to company, until seemingly, every voice joins in the grand old chorus, 'Glory, Glory Hallelujah.' What inspiration it brings. 'The Rebel foot is on thy soil. Maryland, my Maryland,' but 'We are coming, we are coming 300,000 strong.' Alas! alas! that night's march was the only the 107th Regiment made with full ranks. Never again was there such an unbroken touch of elbows among its members, and so the memory of that first march will abide longest and best remembered among all of the surviving comrades."[26]

The old aqueduct bridge mentioned was the Alexandria Aqueduct. This crossed the Potomac to connect the C & O Canal to the Alexandria Canal. During the war this was drained and used as a bridge.[27]

An aqueduct actually looked and was constructed much like a bridge. It was used to keep the canal waterway intact while crossing other water ways. The canal water traversed the aqueduct bridge way.

September 7, 1862 General McClellan left Washington on the 7th of September, and established his headquarters at Rockville.[28]

September 7, 1862 The 107th remained at Rockville where they furnished one company (A) as a Guard for Gen'l McClellan's Head Quarters.[29]

General A.S. Williams writes that his original brigade was with him in name only. "...Instead of 3,000 men they number altogether less than 400 men present! Not a field officer nor adjutant is here! All killed or wounded! Of the 102 officers not over 20 are left to be present! Instead of hopeful and confident feelings we are all depressed with losses and disasters. Instead of an offensive position the enemy is now in Maryland and we are on the defensive. What a change! After such vast preparations and such vast sacrifices. This has been a 'brainless war.' I can't tell you the future. We are accumulating troops this way and shall doubtless have some severe conflicts. If we fail now the North has no hope, no safety that I can see. We have thrown away our power and prestige. We may become the supplicant instead of the avenger...."[30]

President Lincoln directed that three corps of the Army of Virginia be absorbed into the Army of the Potomac. Pope's First Corps now became XI Corps, his Second Corps was changed to XII Corps, and his Third Corps designated I Corps.[31]

September 8, 1862   The 107th marched beyond Rockville and were attached to General Gordon's Brigade, Williams Division, Banks Corps. They camped there until the 11th.[32]

A.S. Williams: "Four other regiments are ordered to us, but they are so green in officers and men that little can be expected."[33]

September 11–12, 1862   Marched in the morning each day camping in advance each day.
September 11, 1862   Resumed march and camped at night near Damascus.
September 12, 1862   Camp near Damascus, Md.[34]

From A.S. Williams: "I have 3000 fresh and gaudy new volunteers. These jolly fellows, who have marched up from Washington without tents and with no shelter but blankets and some overcoats. They think they are suffering, and I fancy, as it is raining tonight, that they are not as comfortable as they were a few weeks ago, as they have not the knack of old soldiers of extemporizing shelters out of rails and blankets and pieces of boards.

"With all the new troops and the reorganization.... There will be a great battle or a great skedaddle on the part of the Rebels. I have great confidence that we shall smash them terribly if they stand, more confidence than I have ever had in any movement of the war."[35]

Sept 12, 1862   The Second Corps, Army of Virginia, was changed to the Twelfth Corps by General Orders No. 129 of the Adjutant-Generals Office. The following shows the corps structure as it relates to the 107th New York.

    1. Maj. Gen. Joseph K. F. Mansfield
    2. Brig. Gen. Alpheus S. Williams
          First Division
    1. Brig. Gen. Alpheus S. Williams
    2. Brig. Gen. Samuel W. Crawford
    3. Brig. Gen. George H. Gordon
          Third Brigade
    1. Brig. Gen. George H. Gordon

  2. Col. Thomas H. Ruger
  27th Indiana, Col. Silas Colgrove
  2d Massachusetts, Col. George L. Andrews
  13th New Jersey, Col. Ezra A. Carman
  107th New York, Col. R.B. Van Valkenburgh
  Zouaves d'Afrique, Pennsylvania
  3d Wisconson, Col. Thomas H. Ruger

September 13, 1862 "On the 13th we marched to Frederick expecting an attack all the way. We forded the Monocacy, arrived in the afternoon and encamped about a mile east of the city."[36]

The main body of the right and center wings of McClellan's Army arrived at Frederick on the 12th and 13th. The enemy had marched out two days before, taking the roads to Boonesboro & Harpers Ferry.[37]

September 14, 1862 "Gen. Mansfield arrived from Washington on the 14th. He was a most veteran-looking officer, with head as white as snow. Mansfield took over as the new commander and A.S. Williams went back to his division command. With Mansfield we were ordered forward from Frederick crossing the Catoctin Mountain by a very rough road. Ascending the mountain, we heard the reports of distant artillary and once on the summit could see that a fierce engagement was going on across the valley and in the gorges of the opposite range of mountains. This was to be the battle of South Mountain."[38]

"We were hurried down over the rough roads and finally about sundown were ordered to bivouac the corps. Before the regiments had filed into the fields, however, a new order came to follow Gen. Sumner's corps over the ploughed fields toward the musketry firing heard in front. The 12th Corps had been ordered to Middletown to report to Gen. McClellan."[39]

September 15, 1862 "At daybreak we moved forward. We passed over that day a portion of the battlefield of South Mountain [through Turner's Gap] and saw many Rebel dead."[40] The 107th camped that night two miles beyond Boonsboro on the 15th — and from there moved towards Sharpsburg.[41]

A letter to Newton from home:
Corning Sept 14 1862
Dear Son

I have received no letter from you since the 24th Augt. and during that time I have often turned away from the post office with disappointment and more — particularly of late — Since the Rebels have driven the Army of Virginia from their advanced position — back under the protection of the fortifications around Washington. I dont know but this retreat and slaughter of our poor fellows by thousands was unavoidable — Perhaps it was another masterly piece of strategy — If so either way I have failed to see it — And another thing I have failed to devise any shadow of exercise for permitting our poor wounded soldiers to lay for three or four days on the battle ground when we were permitted under a flag of truce to go to their relief — The defeat was bad enough — but this last act of seeming neglect — seemed to horrify the whole country — And well it might if true it was barbarious and humanity shudders to contemplate their sufferings — But I may be too uncharitable towards those whose duty it was to attend to this business and hope there is some excuse that will in some measure exonerate the government from the charge of wilful neglect — The last letter received from you by Mary was written — from Rockville last Sunday [Sept 7] and from all the information we can glean from the papers (and that is not much) there is a prospect that you have some heavy work to do in Maryland — But little reliance can be placed in newspapers — statements and in the absence of anything Official we imagine a great many things that may be without any foundation — But the affairs of the country at present look very discouraging and a gloomy feeling seems to prevade the whole community — The fears of more defeats — The loss of all we have gained during the whole summer campaign and in fact more for Maryland was free from Rebels in the spring — (all this) and also the probability that thousands more of lives must be sacrificed to redeem what has been lost — may well cast a gloomy shadow over the whole country. But I can see no way to avoid the dangers and difficulties but to meet them relying on the God of Battles — and of Nations for strength and aid in this time troubles for his power is omnipotent and I believe he will succor thou that call upon him in sincerity — that he may bless and protect you and save our country from further disasters is my earnest prayer. I have nearly filled my sheet with matters that I fear will not interest you much. And can almost see you glancing hastily over it to find some news from home — Well I have but very little to tell — Mother is absent making a visit at Nunda and I think I shall go out after her the last of this week — A letter just arrived from Mrs Stevens — says that Uncle Lewis does not want to come north but his wife does very much — thus all their silver plate is buried — The Union Troops have been there and pulled down their flag and raised the Stars and Stripes.

The excitement of recruiting and the fears of a draft have quite passed away for the present at least. As the quota called for have all been raised in Old Steuben and some over — The Regt of Col Hathaway is to leave Elmira tomorrow — The other Col Hanover will leave soon. We are in hopes of seeing you home this fall at least on a furlough we can hardly expect more — but we often regret your going again into the service. I hope you will write us as often as possible if it is but a few lines to let us know where you are — Respects to Liuts Wilson and Rutter-All well —

As ever Afectionately
Your Father

Captain Newton T. Colby, 107th New York. Colby family collection.

PS Have you got your vest — I paid Sam $1.00 and he promised to have it sent on[42]

While General Lee was concentrating his forces near Sharpsburg, General Jackson captured Harpers Ferry from Colonel Miles with relative ease on the 15th, and was to join up with Lee near Sharpsburg on the 16th.

CHAPTER 10

The 107th New York Regiment at Antietam

"When the Rebels came into Maryland on 4, 5, and 6th of September they proclaimed that they had come to liberate the people of Maryland from the despotism of Lincoln, and intimated that they intended to stay. They discovered, in the first place, that there was either no rebel sentiment in Maryland, or that if there was any it dared not show itself. They got no recruits. What ever prestige they may have derived from their victories at Rappahannock and Manassas was destroyed by their lack of success at South Mountain and Antietam. They invaded the state exultant, hopeful, flushed with triumph; they retired defeated, disappointed, disheartened."[1]

"J. K. F. Mansfield, an engineer officer who never before had commanded large bodies of troops, was picked to command the XII Corps just two days before the battle of Antietam."[2]

From the *Corning Journal*:

Great Battle at Sharpsburg
Headquarters Army of the Potomac
Tuesday Evening Sept. 16

"During this afternoon information was received at headquarters showing that the enemy were crossing the river, and concentrating their forces on the ridge of hills outside of the town of Sharpsburg, to within three miles of the main body of our army. Jackson left Harper's Ferry this morning, his troops commencing to arrive during the afternoon, when it became evident that Lee was disposed to engage our forces in battle at this point.

"Gen. McClellan sent for Franklin's [VI] corps and Couch's Division, who were about 7 miles distant on the other side of Elk Ridge. There was considerable artillery firing during the day on both sides, resulting in our having about 40 men killed and wounded."[3]

Allan Pinkerton, who was known as Major Allan, accompanied a party of cavalry to reconnoiter across the Antietam. It "was discovered that the enemy had changed the position of some of their batteries, while their left and center were upon and in front of the Sharpsburg and Hagerstown turnpike, and the extreme left rested upon the wooded heights near the cross-roads to the north." Upon recrossing the Antietam while returning, Pinkerton's horse was shot from under him.[4]

It was about 4 P.M. when General Hooker began to move his I Corps troops across the Antietam Creek by way of local ford and the upper bridge. He had about 8600 men to position in anticipation of an attack.[5] General Richardson reported that Hooker's troops got into action about dusk. The battle lasted two hours, during which the enemy were driven about a half a mile with considerable loss. The Pennsylvania Reserves, who were in front, suffered much.[6] As the sun began to set, and with diminishing light, Hooker engaged the men of General Hood's Division. The fighting in David Miller's cornfield and the East Woods ended with the coming darkness. Hooker prophetically informed his men, "We are through for tonight, gentlemen, but tomorrow we fight the battle that will decide the fate of the Republic."[7]

The XII Corps had marched from Boonesboro along the Boonesboro Pike to the area near the Pry House, McClellan's Headquarters. They turned westward on the Keedysville Pike, across a small stone bridge, over Little Antietam Creek, to the area around Pry's Mill where they bivouacked. The mill and the surrounding farm buildings were used as hospitals after the battle. It was at this location that General Mansfield had his last meal at the Jacob Cost house.

"About 10 o'clock P.M., the XII Corps were wakened and ordered against loud talking and prohibited all fires as they prepared and moved to the Upper Bridge."[8]

Mansfield's XII Corps then moved over the upper bridge in silence and total darkness. They were to support Hooker's men in the morning.[9]

Gen. A.S. Williams writes, "The regiments had just settled down when ... along came a message to get under arms at once. We passed a stone bridge [upper bridge] over the Antietam and then branched off into the fields. Gen. Mansfield and his escort led the way, but it was so dark and the forests and woods so deep that I could not follow and was obliged to send ahead to stop our leaders repeatedly."[10]

From the upper bridge, the 107th either marched along the Keedysville Pike to the area near the intersection with Smoketown Road, or they went through the Hoffman farm to the area just south of the Line farm. Other regiments camped along Smoketown Road south of the Keedysville Pike. They were on the farms of John Poffenberger, Line and Hoffman, about a mile north of Hooker's position. The 107th camped between the Line and Hoffman farms. "By midnight, the XII Corps had arrived at the cornfields of Martin Line [George Line], where it bedded down in close order by column of companies. A field hospital had already gone into operation at the house — a grim reminder of the soldier's fragile state of life."[11] The night was occupied in getting the troops in their respective positions, while ammunition trains and ambulances were forwarded to the different commands.

At about two o'clock in the morning Gen. Williams got under the corner of a rail fence, but the pickets in front of them kept firing.... He said, "...I shall not soon forget that night, so obscure, so mysterious, so uncertain; with the occasional rapid volleys of pickets and outposts, the low, solemn sound of the command as troops came into position, and withal so sleepy that there was a half-dreaming sensation about it all; but with a certain impression that the morrow was to be great with the future fate of our country. So much responsibility, so much intense, future anxiety! And yet I slept as soundly as though nothing was before me."[12]

Cpl. Arthur S. Fitch, Co. B., 107 N.Y. Vols. Regt., wrote, "...Sept 16, 1862 ... night again, dark, chilly and forboding. There in the clover field wet with dew, facing the grim woods, wherein lie the enemy, the men are bivouacking the 'night before battle.' No shouts or songs now. The stillness of the night is broken by the hostile pickett shots close to the front. What are the thoughts that fill the minds of the men as they lie there, anxiously awaiting the morning? Who can describe them?"[13] Light rain fell during the night and gave way to fog in the early morning hours. It was thought that Hooker and Mansfield, with 8600 and 7200 men, respectively, would outnumber Jackson two to one. This, of course, could only happen if McClellan thought to coordinate the attack.[14]

Early on the morning of the 17th all were waiting for the order to move. Due to the rain and fog, visibility on the field was not very good. It was perceived by the men "as a good omen, they thanked God, exclaiming, 'We have not got to fight beneath a blistering sun.'" However, as the sun began to rise, the fog began to thin and the sights and sounds of the pending battle loomed ahead. Hooker's men had spent the night on the

Joseph Poffenberger farm that was just north of the Miller corn field. The corn field was a large rectangle of tall, mature corn between the East Woods and a rail fence along the Hagarstown Pike. This field would forever be known as "The Cornfield."[15]

Between 6:00 and 7:00 A.M., Gordon's Brigade, including the 107th New York, moved into position just north of the Joseph Poffengerger farm along the Smoketown Road.

By 0600, the I Corps of Joseph "Fighting Joe" Hooker was in motion against Jackson's line, thus inaugurating what was to become the bloodiest day in all American history.

After about an hour of heavy fighting, Hooker's men were suddenly surprised. With the Rebel yell, over 2000 Confederates came charging out of the West Woods. Their terrible volley, in the words of Rufus Dawson, "cut like a scythe through the Federal lines." Hooker's troops were stopped in their tracks and quickly fled the rear. The field was strewn with much carnage and the enemy followed the retreat closely. Hooker knew he was in serious trouble and called to Mansfield's CII Corps to come quickly to his aid. He also committed his reserve of Meade's division comprised of Anderson's and Magilton's brigades.[16]

Gen. A.S. Williams writes the following to his daughters on the 17th: "At the first dawn of day the cannon began work. Gen. Hooker's command was about a mile in front of us and it was his corps upon which the attack began. By a common impulse our men stood to arms. They had slept in ranks and the matter of toilet was not tedious, nor did we have time to linger over the breakfast table. My division being in advance, I was ordered to move up in close column of companies— that is a company front to each regiment and the other companies closed up to within six paces. When so formed a regiment looks like a solid mass. We had moved a dozen rods before the shells and round shot came thick over us and around us. If these had struck our massed regiments dozens of men would have been killed by a single shot.

"I had five new regiments without drill or discipline. Gen. Mansfield was greatly excited. Though an officer of acknowledged gallantry, he had a very nervous temperament and a very impatient manner. Feeling that our heavy masses of raw troops were sadly exposed, I begged him to let me deploy them in line of battle, in which the men present but two ranks or rows instead of twenty, as we were marching, but I could not move him. He was positive that all the new regiments would run away. So on we went over ploughed ground, through cornfields and woods, till the line of infantry fight began to appear.

"It was evident that Hooker's troops were giving way. His general officers were hurrying toward us begging for support in every direction."[17]

After about an hour and a half of artillery fire and continuous fighting, Hooker's men were almost used up. Jackson, however, still had to face two more Union corps.[18]

Major General J.F.K. Mansfield moved his corps toward the battle. This was the first time that Mansfield had commanded such a large number of men and he was concerned about their lack of experience. At least half of them had never seen combat and he was apprehensive as to how they would react. They were kept in compact lines until they were to be deployed.[19]

The 107th New York was one of those inexperienced regiments, having just been formed in July.

7:20-8:00 A.M. XII Corps—"deployed like a huge skirmishing party as Mansfield committed the Corps to the conflict piece meal." Brigadier General George H. Gordon's Brigade followed by Brigadier General Samuel Crawford's Brigade led the corps, which was closed en masse, column of divisions (two company front, fifteen ranks deep). Brigadier General George S. Greene's Division followed right behind.[20] This was a risky formation, especially in light of the exploding artillery shells. Mansfield thought that because so many untested men were going into battle for the first time, they might run to the rear out of fear. To encourage the troops the general shouted words of encouragement: "Ah! Boys. We shall do a fine thing today. We have got them where we want them. They cannot escape by the skin of their teeth."[21] "Gordon's Brigade passed an isolated body of woods to the northeast of the East Woods, the 13th New Jersey and the 107th New York, his two green regiments, peeled off from the column to secure that [left] flank against any confederate thrust from the East Woods. The four remaining regiments marched south by the front into the North Woods, where they halted to realign and unsling knapsacks."[22]

"As Mansfield's Federals drove through the wood they encountered irritating sniper fire from the retreating Rebels dodging from tree to tree or from behind rocks, fallen branches and wood piles."[23]

"General Mansfield did not act nearly as cocky as he had an hour earlier, when, in response to a cheer from Gordon's Brigade, he boasted, "That's right, boys; you may as well cheer. We are going to whip them today! Boys we're going to lick them today!"[24] "Mansfield tried his best to get his troops into position in the East Woods, despite the blanket of smoke covering the area and the fire from the woods and corn."[25] "The 10th Maine, halted in the grassy field on the eastern side of the Smoketown Road, near the northern edge of the East Woods."[26] "Seeing the 10th Maine

10. The 107th New York Regiment at Antietam

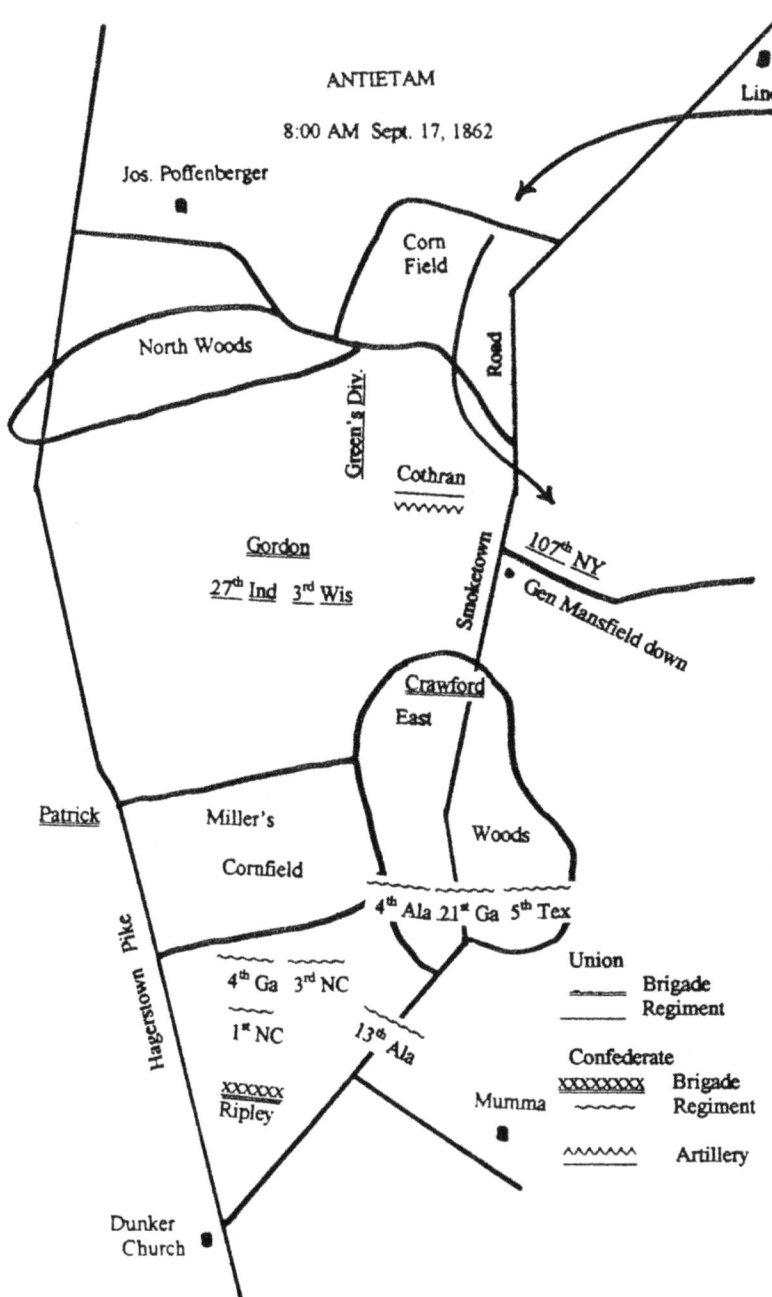

Map of Antietam, September 17, 1862, at 8 a.m. showing position of the XII Corps, 1st div. 3rd Brig.

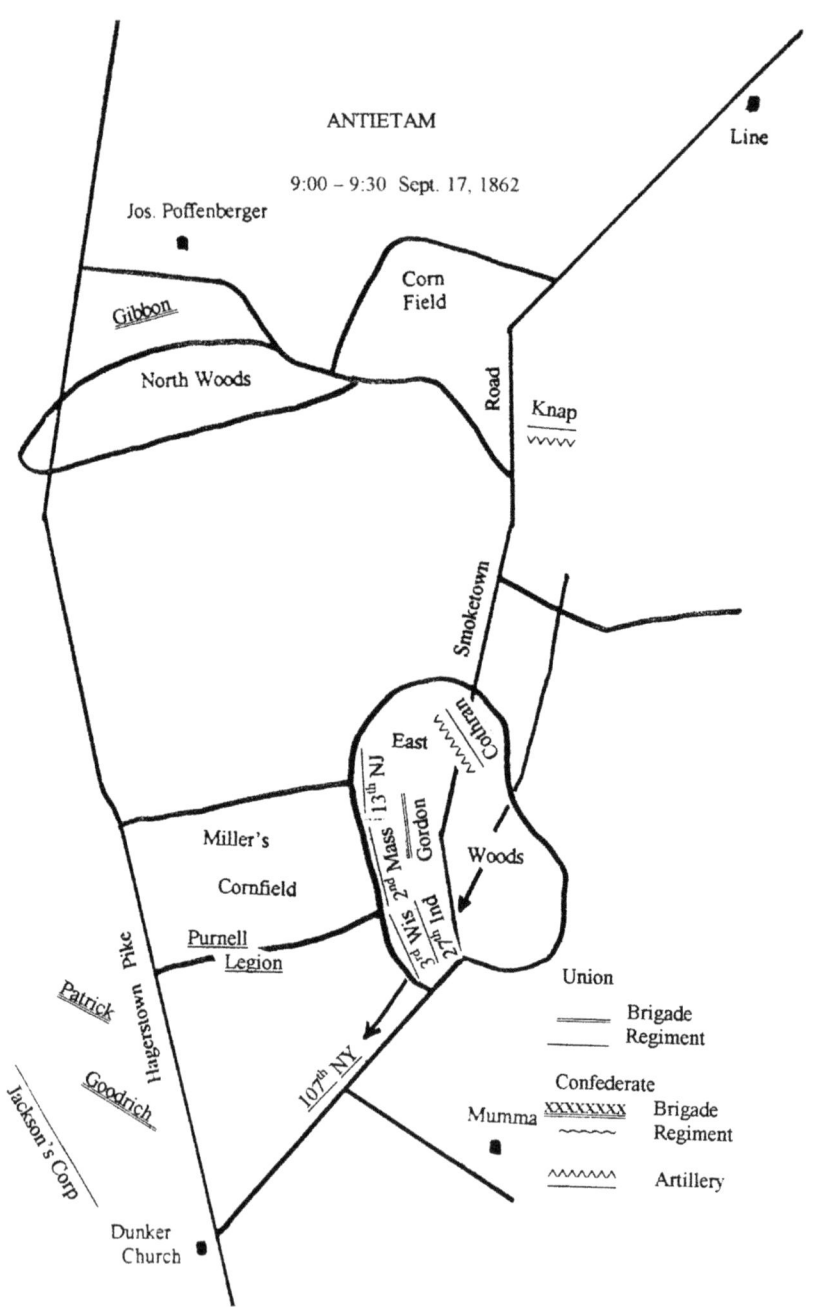

Map of Antietam, September 17, 1862, at 9–9:30 a.m. showing position of the XII Corps, 1st div. 3rd Brig.

10. The 107th New York Regiment at Antietam

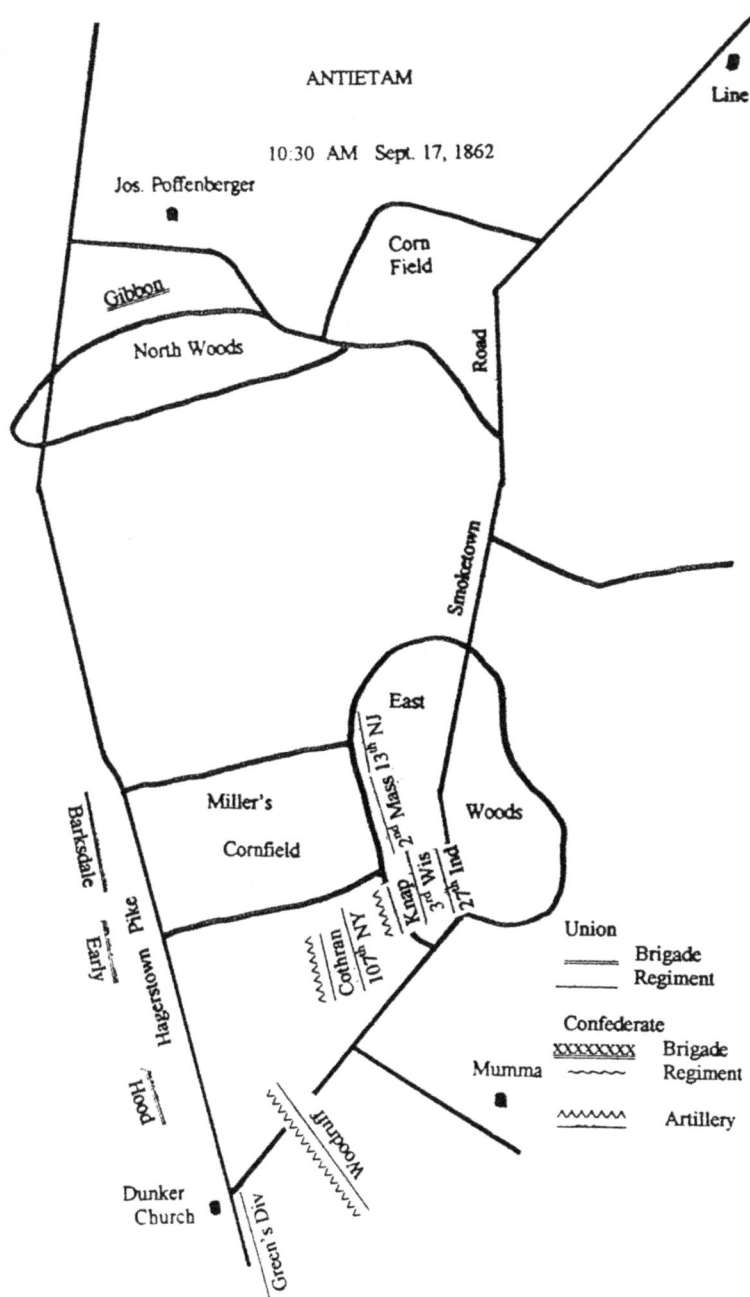

Map of Antietam, September 17, 1862, at 10:30 a.m. showing position of the XII Corps, 1st div. 3rd Brig.

firing into a Cornfield near Smoketown Road, Mansfield supposed they were accidentally shooting at some of Hooker's men attempting to retreat to safety. Interposing himself between what he believed to be friendly forces, Mansfield rode before the Maine regiment calling out, "You are firing into your own men."[27] He commanded the soldiers to cease fire. "You are shooting your friends," he screamed, "There are no Rebs so far advanced."[28] "The men argued the contrary leading the General to scrutinize the opposing force."[29] "He was told that he was wrong and he should see the Rebel snipers in the trees."[30] "Realizing his mistake he exclaimed, "Yes, Yes, you are right."[31] "The general, tottering in the saddle, goaded his bleeding horse north along the Smoketown road until he reached the right of the 125th Pennsylvania. He seemed ill, and several men helped the general dismount. Mansfield, bleeding, was carried to a lone tree in the rear of the line, where he was left to await the arrival of a surgeon."[32]

At about 7:50 A.M., some men and officers of the 10th Maine finally found the unfortunate General Mansfield when their regiment retired from the fray. Sergeants Merritt, Storer Knight, and Adujutant Gould took a blanket and laid the seriously wounded officer on it. They also found a black cook from Hooker's Corps and convinced him to help them get the portly Mansfield into one of the waiting ambulances along Poffenberger's Lane. As they put the dying general into the wagon, Adjutant Gould looked across the field and noticed the 107th New York being led toward the East Woods by General Crawford. Troops were everywhere.[33] General Mansfield was attended to by Dr. Flood, the Surgeon of the 107th New York Regiment. "He had received a shot to the chest that would prove mortal. He was taken to the George Line farm house where he suffered through the night and died the next day."[34]

With General Mansfield down, the command fell upon the shoulders of General Alpheus S. Williams. He had been with Mansfield only minutes before and was somewhat surprised when Informed that he had been wounded. Williams went to General Hooker to be briefed on the situation. As they were talking, Hooker was shot in the foot and had to be taken off the field. Now Williams was on his own. Between 8:40 and 8:50 the Yankees again came under heavy fire from the Corn Field. Hill's Brigade was now able to relieve some of Hood's men.[35] "Gen. Williams began at once to deploy the new regiments, the old ones had already gotten themselves into line. Taking hold of one, he directed Gens. Crawford and Gordon to direct the others. He got his in line pretty well by having a fence to align it on and having accomplished this he ordered the colonel to go forward and open fire the moment he saw the Rebels. Poor fellow! He was killed within ten minutes. His regiment, advancing in line, was split in two by coming in contact with a barn. One part did very well in the woods but the trouble with this regiment and the others was that in attempting to move them forward or back or to make any maneuver they fell into inextricable confusion and fell to the rear, where they were easily rallied. The men were of an excellent stamp, ready and willing, but neither officers nor men knew anything, and there was an absence of the mutual confidence which drill begets. Standing still, they fought bravely."[36] "Eventually Williams had his forces divided to reinforce the depleted commands of Meade and Gibbon with Crawford's brigade being sent to join forces near the Miller farm and Gordon's taking position to the north of the Cornfield."[37]

"In attempting their movement to get into position before the Cornfield, Gordon's brigade was subjected to a galling fire from the enemy. When Hill's detached brigades launched a counterattack against Gordon's men, the Yankees defiantly held."[38]

By about 8:40 "the cornfield and the East Woods were finally in federal hands," having been secured by the 12th Corps. By advancing through the wood, Gen. Gordon's Brigade, "the 13th NJ, 2nd Massachusetts, and 3rd Wisconsin (facing west, in line north to south respectively) had secured the East Woods with the 27th Indiana in reserve." The 107th New York, after passing through the east portion of the East Woods, "was posted where the Smoketown Road entered the woods, facing south.[39] 125th Penna., under Gen. Crawford, advanced [west] just north of Smoketown Road to the post and rail fence at intersection with Hagerstown Pike. [near the Dunker Church][40] "When they engaged the enemy he was in a strip of woods, long but narrow. They drove him from this, across a ploughed field and through a cornfield into another woods, which was full of ravines."[41] 125th's left flank secured the Dunker Church while the right made it to the West Woods.[42]

Gen. A.S. Williams wrote the following: "There the enemy held us in check till 9½ o'clock, when there was a general cessation of musketry. All over the ground the Rebel dead and wounded lay thick, much more numerous than ours, but all were painfully mingled in. The necessities of the case were so great that I obliged to put my whole corps into action at once. The roar of the infantry was beyond anything conceivable to the uninitiated. Imagine from 8,000 to 10,000 men on one side, with probably a larger number on the other, all at once discharging their muskets ... amidst hundreds of pieces of artillary, right and left, were thundering. While the battle was raging fiercest ... Gen Doubleday needed support on our right ... I started a division over and followed them. As I entered the narrow lane running to the right and front a battery opened a cross-fire and Pittman and myself had the excitement of riding a mile or so out and back under its severest salutations ... Finding a battery, I put it in position to meet the flank fire of the Rebel battery and some one else had the good sense to establish another farther in the rear. The two soon silenced this disagreeable customer. At 9½ o'clock Gen. Sumner was announced as near at hand with his corps. As soon as his columns began to arrive Williams withdrew his men by degrees to the shelter of the [east] woods for the purpose of rest, to collect stragglers, and to renew ammunition."[43] "Lieutenant George A Woodruff's Battery I, 1st US Artillery, [Sumner's II Corps] careened down the Smoketown Road and took up a position several hundred yards northeast of Dunker Church. Woodruff could clearly make out fleeing Federals in his front being closely pursued by the enemy. He wasted no time. "Coming in battery, we opened fire with cannister at once," he later wrote. "They still remained in the woods, and we continued our fire, using special case or cannister." Battery 'I' did yoeman's work. During the course of the fighting, the battery discharged 168 rounds of cannister, 75 rounds of spherical case and 27 rounds of solid shot."[44]

"In engaging the worn out remnants of Jackson's command, the Federals of Mansfield's corps had lost 1,800 men, including its commander Joseph Mansfield while winning a significant foothold in the enemy's line. In the end, Hooker and Mansfield essentially wound up fighting separate battles while getting chewed up in the process."[45]

"Sumner's force in the center was soon used up, and Williams was again called to bring up his wearied and hungry men. They advanced to the front and opened fire, but the force opposed was enormously superior. Still they held on, under heavy losses, till one o'clock. Some of the old regiments were fairly broken up in this fight and what was left were consolidated and mixed up afterward with the new regiments. Sumner's men gave way towards the left, when he was drawn out by a rush and his men came scampering to the rear in great confusion. The Rebels followed with a yell but three or four of our batteries being in position they were received with a tornado of cannister which made them vanish before the smoke cloud cleared away.... Guns were discharged at short range, and each cannister contains several hundred balls. They fell in the very front of the line and all along it apparently, stirring up a dust like a thick cloud. When the dust blew away no regiment and not a living man was to be seen. Several of the old regiments had fired nearly forty rounds each man. They had stood up splendidly and had forced back the enemy nearly a mile. The new regiments were badly broken up, but Williams collected about one-half of them and placed them in support of batteries. [this included the 107th N.Y.S.V.] They held the main battle field and all their wounded, except a few in the woods. His troops slept on their arms well to the front...."⁴⁶

Camp of the 107th N.Y.V.
In the field — Sept 21, 1862
Sunday Morning
Dear Father

    I have had but one letter from home in about three weeks— not — I suppose because they have not been written but because our troops have been so constantly on the move — and I assure you I long for home news— Probably you have heard long before this of the battle in which our Regt participated — It was a severe fight and I am happy to say that our Regt has won great credit — Our loss is somewhere about 70 in killed wounded and missing. We were under fire all day — and it is wonderful that our loss is not more than doubled — some description of some parts of the fight may interest you — We had marched all the fore part of the previous night and then lay down a little while back of a piece of woods till day light — I slept very sound and when I woke the battle had begun — Presently we were ordered forward and then stopped again — then forward through a corn field and when we reached the other side we deployed (being massed before) and moved by the left flank into the edge of a piece of woods— The shells of the enemy flew over us here — tearing great limbs off the trees and screaming horribly — making us dodge like fun — Then we were ordered to lie down for perhaps 15 minutes— Genl Gordon — (our brigadier) rode up and telling us to cheer ordered us forward — While laying here — Genl Mansfield rode past us into the open lot in front and when within twenty rods of our line was struck by a bullet — which passed through his body — resulting in his death very shortly after — Our Surgeon Dr Flood attended him where he fell — Well we cheered and charged forward toward a wood — distant perhaps— 75 or 100 rods— As soon as we left the edge of the woods— we were under a heavy fire — but I did not see a man fall — till we entered the woods [East Woods] and then a shell struck into the ranks near where I was— killing and wounding 5 or six — I saw them fall and heard their screams— but on we went and I know not who they were or what became of them — Presently we got through the woods and lay down behind a rail fence — in front of which was one of our batteries— and firing away fast and furious— [the 107th was at the fence on Smoketown Rd, near Mumma's Lane-on the right flank facing towards the Dunker Church was Monroe's Battery and to the left, in the field facing south was Owen's Battery] The rebs tried to silence it with their batteries—

and the shells and shot flew about us terribly — One struck the banner (it was lying on the ground) and tore it nearly to pieces — At last the rebs again fell back and ceased fire for a few minutes and suddenly they tried to turn our right flank — Battery after Battery galloped up — unlimbered and began firing in the new direction — Our Regt charged front to meet the new attack and went to the right — in an open field to support our artillery — [Capt. Cothran's Battery, First New York Light Artillery] The firing here was perfectly awful — Just before us was a row of our cannon firing with the greatest rapidity and within six rods behind us another row — doing the same — The rebels were not more than fifty rods in front in a piece of woods and I could see our shells strike into the woods and burst every minute — when I could get up pluck enough to raise up and look that way — As a general thing however — believe me — dear father — I laid *rather* close and in fact tried to get as thin as was possible and felt somewhat like a pancake — Just then Col Van [Valkenberg] came up and ordered me to deploy my company to the front and see if the enemy were there yet — Well — of course I must obey — and did so — deploying one platoon as skirmishers we moved strait toward the foe — Not a man flinched — and we moved steadily forward — (our artillery ceased firing-for us to go before them) till we mounted a little knoll — when within ten rods of us — up jumped a whole regiment and let drive at us — My men fell to the ground and the volley did no harm whatever — and having accomplished what we were sent out for I returned with my company in good order and again lay down in my place in the regiment — As soon as we had left the ground our artillery poured in grape and cannister and the rebs brought up another battery — so that we were exposed to a terrible cross fire — A shell — or piece of RR iron hit one of my fellows — killing him — passed on and took part of Sergt Johnny Browns foot and tore my sword blade away and I have not seen it since — Two of the men took Brown and Corwin off the field. We were then ordered back to the edge of the woods — [east woods] about 15 rods back and covered ourselves behind the trees and were soon relieved by another regiment — I was entirely used up after the fight and could not absolutely stand on my feet — Lieut Rutter acted bravely and did well — Lieut Wilson was not in the fight — being sick — I could write an hour telling you the incidents — but I have neither time or space — The dead and wounded rebels lay around very thick — I went over the field on horseback — the second day after the fight and such sights you never dreamed of — Wounded rebels were still laying about and they begged me to have them removed — You may be sure — dear father that I was not inhuman — but it was little I could do to relieve them — I saw one rebel — with one side of his face including one eye and ear — blown off —

trying to eat a hard cracker with the well side of his mouth! But I will not try to tell what I saw — We are near Harpers Ferry and where next we go I do not know. Write me often — *Do not let anything I write get published*—for I do not wish to blow my own Bugle — Let others say what they please — I am all right — Give my love to mother and Henry and wife — Tell Mary I have written her several times and look for letters from her anxiously — Of course you have worried about me — but do so no longer — I send this to Washington by our Rutter — and he leaves very soon — I hope we may be sent back to Washington soon for we have marched nearly every day for three weeks and are worn almost out — I have had no change of under cloths for that time and they (the under cloths) are ragged as well as dirty — Take good care of Mary and the little folks for my sake — Write me soon — I would like to see the newspaper account of the fight — but presume I will get hold of a paper soon — I have seen no reason to change my mind as to remaining in the service and heartily wish I was out of it — but there is no chance I suppose for that — Wilson would go if he could and says he dont see why I came back again — but I must close — Love to all and respects to any enquiring friends — and tell any others that "he did not run after all — in the battle" —

Affectionately Your Son
Newton[47]

In the *Journal*:
"We learn that Sergeant John Brown of Capt. Colby's Co., 107th Regiment had his foot taken off by a piece of a shell in the Sharpsburgh battle. Capt. Colby's sword was shot away. We have no particulars farther concerning this Company."

"We regret to learn that Capt. Wilkinson, 107th Regiment, is dangerously ill. We hear that he was stunned by a shell which burst near him and prostrated him mentally and physically."[48]

"A shell struck G Company of the 107th New York. Captain H.G. Brigham (G Co.) watched helplessly as it shredded eleven of his men. Amid the smoke and carnage, he heard sixteen year old Willie Everts shrieking and wailing. The explosion had ripped the boy's legs away. The regiment continued into the woods but the memory of Willie's pleas stayed etched in Captain Brigham's mind forever."[49]

Capt. Arthur Fitch wrote:
"It was while lying here that the regiment encountered a perfect storm of missiles from the enemy's guns, and the beautiful blue banner it carried was torn to pieces by a bursting shell.

"...the regiment lay when ordered to support the batteries in the cleared field in front of the woods ... there was a big pile of stones in front of Co. B, the right Co., ... here the regiment was flattened to the ground as our batteries hurled shot and shell just above our heads during the four long hours the regiment occupied this trying position. Here it was that Theodore Smith was struck by a shell and lost his leg. Capt. Miles, of Co. F, crept up to a stump to get a better view of the enemy's position ... in front the woods about the Dunker Church, where the enemy was posted, and behind, the woods from which the regiment emerged at the beginning of the battle, and to which they retired when relieved ... many of the wounded were carried to the stone house to the rear [Samuel Poffenberger's], where the spring was. It was here that Theo Smith had his leg amputated, and lay for many days with the family still occupying the house ... the Line farm where the regiment bivouacked the night of the 16th.... The morning of the 17th the regiment formed a line, just previous to going forward, a rest was taken. Here it was that Gen. Mansfield rode out and spoke these words: 'Ah! boys, we shall do a fine thing to-day. We have got them where we want them; they cannot escape with the skin of their teeth.' He then rode forward and within ten minutes was shot and mortally wounded. His body was placed in a blanket and carried from the field by our men, passing directly through our line as we stood waiting the order to go forward."[50]

The 107th New York lay at night upon the bloody field of victory, remaining there the next and succeeding day in vicinity of the battle field.[51]

A young surgeon from the Christian Commission in Philadelphia arrived in Sharpsburg on the 18th and wrote the following observation of what he found. "There they lay in all positions—dead, dying, maimed, mangled! Men of both armies now powerless to fight! Silent and still—some of them forever still! Some frowning and bearing their agony with speechless heroism. Some praying for water! Many praying for death! Every available house and barn was filled with the wounded! The surgeons had plenty of work to do as they dressed or amputated limbs forever useless, sewed up gaping wounds, removed bullits, applied splints to fractures, arranged dressings and bandages and administered refreshments as needed. Some of the cowardly men would shoot off the ends of their right forefingers, hoping it would be considered accidental. They inflicted these injuries upon themselves so that they could be protected from the dangers of an engagement."[52]

No. 164: Report of Brig. Gen. Alpheus S. Williams, U.S. Army, commanding Twelfth Army Corps, of the battle of Antietam.

10. The 107th New York Regiment at Antietam

Hdgrs. Twelfth Corps
Army of the Potomac
Sandy Hook, Md.
September 29, 1862

Colonel: I have the honor to submit the following report of the part taken by this corps in the recent action near Sharpsburg, Md., on the 17th instant: Two days before the action, Brigadier-General Mansfield, U.S. Army, assumed command of the corps while on bivouac in the South Mountain Pass.

About 2 o'clock the night before the action, the corps took up position about 1½ miles in rear of General Hooker's corps, near the farm of J. Poffenberger, bivouacking in columns of companies. At the first sound of cannon at daylight on the morning of the 17th instant, the command was put in movement, each regiment, by order of General Mansfield, marching in column of companies, closed in mass. [closed en masse—column of divisions (2 company front, fifteen ranks deep)] In this order the corps moved to the front by batallions in mass, the First Brigade, First Division, leading, over ground of intermingled woods, plowed fields, and cornfields. Before reaching the position of General Hooker's Corps, information was brought that his reserves were all engaged and that he was hard pressed by the enemy. The columns were hastened up and deployed in line of battle with all the rapidity that circumstances would permit. Five of the regiments of the First Division were new and wholly without drill. [This included the 107th NYSV]

The massed battalions had been moved with such haste that the proper intervals for deployment had not been carefully attended to. The old regiments, however, deployed promptly, and the new regiments (both officers and men of which behaved with marked coolness) soon got into line of battle, with more promptitude than could have been expected.

While the deployment was going on, and before the leading regiments were fairly engaged, it was reported to General A.S. Williams that the veteran and distinguished commander of the corps was mortally wounded. He at once reported to Major-General Hooker on the field, took from him such directions as the pressing exigencies would permit, and hastened to make a disposition of the corps to meet them. Crawford's Brigade was directed to deploy to the right, its right regiment extending to the Williamsport [Hagerstown] and Sharpsburg stone pike. Gordon held the center, while Brigadier-General Greene's Division, following the first division in column, was directed to the ridge on the left, extending its line from the lane on Gordon's left to the burned buildings, [Mumma farm] a few rods northerly of the brick church.

While General Greene was moving into position, I was strongly solicited by Brigadier General Gibbon to send re-enforcements to the right to support General [Abner] Doubleday's position. I accordingly detached the Third Brigade of General Greene's division, with orders to report to any general officer found on the field. At the same time I ordered the One hundred and twenty-fourth Pennsylvania Volunteer (Crawford's brigade) to push forward past the farm-house of Mr. Miller, cross the pike into the woods beyond, and hold the ridge as long as practicable.

In the mean time the whole line had formed in good order, and were pushing the enemy from the woods and open fields. The requisitions made upon the corps would permit no reserves, and it may be truly stated that, to cover the points threatened or pressed, every regiment (save Thirteenth New Jersey, held in reserve for a while by General Gordon) was, as early as 6:30 to 7 o'clock A.M. engaged with the enemy.

The enemy at this time had pushed his columns into the open fields in advance of a strip of woods, a few hundred yards wide, which extended along a gentle ridge from the brick church, on the Sharpsburg road, to the farm house of J. Miller, and extending beyond in the same direction to a distance not discernible from my position.

In the rocky ravines of these woods, [West Woods] and in a considerable valley in the rear of them, the enemy covered his supports and brought up his re-enforcements. A prominent hill beyond was a strong position for his artillery. Into these woods, after a severe struggle of an hour and a half to two hours' duration, we drove the enemy. A line of high post-and-rail fence on each side the public road between the church and the farm-house named, a few rods from and nearly parallel with the inner edge of the woods, proved a great obstruction to our rapid pursuit, checking up our line until the enemy could bring up his strong re-enforcements.

All the regiments of this corps were engaged, and had been under arms from daylight, without food; still, they held their position, exposed part of the time to an enfilading fire of musketry and artillery in front. In the mean time Brigadier-General Greene, on the left, with two small brigades of his division, numbering only about 1,700 men, had successfully resisted several attacks, and at about 8 o'clock A.M., making a dash, had seized upon the woods where they abut upon the road at the church before mentioned. These he gallantly held for several hours.

I greatly regretted that his repeated calls for aid could be answered only by sending the Thirteenth New Jersey, and subsequently the Twenty-seventh Indiana and the Purnell Legion, of the Third Brigade. Impressed with the importance of holding this position, I made several efforts to recall the residue of the Third Brigade of his division to his assistance, as well as to procure re-enforcements from other sources, but did not succeed.

At nearly 9 o'clock A.M., it being reported that a portion of the Second Corps (Major-General Summer's) was advancing to our support, I dispatched a staff officer to apprise him of our position and the situation of affairs. Soon after, the firing on both sides wholly ceased. Some of the old regiments had emptied their boxes of ammunition, and all were greatly exhausted by the labors of the day and of the preceeding night. As the line of General Sedgwick's division appeared, the regiments of the First Division of this corps were withdrawn to the first line of woods in the rear [East Woods], within supporting distance of several batteries, and directed to replenish their cartridge-boxes and to rest the men. A portion of the One hundred and twenty-fourth Pennsylvania Volunteers continued, however, to hold the woods near Miller's house until ordered, without my knowledge, to withdraw, by some officer unknown to the commanding officer of the regiment. Greene's command had also the possession of the woods at the other end near the church.

General Sedgwick's gallant division and the veteran commander of the Second Corps were received by hearty cheers of our men. This division pushed forward without a halt, and dashed against the strong position of the enemy. The resistance was, if possible, more formidable than ever, and, after a brief but severe contest, I was ordered to send to the front all of my command immediately available.

As General Gordon held his brigade in line most convienent for a movement to the point indicated, he was ordered to advance at once, which was done cheerfully and promptly. The troops which the support was intended for had, however, withdrawn, or changed position toward the right. The regiments of Gordon's brigade brought into action this second time, I regret to add, suffered severly, and were obliged to retire after a stubborn contest. The enemy did not follow, and Gordon's regiments again took position, in good order, behind our batteries.

The enemy, gathering his strongest columns in the woods, made several efforts to dislodge General Greene's command in the left extremity of the woods, as well as to seize upon our batteries in front. All were unsuccessful until about 1.30 P.M. when, by a desparate effort, they forced our wearied forces to retire from the woods, making, at the same time, a rapid dash for our batteries. They met with terrible slaughter by canister at point-blank range, as well as by musketry from the supports, fell back in confusion, and gave up all further efforts to advance beyond their stronghold.

Soon after this, General William F. Smith arrived with his division, and, moving through our lines to the front, gave me an opportunity to withdraw those of this corps which had been most engaged a few rods to the rear, where they could find refreshments and rest. Several of the new regiments were left in support of the batteries.

General Greene's division and Gordon's brigade were subsequently sent to the front in support of a portion of General Franklin's corps, and remained in that position through the night. Of the batteries of this corps, two (Fourth and Sixth Maine) were posted by Captain Best, U.S. Army, chief of artillery, under orders of General Mansfield, on hills adjacent to general headquarters. Knap's Pennsylvania, Cothran's New York, and Hampton's Pittsburg batteries were ordered to the front as soon as the command of corps devolved to me. Knap and Cothran took post in front of the woods occupied by the enemy, Hampton farther to the left, near General Greene's position. These batteries were bravely and excellently served from morning till late in the afternoon. The enemy repeatedly attempted to seize them, but always met with bloody punishment. One section of Knap's, temporarily detached for the aid of General Greene, unfortunately was ordered into the woods, where it fell under heavy infantry fire, by which men and horses were lost and one piece necessarily abandoned. This battery subsequently brought from the field a 12-pounder howitzer of the enemy [on the 19th].

I refer to the report of Captain Best, forwarded herewith, for more specific mention of the valuable services of these batteries. I append hereto a list of casualties of the corps, showing a loss of 1,744, of which 85 are reported missing.

I have the honor to be, colonel, with much respect,
your obedient servant,
A.S. Williams, Brigadier-General Commanding.
Lieut. Col. J.H. Taylor
Chief of Staff and Assistant Adjutant-General[53]

From the Report of Capt. Clermont L. Best, Fourth U.S. Artillery, Chief of Artillery, of the battle of Antietam, 12th Corps, we hear:
"At 2 A.M. on the morning of the 17th, the corps being then near the battle ground, I was ordered by General Mansfield to proceed in person to the rear, to post two batteries of the corps on some hills adjacent to the headquarters of General McCellan, to be pointed out by a staff officer. After performing this service, posting the Fourth Maine Battery and the Sixth Maine Battery, I proceeded to the field, and found that General Mansfield and General Williams, succeeding him, had already posted the

rifled batteries of Knap and Cothran in front of the infantry and near the enemy. Captain Knap commenced fire at 7 A.M. slowly and deliberately, the enemy advancing against him several times between that and 12m., but each time repulsed with canister. At 12 m. one section of his battery, under Lieutenant McGill, was ordered by General Greene forward to assist Colonel Tyndale in holding a wood. Colonel Tyndale ordered one piece of this section to enter the wood, in the act of which it was met with such a destructive fire from the enemy, wounding 4 cannoneers and killing 3 horses, that the piece had to be abandoned, and was lost. Captain Knap continued working the remaining five guns till 3 P.M., at which time he withdrew from the field, wanting ammunition.

"Captain Cothran was assigned a position near the center of the line of battle, supported by the One hundred and seventh New York Volunteers, and was exposed to the enemy's fire from 9 A.M. till 3 P.M., using, at times, canister rapidly. He also withdrew, out of ammunition. Captain Hampton's battery was placed in position near Dunkard Church, and expended 217 rounds against the woods in which said church is located.

"The respective captains named speak in confident terms of the gallantry of their officers and men during the varied fortunes of that day. The gallantry of the captains themselves has been established on this as well as on previous fields.

"C. L. Best, Captain and Chief of Artillary, Bank's Corps
S.E. Pittman, First Lieutenant and Acting Assistant Adjutant-General."[54]

On Sept. 12, 1862, the Second Corps [Bank's corp] of the Army of Virginia became the Twelfth Corps of the Army of the Potomac. Capt. Best evidently still used the designation of Bank's Corp at this time.

Capt. Colby and the 107th N.Y. had been deployed in the field between Cothran's and Knap's batteries and for several hours were under enemy artillery fire.

From the Report of Bridg. Gen. George H. Gordon, U.S. Army, Commanding Third Brigade, of the battle of Antietam we learn:

"Just after the break of day we were aroused from a brief slumber by sharp firing of musketry in front of General Hooker's position. The corps, then commanded by the lamented General Mansfield, was by that officer immediately put in motion. My brigade, formed in columns of battalions closed in mass, I directed toward a battery which I was ordered to support, but before reaching the same I received a countermanding order to move forward with all possible dispatch to the support of General Hooker, then severely pressed. I moved accordingly my deployed masses by the flank at double-quick, gradually gaining deployment distance, thus throwing forward in line of battle on the right the Second Massachusetts Regiment, Colonel Andrews; in the center the Third Wisconsin, Colonel Ruger; on the left the Twenty-seventh Indiana, Colonel Colgrove. The One hundred and seventh New York, Colonel Van Valkenburgh, I held in reserve, throwing them into the edge of a piece of woods on the left, which I was informed by an aide of General Hooker, who met me advancing, was to be held at all hazards. The only remaining regiment of my brigade, the Thirteenth New Jersey, I had, by direction of General Mansfield, thrown into the edge of a piece of woods behind my first position as a reserve. This regiment remained as posted during the deployment of my line and the posting of the One hundred and seventh New York.

"While moving forward the three regiments referred to, an aide of General Hooker's, galloping rapidly toward my command, begged me to hurry forward. It was apparent, from the steady approach of the sound of musketry, that the enemy were advancing. Their shouts of exultation could be distinctly heard as the line of my deployed battalion, sustained on the right by Crawford's brigade and on the left by Greene's division, both of our own corps, advanced boldly to the front. Before the impetuous charge and the withering fire of our line, the enemy halted, from whence he had emerged. I immediately ordered the One hundred and Seventh New York to support the movement of my advance line, at the same time sending my aide, Captain Wheaton, to bring up the Thirteenth New Jersey. We now held possession of the field, had driven the enemy into the concealment of the woods, and, by a partial change of front forward on our left, were advancing toward the center of the general line of battle.

"My brigade was now drawn up in two lines. In the first, the Second Massachusetts and One hundred and seventh New York Regiments; in the rear, the Third Wisconsin and Twenty-seventh Indiana. These latter regiments had suffered considerably. In the others the casualties had been unusually light. We were at this time re-enforced by General Sumner's corps, who, coming with shouts to the field, pushed across into the woods containing the enemy, and engaged him with ardor.

"By direction of General Williams, I formed my brigade in line of battle in the edge of the woods through which we had charged. General Sumner's soon became warmly engaged. It was apparent that the rebels had received very strong re-enforcements. The tide of the battle again turned. Our forces were compelled to fall slowly back behind the batteries posted in front of the woods the enemy had tried vainly to enter. More than driving our forces from the woods the enemy did not essay, or if he did, was foiled. The next movement of my brigade I am called on to report was ordered by General Sumner, through General Williams. It was to move up toward the woods in front, to support the troops there. The order, most urgent and imperitive, furnished the only information I possessed that our forces again entered the woods in our front. I deemed it of the utmost importance that my command should move forward with the least possible delay. I therefore in person gave the order to the regiment nearest me, without the formation of my entire brigade, intending to bring up other regiments to support or continue the line, as circumstances might require.

"The Second Massachusetts and the Thirteenth New Jersey Regiments were immediately put in motion. The Third Wisconsin and Twenty-seventh Indiana Regiments, which, as before stated, had suffered seriously in a previous encounter with the enemy, were lying about 200 yards in front, concealed from view, of the enemy by a slight ridge. The One hundred and seventh New York was posted some distance to the left. The Second Massachuetts and Thirteenth New Jersey pushed forward, with great alacrity, sufficiently far to find the troops to be supported and had retired, that a large force of the enemy lay concealed in the woods, while a not inconsiderable number showed themselves in the open field beyond. These regiments were received with a galling fire, which they sustained and returned for a brief period, then fell back upon their supports. So strong was the enemy, that an addition of any force I could command would only have caused further sacrifice, without gain.

"The loss in the Second Massachuetts was severe. Here fell, mortally wounded, Lieut. Col. Wilder Dwight, of this regiment, bravely fighting for his country. An official paper is not the place to express the sadness the death of this gallant officer brings to the regiment, in which his presence was so much felt, as well as to many friends serving in the army, to whom he was much endeared.

"I halted my command to report to you, sir, the position of the enemy, and was ordered to form a supporting line behind batteries in position on the left. The rebel lines again advancing, I then forwarded a portion of my brigade to support those nearly in front, while the One hundred and seventh New York Regiment was directed to support Captain Cothran's battery on the left. This fine regiment, but just organized and brought into the field, in this battle for the first time under fire, moved with steadiness to its perilous position, and maintained its ground until recalled, though exposed to a front fire from the enemy and a fire over its head from batteries in its rear.

"About this time, in the order of the events as narrated, I received an urgent call from General Greene, commanding the Second Division of our corps, to send him any re-enforcements I might have and could spare.

General Greene at this time was gallantly holding a portion of the woods to the left, the right of which was held by the enemy in force. I directed the Thirteenth New Jersey, Colonel Carman, to support him. This regiment, also for the first time this day under fire, moved boldly and in an orderly manner toward General Greene's position, and I am much gratified to report that the general has spoken to me of their conduct in terms of high commendation. The services of my brigade during a portion of the remainder of the day were confined to forming a supporting line to fresher troops in our front.

"Thus terminated a bloody and obstinate contest. From sunrise to sunset the waves of battle ebbed and flowed. Men wrestled with each other in lines of regiments, brigades, and divisions, while regiment, brigade, and division faded away under a terrible fire, leaving long lines of dead to mark where stood the living. Fields of corn were trampled into shreds, forests were battered and scathed, huge limbs sent crashing to the earth, rent by shell or round shot. Grape and cannister mingled their hissing scream in this hellish carnival, yet within all this and through it all the patriots of the North wrestled with hearts strong and nerve unshaken-wrestled with rebel hordes that thronged and pressed upon them as to destruction; never yeilding, though sometimes halting to gather up their strength; then with one mighty bound throwing themselves upon their foes, to drive them into their protecting forest beyond. We slept upon the bloody field of our victory.

"I cannot to highly praise the conduct of my brigade of regiments, old and new.

"The Second Massachuetts, Colonel Andrews; the Third Wisconsin, Colonel Ruger; the Twenty-seventh Indiana, Colonel Colgrove, I had a right to expect much of. I was not disappointed. Veterans of Winchester and Cedar Mountain, they can add up to their laurels the battle of Antietam Creek. In this battle, I believe unparalleled in this war in severity and duration, from sunrise to sunset ever under fire, at times very severly, never free from musketry or artillary, officers and men behaved with the most praise worthy intrepidity and coolness. The One hundred and seventh New York, Colonel Van Valkenburgh, and the Thirteenth New Jersey, Colonel Carman, being new troops, might well stand appalled at such exposure, but they did not flinch in the discharge of their duties. I have no words but those of praise for their conduct. They fought like veteran soldiers. They were led by those who inspired them with courage, and they followed with a determination to conquer or die. If I make special mention of the One hundred and seventh New York Volunteers, of my brigade, it is that I speak of its colonel and lieutenant-colonel, Colonel Van

10. The 107th New York Regiment at Antietam

Valkenburgh and Lieutenant-Colonel Diven, both of whom, members of the present Congress, have left their Congressional duties to organize and bring into the field this fine regiment for their country's service. The example of these fine gentlemen, leading their men into the fight, cheering them onward, themselves thoughtless of exposure, prominent in the advance, bearing extraordinary fatigues without a murmur, shows a willingness to sacrifice their comfort and their lives for their country. Let others of our prominent men do as they have done, are doing, and the rank and file of our country will throng to follow such earnest leaders.

"I am, sir, very respectfully, your obedient servent.
Geo. H. Gordon, Brig. Gen., First Div., Twelfth (late Bank's) Corps
General Alpheus S. Williams, Commanding Twelfth Corps."[55]

No. 178: Report of Col. Robert B. Van Valkenburgh, 107th New York Infantry, of the battle of Antietam.

Hdqrs. One Hundred and Seventh Regt. N.Y. Vols.
Near Maryland Heights, September 21, 1862
[To General George H. Gordon]

GENERAL: On the morning of the 17th instant we were formed in line of battle, under your immediate supervision, in the corn-field, nearly opposite the woods which were then in possession of the rebels. After being thus formed we were moved by the left flank into the woods upon the left of the corn-field, and directed to hold at all hazards. Soon, however, the enemy gave way in front, and by your direction my command charged across the intervening plowed field at double-quick, passing entirely through the narrow belt of woods which had been the scene of conflict, and reached the lane and fence upon the opposite side. During the whole time we had been under constant fire, and as we crossed the belt of woods were under a perfect hail-storm of shell, round shot, and musketry. We were then ordered to shield ourselves from the enemy's fire by lying down near the fence. While here we lost a number of our men in killed and wounded. In about an hour we received an order from you to retire into the woods and again form line of battle, which I was in the act of obeying when General Gibbon, as I understand by your directions, ordered me to return and support Cothran's battery, which was doing good execution upon the right of the woods. I obeyed the order, formed my men in line of battle in front of the enemy, marched up to the battery, occupied the position assigned to us until past 3 o'clock, when the battery and my regiment were relieved by General Slocum's division. We were under severe fire from early morning until 4 o'clock. The officers and men, so far as I know, of the One hundred and seventh Regiment behaved well, and obeyed every order with alacrity. During the time I was supporting Cothran's battery, General Greene directed me to send two companies as skirmishers into the woods immediately in front. I detailed Company I, Captain Colby, and Company E, Captain Morgan, to that duty. They did it in gallant style, but found the road and woods teeming with rebels. Capt. E. Chalmers Clark [Co.H.] a brave officer, while in the active discharge of his duty on the field, fell seriously wounded through the left breast by a musket-ball. Capt. W. F. Fox [Co.C.] was injured by the concussion of a shell, and Lieutenant Gleason [Co. G.] was wounded in the leg. I desire to commend the coolness and bravery of Captain Cothran, who was in command of the battery. His decision and promptness, in my opinion, contributed in a great measure to the sustaining of that position.

I am, general, yours, very respectfully,
R. B. Van Valkenburgh,
Col., Comdg.
One hundred and seventh Regt.
New York Vols.
General George H. Gordon[56]

No. 166: Report of Capt. George W. Cothran, Battery M, First New York Light Artillary, of the battle of Antietam:

On the Battle Field
Near Keedysville, Md.,
September 18, 1862

Captain: About 9 A.M., on the 17th instant, I was ordered to proceed with my battery to the front. I arrived at the scene of action while the contest was raging the fiercest, and took the most favorable position I could in the open field to the right of the woods, [East Woods] near the center of the battle. My battery was supported by the One hundred and seventh Regiment New York Volunteers, Col. R.B. Van Valkenburgh. I maintained my position — a very important one — from 9 A.M. until near 1 P.M., when I was relieved by a battery sent for that purpose by General Franklin, who just came up with his command. When I gave way our last shot had been fired. Twice the enemy attempted to charge us in front, but we drove them back each time, without calling upon our support to rise from the ground or to fire a gun. During the whole time we occupied our position we were subjected to a galling fire from the enemy's infantry and artillary. The enemy were frequently within canister range, when we used canister upon them freely and with telling effect. During the day's engagement two batteries opened fire upon us, which were soon silenced, and when we retired from the field for ammunition the enemy's fire was slow and irregular. I have just returned from the scene of yesterday's conflict, and I found the ground where we fired canister literally strewn with the enemy's dead. Our fire was very destructive to the enemy. Our loss consisted of 1 corporal and 5 men wounded. We also lost 4 horses killed. My officers and men behaved with the utmost coolness, and manfully worked the guns amidst the most terrific musketry. But two of my officers (Second Lieutenants Hodgkins and Robinson) were with me, and they were very courageous and efficient. The One hundred and seventh Regiment New York Volunteers, Col. R.B. Van Valkenburgh, is entitled to great credit for both coolness and courage, and the admirable manner in which it supported my battery during the fight. This being the first time this regiment was under fire, I most cheerfully bear testimony to the excellent bearing of both officers and men while occupying the uncomfortable position of being the recipients of the enemy's fire while they were unable to return it.

I am, with great respect, your obedient servent,
Geo. W. Cothran
Captain Battery M, First New York Artillary
Capt. H.B. Scott,
Actg. Asst. Adjt. Gen., General Gordan's Brigade.[57]

General A.S. Williams, after Antietam, wrote the following to his daughters: "The newspapers will give you further particulars, but as far as I have seen them, nothing reliable.... The 'big staff generals' get the first ear and nobody is heard of and no corps mentioned till their voracious maws are filled with puffing. I see it stated that Sumner's Corps relieved Hooker's. So far is this from true that my corps was engaged from sunrise till 9½ o'clock before Sumner came up, though he was to be on the ground at daylight."[58]

Evidently someone was jealous of Capt. Colby's recognition for his part in the action and tried to smear his name in the home newspapers. Such poor reporting was typical of the time period. Here a fellow officer sets the record straight.

Camp of the 107th Regiment
Oct. 10th, 1862

Editor *Corning Journal*—Having noticed in an Elmira paper a letter from an officer of our Regiment, which from clauses contained, might give side to unpleasant feelings among Capt. Colby's friends, I take the prudent opportunity of noticing it. The letter reffered to, in giving an account of our movements, during the late battle, says, among things, that Capt. Colby when ordered out with his Company as skirmishers did not deploy his men, that they only went half way out, that then they skedaddled back to the Regiment. Now this must be a mistake on the part of the officer who wrote the letter. Capt. Colby's Company joins mine when in line, I was with the Regiment during the whole of the action, and noticed his Company particularly. I heard the order for them to act as skirmishers, saw the Capt. cooly form the two platoons—giving one to Lieut. Rutter, and taking command of the other himself. He then deployed his men in good style, and passed out of sight. Soon a severe volley of musketry passing directly over the right wing, (which wing Capt. C. represented) told that he had accomplished his purpose, and found the location of the enemy. After a reasonable time had elapsed, he returned with his Company, the whole party marching in good order, their safety testifying to the cool and soldierly manner with which they had been handled. They did not skedaddle back, but came back in proper order. The Colonel thanked them on the spot before the whole Regiment. This is not my version only, but coincides with that of all of the line officers with whom I have conversed regarding the letter. I dislike anything which savors of a newspaper controversy, but on account of my own feelings towards Capt. C. as a fellow officer—and knowing well, that such a rumor uncontradicted would touch the pride of our Corning friends, I respectfully call attention to the facts of the case. Yours truly,

Capt. Co. C. 107th, N.Y.S.V.[59]
[The Capt. of Co. C was William F. Fox]

A large leather-bound family Bible that belonged to the Dunker Church was donated in 1851 by the Daniel Miller family. The day after the battle, on Sept. 18th, a Sergeant Nathan Dykeman, 107th N.Y. Reg., Co H took the Bible. It remained in his family in Schuyler County, New York until 1903 when it was purchased by his regiment from his sister. They felt that it should be returned. It is often on display at the visitor center at the national park.[60] According to his military records, Sgt. Nathan F. Dykeman was killed by a locomotive in Washington on May 29, 1865, after surviving the war.[61] Sgt. Dykeman along with two other men were reportedly walking along the tracks. An approaching train caused them to step off the tracks, Dykeman to one side and the others to the opposite. Unfortunately for Sgt. Dykeman there was a train coming the other direction also and he was killed.

10. The 107th New York Regiment at Antietam

The 107th in Wednesday's Battle

From the *Elmira Press*: [We are kindly permitted to publish the following letter, written in haste, from Lieut. Col. Diven, to his son. It will be read with great interest.]

BATTLE FIELD, Sept. 18th, 1862. The news of the great fight yesterday will have reached you before this. But what you will be most specially interested in, I sent by telegraph last night i.e. that I am well. All boys are writing home about their fight, and a queer medley would their letters be, taken together. You will expect me to give my account of the battle. I cannot, and advise you to read very little, other than general results, until the offical reports are published.

I know just what our Regiment and a battery which we were supporting did; beyond that I know very little. I will tell you just what our Regiment did. We were placed in column by company, at about six in the morning, and started forward on quick time; the firing was then very sharp in front, both infantry and artillery. We marched across an open field and corn field, when we came to a fence; the fence had been opened only for files of four. We were ordered to pull down the fence, and at the same time form our line of battle. The fence was very strong, and resisted the force of all the men that could get hold of the rails, and I ordered the right wing, where I was, to climb it. We were nearly across, when we were ordered to face to the left and march in line to a piece of wood, the front line of which was in line with the fence we were crossing. The left marched behind the fence, the right in front, until it came to the corner of the wood where the fence was open, when the left passed through, and the line of battle was formed behind the fence fronting the wood. As we were taking the position, Col. Van Valkenburgh called to me for the doctor — that Mansfield was shot. I saw them picking him up and bearing him from the field. I found and sent Dr. Flood. We lay down behind the fence; the fire, shells and shot in our front was incessant, but we were in little danger. True, it was here I ran the narrowest chance, a fragment of shell bursting my sleeve. The enemy were driven from the wood in front about this time, and our wounded men came back very thick. As the enemy left the wood in front, we were ordered to advance in line of battle. The first field was ploughed, and as we double-quicked through it, it winded our men sadly. From the ploughed field we passed the wood from which the enemy had been dislodged, a cornfield and a stubble; passing through the stubble we were subjected to a galling fire from the woods on our right, and our line was in considerable confusion. Reaching a lane, we crossed the first fence, and laid down in the lane behind the next. [Smoketown Rd near Mumma's

Lane] This was no comfortable position, as the enemy had a battery exactly in range with the road. Shell and shot were flying briskly over our heads, occasionlly striking. A shell burst in the middle of our beautiful banner, and it is a tatter. We lay here fifteen or twenty minutes, when we were ordered into a wood a little to the rear [east woods] and to the stubble field which we had crossed. [where we would defend the artillery] While we lay in this lane, a battery of Parrot rifled guns had been planted in the stubble field, and a Pennsylvania regiment ordered to support it. This regiment gave way just as we were passing, and we were ordered to take its place. In obedience to the order, we countermarched and formed in rear of the guns amid a very sharp fire of musketry from the woods. [west woods] When formed we lay flat on our faces, and remained in this position until 2 o'clock. Much of the time the shell and shot flew rapidly over us, and one occasionlly struck around us, and sadder still struck some of our boys. At times the musketry was fearful over our heads. I can compare it to nothing but a swarm of bees passing over us, yet few were hit unless they raised from their prostrate position. As we lay under this fire I was requested to go inform our Brigadier General where we were — we having been ordered to our position without Gen. Gordon's knowledge. I found him forming his brigade in a new position, and he told me to have the regiment brought in, I went back to tell Col. V., and when I arrived saw at a glance that our regiment could not be moved, and hastened back to inform the General. He said it was right — let them remain. I came back and found the regiment had shifted position, mainly on account of our guns planted in the rear and firing over them. It is said we lost two men from this cause. Soon after the battery we supported had exhausted its ammunition, and became to much heated to be worked. It was relieved, and we with it. Our men behaved well. I think each officer did his duty — I can almost say the same of each private. We were complimented by the General and warmly by the Captain of the battery we were supporting. But if we were to be praised, what should we say of them?

Capt. Cotheron [Cothran], of Lockport, of the battery, while we were hugging the ground sat upon his horse, and went from gun to gun, directing their aim, all the while in a more exposed situation than we were — than we would have been, had we kept our horses or feet. And when I went to Gen. Gordon the second time and found him in the woods upon his horse, amid war of bursting shell, and the bark and limbs flying as though the lightning was playing with the trees — I think he was not out of his saddle during the day — I confess I felt a little ashamed of having sent back my horse. But we were advised to do it by experienced officers, and all did so. We performed our duty, as things were, just as well. But I can imagine places where I could not, and think I never shall fight again without my horse.

We have lost in killed eight or ten, and in wounded about fifty. Our loss is nothing to some regiments. Capt. Clark of Havana Co. [Co. H.], was shot through the lungs, and I fear will not recover. It is not saying too much for him, to say he is one of the best Captains in the service. [Capt. Clark was discharged for disability, Dec. 24, 1862]

One incident in the day should not be forgotten. Gen. Green sent for Col. Van Valkenburgh to the left of our line, asking for two companies of skirmishers— The enemy in the woods we were shelling had nearly ceased firing, and it was desirable to know their position. The Col. sent Capt. Colby's and Capt. Morgan's Companies [Co's I & E]. It was a thick wood and the stronghold of the enemy they were to skirmish, and they went forth bravely to the work. Colby and Lieut. [Capt.] Morgan deserve high praise for the manner in which they organized and led them forward. The guards cheered them as they passed and we held our breath with anxiety to hear if they awakened the enemy. We did not wait long before we heard such a volley of musketry as none of us had ever heard before, and the shriek of bullets over our heads was amazing. We gave up our gallant skirmishers as lost, when they came trotting back unscathed, save that Lieut. Rutter had his sword shot away, and one private had his gun damaged by a bullet. I have given you all I know of the exploits of our regiment.[62]

Gen. A.S. Williams writes on why possibly the 107th and others did not receive much recognition: "In the last battle we had, I think, some ten or eleven general officers killed or wounded. My only wonder is that anyone escaped. I was myself under fire from sunrise to nearly 2 o'clock P.M. We went in without breakfast and came out without dinner. The major generals with big staffs will gobble up all the glory, judging from newspaper reports. But there is an unwritten history of these battles that somebody will be obliged to set right someday. Generals are amazingly puffed who are not ten minutes on the field. Corps are praised for services done by others. Commands that were hours behind the line, when the battle raged the fiercest, are carrying off the reputation (in newspapers) of saving other corps from defeat. These reports are got from staff officers of the absent corps. The reporters are often of the staff...."

Thus ended the first phase of the Battle of Antietam. The day continued with action at the Bloody Lane and the Lower (Burnside's) Bridge. The 107th New York was not active in this work.

General Williams continued: "If McClellan's plan had been carried out with more coolness by some of our commanding generals, we should have grabbed half their army. But we threw away our power by impulsive and hasty attacks on wrong points. Hundreds of lives were foolishly sacrificed by generals I see most praised, generals who would come up with their commands and pitch in at the first point without consultation with those who knew the ground or without reconnoitering or looking for the effective points of attacks. Our men fought gloriously and we taught the rascals a lesson, which they much needed after Pope's disaster. They out-numbered us without doubt, and expected to thrash us soundly and drive us all pell mell back towards Washington. As it was, they sneaked out of 'my Maryland' at night leaving their dead and wounded on the field. Even dead generals were left within their lines unburied. Their invasion of Maryland has been a sad business for them."[63]

"This had been an eventful day in the history of the rebellion. A battle had taken place in which the Army of the Potomac had again been victorious, and which exceeded in extent any battle heretofore fought on this continent."[64]

The 107th New York lost 7 killed, 51 wounded, and 5 missing for a total loss of 63 men.[65]

From the *Corning Journal*, October 23, 1862:

Last Good Bye to a Brother Soldier

Farewell, farewell, is often heard,
From the lips of those who part.
'Tis a whispering tone, 'tis a gentle word;
But it comes not from the heart.
It may serve for a lover's closing lay,
To be sung neath a summer's sky.
But give to me the lips that say,
The honest word, good bye.

Adieu, adieu, may greet the ear,
In the guise of courtly speech;
But when we love the kind and dear,
'Tis not what the soul should teach;
Where'er we grasp the hands of those,
We would have forever neigh;
The flame of friendship burns and glows,
In the warm, frank words, good bye

The mother sending forth her child,
To meet with cares and strife;
Breathes through her tears her doubt and fears,
For the loved one's future life;
No cold "adieu," no "farewell" lines,

Within her choking sigh,
But the deepest sob of anguish gives,
God bless thee, boy! good bye.

Go watch the pale and dying one,
When the glance has lost its beam —
When the brow is cold as the marble-stone,
And the world a passing dream;
And the latest pressure of the land,
The work of the closing eye.
Yield what the heart must understand,
A long and last "good bye."

J.G.L. 107th Regt. N.Y.V.[66]

Possibly John G. Lowe, musician, who deserted October 23, 1862, the date of this printing.

September 18, 1862 "The day was passed in comparative quietness on both sides. The burial parties would exchange the dead and wounded with the Rebels in the woods."[67]

"Horrors of the Battlefield" a world correspondent says: "The severest fighting of the war was followed by the most appalling sights upon the battle-field. Never, I believe, was the ground strewn with the bodies of the dead and dying in greater numbers or in more shocking attitudes. Let those who desire to witness a great battle, and gratify themselves with the sublimest spectacle which mortals ever gaze upon, hear but once the cries and groans of the wounded, and see the piles of dead men, in attitudes which show the writhing agony in which they died—faces distorted with the pains which afflicted the dead in their last moments, begrimed and covered with clotted blood, arms and legs torn from the body or the body itself torn assunder, and all the scenes upon the field of battle which fill one with horror and sadness, and they will be content to deprive themselves in future of the sublimity of a battle scene, when they think upon the horrors of the field where the dead lie in heaps unburied, and the dying and wounded uncared for beside them. The faces of those who had fallen in the battle were, after more than a day's exposure, so black that no one would ever suspect that they had been white. All looked like negroes, and as they lay in piles where they had fallen, one upon another, they filled the by-stander with a sense of horror. In the road they lay scattered all around, and the stench which arose from the bodies decomposing in the sun was almost unendurable. Passing after night from Sharpsburg to Hagerstown upon the turnpike, it required the greatest care to keep my horse from trampoling upon the dead, so thickly were they strewn around. Along the line for not more than a mile at least one thousand five hundred lay unburied."[68]

The following is a list of the killed and wounded in the 107th: *Killed—* John H. French, Co. A; Henry Harrington, Co. B; Pat Callaghan, Co. D; John Kallahart, Jesse E. Stevens, and Wm. Everet, Co. G; Cyrus J. Covill, Co. H; Dan'l J. Corwine, Co. I. *Wounded—* Co. A. Rob't Goldsmith, F. Brown, Rufus Harndon, John Egbert, Wm. Broas. Co. B-Charles Kilmer, Wm. M. Hurd, Geo. W. Davis, Jas. Defoe, J. Churchill, Elijah Coles, Amos Decker, Chas. Terwilliger. Co. C-Peter Austin, L.W. Osborne, D.D. Leavenworth, A.D. Bagley, E.D. Fay, J.V. Churchill. Co. D-B. Beardsley, Frank Brandenburg, Geo. Burgis, B.F. Rogers, Robt. Smith. Co. E-David Crow, S.Bennett, John Liston. Co. F-John E. Hoag, Asa Brownell, T.G. Smith. Co. G-A. Mosher, A. Johnson, T. Parish, A. Fisk, R.J. Henderson, V. Benedict, E. Gleason, N.A. Robinson. Co. H-Capt. E.C. Clark, S. Edwards, S.P. Darly, O.G. Gardner, M.S. Dawson, J.S. Gregory, J.J. Emmaus. Co. I-J.M. Brown, H. Castor. Co. K-E.H. Babcock, J. Japheth, S. Cole, Wm.H. Lamphere, O. Bathrick. *Missing-*Joseph Herrick, Co. C; Moses Slawson, Co. D; Wm. Tongue and Clark Crum, Co. E; Nicholas LeRoy, Co. G-Elmira Adv.[69]

On the afternoon of the 18th [20th], "I [General A.S. Williams] received orders to occupy Maryland Heights with my corps. They are opposite Harpers Ferry, and had just been surrendered by Col. Miles. I marched till 2 o'clock in the morning, halted till daylight, men sleeping in the road. I slept in a hay barn. Started at sunrise up the Heights and marched along a rocky path on the ridge to the Heights overlooking Harpers Ferry. Occupied Heights without opposition. Found there was no water there; left a strong guard and took the command down the mountain on the east side. Sent a brigade over the river and a regiment to Sandy Hook. I have sent one division over the river to Loudon Heights and one [the 107th] part way up Maryland Heights in front. Just before reaching the Heights we passed the recent battlefield between a portion of Miles' infantry and the Rebels. The country people were picking up arms, and the stench proved abundantly what was said by them, that many were still unburied."[70]

CHAPTER 11

The 107th New York Regiment at Harpers Ferry

General Williams describes the Harpers Ferry encampment with the following: "The white shelter tents cover now an immense area in this vicinity. As seen from Maryland Heights, which terminates in an abrupt bluff on the very edge of the Potomac, the view is really magnificant and grand. On the west side the whole valley of the Shenandoah spreads out between the two rivers and mountain ranges away up to the bluff near Strasburg and Front Royal, sixty miles away. For several miles along the interior slope of Bolivar Heights, which run across the triangle between the Potomac and the Shenandoah, the tents d'bris of Sumner's corps shine in the purest white. Away south on Loudon Heights, higher than Bolivar, are seen the tents of the 2nd Division of my corps. On the east, along up Pleasant Valley for four or five miles, are thickly dotted the camps of my corps and Burnside's. Half way down the Maryland Heights on a considerable plateau, where are the big-ship Dahlgren guns of one hundred-pound caliber and the thirty-pound Parrotts, are thickly posted two brigades of the 1st Division of my corps...."[1]

This camp sight, near the Dahlgren guns, is described by Capt. Colby in his following letter. From this camp Newton directed picket duty along the Potomac.

Camp of the 107 Regt NY Vols
Near Harpers Ferry Sept 27, 1862
Dear Father

Having an opportunity of sending you a couple of mementos of our fight on Wednesday last — which I picked up on the field — One is a rebel cavalry officers sabre and the other a sabre bayonet — I thought I would send them thinking they would interest you — They were obtained near the "cornfield" (the most fiercely contested ground on the field) and when the rebel dead lay thick and in piles — It looked as if an entire rebel regiment had fallen there and it was over that ground too — where I deployed my boys as skirmishers — I see that Col Diven mentions us in a letter to the Elmira paper giving us some credit for it and hope you will be pleased with my performance in the fight — Candor compels me to say that I most heartily deserve to be excused from any further battles — however — for they are really terrible matter of fact arrangements and are not at all romantic or desirable — I send to you today an Elmira paper containing Diven's letter and account of the fight — I have to regret the loss of my sword and must I suppose lay out $15 to buy another — as I do not wish to use the one presented me by my old company — I value it highly and do not wish to have it spoiled or lost here — Tell Mary to take care of it and not let it rust — or scratched by scouring —

Well — we are laying here on Maryland Heights about 1½ miles from Harpers Ferry and on the Maryland side of the Potomac and is in the point of land between the Potomac and the Shenandoah river — the two rivers coming together there — Harpers Ferry is at present a mere skeleton of what it was — it having been "destroyed" twice — The engine house where the old enthusiast — John Brown — was captured is still pointed out by the citizens — It is very rocky and mountainous all about here — but a little back it is a very fair country — raising splended crops of wheat and producing the finest varieties of fruit —

To change the subject and think of myself I am so tired and sick of this life that I hardly know what to do — I wish I could get out of it some way — but I see no possible chance — and that makes me all the more restless — I would like it very much if I could get out of active service in the field and secure some more quiet place in the city — (Washington) where I might get the *pay* which is so necessary to me — without the fatigue and expenses of the last year and a half — It seems as though I was as well entitled to it as any one and more than some — but I suppose I have not political strength enough — to obtain it — How can I get out of it? Can you suggest some way? I care not a fig what *"they say"* but am forced to care somewhat for ways and means to live and etc. Not a cent of pay yet and when it will come I can not say — Do they think the war will close — or that it looks like coming to an end some time? I fear that there is no end very near to this war and if not I assume that there will be great suffering everywhere — even at the north. I much desire to save the little amount I have in the bank and not touch it — in the hope that I may be able to add to it — for a nest egg — but I fear you will have to use some of it — Do the best you can — I am sorry to hear that Henry is in the Dickenson House. I hoped he could get some better employment — Give him my love and regards — Keep the sword and bayonet till I come (if ever that happens) and show them to Mary and Mother and any friends —

Give my love to Mother and *write* I have not a letter from you and this is the *fourth* one I have written you —

Affectionately your son
Newton[2]

Camp of the 107 NYV
Near Harpers Ferry
Sept 30, 1862
Dear Father

Yesterday your long looked for and very welcome letter came to hand containing the box of pills — I was glad to get the pills as I have been a trifle under the weather with bowel complaints but am now much better — I was surprised that you should complain at my not writing — as I had done so — three times and if you have not received three I do not understand it — though I suspect that our mail is not very reliable — we are here at Harpers Ferry — or near it — and may stay a week or month and may not another day — the health of the regiment is not good — there being a larger number of sick — I think that this location is an unhealthy one — being on the side of a mountain where the sun does not reach us till 9 or 10 oclock — then comes down very hot all of a sudden — and then too — on the mountain top — the dead lie on the ground still unburied — it being so rocky that there is actually not dirt enough to cover the bodies — They tried to burn them — but only partially sucessful — you say that Mary needs money and that you will be obliged to draw on the little store in the bank — but I earnestly hope she can get along without disturbing that — as I much desired to keep that for a "nest egg" — but if you can not get along without — why I suppose you will have to take it — I have not got a cent of pay yet and do not know when I can but expect it at all the time — I hope to have some ahead before long — but it seems to be nearly useless for me to attempt it — I mean to make government pay me for getting up this company — if possible — I wish I could get Graves Bill for room rent — somehow — as they would pay that — but will not pay for some of my other actual expenditures—can it be arranged? I sent you by Mr LLoyd Paxton of Rupert, Pa. a cavalry sabre and a sabre bayonet. The sabre bayonet I picked up on the battle field myself and the sabre is a rebel one and was picked up by one of our Cavalry men—who accompanied a flag of truce which we sent out to accompany the Rebel flag of truce sent from their side to obtain permission to bury their dead—I wish you to keep them only until I come if ever—Mr Lloyd Paxton who takes them to you is a friend of Lieut Rutters—and in addition to being wealthy is an intelligent and refined gentleman and if he should call on you I bespeak your regard and attention to his wants—he said he would take the sabres as far as Elmira at least and perhaps to your hands in Corning and promised to call on Mary too—Tell her so for me—I think him a gentleman and am sure you will like him—He is a bachelor and seems to think more of Rutter as if he was his own brother. I am glad to hear that you have obtained the place of assessor and think it will be more healthy employment than being confined in doors—Uncle Luke—you say is well and I am much pleased to hear it—I believe I must write him a letter—I hope Wadsworth will be elected Govenor—and then I hope Van V will be made Govenor of Washington—in place of Wadsworth—as that would bring us back to the city—where we could be more comfortable—Lieut Rutters sword—as well as my own was shot and injured and he has sent it home and his Elmira friends—who gave it to him are I understand to give him another—My sword went to pot I guess—probably torn to pieces—one of Capt Fox's men said he saw the hilt laying on the ground—I have an empty sheath left—and suppose I must buy another—perhaps I can get along without buying and use the Qrmaster's (Ed Graves) for a time at least—Rutter acted *very* well under fire and is a gallant boy—Give my love to mother and Henry—Tell Henry to write—It is rummored here that the rebs have sent peace comissioners to ask for peace—but I guess it is like most camp rumors—false—I have got a horse that I secured on the battle field and mean to keep him and send him home if I can—He is very poor now—but is young and will make a good one if he is taken care of—The weather here is very warm in the day time and cold at night—regular fever and agree style [sic]—You ask me to describe the fight and I believe I did so as far as I could in a previous letter and if it does not come to hand write and I will try and repeat it—As you say I witnessed some awful sights such as I hope never to see again—but they affected me much less than I would have thought possible—Dead men became a common sight and I could have gone to sleep with them on every side—so much does "use breed a habit in a man"—Some of the Rebels lay in the sun a day or two and turned so black that they were actually taken as Negroes—until you noticed their skin under their clothing—

11. The 107th New York Regiment at Harpers Ferry

Now then please write often — and believe me dear Father
Very Affectionately Your Son
Newton[3]

The 107th Regiment remained in camp at Maryland Heights until the evening of the 29th. They suffered great sickness and a large percentage of deaths in the ranks, about 300 being sick.[4]

On Oct. 1, President Lincoln visited the Fifth Corps to speak with General McClellan. The Fifth corps was camped near Antietam Ford just south of Sharpsburg and included Lt. Col Chamberlain and the 20th Maine that would become famous at Little Round Top.[5]

Camp of the 107th Regt NY Vols
Maryland Heights Oct 9, 1862
Dear Father

Your truly welcome letter came duly to hand this evening — and was of great service in raising my rather depressed spirits — As you will observe by the date — I am still at Maryland Heights — but do not expect to be here many days more — as from what I can learn — there will soon be another forward move and perhaps a battle — You ask me to write in case there is a fight and say if I am safe and I reply — of course I will and did too after the battle of Antietam — I wrote either the same night or the next day — but I fear you did not receive the letter — I also wrote you the facts in regard to Wilson — but I see you have not got that letter either — and will repeat them — Wilson had been under the Doctors care for several days previous to the fight and the night before the fight we started from our bivouac about 12 or 1 oclock in the night and Wilson who had gone to a house to stay did not know we had left till early in the morning. He then got into an ambulance and started after us and reached near the battle field — after we had gone into the fight and although sick and really not able to do so — started to find the Regiment and Company which as you may immagine was no very easy task — and while doing this and distant *not over* half a mile from us — he met Tuthill — He was not leaning against a fence — but was going toward the field of battle — He could not find where we were at once — (not very strange when you consider that our own Brig Genl — was unable to say where we were) He did find us however — when we had been ordered back to rest and eat — and took charge of the company that night — for I was about used up with fatigue and c — and had charge of it till morning — acquitting himself with credit — Please deny for me — that he acted cowardly — most decidedly — He is a good officer and for one that has had no more experience is well posted and is efficient and active in the discharge of his duties — So much for putting at rest a slander — So Uncle L is married again? Well I am really surprised — and delighted too — for I have before heard of her many good qualities.

Oct 10, 1862

I did not get to finish this letter last night and resume it now — Strange that I should be called upon to defend my reputation against a cowardly and unprovoked attack — made on me by a Capt Morgan in this Regt — in the Elmira papers — I presume you have either seen or heard of the attack — It is false from beginning to end — as far as it relates to my company and I have laid the case before the Col and Lt Col and they say I shall be made all right — I told them that I would not do another hours duty until they took notice of it and punished the lying hound — and that they only advanced about half way and then skidadled back to the Regiment — All of which — every officer in the Regiment knows is false and an out and out lie — Lt Col Diven has assured me that he shall retract it as publically as he stated it or his place in the Regiment would be made a very uncomfortable one — Nearly every officer in the regiment has expressed both astonishment and indignation at the bare faced lie — I can not say what the motive is for such an attack — for I never searcily [sic] had anything to do with him — and never that I am aware of said or done aught that could offend him — I had treated him civily — but had never liked his appearance — He has been twice under arrest since we left Elmira and is evidently — both a coward and a liar. Our best Captains in the line — offered voluntarily to get the signatures of the line officers to a paper stating that the assertion of Morgan was false — and I think I will accept the offer — With regard to the Sword and sabre bayonet I sent you I regret to say that Mr Paxton had them both taken from him by a officer of the guard at Washington — Mr Paxton wrote me and expressed much regret — at the loss — for which he of course was not at all chargable. I fear he will think I blame him — but I do not in the least — He is too much of a gentleman to do anything unfair or dishonorable — I shall try and recover them if possible — but I can no more get permission to go to Washington than I can fly — Our men are very unhealthy and several have died here — I have lost none by sickness yet — but we have not got over 250 men fit for duty — out of the 1000 that we brot here! We have a funeral nearly every day — My men lie on the ground without shelter (except bush tents which are no protection against rain) and many of them without overcoats or blankets — and it is not strange they sicken — I have complained to the Col. and

11. The 107th New York Regiment at Harpers Ferry

beseiged the Quartermaster for something to protect my men from rain and cold nights—but with no success—Just now one of my Corporals brought me some hard bread as a sample of what they had to eat and on breaking it open I found it was alive with bugs and worms!! I have been shown beef which had been issued to my men—that was alive with maggots—Now—whose fault this is I will not pretend to say—but I do say that it is shameful and disgraceful—Just as we went into the Antietam fight—the men were ordered to take off and pile up their overcoats-tents and blankets and of course—after the battle they were missing—which accounts for there being without them—Also when we left our Camp near Washington the Companies were ordered to leave their baggage—consisting of carpet bags and trunks and knapsacks behind and were told that a guard would be left and that they would be perfectly safe—We sent for all that baggage the other day and it has just come to hand—and such a looking lot of plunder I never saw—Scaracly a man in the regiment but had lost something—My own loss being three flannel shirts and a blanket—and this was light compared to most others—Knapsacks had been torn open and plundered of anything valuable and c and c. I am disgusted with such wretched work—but I will not blame any one just now—I am gathering some few facts for future use.

Saturday Oct 11, 1862

Again I have been obliged to stop and again I resume this letter and hope to finish it—Last evening I was surprised at receiving by express—an elegant sword—a present from Liut Rutters friend Mr Lloyd Paxton—I assure you it was an entire surprise and very unexpected—He also presented Liut Rutter with one—Mine is a bronze scabbord and is beautifully trimmed and is really beautiful—I wish I could show it to you all—while it is new and beautiful but I presume before you see it—it will be old and battered all up—The Colonel leaves us about the 20th and there is a great fight in prospect over the post of Major there being five or six candidates—I have made considerable effort to get it—I wrote to Walker and Thompson and asked their assistance—but they are rather cold friends and I am prepared to fail—and if so I shall diliberately get out of service *any how* and *any way*—I do not really care whether I fail or not—for things in this regiment are badly mixed—and I predict trouble in it—do what they will—Smith—the Major is a conceited ass—Diven—a fine man—but with little or no military experience—and most of the line officers not at all posted in their duties. Capt Miles of Addison [NY] (you know him—a fine old man) a good friend of mine and I respect him very much—Capt Fox is also very friendly and I think he is a fine fellow and his brother too

Liut Fox — Capt Fox seriously injured at Antietam by a shell which burst close over his head — He was actually deranged for a short time — the effects of a shell bursting so close are sometimes very strange — For instance one of my men who had one explode near his head — has lost his speech and has not been able to speak a word up to this time! He is still in Hospital — There is little here in the way of news — I packed in a box and will send you right away — a fine Remington Rifle — with sabre bayonet complete — It is all to pieces as it was necessary to take it apart to pack it — Possibly I may pay the charges on it to Corning — but do not know as I can raise money enough — so if I do not prepay — you can use my money to do so — I also put in the box two of my books which I did not need and an old sword belt — I tell you what Father — I am sick of being in the Army and long to be at home where I can have peace and quiet — I will not stand it a great while longer — under any circumstances — So you may look out for me one of these days — I wish you could see my splended new sword — It is a perfect beauty — Why Mr Paxton should give me a sword I certainly can not imagine — I expect however that he wishes me to aid and care for Lieut Rutter — but I needed no such inducement for I esteem him and would do anything for him I could — I guess you will think this letter overlong — but never mind — I am watching some prominent folks here closely and have once or twice nearly made up my mind to act against them and against their being elected to high offices — but I will write you again soon — I am not very well but am not sick — Write very soon and tell me if you got the gun-

Affectionately Your Son
Newton[6]

Camp of the 107 Rgt N Y Vols
Maryland Heights Oct 11, 1862
Dear Father

    I send you herewith a Remington Rifle with sabre bayonet — picked up on the battle field and I have cleaned it and it is in good condition — In putting it together — lay the barrel in the stock — then slip on the lower brass band and then the upper one — then the steel ring which holds the bayonet on (to put this ring on you will have to loosen the screw in it) Then screw on the lock and barrell — It is a fine gun and I desire you to take good care of it for me — Pay charges out of any money of mine you may have — as I have not got any — I hope you will notify me at once of its safe arrival — I mail a letter to you to day also — Has Mary gone to

Nunda or why do I fail to hear from her? Do not let the gun get rusty — I will try and recover the sword and sabre bayonet I sent you.

Give my love to Mother Henry and wife-
In Haste Yours Affectionately
Newton[7]

Camp of the 107th Maryland Heights
Oct 21st 1862
Dear Father

It is long since one of your letters has gladdened my vision and to remind you of the pleasure they afford me I now write — hoping to thereby urge some intention of yours into action. I have been doing the daily dull routine of camp duty and I confess that each day adds to and increases the dislike and disgust I have latterly had for this service — There is no mistake in the matter — that we are here — only to pander to the political aspirations of some men or set of men — and that the war with its immense cost of blood and money — is a mere political machine — to be continued long — or made short — as shall most conduce to the interests of the managers. Occasionally — the evidences of the truth of this leak out — and as far as I am personally concerned — I care little for the war and profess no enthusiasm and patriotism — only aiming to make the utmost I can out of it — with the least risk of life and health — I believe that most men in the army now think as I do — I see that Mary has gone to Nunda and suppose you were obliged to attack my reserve in the bank — and if so — please tell me in your next how much there is left. I think you had better use what is necessary to lay in a good stock of wood for winter — as well as potatoes-pork-butter-flour-beef-sugar and etc — I think it would be a good idea to buy 3 or 4 barrells of good flour — as I notice it has an upward tending in the market — but I leave it to your judgement — get plenty of butter and potatoes and some apples too — and above all a good soo pig — Yesterday while on pickett duty along the bank of the Potomac I lost a Lieutenant and one private — both taken prisoners by the rebs — I had two lieuts — and thirty men from Co H with thirty more of my own men detailed for pickett duty under my command and while performing this duty — Lieut Sailor [Saylor] very unwisely and in the face of his orders and instructions got into a boat and went across the river to a large house to get some eatables — and while in the house was taken by three rebel cavalrymen — The women of the house ran down to the river bank and screamed to us to come over and save him — but we had no boat to cross on and if we had I should have been cashiered for going, so I was obliged to let him slide — He will be dismissed the service for disobeying orders of course and it will serve him right — He did a foolish — unmilitary thing and it occasions much laugh at his expense — Have you seen Van Valkenburg? Will he get a full party vote in Steuben? Quite a number here do not hesitate to blame him for leaving us and say hard things of him — He has got nicely out of it and I wish I too could do the same. Cant you get me a place as drill master to the drafted men in Elmira? Please try — and try hard — Ask Van to get it for me — he will know I am competent — and some one must have it. I would rather have it — than to get promoted to Major here — The truth is — in my opinion and the opinion of many others here — the battle of Antietam — cured Van of any idea of being a Colonel — or anything else — in real war and fighting — Too much swine — for 12½ cents — Do not mention this however — But I am sleepy and must "retire" i.e. pull off my coat and boots — which is all the undressing I have done for two months. The rain pattering on my tent sounds drowsy and I bid you affectionately — good night.

Oct 22

Having just finished the morning drill I set down to complete this letter — With reference to my winter stores — if possible I desire you to get a full supply — Enough to last till next summer of such things as will keep — for I expect that everything in the way of provisions will be very high — Use the funds in the bank — for I have not received a cent of pay and do not know when I shall — but when it does come there will be all the more of it together — What do you think of putting blinds on my house? Cant it be done cheap now when building and all is dull? I have always intended to put then on — One thing be sure and have done and that is hire some good man to make a good large strawberry bed and set out the plants now — at once. Make it down by the house where I had the others — Cover those grape vines too — laying them on the ground — Write me what it will cost to put blinds on and I think I will have it done while Mary is away — What is Henry doing? I hope he is steady and trying to get along —

I must close in order to be in time for the mail — I hope you will write often, I received Henrys letter and will reply to it very soon — Give my love to Mother and Henry and Emma and try and see if you can comply with numerous requests of this epistle.

Believe me affectionately Your son
Newton[8]

Paymaster arrived Oct. 22[9]

11. The 107th New York Regiment at Harpers Ferry

From the *Journal*, October 23, 1862:

"We publish on the first page the resolutions adopted by Co. A., 107th Regiment, in reference to the death of Henry P. Smith of said Co., second son of Dr. S.H. Smith of Caton. The deceased left home two months ago to do his part in sustaining the Government. He passed through the terrible battle of Antietam, unharmed, but the exertion and the subsequent hardships and exposures proved too much for his vigorous frame—and an attack of violent disease soon followed. His father was telegraphed, but as both could not leave, his mother at once went to the camp near Harper's Ferry, reaching there a day or two before he died. She brought his body home on Thursday of last week, and he was buried on Friday morning at Caton Centre. The friends and acquaintances of the young patriot will ever cherish his memory. He is another victim of the slave-holders rebellion."[10]

Camp of the 107th NY Vols
Maryland Heights Oct 25, 1862
Dear Father

Yesterday I received a long good letter from you and it was thrice welcome as I had not heard from home in some time. Mary does not write as often as usual and I get but few letters from home—so they are welcome and yours always are—This morning at daylight orders for us to advance have been received and we are all packed up and momentarily expecting the order to fall in—I assure you that I speak the truth—when I tell you that as far as my observation goes—the army receives the order to advance with no enthusiasm or spirit—in fact they go unwillingly—I believe the order is condemned by McCellan himself—and I know that our regiment is in the worst possible shape for a fight—but in obedience to political clamor and wire pulling—we—the machines must start—suffer exposure—risk life and health and then be cursed if we fail—I will be an officer in this army just as long as I am actually obliged to and not a minute longer—I have no hope of getting the position in the field and in fact I care no great for it—because there will be a row over it—get it who will—Diven has got his comission as Col and Smith as Liut Col—but nothing is known about who is to be Major—though I presume it is all settled now—I asked Diven if he could not get me a clerkship in Washington—and he said he would cheerfully assist me in any way I wished—but thought the chances were not first rate—Well—I will not remain here—so put your wits at work and see what I can get into for a business—I may remain till into Jany if I am well—in order to get all the pay I can—but would come sooner if a good pretext could be had for leaving. If we have a fight — as is predicted tomorrow and I come out again all right I will write you by the first opportunity but should you fail to get the letter dont worry — as chances of sending letters from a battle field are not plenty by any means — I hope we shall succeed but I do not feel over confident — I wish you to get full supplies of flour potatoes — butter — eggs — apples — pork and c and c — When gold brings its present premium I think there is prospect of high prices — I think you better buy 4 bbls flour for winter use — and put them in my house — Perhaps you can judge better then I can — where you are — but it looks that way to me — Do it — if you do not think it bad policy — Flour is not high at 6 or 7 dollars — any way — and is about as good as money — Pork is very "handy to have in the house" too

Afternoon Oct 25

Since writing the above — orders have been received for our regiment to stay here on the heights — the result of the inteference of Dr Beadle of Elmira — Who came here and went to head quarters of the Army Corps and represented the condition of our regiment and they allowed the Regt to remain. Bully — for Zacy Beadle — It seems that the folks at home are hearing of our condition and are moving to help us — Day before yesterday I had one of my men die in the hospital — His name was Beman [Gideon Beaman, wagoner] from Wayland — a fine young man too — I went over to Harper's Ferry and we buried him with military honors — He had been sick a couple of weeks with Typhoid Fever — I have another who can not live — and he is from Wayland too — His name is Johnson [William or Samuel] I have several deserters — and among them is Sam H Matt — [Samuel Mott] of Corning and a fellow by the name of Harrison — [William Harrison] some relation to Pete McNeil — He is a worthless hound and is no loss — I will leave this letter to finish in the morning — and go to bed — quite satisfied to be in good quarters — instead of out doors and on the march — Thos H Beecher preaches here tomorrow and if I dont go on pickett I shall hear him — so good night-

Oct 26th Sunday 1862

Today being Sunday — I could not mail the letter I had written to you — so I will add a few words — I see by reference to yours that you have not yet received the Gun I sent you — and come to ascertain about it — I find that it only left here day before yesterday and I hope it will come to hand all right — Perhaps you had better have the gunsmith put it together and if rusty or dirty have him put it in order — It is a valuable gun — I have heard of another that I think I can get and if so will send it to you — It is

11. The 107th New York Regiment at Harpers Ferry 187

a Sharps Rifle — breech loading — and will cost me only the express charges to send it home — The horse I mentioned having — has been stolen — I had no place to keep him and could get none — I tried among the farmers but could not succeed No great loss — for he was branded U.S. and might have been claimed by the Govt anytime — The next one I get will not be a branded one and then I can at once send him home — It rains like mischief today and but for our stone fire place would be very cold — The regular's are raising "hub" with our volunteer soldiers — Yesterday — a "regular" sergeant came by our camp and getting a number of our men around him began to coax them to enlist with him in the regular service — telling them to "come along and never mind their officers" — and that they would get "bigger pay" — and "get furloughs" to go home and c and c — He succeeded in inducing 15 or 20 to follow him — Happening to hear of it — and being Officer of the day — I ordered the officer of the gaurd to follow him on the double quick and arrest the whole party and bring them back — I then reported the occurrance to Lt Col Diven — who ordered me to report it to Genl Gordon — I did so at once and the General said he hoped I could catch them — but added that the Sergeant had the law on his side and was doing only what the War Department had authorized-!! He read me an order — which permits regular officers to enlist our men from us at any time — They can even take them while on post doing gaurd duty! The men so enlisted to serve only the expiration of the time for which they originally enlisted — Where they have lied and coaxed them away — they send back to us for their pay and clothing accounts and force us to give them a discharge and they are then re enlisted! It seems that the Government is trying to break up the volunteer force — Col Diven says that he will arrest and treat as a deserter any man in this Regt who leaves to enlist elsewhere — I forgot to say that the officer of the Gaurd could not overtake them and so I suppose they are lost to us — None of my men went however — Diven undertook a battalion drill the other day and made wretched work of it — I guess the Major put him up to it — so as to get the officers down on him — but he need not imagine he can ever be the Col of this Regt — for it is impossible — I guess things will take such a shape that I can honorably withdraw before long — I hope so — and only wish I had some good business — to fall back on — Wilson says he will resign at the very first chance — He is awful sick of military and has been for a long time — Lt Rutter is sick yet and has the jaundice — Write me very soon and tell me what you think of buying the flour and c Give my love to Mother and tell her I will send her the blankets if I can get them — but we dont get such blankets as we used to — They are coarse and dark colored —

Give my love to Henry and Emma and believe me

Yours Affectionately — Newton

Written on the outside of the letter: "I am out of stamps—so you must pay postage — They can not be got here —"[11]

On some of Captain Colby's letters he would write on the outside of the envelope the following:

Soldiers Letter
N.T. Colby Capt.
107th N.Y. Vols.

The mail service would mark it "Due 3" to be paid by the recipient.

Part of a letter from General A.S. Williams to his daughters, Oct. 26, 1862: "We are lacking much. There seems to be an unaccountable delay in forwarding supplies. We want shoes and blankets and overcoats—indeed, almost everything. I have sent requisition upon requisition; officers to Washington; made reports and complaints, and yet we are not half supplied. I see the papers speak of our splendid preparations. Crazy fools! I wish they were obliged to sleep, as my poor devils do tonight, in a cold, shivering rain, without overcoat or blanket and under one of those missnamed 'shelter-tents'; a mere sieve, which filters the water over one in a nasty mist and gives no warmth. I wish these crazy fools were compelled to march over these stony roads barefooted, as hundreds of my men must if we go tomorrow."[12]

Parts of a letter from Chaplain Beecher:

From *The Elmira Advertiser*,
October 28th, 1862 —1 o'clock P.M.

Dear Fairman: — Having finished a visit to the 107th Regiment — Col. Diven — I am now sitting on the stone wall amid the ruins of Harper's Ferry. An hour ago I was by the graveside of Marcus Dawson, of Co. D. [Dawson was later buried in Antietam National Cemetery] There upon a point commanding a view of the Shenandoah Valley for miles— lie fourteen men of the 107th, fallen by fever and now at rest. A truer sacrifice to principle earth rarely sends before God, and a fairer altar never received the gift. I know nothing of Dawson save that as a Christian I have assisted in burying him. But I saw in the hospital the body of a young man, three days dead, whom I myself enlisted. I have his name in one of my old books, and as I looked upon his blanket shroud, I earnestly tested myself, was I

11. The 107th New York Regiment at Harpers Ferry

Top: A normal mailing when stamps were available. *Middle:* A letter marked "Soldier's Letter" in the upper left corner was sent with postage due. *Bottom:* Letter sent to a soldier's home by way of another soldier who was going home.

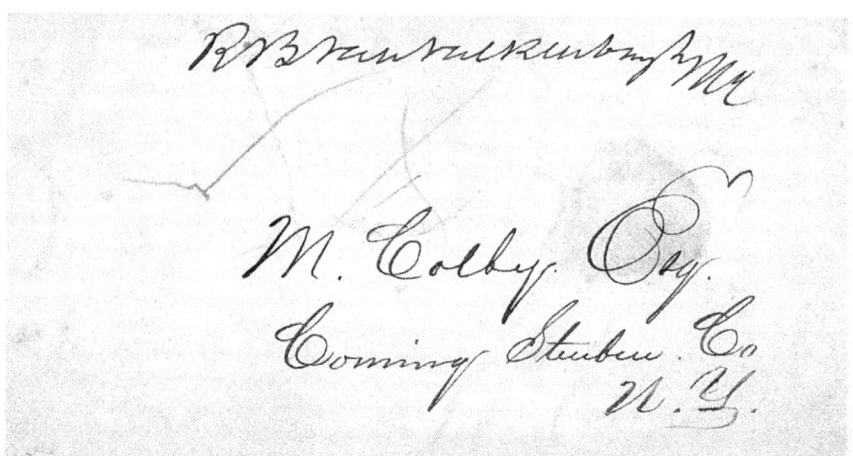

Two examples of envelopes franked by congressmen Lt. Col. A.S. Diven of the 107th New York and Col. R.B. Van Valkenburgh of the 107th New York, respectively. Colby family collection.

right in telling him to enlist? I called to my mind my speeches and my pleedings, and my statements of duty. I thank God that I have not one word to repent of.

    These solomn scenes I saw in fancy, while I journeyed among the hills of Steuben and Senyler. Many an hour have I spent, ere leaving dear home, seeing in fancy the fence-side hospitals, and stable shake downs, and floor-cots of military hospitals. I saw the boney, sick men with dull eyes. I saw the huddled graves more plainly than now. And yet I said "respect the powers that be, for there is no power but of God, and the powers that be, are ordained of God." The President calls for troops, wo is me if I read the Bible and fail to obey. It is well with the boys that sleep! It is well!

Let me add that the hardest is over with the 107th boys. Their sick list is still large, say 230; but this list is diminishing. One or two fatally sick, but no more. The hospitals are daily improving in comfort, and the men in cheerfulness. Col. Diven is still feeble, but energetic, and the regiment will have rest for a time.[13]

"Dr. Flood, surgeon of the 107th Regiment was in Elmira last week, and procured a large quantity of vegetables gratuitously furnished at his suggestion, for the Regiment. He said that scurvy prevailed for the lack of potatoes, onions, black pepper, mustard and some whisky for medical purposes."[14]

CHAPTER 12

Antietam Ford

October 29, 1862 The 107th left Maryland Heights at night and bivouacked next morning near Antietam Ford, on the Potomac, guarding the ford.[1] Lt. Col. Chamberlain and the 20th Maine spent the lovely month of October 1862 training at the camp near Antietam Ford. He was later to become famous at Little Round Top during the battle of Gettysburg. With magnificent weather on October 30, the Fifth Corps, including the 20th Maine, left Antietam Ford for Snickersville, near Snicker's Gap.[2] On that same morning the 107th marched with the 3rd Brig. (Gen. Gordon's) towards Sharpsburg, Md. They marched back to the ford the same afternoon and pitched camp near the same. They remained here with the 3rd Wisconson Vols. and a section of artillary guarding the Antietam Ford about 4 miles below the Antietam battle field.[3]

Antietam Ford was near where the Antietam Creek empties into the Potomac River several miles below the battlefield. At this location the 107th New York and the 3rd Wisconsin performed picket duty to prevent the rebels from crossing the Potomac again.

Upon visiting this camp site the following was written by Mrs. G.L. Smith, wife of Lt. Col. Gabriel Smith, who was accompanied on this trip by Mrs. Diven. "The scenery is beautiful and the camp was near an old, abandoned blast furnace and iron works. The principal furnace was of brick on the outside, many of which had been utilized by the soldiers to build chimneys to their tents or quarters. Many of them had built little squares of poles and earth about their tents on the top for a roof and had dug a hole in the ground for a fireplace, building a brick chimney up from one side of it to carry off the smoke. Such quarters looked very cozy and comfortable on the inside."[4]

12. Antietam Ford

Camp of the 107 Regt N Y V
Near Sharpsburg Nov 1st 1862
Dear Father

    For the first time in several days I have an opportunity of writing and I avail myself of the chance to give you some idea of our whereabouts— You know I wrote you that Tracy Beadle of Elmira had been to see us and appreciating our condition had been to the General commanding the corps and got an order for us to be left in our quarters when the Army moved. Well we thought of course that we should remain there and accordingly built log houses and c, taking great pains to be comfortable—I had been several days hard at work building a nice log shanty and had a tip top stone fire place made and on Saturday afternoon moved into it—The fire place drawed beautifully and I was feeling good over it—when suddenly an order came to be ready to move in two hours!—and by Jove—just after dark we left Maryland Heights and trudged off in the direction of Sharpsburg. The night was cold and chilly—but the exertion of climbing up and down hill—soon made me sweat profusely and then while very warm and sweaty—we halted by the road side for an hour or more and I was soon shivering with cold. After tramping all night nearly—we reached Antietam Forge—a little place on the Potomac—Here we halted for half an hour and then about faced and marched back a mile or so and turned off the road into a field and wrapping up in our blankets laid on the ground till daylight—I found my blanket white with frost and felt stiff and sore.

    However we started off again and after marching five or six miles again halted and lay down in a field for an hour or so and then our regiment and another ordered to return again and back we came to where we lay in the field—Stopped an hour or so and then marched up a hill from the top of which we can see the river and considerable of the country on the other side and encamped and here we are now—Our Regiment is very much demoralized and reduced by sickness and desertion—The companies average about 30 able men—Each and even these are discouraged and disheartened—We have no confidence in our Field Officers not but they are good men—but they evince no knowledge whatever of their duties and we are afloat as to discipline and drill—The Regiment—as available troops—have been utterly demoralized and rendered unfit for duty and it is—in my opinion directly chargable to Van Valkenburg—The influence of his example—in leaving—has been most disastrous—for the men all say—that when things began to look gloomy—he backed out and left them—there is no way for them to get out and they must stay and catch it. The pretext of his nomination's making it necessary is all fudge — and as to his wife's illness — so is that — for she has been sick for months — Almost without exception both Officers and men — hope he will be beaten and not get elected — I hope so — and if I could would do anything in my power to prevent it — I have learned since he left that he is down on me and that instead of asking Genl Patrick to retain me on his staff — he did nothing and in fact opposed it!! He said I had opposed him once and had said he would sell himself if he could — in Congress — I did certainly say so — once — and have always thought so — and I believe he has sold himself for money — more than once — I think he is a politically dishonest knave — I wish I was at home — I would do my utmost to defeat him. But enough of him — only every Father who has a son and every one who has friends or relatives in this Regiment ought to *vote plumb against him* — We have a fine place to camp in — much better than at Maryland Heights — but probably shall have to leave it before long — We do picket duty along the Potomac at the very place where Stewarts Cavalry crossed on their last raid into Maryland — The Rebel pickets are occasionally visable on the other side and some picket firing takes place across the river which is about 60 rods wide — Write me — directing as before — as often as you can — no pay yet and do not know when we shall get it — I caught a severe cold on the march and have been a little under the weather — but nothing serious — I hope —

Give my love to Mother — Henry and Emma and believe me

Very Affectionately Yours
Newton[5]

General A.S. Williams once wrote about picket duty: "It is a hard duty, as the poor fellows are not allowed fires and the weather has been inclement. Still they go on with wonderful cheerfulness. There is a strange excitement in the prospect of shooting at one another across the river. We have had, however, very little picket firing and do not encourage it. The Rebels appear on the opposite bank, but so long as they remain quiet we do not trouble them."[6]

Nov 7, 1862 Burnside replaced McClellan as commander of the Army of the Potomac.[7]

Head Quarters 107th Reg N.Y. Vols
Camp near Antietam Ford, Md

12. Antietam Ford

Nov. 9, 1862

General Order No. 9: The camps of the 107th NYV and 3d Wisc. Vol. will procure all wood for fuel or other purposes from the woods south of the camps— no rails or timber from other wood lands must be taken. Guards will report any one violating the above order and will not allow wood of any kind to be carried into camps from any place other than the woods indicated.

Bu command of
Col. Alex S. Diven
Hull Fenton Adjutant[8]

Camp of the 107th N.Y. Vols
Near Antietam Ford, Md. Nov 11th 1862
Dearest Wife

I have at last received some letters from home — dear home that seems so far away — so loved — an little can you — dear wife tell the comfort that words can carry — when they come from the loving hearts of the home fire side — Long — weary days have come and gone since I have heard from you and my anxiety had become a wretched heavy feeling. I have been much employed lately and camp duties come oftener than usual — owing to the fact that a great number of our Officers are absent and sick — I hope to be able to come home by the middle of December — Either permanently or on leave — though I presume If I make up my mind to resign — that I shall stay till Jany — at least — but this is all speculation — as I shall be goverened entirely by circumstances.

We are still here near Antietam Ford on the Potomac — above Harpers Ferry — to prevent any more rebel raids into Maryland — something like locking the barn after the horse has been stolen — McCellans removal took us all by surprise — and we expect nothing now except long marches — in the cold and mud — fighting and freezing and starving — to satisfy the ambition of some new General — This is a fine thing for the Generals — but I immagine that there is but little thought about caring for the men — or even for the interests of our country — Now and then a man can be found who really came for the sake of principle — but a short experience convinces them that they have been badly sold — There is very little here — in the way of news and my leisure moments are generally employed in thinking of you dearest and building air castles — as to what we will do in the future. Doubtless you would laugh if you could read my thoughts upon such occasions — but with your merriment — then would mingle some great satisfaction too — for you would see how truly and how well I love my absent darling — God grant that ere long we can once more go here and there together — and close our eyes each night side by side and sleep the sweeter for the consolation of each others presence — I must here pause — as our band are making the preliminary call for dress parade — When I come back I will tell you something — about my trials in trying to get a fire place in my tent and how near I came to freezing in the snow storm we had the other day — Well here am I to tell you as I promised and to begin — it suddenly grew cold and began to snow and I had nothing but a common tent and no fire — So I went down to an old ruined forge or furnace and got some pieces of iron and lugged them a mile or two in the storm — and dug a hole and covered it with the iron and at great labor fixed a chimney of stones and mud and barrells and then — with great expectations of comfort — built a fire and had the satisfaction of seeing the smoke pour into the tent in a huge volume — Very fine stove — but the draft was on the wrong end — Well I had to put out the fire of course and sleep cold again — I fussed and fixed it over and at last have got a fire place that I can have a fire in when the wind was in the right direction — and then only — This is one of the many trials and I actually believe that this is only a small part of what lies before me if I remain in this regiment — It has already done and suffered more than any other now in the service — for the length of time it has — been there — and now doubtless we must again tramp — A soldiers life — especially a foot soldiers — is and always has been disagreeable to me and ere long I shall bid it good bye and I hope return to live at home. It is snowing again — and we have had but one fair day since last fall — Well I look forward anxiously to the time when I may return to my home — but I wish to do so creditably — If I stay here much longer I intend to get Father to get a carpenter to put blinds on my house — that is — when I am out of debt — It does not seem to me that will be very soon though — Nearly a year in the service and only paying debts all the time! It is enough to discourage one man — Never mind — I hope for the best and the best — in my opinion is to be able to get the place I am after — for it is a good one — but I will not say what it is — for I hardly think I shall succeed —

N^9

In the above letter Capt. Colby talks of getting iron for his fireplace from an old furnace. Less than a mile over the Antietam Iron Works Bridge was a dormant iron works at this time. The foundations and two buildings (a stable for mules and the company store) are still visible today and the old stone bridge is still in use. The iron deposits near the village of Antietam, the local hardwoods for charcoal and the available water power of Antietam Creek made this an ideal location for a furnace. The first furnace opened in 1765 and made cannons, cannon balls and muskets for the Revolutionary War. The present ruins are thought to have begun operation about 1822 and included rolling and slitting mills, a sheet-iron mill, a shingle mill, paddle-mill, and an extensive nail factory. It is also thought that the mill did not operate from about 1857 to 1879 when it resumed operation. The ore for the mills was obtained from both the Virginia and Maryland sides of the river.[10] Much of the hardwoods came from the high ridge overlooking Sharpsburg near where Gen. McClellan had his lookout post. After the hard woods were stripped from this ridge it was turned into a huge orchard. This was in the vicinity of what is now the Antietam Overlook Farm Bed and Breakfast.

While visiting their husbands Mrs. Diven and Mrs. G.L. Smith would visit the Antietam battlefield often. "They saw many newly made graves and unburied horses. The signs of the fearful fight were thick over the field, trees torn by shot and shell, and with bullit marks showing upon them almost as thick as rain-drops, brick walls with many an opening knocked through them by the cannon; bloody and splintered fences which one side had defended against the other, and against which wounded soldiers had leaned."[11]

Camp of the 107th N Y Vols
Near Antietam Ford Md Nov 13th 1862
Dear Father

Your long looked for letter came to hand day before yesterday and I hasten to reply in order to hear from you again soon. Camp life wears on as usual — and the constantly recurring routine of duties are varied scarcely at all — Pickett is our chief employment just now — as we are guarding the chief fords across the Potomac — Yesterday — or rather last evening — information was sent to us that the enemy had again crossed the Potomac at or above Williamsport and we were ordered to look out for them — so that they should not get back by the fords we are holding — I do not believe they will find it for their interest to try *here*— any hour. How long we shall remain here is quite doubtful — as it is generally thought that McCellans removal — which by the way took us by surprise — indicates a stirring winter campaign and if so — we shall doubtless be included among the "sufferers." I say "sufferers"—for a winter campaign is no joke — Some new man will of course be made Commander in Chief and of course he will have to attempt some vast undertaking in spite of cold and wet and mud — and in fact the colder and muddier and stormyer [sic] it is the sooner will he make his attempt and thereby gain the more credit — Well I suppose we must abide the consequences — be they what they may — We have had a snow storm here — which did not add to our comfort in the slightest — The weather was quite cold too — I see by the election returns that Van V — suffered not a little and do not wonder at it — though I have not ommitted myself here — as it might injure me sometime — He never would do anything for me however and I am under no obligation to him whatever — You say correctly I think — that the position of Major is for sale to the highest bidder — and he who gets it — must pay well for it — either in dollars and cents or in political support and unfortunately I am poor in both — So I calculate to see some one else take it — If they decided to let competency be the test I *might* have some chance — but of course it will be here as it has ever been — We get no pay yet and there are even no rumors of its coming soon — I have a little over three months pay due me — which ought to amount to nearly $400 — but I do not know what my pay is exactly now Out of this I owe considerable — as living costs very high — double what it need to — I desire to ascertain some way — if I can not obtain pay for the time and money spent in getting up my company and I think I will address the Adjutant General of the State on the subject — I think the state ought to pay me about $500 — and I shall make a big try to obtain it — believing that it would be handy to have — Suppose you talk with Charley Thompson about it and tell him to get C.B. Walker to write Col Diven a letter asking my appointment as Major — and to write to Lt Col Smith — himself — I have made up my mind to study politics — so as to be able to pay off some debts I owe — and I will make it a subject of deep hard study too — politics control all appointments — both here and at home — I begin to see — much to my surprise that our public men are not an average — men of great talants — or possessed of more acquired abilities than many who are never thought of in connection with places of honor and profit — I see to with sorrow — that our most important public offices are filled with men whose only real ability — is that of low cunning and intrique and I forsee the time at no distant day either — when the result will be a universal acknowledgement of the failure of our form of government. Vox populi est vox dei — [the voice of the people is the voice of God] is very fine in theory — but the experiences of the American Republic — where the maxim has been reduced to actual practice illustrates its fallacy — I only state my real convictions — when I say that a monarchial government — with an aristocricy — limited by wise regulations and which shall offer the highest and most permanent rewards to individual exertions and merit — is after all the nearest to perfection — Now — there is little or nothing to stimulate to great and splended achievement except the accumulation of money — (after the Shakesperian Model Shylock and that can hardly be deemed "great" — or "splendid") or the exertion which results in the temporary acquirement of office — Money can be left to your heirs — and yet produce no permanent good — for it may be dissapated and squandered and office and political power — pass away with every breath of popular clamor — but once establish an honorable grade of rank to which any may aspire by the possession of virtue — talents and energy — and which can be transmitted to your children and you offer the highest and most permanent inducements to exertion — to virtue — and to genius. Pardon me for this prosy attempt to theorise upon such, such an ideal subject and permit me to bring back to more useful subjects — this rambling effusion.

You speak of coming down here in December and I should much like to have you come — I do not anticipate remaining in the service after Diven shall have put some ignorant officer over me in the post of Major — or if he gets some one who is well posted *outside* of the Regiment — which I think will be the case — I will tell you the history of this wrangle when I see you — for some of its features are rather queer. After all — if I was appointed — it would make it necessary for me to remain a long time in the service — and not being in love with it — I care but little for the position — Especially as I think it will afford me a fair chance to resign and come home — I say but very little about it — Tell Hungerford that I have appointed Gansevoort [Robert H Gansevoort] to a Sergeants position — as I promised him — and did it by reducing a Sergeant to the ranks — Gansevoort is a fine fellow and is worthy a comission — I have also reduced three Corporals and appointed three others — Did I ever tell you that Hungerford wrote me — asking me to promote Gansevoort? He did and of course I did promise to and have fulfilled the promise and if Wilson resigns as he says he will — and G_ will give me something handsome — I shouldent much wonder if he was promoted again — This however is *strictly* confidential — I go in for the greatest promotion for the highest pay — just like everybody else in the army — What do you think of putting blinds on the house? You have never answered that question — Romlee's wife — from Knoxville — is here — came yesterday. The Adjuntant of our Regiment — Hall Fanton — a lame man from Schuyler Co is making great effort to get the place of Major and with good prospects of success too — as he is backed strongly at the house by Charley Cook. The idea of giving him the place is ridiculous as he is not at all posted and is only a Lieut — and if he gets it — I shall come home at once — I could get out easily — with some home backing—like Walker, Thompson and etc—but they probably are not willing to back me and I shall live to pay them I hope. Elmira and Chemung Co—have been doing a fine thing for us—in sending a whole car load of potatoes-onions—and etc for the use of the regiment—Corning ought to send my company some tobacco and etc—they have not a cent of money and the sutler [a camp follower who peddled provisions to soldiers] refuses to take their orders (as is customary) and they absolutely suffer for it—I have given away at least five dollars worth—but that went but little ways among so many—Tell Sim Van Etten to take up a collection and send it on in smoking and chewing and plug tobacco—The men can appreciate it and I assure you—Have it done if possible at once. I have to pay 8 cents for an ordinary 3 cent paper and 30 c per plug—Direct it to my care at Harper's Ferry Md.

Send all letters for me also to Harper's Ferry—instead of Washington—as we have an arrangement by which all letters for one regiment are to go there—Corning ought not to be out done—and I desire to make my men as comfortable as possible—The health of the men is much improved and they only need some little comforts to be in pretty fair condition.

Give my love to mother and tell her I hope to see her before long—Remember me to Henry and wife—I hope he is steady and that he will or has now got a good situation—

Write soon and believe me
Affectionately Yours Newton[12]

"Mittens—Col. Diven has written to Elmira, stating that the 107th Regiment is greatly in need of mittens. As Capt. Colby's Co. is in this Regiment, this appeal comes to this community [Corning] to do its share in the good work. Col. D. says: 'The sentinel while on guard must be always on his feet, and always carry his gun. The Government furnishes no mittens. You can imagine the hardships of walking in a cold night or day, the bare hand always on the gun, which cannot be supported except by keeping the hand in contact with the iron of the barrel or the mountings. We want common knit yarn mittens, coming well up on the wrist. We want these for 800 men. I but name the want.'"[13]

"The Ladies of the Soldier's Relief Society of Corning will give a Thanksgiving supper for the benefit of sick and wounded soldiers at Concert Hall, the 27th, thanksgiving evening. All interested for our brave soldiers are invited to attend."

By order of Committee.
C. Stewart, Sec'y.[14]

"The *Elmira Advertiser* publishes an interesting letter from Capt. L. Baldwin, of the 107th Regiment. He is senior Captain, and we trust will be promoted to the post of Major made vacant by Maj. Smith's appointment to the Lt. Colonelcy. He gives a statement of the men fit for duty, that the 107th has 476 men and eighteen line officers ready for duty, out of one thousand and odd that left Elmira in August last. There are reported sick 179, and absent sick 156, making a total of 811 accounted for; the rest have been killed, wounded, died of disease, discharged and deserted — of the latter quite a number. Of course the field officers are on hand, as usual, and not included in the above. that Co. I (Capt. Colby) has but 41 non-commissioned officers and privates, and but two officers, fit for duty."[15]

1st Sergt. Edwin Weller of Co. H. wrote home the following from Antietam, Nov. 21, 1862: "We heard yesterday for the first time since he was taken prisoner from Lieut. L.O. Saylor, he has been paroled, [by the Confederates] and is at the Camp of Paroled prisoners at Annapolis waiting to be exchanged."[16]

The following order was issued sometime later listing the disposition of several soldiers:

General Orders No. 195
Dismissed from the service

The name of Lewis O. Saylor, 2d Lieutenant, 107th New York Vols., Company H., for being captured when across the Potomac contrary to orders.[17]

Lieut. Col. Smith, of the 107th Regiment, thus refers in a letter to Elmira, to the necessity for mittens. We hope the ladies will move in this matter and send Capt. Colby enough for his company, as we suggested last week. The difficulty of obtaining yarn may prevent. We do not believe that any lack of patriotism exists. He says: "Our men have not been paid one cent since they left home, and they have no money to buy mittens with, and when I mentioned my application to Elmira they seemed to think the question settled and the mittens sure to come. If any among you think they are not needed just let him come here and walk a beat of one hundred and twenty-five paces on two hour reliefs, for the whole twenty-four hours day and night, and grasp with uncovered hands a cold musket barrel, with plenty of snow upon the ground and more falling, and all the time freezing besides, and I am sure he would never again question their necessity."[18]

Head Quarters 107th Reg. N.Y. Vols.
Camp near Antietam Ford

The following extract from instructions received from Brigade Head Quarters is republished for the direction of officers having charge of pickets and guards:

EXTRACT XVI: The partakin of goods from this side (Maryland) to Virginia or from Virginia to this side within the jurisdiction of this command is strictly prohibited. Should any person violate this order or attempt to do so, such person will be arrested; his goods together with the coat, a wagon and team used in transporting the same will be seized, and sent to the Provost Marshalls Office in this place (Sharpsburgh) accompanied with a full statement (in writing) of all the facts connected with the transaction.

By Command
Col. Alex S. Diven
Hull Fenten Adjutant

Mem.: Handed copy of above to Capt. Colby 107th NY in command of picket line Dec 4th at Guard Mounting and copy also same form to Capt. A.M. Gill, 107th Field Officer of the day.[19]

Head Quarters Picket Gaurd
Antietam Ford, Md Dec. 4, 1862
Dear Father

Seated on a bank—which slopes toward the Potomac and perhaps ten rods from that river—I am trying to write to you—The day is warm and the sun shines out cheerfully and with the exception of the leafless trees—There is little indication of winter—Between my position and the river—is the Chesapeke and Ohio Canal—which here follows the river closely—and along the heel path—our sentinals are slowly marching backward and forward—their bright muskets glistening in the sun—as far as the eye can reach in both directions—The river and canal here resemble—almost exactly the Chemung river and canal below Corning—by Johnathan Browns I have just stationed my guards and relieved the old one and now I sit here to answer yours which came to hand last night—and which I have so long looked for—I have wondered not a little—why it was—that I get no letters from any one—Yours is the only one I have received in weeks—Mary has almost ceased to write for some reason—I know not why—and having written her several without receiving any reply I have quietly decided to write no more until I receive some replies—It is true—our mail is irregular—but Wilson and Rutter get letters about twice a week and of course I could too if they were sent—

12. Antietam Ford

The question of the Major ship is still unsetteled and though I suppose I have but little chance for it — yet I desire to stay until it is fixed and then — failing to be promoted — I can have a pretext at resigning — Especially — as it is admitted that I am the most competent of any one in line — by Cols Diven and Smith and nearly the entire line — This however has little to do with it — as political power decides upon the merit of an officer and promotes — To tell you the truth — however — I agree with you in saying it costs more than it comes to — unless I make up my mind to follow the service always — and with the exception of always being away from home — it would please me to do so — I expect to apply for a leave of absence about the middle of this month — Wilson has resigned — but his papers are not yet approved and it will take two or three weeks before they can get around — and I shall make a *"plum"* thereby — if I have no bad luck — I owe quite a sum for board and c — but I have due me to day — about $500 and if we get no pay — till Jany 1st I shall have over $600 due me — Of course I can not go home until we are paid and we expect the paymaster daily — He will only pay us to Aug 31st — however — I will write to you just as soon as I think you had better start to come — (if at all) and give you fair notice — But if I can come home — will you then wish to come? Perhaps you would like to see Washington while Congress is in session — and perhaps it will pay you the expense of coming any way — Charley Walker has either been misrepresented to me — or else — he did not tell you the truth — when he said the Senior Captain was to be the major — and c — Charley Thompson wrote me saying that Walker had requested my appointment — when he was in Albany — and that he (Thompson) had also written to some friend of his in Albany to appoint me — or to get me appointed — The Senior Captain — (Baldwin) is from Elmira and if he gets it — then all our field officers are from Elmira — Col — Lt Col — Major and Surgeon — Baldwin is a clever fellow — but has no military knowledge or experience — The other day — when the regiment was being reviewed by Genl Gordon — Baldwin marched his company past at "Present Arms"! Ye Gods — "Present Arms" — when on the march!! You see he is not *very thoughrosley* [sic] posted — Steuben Co — with 5 companies in the regiment has one officer only — ranking as Liut — Chemung Co — with only 4 companies has 1 Col-1 Lt Col — 1 Surgeon with the rank of Major and Schuyler Co — with only 1 company has 2 staff officers (Adujutent — assistant Surgeon) ranking as Liuts — but enough of this — Whoever informed you that my company was reduced to thirty or forty men lied — I have 64 men here and have in the different Hospitals about ten or twelve more — I have lost some by desertion it is true — but other companies are no better off than I — in that respect — I have had one man come back voluntarily — after deserting — We are not able — as a regiment to turn out over — between 4 and 500 men — which would be an average of 40 or 50 men to the company — so you see I have more than an average — But of course there must be some lying going on — I think I will not have blinds put on my house until I come home — You ask if there is anything I need and I reply that there is not at present — I am trying to get along cheaply and economically — I wear the same old coat — that I wore in the 23rd — with a pair of Privates pants — I had the luck to have nearly all my shirts stolen (I only brought two or three along — leaving the rest in my trunk at Washington) and I never wear such as I draw of the Gov for my men — but — a new coat would cost $25 — and I get along well enough — here — and if I do not stay long — I shall not need any and If I do I can buy one any time — So dont waste any money in buying things for me — I am going to New York if I come home — certain — Tell Cochran for me that I have received no pay yet or I would pay him the balance I owe him — If I come I shall take Mary and go to the city — and be gone a few days — just for the notion of it — How is Mother? Tell her that if I can get away — I will drop in on her one of these mornings — We have been rather apprehensive of an attack here for a few days past — but have seen nothing of the enemy lately —

Give my love to Mother and Henry and wife — Write often —

I will write as soon as I can tell you anything with certainty about coming home-

Very Affectionately Yours
Newton[20]

Published by request in the *Corning Journal*, Dec. 11, were directions for knitting mittens with a finger. The directions were published by the order of the Ladie's Soldiers Relief Association of Elmira.[21]

Camp of the 107th Regt N Y Vols
Near Antietam Ford Dec 9, 1862
Dear Father

Van Etten leaves here for Corning today and I avail myself of the chance to drop you a line though you did not send me any when he came here — I received a letter from Henry today — in which he speaks of having enlisted in the Guards and says too — that you talk of "doing" the Capts position I think you will regret it if you do — for you are illy adapted to endure the food and beds and etc Your health will fail you — then if you should be called into the field — you would either suffer in reputation for resigning — or by exposure and sickness — No-No — permit me to represent the family in the military line and you stay by the families — There is no decision public yet — as to how the majorship shall be settled —

There is news in Camp — Diven has gone to Washington — but is expected back soon and will I think resign his place before long — though he says he prefers to be here — I wish he would try to get us to Washington — but there is no hope of it I suppose — am of the opinion that the fighting will soon be finished — probably after one more general set to — and I confess I shall not be sorry — There are some unwritten pages in the history of this regiment — that will some day be published. Lt Col Smith just came in and notified me to be ready to move at a moments notice! Splended time to move — snow and mud on all sides — but so it goes — Well I have not the slightest idea where they desire us to tramp to — but wont we catch it? I will try and notify you of our destination as soon as I find it out — Do not attempt to come here until you here from me again — I will leave this open till the last minute and try and discover our destination.[22]

This letter was unsigned.

In Newton's haste to give this letter to his father and the following one to a niece to Van Etten to carry home he forgot to sign them. He acknowledges this in the next letter to his father on the 15th: "It is next to impossible to write without soiling paper please excuse it!"

Camp on the 107th Regt N.Y. Vols
Near Antietam Ford, Md Dec 9, 1862
My dear niece

Long weary marches — the constant and necessary duty of camp — the absence of writing material frequently — and the amount of my absolutely necessary correspondance — have together conspired to prevent my writing to you — up to this time — and now — having the requisite leisure I hasten to disabuse your mind of any impressions that may from my long silence — Your Aunt Mary having been with you for several weeks past — I conclude you are not ignorant of some portions of my experience since entering the service the last time and therefore I need not repeat it here — To this hour — I have not ceased to be thankful — that I passed safely through the bloody day at Antietam — when not less than 20,000 dead attested the fury of the fight — Believe me — my dear girl — it left its strong impressions — and they will be fresh to the last hour of life. Regiment after regiment charged past us — their cheers making the blood tingle to our finger's ends — and we wondered how much longer we must wait before we too could gloriously dash forward upon the rebel cuss that held a piece of woods just on our front and win *our* page in history — and not long had we to wait — It could not have been past eight in the morning — when I saw our gallant Brigadier General emerge from the smoke in front and spurring up to where we lay — ordered us to "up and at them" — and away we went with the maddest cheers — and the wildest fiercest excitement of a battle — The gambler who risks his whole fortune in some game of chance — approaches in a remote degree — but only remote — as the stake in battle is life and honor — About four in the afternoon fresh troops relieved us and we left the front — exhausted and weary — but thank God — unbroken and in good order — having *always* maintained our position and twice forcing back the rebels from theirs — Upon one occasion — a Pennsylvania regiment — which was supporting a battery near us — broke and disgracefully ran — and then we were ordered into its place and successfully held the ground — But here I am doing just what I promised not to! Pardon me — for I know that this does not interest you and I will talk of other matters. Has your Aunt gone....

Remainder of letter missing[23]

For the *Journal*:

Parts of a letter from Chaplain E.F. Crane:
From the 107th Regiment
Antietam Ford, Dec., fifth, 1862
My Dear Friend:

Our Regiment is fast recovering from the sad effects of sickness and battle, and we begin to lengthen our lines at dress parade and battallion drill. But Oh! sad to tell, that many of our brave boys have found a grave in stranger soil and many more must soon go to their homes, broken down with disease, or maimed in body.

We were cheered the other day, at the unexpected presence of your fellow townsman, Simon Van Etten, who made many of the Reg't glad, not only by his presence, but by the large amount of supplies he brought with him. It would have done you good to have seen the crowd around, as he was dealing out to each soldier the rich delicacies he had in store.

Think of it as you may, there is nothing that cheers a soldier more than a letter, or a box from friends at home, this side of seeing the friends themselves.

Our worthy young friend, Quarter-Master Graves, has been promoted to Brigade Q.M. and hence is a member of General Gordon's Staff. A grand compliment this, to enterprising mind.

Capt. Colby, of Co. I., is one of the best officers in the Reg't. He is, decidedly, a credit to the town from which he and his company emenates. He has a good lot of men left him to command, the cowards having all deserted. It is quite probable, that as a Reg't, we are now in Winter Quarters. Our men have been very busy in pre-paring themselves huts for their accomodations and they have made themselves quite comfortable.

Our men are now engaged in picketing this part of the canal and river, and they are suffering, to-day, very much from a cold, severe snow storm, that commenced here yesterday. The snow is about four inches deep, and the cold, north wind, which is blowing almost a gale, makes it play very lively. But this picketing must be done, whether there is any real necessity for it or not. Officers and men alike, must turn out, and the voice of the Sergeant may be heard above the whistling winds, "turn out, second relief—turn out first relief," and the tramp of the squad may be heard marching off to duty.

I would not have you think that there is no necessity for our picketing at this place, because it was only Thursday, of this week, that our men saw a platoon of guerrillas on the opposite side of the river. But they did not shoot. From all we can learn, there are not many such near us, and the truth is, we have about as much to fear from northern guerrillas as we have from geurrilla of the south.

Please remember me, kindly, to all enquiring friends, and if Uncle Sam sees fit to grant me leave of absence this winter, I intend to visit Corning and make a general report of the Reg't.

My own health is, now, very good, and I love the work in which I am engaged.

Yours truly,
E.F. Crane, Chaplain of the 107th Reg't., N.Y.V.

P.S. Dec. 11th, we are now on the way to the valley of the Rappahannock.[24]

CHAPTER 13

Near Fairfax Station and On to Chancellorsville

It was a common practice to have troops march and counter march over the same paths, without any apparent reason. The commanding generals sometimes had a reason, but the men in the ranks often knew nothing.

Dec. 10, 1862   The 107th broke up camp at Antietam Ford, Md., marched for Va., bivouacked with 3rd Brigade (Genl. Gordon's) on the road to Harpers Ferry after marching 4 miles.

Dec. 11, 1862   Marched early in morning, crossing the Potomac at Harpers Ferry at sunrise, passed over the Shenandoah, thence around the base of the Blue Ridge into Loudon Valley. Bivouacked that night near Hillsboro—eleven miles from Harper's Ferry.

Dec. 12, 1862   Marched all day, passing through Hillsboro, bivouacking at night 3 miles west of Leesburg.

Dec. 13, 1862   Sunday — Marched 19 miles bivouacing on the Fairfax Pike.[1] Near Chantilly, thawed snow made the roads almost impassable.[2]

Dec. 14, 1862   Passed through Fairfax Court House, bivouacking at night near Fairfax Station, Va.[3] "We have rumors of great fighting at Fredericksburg and severe losses" (about 10,000 Union and 5,000 Rebels were killed or wounded on 12/13).[4]

Bivouac of the 107 N Y V
Near Fairfax Station Va, Dec 15, 1862

13. Near Fairfax Station and On to Chancellorsville

Dear Father

 Having a chance of writing a few lines I thought I would try and let you know where we are — I wrote you just before leaving Antietam — but could not then tell you where we were going — We are bound to Fredericksburg — This is the ~~fifth~~ sixth days march and I need not say we have endured hard fare and hard marching — and we have about four days more before us — which will be worse still — I am so sore and lame I can hardly move — I am writing before sunrise and can hardly see the lines on the paper — We are in Slocums ~~Division~~ Corps — Williams Division and Gordons Brigade — The order has come to fall in and I must stop — I have not heard from home in a long time — Wilson leaves us here — though he has not yet got his papers — but soon will probably — Rutter and I go through — I hardly think I can stand it — but will do all I can — It is no small thing I assure you and It looks like a storm — Give my love to Mother and Henry — Has Mary returned yet? Give her my love and tell her to write very soon — If I can I will quit this miserable service when we get to Fredericksburg — No Major announced yet but it is thought here that some outside man has been appointed — Diven told me this morning that we would know who it was very soon — The rebel cavalry have hung around us all the way and attacked our train yesterday — but were repulsed — It is rumored that there has been severe fighting at Fredericksburg — but I have not seen a paper in a week — We have at least 20,000 men in this corps and unless I am much mistakened — we take their "Johnny little Richmond" this time — Take care of my wife and children a little while longer and if I am spared I will come home soon and hope to take that care off your hands — This Regiment has been kicked around and dragged about not a little — Its a big thing to have members of Congress to command it! because they can *favor* us greatly!! Oh yes — especially when they dont know anything about military matters — Write soon — Remember me kindly to any enquiring friends — especially Curtiss — Austins — Denton — and c and c I can not write again until we reach F — — burg and will then — as soon as possible — No pay yet — I sent my new sword by Van Etten and a gun to Thompson — I forgot to sign the letters I wrote you and sent by him — That is the sword given me by LLoyd Paxton — and I prize it highly —

I must bid you good bye
Affectionately Your Son
Newton

I am as ragged as a bear —
I also sent my commission by Van Etten[5]

Dec. 15, 1862   Monday — The sick and those unable to march of the Regt. were sent by rails to Alexandria (40 in all); others under charge of Lt. Col. Smith marched southward to beyond the Occoquan Creek, bivouacking at night 3 miles beyond Wolf Run Shoals.[6]

Dec. 16, 1862   "Before daylight my troops [Gen. A.S. Williams] were in motion. About 12 o'clock I received orders to halt until furthur orders."

Dec. 17, 1862   "I [Gen. A.S. Williams] was notified to countermarch this morning. It had rained the night before and during the morning the roads were indescribable. I ordered the troops to march before daylight and all three brigades succeeded in reaching Fairfax before night."[7]

Dec. 28, 1862   [Sunday] When in light marching order the Regt. started for the Occoquan Creek again, bivouacking that night on its north shore. Remained there until noon on the 29th.

Dec. 29, 1862   [Monday] "Resuming march we arrived back in an old camp at Fairfax Station at about 4 P.M., marching the whole distance without a halt. The whole distance marched by the Regt since breaking up camp at Antietam Ford [Dec 10] being somewhat more than one hundred miles.[8]

Camp of the 107th N.Y.V.
Near Fairfax Sta. Dec. 30, 1862
Dear Father

The Chaplain — Elder Crane being on the eve of going home — I will avail myself of the chance and write you a few lines— Last Saturday I went to Washington [28th and 29th] and while there the rebels made a dash and our regiment was ordered to march and did march to Occoquan Creek and then came back again without seeing anything of the rebs— I had good luck to escape the toil and exposure — by being absent — but I assure you I was very uneasy and did my utmost to get back — but it was impossible — so I stayed in the City till to day — The rebels— in making their escape — passed through Fairfax — within a mile or so of our camp — They are bold riders— I assure you — There is but little news here— I received a letter from Seymour Denton to day — asking me to appoint John Sheppard — my orderly — to a lieutenancy and Col Divin showed me letters from Judge Johnson — Charley Thompson — Seymour Denton — and others asking the same thing of him — It complicates matters very much — as I would do almost anything to oblige Denton — but if I do so— in this matter — it will be at a sacrifice of $100 — and poor as I am — it is no small sacrifice — What do you advise? Robert Gansevoort of Bath — who has once

13. Near Fairfax Station and On to Chancellorsville

Certificate presented to Newton T. Colby on December 31, 1862, making him Major of the 107th Regiment Infantry.

been in the service as a Lieutenant and who is a Sergt in my company now — wants it and I think would make the best officer — Sheppard is honest — reliable — steady but lacks force and energy — Col Diven leaves it to me entirely — to say who it shall be —

Please say nothing of this to any one — If you could find time write a little more often I could appreciate it — As I am very anxious to hear from you — I want to come home very badly and see you all — but I suppose it will not be possible until we get somewhere — where we expect to stay for the winter — and then beside that I have received no pay yet — Government — ought to be so poorly served — as they serve us in keeping back the money earned by hard knocks. I am sick of soldiering — *in the line* especially — and shall decline to continue in it much longer — What does Wilson have to say? He seemed to be much pleased to get out — and between you and I — I was not greatly disturbed by his leaving — I never had any trouble with him — though I failed to fall in love with him — How does Henry get along — and what is he doing? I hope he is getting ahead — as I fear we are to see hard times before long — I am fearful — that Green

Major Newton T. Colby. Courtesy Paul Newton Colby, Jr.

backs will collapse and be worthless and I shall have mine invested somehow — What do you think of it? Give my love to mother — how I wish to see her — well I may *perhaps* — in January — By the way if you want a minister — I think you could get Elder Crane — for I believe he does not care to stay here — Any how — get him to preach in Corning — one sabbath while he is home — He goes by order of the Genl to try and find some of our deserters — My boys are all pretty well and can do their duty as well as the best-

But I must close — Write often and believe me

Affectionately your son
Newton[9]

From the *Corning Journal*:
12/31/1862 Newton Colby-Major on Field Staff[10]
"We are glad to notice that Capt. N.T. Colby, 107th Reg., has been promoted to the post of Major, to date from Oct. 22d."[11]

"Lt. Col. G.L. Smith [Gabriel] and Chaplain Crane, of the 107th Regiment, are with us — the former on a sick furlough. He has been unwell for some time, and the Surgeon considered a respite from active service absolutely imperative. Mr. Crane will return in a few days. They report the Regiment in an improved condition, though it has of late been compelled to undergo many hardships and de-privations."[12] "Elder Crane preached in the Baptist Church [Corning], Sunday morning and evening."[13] "Capt. E.C. Clark of the 107th Reg't, severly wounded at Antietam, has been obliged to resign in consequence, and has returned to Havana" [NY].¹⁴

Head Quarters 107th N.Y. Vols
Fairfax Sta. Va. Jany 16, 1863
Dear Father and Mother

Your last letter came to hand two or three days since and I should have answered it earlier — but I have had no small amount of business to transact — Col Diven being absent and Lt Col Smith also — I have been obliged to do all that has been done — The regiment has been drilled each afternoon — and c and c. Some of the Captains feel very bad because they did not get the promotion and have tendered their resignations — My old enemy — Morgan — is busy — urging the officers to resign and has succeeded to the extent of 3 or 4 and perhaps will induce others — He is a low fellow — of no character — and I never notice him — and am not disturbed by his conduct — In fact if they all resign I care not. Once more we are to march — orders having been received to cook the rations — can not guess where — but it will be *hard* — in any direction — as the roads are terrible — I expect orders hourly to move — though it is now nearly nine in the evening — I am very much disappointed — as I had anticipated a visit from you and Mary — but of course you can not come now — Tell Charley Thompson that I have not been able to get to Washington since my promotion and I have no horse of my own — or uniform — I think you would smile to see me for I am quite ragged — I wear the same old coat — I had while in the 23rd and it has nearly come to pieces. If they have my measure in Corning I desire you to see what they will charge for an ordinary fatigue coat of heavy dark blue beaver (or something of that kind) of cloth made double breasted — and frock style — with turn down collar — If I can get one for $12 or $14 — I think I will have one made — I shall have to pay at least $25 — here — for my uniform coat and then I ought not to wear it all the time and ought to have the fatigue coat I mention — Write me what you think about it — My horse will cost me $116 and saddle and briddle and c $30. You see it costs like the Dickens — If we get anywhere — where I can be got at — I desire you and Mary to come down — Col Diven goes to Washington Monday mornings and stays — (in congress) till Friday or Saturday — or rather I should say he has done so and expected to continue — but I suppose he will have to come back now and go with the Regt — He thought we were to stay here some time — but I always expected and feared we should not and it proves I was nearest right — All sorts of rumors prevail as to our destination — Some say — North Carolina — others—Fredericksburg—Gordonsville—Thoroughfare Gap—Harpers Ferry and c and c "ad infinitum." I have just received another order and it settles the matter as to moving and we shall doubtless move tomorrow—Alas for me—for it will be tough—I assure you—Well—write often—and I will write you as soon I can do so—On the march—I have no opportunity—so do not be disappointed if you do not hear from me—Give my love to Mother and Henry—and his wife—and tell them I would greatly like to see them—but I can not tell now—when I can expect to get a "leave"—My trunk and lots of clothes are at Mrs Andersons and I have an overcoat at Mrs Bishops—No 316 Delaware Avenue (where Col Smith stops)—Write often and believe me

Very Affectionately your Son
Newton[15]

Burnside's "Mud March" took place Jan 19-24.

Jan 19, 1863 The 107th marched from Fairfax Station, Va., to Occoquan Creek and bivouacked at 9 P.M.[16] "Weather cold and road frozen in roughest state." Encamped about 2 miles beyond Wolf Run Shoals, at Beacon Race Church.[17]

Jan. 20, 1863 Marched at 7 A.M. for Dumfries, bivouacked at 6 P.M. at Dumfries[18] (14 miles south side of Quantico Creek). "Road still rough and weather cold threatening snow—a cold north east rain began before dark with a very tempest of wind. The few tents our men had were soon flattened and camp fires put out. All night the cold rain kept up and the wind howeled."[19]

Jan. 21, 1863 Marched at 7:30 A.M., forded Quantico Creek, camped at 4 P.M.[20] "The frost had all gone and mud of the stickiest and nastiest kind had taken its place. The rain was still pouring, but we began our march at 7 o'clock. On either side of the road was the densest forest of scrub pines, a perfect thicket."[21] "One can't go a mile without drowning mules in mud-holes. It is solemnly true we lost mules in the middle of the road, sinking out of sight in the mud-holes. A few bubbles of air, a stirring of the watery mud, indicated the last expiring efforts of many a poor long-ears."[22]

Major Colby was fortunate not to have made the preceding trip as he was detailed to special duty as shown in the following letter.

13. Near Fairfax Station and On to Chancellorsville 215

Fairfax Sta Va Jany 21, 1863
Dr Father

I am at this place and waiting — in order to go on and overtake the Regt which moved towards Fredericksburg — yesterday morning — Our Paymaster — Maj Campbell and Maj Diven (the Col's son) are with me — We have a Cavalry Escort of thirty men and hope to overtake the Regt tomorrow — The going is awful — Maj Campbell has with him about $90,000. It would make a good haul for the Rebs — if they captured us eh? But I must close as we are just starting

Give my love to Mary and to Mother and Henry-

In haste Ever Yours Newton[23]

Jan. 22, 1863 Marched at 7 A.M. through rain and mud over almost impassable roads until 6 P.M., camped near Acquia Creek.

Jan. 23, 1863 Marched at 1 P.M. and camped at 7 P.M. near Stafford Court House.[24] Stafford Court House — "like most of Virginia's 'court houses,' was a place of three old houses, a small, dilapidated court house and a jail about eight feet square."[25]

Jan. 24, 1863 Received pay.[26]

Head Qrts. 107. NYV.
Near Stafford Court House Va.
Jany 25, 1863
Dearest Wife

Inasmuch as Maj Campbell did not start as he expected I have a chance to say a word or two more — We have not moved yet — and the opinion is that we shall not — at least right off — Col Divin goes back to Washington with Maj Campbell — leaving me in command — The Col thinks there will be no fighting for the present — but I should not be at all surprised if there was — He says he would not go on any account — if there was to be a formal move — Darling wife — I do long to see you to be near you — but fate seems to forbid just now — but I live in the hope that something will turn up — to permit me to get a leave — I could sit for hours and tell you of "the dangers I have passed" and the scenes I have witnessed — Nothing could make me happier than to thus pass whole days — Darling keep up your courage and have faith in better days — when we may be united — They are nearly ready and I must hurry and close — Dearest one I can only say from

my heart I love you truly and purely — Write very often. Kiss our little ones-
Love to Father and Mother
1200 kisses for your dear self and believe me

Ever Yours only
Newton[27]

Jan. 26, 1863   Maj. Gen. Joseph Hooker succeeded Burnside as commander of the Army of the Potomac.[28]

Head Quarters 107th Regt NYV
Near Stafford Court House, Va
Jan. 26, 1863

General Order No. 3: I — Commandants of companies of this regiment here after and till further notice — will be held responsible for reporting when they allow more than three men of their respective companies to be absent from the camp at one time, the absence of a non-commissioned officer and privates of this regiment have grown into an evil and retards the filling of the details, the prompt performance of duty assigned to the command and it must be abated.

II — Anyone found gambling in this camp, by an officer of this command, will be by him forth with ordered under arrest, and the fact at once reported to the commanding officer. Any officer guilty of neglect of duty in this regard, it will be the duty of the Colonel or officer in command to report.

By command of Major N.T. Colby commanding
Hull Fenten Adjutant[29]

Jan. 27, 1862   Marched to Hope Landing near Acquia Creek. The Regiment suffered much sickness.[30]

General Hooker reorganized. His corps commanders were now John F Reynolds (I), Darius Couch (II), Daniel Sickles (III), George G Meade (V), John Sedgwick (VI), Oliver O Howard (XI), Henry Slocum (XII), and Alfred Pleasanton (Cavalry).[31]

Head Quarters 107th N Y Vols
New Hope Landing, Va Jany 31, 1863

13. Near Fairfax Station and On to Chancellorsville

Dear Father,

Your very welcome letter came to hand last evening and I was much pleased to hear from you and the folks at home — I have been absent so long that I have almost forgotten how you all look —

I am at present in Command — Cols Divin and Smith both being absent and with little prospect of returning soon — Smith is now in Washington and though Col Diven wrote me — saying that he would rejoin us soon — yet I fear he will not do so permanently — or long enough to allow me to go home — as I am told his health is very poor. Col. Diven will not be with us much if any — until after this session of Congress is over and then you see I am fast — From present appearances I think our Army can not move very soon as the roads are impassable — and I could get away better now than by and by when the roads are good — if there was only some Field Officer to relieve me — I *must come some* way and soon too.

I did not draw all my pay — having two months Capts pay and one month pay as Major — now due me — and out of the pay I drew I owed for the watch I sent you — and quite a larger bill for board and a new coat for my new rank and some horse equipings and etc — I also had to get a new pair of boots and etc and had I paid *all* my debts I could not have sent hardly anything — as I owe nearly $100 — now — No pay for six mos and having to get everything on credit makes large bills — especially now when everything is so high — My expenses are less than the average of officers in the Regt. and I try to econimize.

Col Diven seems to have confidence in me too and I would not have him feel that it was misplaced for worlds He is truly as you said a Gentleman — and I respect him much. We are situated on a bluff — on the Potomac and the view is really splended — At the foot of the hill where our quarters are is Alquia Creek — which-here-is as large as the Chenny and separated from it by a long narrow strip of land is the broad old Potomac — running nearly parallel with the creek — till they both meet about two miles below and in plain sight. Steamers and sail vessels without numbers are continually passing and repassing — If I could get a "leave of absence" I could go direct to Washington by boat — and it would be very quick and easy — but I almost despair of getting it — They tell me that I will get another grade if Smith resigns — but I had actually rather come home than to get it by staying here much longer — I have made no decision in reference to vacant Lieutenancy in my old company — in fact I am "non pleased" — I rather think Sheppard ought to have it — Two Capts-(Baldwin and Morgan) who resigned because I was "jumped" over them — have had their papers returned — "disapproved" and I think *Baldwin* is glad of it —

Wilkinson resigned *professedly* on account of ill health — his papers being accompanied by a medical certificate of disability — has been honorably discharged Non of the Steuben officers have resigned — Capt Miles who sits by — Wants to be kindly remembered to you — He is a fine old gentleman and a good friend of mine.

I have been rather unwell for a few days and the Dr tried to make me believe I was threatened with fever and prevailed upon me to take a thorough physic and it worked off very finely and I feel all right again — My tent took fire in the night a night or two since and I had a rather close call — My shirt was burned through in several places — but the skin escaped — owing to my wearing two shirts — but Adjutant Fanton who quarters with me was not so fortunate — for a piece of the burning tent cloth fell around his neck and burned him severly — I assure you it is no joke — to have to grab your briches and run out into the snow — a la shirt tail — to make your toilet — on a freezing cold night — But as Beacher said-"for this also came I into the service" There is nothing here in the way of news and in fact I presume you are better posted than I — I have purchased no horse yet — and am still using Van Volkenburg's — He "Hoss" is a fine one but poor riding animal — being hard in both the gallop and trot. I am anxious about Henry and really hope he will gradually get better — He must be very careful and not be out late nights — and avoid exposure and fatigue for a time — Have him bathe frequently and *carefully* too- — and he will feel better — I will come home if possible and I can doctor him. Give my love to Mother and tell her that her Soldier boy often thinks of her and desires to see her — I can almost see her now busy with some care for her children — as she always is. God Bless her and you all. Write often Father and believe me

Yours affectionately, your son
Newton[32]

The 107th Regiment New York Vol. remained at Hope Landing, Va. from 2/1/1863 to 4/18/1863.[33]

Head Quarters 107th Regt NY Vols.
camp near Hope Landing, Va.
Feb. 2, 1863

General Order No. 7: Several companies comprising this regiment will be assembled in the companies streets for muster and inspection tomorrow at 9 A.M. The signal for which will be given on the bugle. 15 minutes before 10 assembly will be sounded, when the companies will march to the open space near the landing. The line will be designated by markers and regimental colors. The men will parade with knapsacks with their overcoats snuggly rolled and strapped on them, and with haversacks and canteens.

Commissioned officers will appear in full uniform with sash and gloves if possible, and the staff will report at this head quarters at 9½ A.M.

By command of

Major N.T. Colby Comanding Regt.
Hull Fenten Adjutant[34]

Head Quarters 107th Regt NY Vols.
Camp near Hope Landing, Va.
Feb. 10, 1863

General Orders No. 4: I — The great number of men absent from camp, without leave, renders it necessary to restrict this abuse and the commissioned officers of each company are required to see that the following regulations are strictly enforced.

II — Roll calls will be had in each company three times per day as follows: Reveille at 7 A.M.; Dinner call at 12½ M; Tattoo at 8 P.M.

The bugle call will be the signal for the companies to fall into line, and no man will be deemed present who does not fall in and answer to his name from the ranks. Orderly Sergeants will report all absent without leave to these head quarters. At least one commissioned officer will be present and personally oversee the calling of roll each time.

III — Hereafter, commandants of the companies will approve the pass of one man only from their ranks, and these passes will be left the night before the day that they are to be used, with the adjutant for approval. Any enlisted man absent without such a pass, duly approved, will be subject to arrest and punishment.

IIII — Hereafter the guard of each day will report to the officer of the day, on the second day after, as police under command of officer of the guards.

By order of

Major N.T. Colby Commanding Regt.
J.R. Lindsay Act. Adjt.[35]

Chaplain Crane of the 107th Reg't in a letter to the *Elmira Press*, thus speaks of Major N.T. Colby: "Col. Diven is spending the most of the time, while we are laying here, in his seat in Congress, and the Regiment is in command of our newly commissioned Major, who is giving universal satisfaction, Major Colby is destined to make his mark as an officer, and in my opinion the wisdom of our Colonel is fully justified in the recommendation of his appointment."[36]

February 16, 1863   We are still in the mud.
February 22, 1863   Most tempestous day, snow, cold and very high wind. Washington's Birthday — we expect to have a grand division parade and review, with salutes.[37]

Head Quarters 107th Regt NY Vols.
Near Hope Landing, Va.
March 3, 1863

General Order No. 9: The earnest attention of both officers and men and is directed to the following orders and officers of the day and the guard will see that they are strictly carried out.

I — Hereafter the men detailed guard will appear at guard mounting with canteens and haversacks and be provided with one days cooked rations.

II — No guard will be allowed to leave the guard house for a longer period than ten minutes upon any pretext except to get on post.

III — Whenever the weather permits, arms will be stacked in front of the guard house and the men under the direction of the officer of the guard attend to the policing of the ground and in the appearance of the guard house.

IIII — The officer of the guard must remain with the guard and will be held responsible that article 33, revised Army Regulations, is enforced and for the regular and prompt discharge of all duties pertaining to the guard. The article above refered to must be read to the men at least once during their tour of duty.

V — Officers of the day will frequently visit the guard during the day and at least once after 12 at night, and will be held responsible for all noise and disturbance after dark.

VI — Any sentinal found sitting down, or otherwise neglecting his duty will be punished according to the usual discretion of the officers of the guard.

VII — A copy of this order will be posted in the guard house and kept there for which the officer of the guard will be responsible.

By order

Major N.T. Colby Commanding
J.R. Lindsay Lt., Act. Adjt.[38]

March 5, 1863   Gen. Williams reviewed his division.

13. Near Fairfax Station and On to Chancellorsville

March 6, 1863   General Hooker was here to review Gen. Williams' division but affair postponed due to rain.

March 7, 1863   Foggy and showery.[39]

Head Quarters 3rd Brigade
Stafford Court House, Va.
March 11, 1863

Special Order No. 27: The ammunition report of the 3rd Wisc., 13th N.J., and 107th N.Y. Vols., showing a deficiency of ammunition. The commanders there of will immediately procure sufficient to make their proper complement. All company commands per 60 rounds per man, the commanding officers of said regiments are reminded that it is their duty to have 60 rounds per man, on hand, in their regiment.

By command of Col. T.H. Ruger
Comdg. Brig[40]

"By a general order of Gen. Hooker, for the promotion of increased discipline, it is designated that no more furloughs will be granted to the 23d and 107th among other New York Regiments enumerated. All officers absent from duty are ordered back to their respective regiments immediately." *Elmira Advertiser.*[41]

March 20, 1863   "Quite a snow storm today—yesterday General Hooker reviewed Gen. William's division and pronounced it a 'splended division.'—The day before [3/18] Williams division was reviewed by General Slocum and the day before that [3/17] Williams reviewed a brigade."[42]

Chaplain Crane of the 107th Regiment in a letter to the *Elmira Advertiser* thus refers to a visit from Major Dickinson: "The Colonel has just returned to camp, and the Hon. A.B. Dickinson came up in company with him. Mr. D. looks very hale and hearty and to day he was out to witness the Battalion drill, and how I wish you could have seen our men perform their evolutions—Why, if they had been veterans in good earnest, they could not have done better; so it seemed to me. After Major Colby had put them through for about an hour, they were formed in a hollow square, and Mr. D. was invited to make a speech, which he did to the satisfaction of all who heard him. His words were of the most encouraging character; hopeful in every respect, with assurances that the people of the United States would sustain the Government, and that the rebellion would soon be put down, and that too, without foreign intervention. When he closed his remarks, he was honored with three rousing cheers and a 'tigers' after which our time honored flag was remembered in the same manner."[43]

"From the 107th Regiment N.Y.S.V.—We gladly give place to the following which has been transmitted to us with a request to insert:

"Camp 107th Regt. N.Y.S.V.
Hope landing, Va. March 28, 1863

"At a meeting of the officers of the 107th Regt. N.Y.S.V., on the occasion of the resignation and departure of Captain James H. Miles, Col. A.S. Diven was called to the chair, and Captain H.D. Donnelly chosen as Secretary.

"Major N.T. Colby, then made some very appropriate remarks, stating the object of the meeting, and his regret that the Captain was about to leave the Regt. After which, remarks were made by Captain Baldwin and others. Captain Miles responded in a brief but affecting manner. Major N.T. Colby, Captains N.E. Rutter, and H.D. Donnelly were appointed a committee to draft resolutions appropriate to the occasion."[44]

March 28, 1863 Major Newton Colby was promoted to Lt. Col.[45]

March 31, 1863 Gen. Williams wrote to his daughter—"Did I tell you how highly my division was complimented by General Hooker and staff at the recent review? He pronounced it the best he had seen in the army."[46]

"Sergeant Ferguson, Co. I., 107th Reg. in a 'poetical' letter recites the exploits of John Brown, Sergeant of same Co. Both were in the hospital at Frederick City, Md.

"P.S.-John arrived this evening, having been honorably discharged in consequence of being disabled from an injury to one of his feet, caused by a fragment of a shell, at Antietam.

"We copy the last stanza of the 'pome.'

> "The Corning boys were not slow,
> They were ready at every command,
> John Brown fought till he lost his toe
> To save old Maryland."[47]

Snow fell Easter Sunday, April 5.[48]

Gen. Williams reports, "We have had ten days of reviews—the President and Mrs. Lincoln and family came down and spent a week or more, reviewing the troops."[49]

April 14, 1863 Roads finally improving—however, pouring rain today.[50]

"Henry Insho, Commissary Sergeant of the 107th Reg. died last Friday, at the residence of his parents, near Lawrence. He was a clerk in the Eire Railway Office Corning, when the Regiment was formed and enlisted in Co. I, and was soon promoted to the position above stated. We learn that he was about to receive a commission as 2d. Lieut., so well had he discharged his duties. He died of fever while on a visit home. His age was twenty-two years."[51]

"Lieut. Col. Colby of the Regiment is home on a brief furlough. He went out as Captain of Co. I, and by his manifest fitness for the position, was promoted to the post of Major, when a vacancy occurred, and he is now commissioned as Lieut. Col. He is amply qualified by experience and ability for the duties of his new position."[52]

Lt. Col. Newton T. Colby. Colby family collection.

CHAPTER 14

The Chancellorsville Campaign

On the 26th of April, the 107th New York with the Twelfth Corps broke camp at Hope Landing and marched to Stafford Court House, Virginia. The camp that they left had taken its toll on the regiment as there was much sickness and death. The many dead were buried at Hope Landing and later removed to the Fredericksburg Cemetery. A large stone that had been in place at their camp is now on display at Chatham House across the river from Fredericksburg. The physical work and weather conditions that they would face in the next few weeks would be second in severity only to the enemy.

Lt. Col. Colby did not complain of any illness at this time but he had been warned sometime past to take care of himself. He appeared to be on the verge of coming down with the fever but seemed to avoid it while at Hope Landing. We have but one letter from Colby, dated April 29, concerning the Chancellorsville campaign. Due to fatigue, weather and an already weakened constitution he eventually contracted the fever.

The 12th Corps moved on the 27th, marching 12 miles to Hartwood Church.[1]

Brig. Gen. A.S. Williams wrote: "My division struck tents at daylight, carrying on the person of each man and officer eight days' rations, which means hard bread, coffee, and sugar which filled not only haversacks but knapsacks—left wagons behind—Ammunition was packed on seventy old mules—pleasant day—terrible roads—pioneer corps were busy at work cutting new roads through the pines—Reached Hartwood CH (3 P.M.) encamped, each brigade in the woods, on a pretty little rivulet. It was rather a 'bivouac,' though most of our men carried their shelter tents."[2]

Tuesday, April 28, 1863   The 12th Corps marched 19 miles to Kelleys Ford on the Rappahannock.³

Brig. Gen. A.S. Williams continued: "We marched at sunrise, following closely the 11th Corp towards Kelly's Ford. it rained later in the day — misty, drizzling cold rain — I had not moved more than two miles before I ran against the rear (artillery and trains) of the 11th Corps (Howard's) and was obliged to halt for an hour and a half, massing my three brigades in some open fields where the 11th had bivouached. Starting again I reached about noon a place called Grove Church. Massing my men I ordered them to cook dinners and make coffee, giving them an hour to do it." When the men moved out, rain had begun: "Roads were exceedingly slippery, but in spite of all delays and hard traveling I had my three brigades encamped in the woods near the ford by 3 o'clock P.M. We were to cross the Rappahanock on pontoons, and take route to Germanna Ford on Rapidan. ...Two considerable rivers to be crossed and several large and ugly streams in face of the enemy.... We saw the pontoons laid in two or three hours without much opposition. Major-General Slocum, as the ranking major general, commanded the three corps until they were united at Chancellorsville, and [A.S. Williams], for the sixth time became commander of the 12th Corps. The Corps was ordered to advance on the morrow and that we must at all hazards pass the Rapidan."⁴

Wednesday April 29, 1863

"Hooker's plan initially was to disrupt the confederate lines of communication using Stoneman's Cavalry to lure Lee out & thus trapping him between the Union cavalry and infantry. Heavy rain put an end to that idea, the cavalry could not reliably cross the swollen Rapidan. The revised plan was to have three corps stage a demonstration below Fredericksburg, then throw the main bulk of the Union forces (Meade, Howard, & Slocum) on the Confederates left flank after crossing both the Rappahannock and Rapidan. Kelly's Ford, on the Rapidan is about 16 miles upstream of the confluence; Meade, Howard, & Slocum were to cross there, and then split so that Howard and Slocum crossed the Rappahannock at Germanna Ford (about 10 miles upstream from the confluence) while Meade crossed at Ely's Ford, just over 4 miles upstream of the confluence. Sickle's men then joined them by crossing the Rappahannock at U.S. Ford, about a mile down stream from the confluence."⁵

General Williams reported: "Before it was fairly light [about 4:30]— 3rd Brigade (General Ruger's) [of the 1st Division 12th Corps, which included the 107th], was to be the advanced guard, was moving toward the bridge. As we approached the river the sound of cannon and small arms not far to our right, up the river, became more and more frequent and distant. We were, however, all across by 6 o'clock.[6] We now took the road for Germanna Ford, on the Rapidan. The First Division of the Twelfth Corps leading." [7]

Kellys Ford Va. April 29, 1863
Dear Father

You will see by the date of this we have left our Camp at Hope Landing — We have marched two days and this morning crossed the Rappahannock without opposition from the Rebels. Why I know not — unless they expect to get us in a worse place — We have four Army Corps with us — say about 40,000 men — and I think our destination is either Culpeper or Gordonsville — but can not expect to get either place without heavy fighting — Our Corps Commander [Major General Henry Slocum] is in command of all the troops and Hooker who was here last night — has — they say gone back to Fredericksburg — My idea is that our folks will advance on Richmond by Suffolk and backwater — by Fredericksburg and by Gordonsville — three routes — I am sanguine we shall beat them — but it will cost heavily — I send you my watch — Elder Crane takes it to Washington will there express it to you — Keep it for me and we will fix up our matters when I come home — The march has prevented my writing to Henry — but tell him that I will do so as soon as I am able — I hope to come out all right and sound — but of course there is no telling — I heard the first cannon just as I write — so the enemy are probably close by — We are falling in and the shots are more frequent.

Give my love to Mother

Ever Yours
Newton[8]

General Williams went on: "...something less than 200 cavalry preceded us as an advance guard, and soon began the crack of carbines with cavalry pickets of the Rebels."[9] Ruger's Brigade (including the 107th) was pushed forward as an advance guard, with skirmishers well to the front, and two regiments moving by the right of companies to the front on either side of the road. [10] "A few miles out we had to ford a small stream swollen by yesterday's rain, wetting the feet of the men, but no obstacle to our march. I [Williams] moved a long line of skirmishers stretching a mile on

14. The Chancellorsville Campaign

either side of the road and then two regiments marching in the fields by the lead of companies. Other regiments and brigades followed the road.... About 2 o'clock we began to approach the hills which overlook the course of the Rapidan. The crack of rifles increased in volume."[11]

"We pushed the inconsiderable opposition rapidly to the Rapidan, and, by a sudden deployment of two regiments to the right and left of the front, so enveloped the line of retreat that nearly the whole force of the enemy (bridge-builders and guard) surrendered after a feeble resistance; about 125 prisoners were taken. The Rapidan at this point is not very broad, but its banks are high and the ford deep, rocky, and rapid. The First Division began at once with marked spirit and cheerfulness to ford the river"[12]; "...the infantry came up and finding the shallowest track went in with a scream and a yell, holding one another's hands and wading to their armpits with cartridge boxes slung on their bayonets."[13]

"By late afternoon on the twenty-ninth, after crossing the Rappahannock and Rapidan rivers, Hooker concentrated his Union forces near Chancellorsville...."[14] "We were established in a strong position in bivouac through the woods, across the peninsula formed by a sharp curve of the stream. Bridge-builders were detached on reaching the river, and in an hour or so a practical bridge for infantry was constructed, over which the Second Division and Eleventh Corps passed dry-shod.[15]

"The rain began to fall before night, but as we were all pretty wet and our boots full of water, it mattered little and the men were as cheerful as in gayest sunshine ... wet feet, wet clothes, wet blankets, and on wet ground."[16]

From the regimental papers of the 107th regimental New York:

April 29, 1863 The regiment marched to and across the Rapidan.[17] "By the morning of April 30, Hooker would have about 54,000 men at Lee's rear."[18]

Thursday, April 30, 1863 "...a dismal, drizzling morning ... at 8 o'clock Gen. Williams was ordered to start to advance toward Chancellorsville and feel carefully the way ... the road was an old, worn-out plank road, full of holes and gullies and very slippery from the rain, the mud on the planks were left being a foot or so deep."[19]

Chancellorsville was a single house whose place in history is due to its position at the crossing of two main highways. General Hooker made it his headquarters, and around it surged the terrific battle of May 1-3.[20]

General Williams wrote: "We commenced taking up position as soon as we arrived. Our left was directly in front of the Chancellorsville house in some rifle pits made by the Rebels, running in a circular shape through a belt of woods and crossing a deep ravine near a place called Fairview, ran through the woods beyond and struck the plank road, on which we had been marching, a mile and a half west of Chancellorsville.[21] Geary's division took the advance, and moved with very little opposition. Near Old Wilderness Tavern the enemy's cavalry, with a section of artillery, made some demonstration on our right, which was easily brushed away by a regiment of infantry sent in turn from each division, while the command and trains were passing, to hold the road that intersects from the south at this point. The line was continued on by the First Division in a circular line to a point on the Old Wilderness Plank road, about 1½ miles west. Barricades or breastworks of logs and rifle-pits were at once made and trees felled at proper points as abatis. An advanced line of barricades and small intrenchments were made by General Ruger to cover the open space half a mile or so in our front, where the enemy had manifested a disposition to annoy us, and from which on subsequent days he inflicted great damage on our lines."[22]

Col. A.S. Diven, 107th New York, reported: "We arrived in Chancellorsville on Thursday April 30, and after forming with the Brigade in line of battle, I was ordered to place my regiment to support New York Battery No. 1, in position at the white house and graveyard south of the Plank road. I formed in the skirt of the wood, along a slight ravine near the left of the battery, and bivouacked for the night. We occupied this position until about noon Friday, when I joined the brigade on its advance with the division along the Plank road."[23]

General Hooker took supper with General Slocum.[24]

General Williams observed: "It was a pleasant moonlit night.... It was a gay and cheerful scene. We had been successful ... thought it to be an overwhelming victory. General Hooker complimented the operations of 5th, 11th, and 12th Corps."[25]

Friday, May 1, 1863 "Meade, Sickles, Couch, Howard and corps commanders were all at Hooker's headquarters at the Chancellors House. Hooker had said "God Almighty could not prevent his destroying the Rebel Army."[26]

When General Williams resumed command of the First Division, he was ordered by the major-general commanding the corps to proceed down the Plank road toward Fredericksburg, sweeping the woods and fields. He reported: "The poor fellows, had marched an average of fifteen miles a day over hard, muddy roads and were carrying sixty pounds on their backs for four days, they were not only not weary or disheartened, but they seemed panting to meet the Rebels. They had marched without stragglers and they went out to battle without skulkers. They marched out some two miles, Williams' division on the left of the road, Geary's on the right and marched through the densest kind of pine thickets and underbrush. The Rebels were throwing shells at them and their pickets were popping away at their skirmishers. On they went and finally came to an open field, across which Knipe rushed his brigade and seized a belt of wood beyond. Here the engagement on the right became brisk and Williams halted Knipe to connect their line on the left and put the reserve in position. Rebel earthworks were just ahead and they had lost but few men, luckily their shell and shot had gone over them."[27] "During most of our advance we were under artillery fire, which however, inflicted no injury. I had crossed some open fields, perhaps 2 miles in advance on Chancellorsville, to a point where the first sight was obtained of the enemy's intrenchments and rifle-pits, and had halted Knipe's brigade to establish my line and put the reserve brigade in position. My skirmishers were sharply engaged with those of the enemy, and the troops seemed never so eager to engage, when an order was received to return to my original position, which was done in good order and without loss. Two or 3 men were killed and 7 or 8 wounded among my skirmishers in the advance."[28]

"Hooker now had 3 corps in the battle area ... but unnerved by the aggressiveness of the less numerous confederates — he had withdrawn his troops to the area near Chancellorsville, placing his least reliable formation, XI corps, on the right flank."[29]

General Ruger reported his division had moved forward toward the enemy, in the direction of Fredericksburg. The line was ordered back just as the skirmishers of the First Brigade had become engaged. The skirmishers of the One hundred and seventh New York were fired on while retiring, and returned the fire.[30]

Col. A.S. Diven of the 107th N.Y. reported: "Joined the brigade on its advance with the division along Plank road. When the line of battle was formed to the left of the road, we were formed in double column in mass on the second line of battle, in the rear of the Second Massachusetts, deployed on the first line. We occupied this position until ordered to fall back. We had, before entering the wood from which we retired, left our knapsacks, and were ordered to take them on our retreat. We had not, however, retired on the same ground by which we had advanced, and were some 400 paces past our knapsacks when we received this order. We faced about, and marched back in the direction of the knapsacks. This brought us to the rear in the retreat, and as I approached the wood where the knapsacks lay, I sent forward Captain Sill and Lieutenant Swayn with a body of skirmishers. Just as our men were taking their knapsacks, our skirmishers were fired upon. They returned the fire with spirit, and did not appear to hear my order to fall back. I hastened up to them, and they obeyed my orders to retire, with reluctance. I am confident they killed several of the enemy, as they were marksmen, and fired with deliberate aim, some of them as many as five times. We rejoined the brigade on the Plank road, and marched to where the line of battle had been established; we on the left of the brigade, the Thirteenth New Jersey on our right. While our men were lying in line of battle here, I was receiving instructions from General Ruger, he sitting upon his horse, when a shell exploded, throwing the earth upon us, and mortally wounding Captain Rutter, of Company I, a promising young officer, beloved by all his comrades for his bravery and other virtues."[31] "Capt. Rutter was mortally wounded by an eight pound shell, which did not burst."[32] "We slept on our arms in this position during the night, and in the morning commenced throwing up breastworks."[33]

According to Col. Hawley the Third Wisconson were not as fortunate. They left their knapsacks also but were not able to retrieve them. They lost knapsacks, shelter-tents, change of clothing, rations of the men, and most of the bedding of officers.[34]

During the night the 12th Corps strengthened and extended their barricades and rifle-pits, and connected the line with the Plank road near an unfinished church, west of Chancellorsville. "The enemy opened a battery from their left front, which was soon silenced by the artillery under Captain Best, chief of artillery of the corps. The enemy's picketts, which attempted to crowd our lines, were also driven back, but I regret to say, with the loss of Lieutenant-Colonel Scott, Third Wisconson Volunteers, and Lieutenant-Colonel Norton, One hundred and twenty-third New York Volunteers, severly, if not mortally, wounded."[35]

Saturday, May 2, 1863

"On the eve of battle, jokes were played; the laughter and jest were as common as if we had been a party of picnickers instead of armed men awaiting the onslaught of thousands in deadly conflict. Morning was of densest fog. The 12th corps breakfasted, as on every morning during the operations, before daylight and as a battle seemed inevitable. They were ordered to strike their few tents and have everything packed for a movement to clear the front. By sunrise their whole front was covered by a very good breastwork of logs."[36]

"General 'Stonewall'" Jackson was then moving his artillery and

14. *The Chancellorsville Campaign* 231

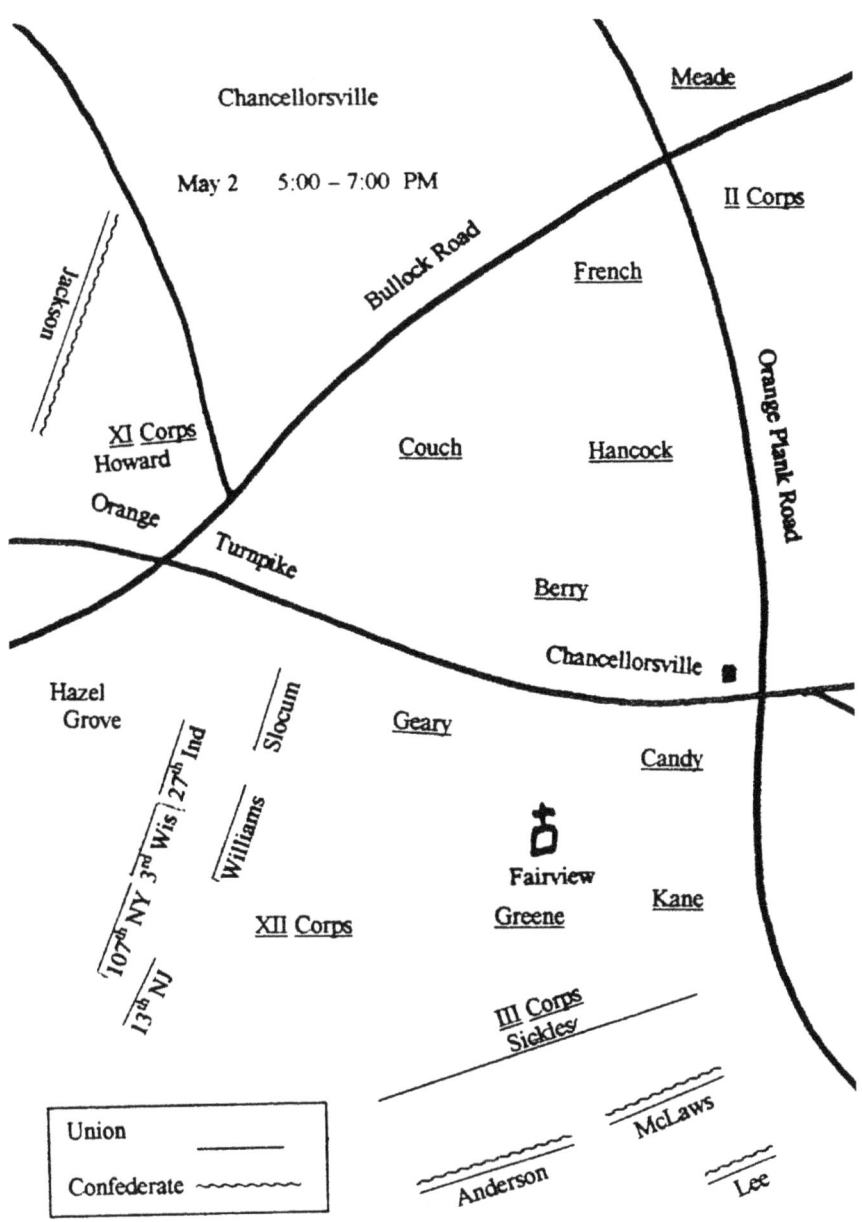

Map of Chancellorsville, May 2, 1862, at 5:00–7:00 P.M.

infantry by a crossroad around our front towards the right and rear of the 11th corps."[37]

Noise of enemy movements was heard all night: "rumor was that at General Hooker's headquarters it was believed the enemy were retreating toward Orange Court House." General Williams "was a dis-believer in the retreat and finally made Knipe send out two or three well known scouts of his command. They returned after an hour and reported" the enemy was massing to the right. He was "entirely satisfied that they were to be attacked from that point."[38] "General Hooker finally accepting the fact that there might be an attack from the right moved the 1st Div. of Slocum's 12th corps, Brig-Gen. A.S. Williams commanding, to fortify a line against the west."[39] "General Williams was aroused from sleep about 1 o'clock P.M. and was told to get his command under arms. He presently came under orders to move out towards his left and front, go two or three miles down through the woods and strike the Fredericksburg plank road as far as possible from Chancellorsville, and then sweep both sides of the plank road towards Chancellorsville house. General Williams was to strike them to the right and rear and drive them towards Geary's barricades. The underbrush was densely thick, almost impenetrable to man. The skirmishers were soon engaged in front, showing that the Rebels were well posted in our movement. They had proceeded perhaps two miles from their camp; Knipe's brigade on the right was sharply engaged, and they were driving the enemy before them. An order was brought to General Williams to return at once and reoccupy his old line."[40]

"Lee had sent Jackson with cavalry and infantry on a march taking them around to the right rear of the Union line. At about 4 o'clock the Third Corps of General Sickles was moved out to the right of the 12th corps and encountered Jackson's cavalry. The message was sent to General Slocum that Jackson was in retreat and that he should advance his line and capture all he could."[41]

Hooker thought that the Rebels were in retreat.... "After an all day march, Jackson had gone into position, hidden by the dense under brush, on the Union right flank."[42]

"When Sickles moved his brigade to attack Jackson's rear guard on the Catherine Furnace Road [while Jackson was circling the Union right] he created a gap about a mile long from Hazel Grove to the right of the Twelfth Corps."[43] "What they did not realize was that it was only Jackson's rearguard as he was encircling the union right. After about 9 hours Jackson was in position on the Union right rear. ...At about 6 P.M. the Confederates charged the Union camp from the wilderness. The union was totally unprepared as they relaxed in camp for the evening. They didn't believe the wilderness was penetrable and did not heed a warning."[44]

14. The Chancellorsville Campaign

The 11th corps on the right was being attacked almost in the rear of the 12th Corps. As Williams cleared the underbrush where the open space lies in front of Fairview and behind the woods where his entrenchments were, he saw the immense mass of fugitives and heard the yells of the pursuing Rebels. There was mass confusion among officers and men and he saw at once that all effort to organize such a body of men was fruitless. The pursuing Rebels were advancing.[45] It was now becoming dark. There was heavy fire on the right. The 11th corps had broken.

Col. Diven was directed by an orderly of General Ruger to change his position and to form on the left of the Second Massachusetts. He gave the order to march by the left flank and led the way. When he arrived at the new position he realized he only had two companies with him. Going in pursuit of the rest of his regiment he found them in much confusion and broken in to fragments. With the help of Captain Scott he was able to get them into line.[46] "As soon as the two leading rebel brigades cleared the underbrush, they were met by a battle line that had been set up directly in front of them. Without a halt, and with a cheer that made the woods and the open space ring, the whole line rushed into the woods. The Rebel advance was checked at once and fell back within fifteen minutes, almost without resistance.

"It was the fire of Hooker's massed artillery at Fairview Cemetery"[47] "and the 1st Division, 12th corps, that had stopped an exalting enemy pursuing a disorganized and broken corps and which had reached within half a mile or less of the headquarters of the commander of the army!"[48]

Col. Diven reported that his major had been wounded the previous day and that he had no adjutant or sergeant-major and his lieutenant-colonel [Colby] had left him this morning, saying he wanted to see Captain Rutter, who was mortally wounded and eventually died this day. Although Lt. Col. Colby had promised faithfully not to be gone over half an hour, due to his own illness he did not return to the regiment until Tuesday.[49]

Because of the illness that Lt. Col. Colby had been fighting for some time and the exposure and fatigue that the regiment was experiencing, he was finally weakened by typhoid fever during this campaign. Colby went to the hospital on Saturday morning, May 2, to be with his close friend, Major Rutter, who had been mortally wounded the previous day. However, because of his own weakened condition, Colby was unable to return to his regiment until sometime Tuesday, May 5. He may have also had a hand in seeing to it that Rutter's body was returned to Elmira where he was reported buried on May 4.

"It was about 8 P.M. that Jackson was wounded by his own troops while making a reconnaissance in front of his own lines. Jackson died on May 10th of complications resulting in pneumonia."[50]

Williams ordered a new line to be taken up along the interior edge of the woods in front of the ravine near Fairview. "The night was passed in throwing up along our whole line such defenses of logs and earth as was possible from the scarcity of tools at hand. The ammunition was also fully replenished to all the regiments from the division pack train. They slept on our arms in position along the road."[51]

"All became silent — after midnight, air became unpleasantly cold ... back at the log shanty at Fairview it was full of wounded, and around the fires fellows boiling coffee in large camp kettles."[52]

On the morning of [Sunday] May 3, General A.S. Williams reported his line was as follows: "two regiments connected to the left of Berry's Brigade, just in advance of Fairview on the Plank road from Chancellorsville to the Wilderness. Ruger's brigade completed the line along the inner edge of the woods to the angle of our breastworks, where it crossed the ravine eastward, to connect with Geary's Division in the woods in front of Chancellorsville."[53]

"Hazel Grove was occupied on Sunday, May 3, by Gen. J.E.B. Stuart after Gen. Sickles' Third corps had been pulled back to connect with the Twelfth Corps. With 30 guns, Stuart shelled the Third and Twelfth Corps."[54] "The 107th, after laying under fire about one hour, four of our left companies ordered to advance to support the 27th Indiana, who were surounded; in about ½ hour the rest of our regiment advanced, and then we opened fire which we kept up for 1½ hour. It was here that our regiment met with the most of its loss in killed and wounded."[55] "By afternoon the Rebels were north of River Rd and Plank rd — between Chancellorsville and Wilderness church. The yankees were in a strong position, however, surrounded except for north path to U.S. Ford."[56]

"Hooker for some reason had not taken up the offensive again even though he greatly out numbered the Rebel troops, now he was beaten and contained by a lesser force."[57]

Monday, May 4, 1863 Another warm, sunny day. "General Williams fortified his position as best he could, and knowing the 11th was on his right, he feared the enemy might break through there and wanted to be ready."[58] "Lee attacked in the afternoon but the Union was able to withstand the attack — this was the last battle of the campaign — the Union held off until nightfall, — withdrawing in good order across the Rappahannock (via Scott's Ford) under cover of darkness."[59]

Tuesday, May 5, 1863 Lt. Col. Colby returned to his regiment after being at the hospital since Saturday. Williams wrote: "we ate broiled pork on sticks and hardtack."[60] "As it looked like rain we put up our tents,"[61]

14. The Chancellorsville Campaign

"we had a very severe storm about 3 o'clock brought on a heavy storm of thunder, lightning, and rain, followed by a steady cold rainstorm."[62] "About 8 o'clock orders came to strike tents without noise; stood in line until 2 o'clock A.M."[63] "The rain continued to pour ... the bridge was washed away once only to be repaired."[64] "They had made two bridges out of what had been four before the rain."[65] "We were ordered to pitch tents again; broke camp at 4 o'clock A.M."[66]

"It wasn't until after daylight [May 6] that William's corp was able to cross."[67]

Gen. A.S. Williams, including A.S. Diven's 107th NY, recrossed the Rappahannock at the United States Ford using the pontoon bridges. They were the rearmost division of the army except the rear guard of Meade's Fifth Corps.[68] "The roads were now very muddy, and it was still raining."[69] Williams' division reoccupied its old camp at Stafford Court House.[70]

By Thursday, May 7, General Williams, who was back at Stafford Court House, whence he departed two weeks before, writes: "After ten days of great hardship, exposure, and privations we are back again with a diminished and dispirited army. We crossed the Rappahanock yesterday morning the whole army moving after midnight over pontoon bridges. My division was the last to escape, except the rear guard."[71]

"I am by no means cheerful because I think this last [battle] has been the greatest of all bunglings in this war. I despair of ever accomplishing anything so long as generals are made as they have been."[72]

General Williams was very critical of the way that officers were promoted to generalships while men in the field such as himself were passed over. Many officers seemed to have good press men and often received credit for the efforts of others.

From the *Corning Journal*:
"107th Regiment — We have no news further than the death of Captain. Rutter, of Elmira Co. I. (Corning Co.): Capt. Nathaniel E. Rutter, Co. I., 107th Regiment was killed near Chanscellorville, Va., by a shell on Friday. He was from Elmira, where he was buried yesterday. [May 4] He was Capt. of the Corning Co. I., having been promoted when Lieut. Col. Colby became major. He is said to have been a worthy and competant officer. He was but 22 years old."[73]

"Disease during the war was a major killer of our fighting men in the field. One type of disease was typhoid and paratyphoid which claimed many lives were lumped together with malaria as 'typhomalarial fever.' The use of quinine as an anti malarial agent was known but was not readily in the fields."[74]

May 10, 1863 Lt. Col Newton Colby developed typhoid fever—brought on by exposure at Chancellorsville.

May 13, 1862 Regt left Stafford C H and marched to Edwards Ferry.[75]

A letter to the *Elmira Advertiser* says that "Capt. N. N. Sill, of the 107th was shot through the calf of the leg in the recent battle on the Rappahannock four persons beside Captain Rutter were killed, 54 wounded, and 23 missing. In Co. I., we notice that Corporal Bruce is missing, E.C. Rowley, do., James Kenaly wounded, Dexter Berry lost his speech from concussion by the explosion of a shell."[76]

The *Elmira Press* reported that Col. Diven of the 107th had resigned and that Lt. Col. Colby would doubtless be appointed Colonel.[77] Unfortunately, this never came to be, as Lt. Col. Colby was stricken with typhoid fever and was forced to leave the regiment.

The following information is from an Invalid claim for pension dated October 4, 1879. This establishes the presence of Lt. Col. Newton T. Colby at the battle of Chancellorsville: "I was never seriously ill or treated for disease while in the Army until March or April 1863 — That I am able to fix accurately the date of the first attack — inasmuch as all my papers and memoranda were carried away when the regiment left me — sick and delirious at or near Stafford Court House Va.-and I never saw them after — but that I truly believe it was some time in March or April — because the regiment went on to Chancellorsville campaign not long thereafter — That at or near the time referred to I remember that the Surgeon Dr Flood said to me 'You are looking badly — if you are not careful you will be down with this fever' — and that he then prescribed for me — that the regiment was then located at Hope Landing on Acquia Bay — by the side of an extensive marsh and that Typhoid fever greatly prevailed in the Regiment and that very many deaths occurred from it there. That I firmly believe that I contracted the disease while there and that I was not well from that time until after the battle of Chancellorsville and when the regiment reached Stafford Court House. Though I endeavored to keep up — and did not take to bed until reaching said location where I was very ill — during which illness the Regiment moved away leaving me here too sick to be moved and that I was treated by the Regimental Surgeon...."[78]

When Colby's regiment moved on, he was left at Stafford Ct House. Newton's brother Henry became aware of Newton's illness and went to Virginia to attend to him. The following letter is from Henry to their father Merrill back home; spelling and grammar are original.

14. The Chancellorsville Campaign

Read this to your self first
Mrs. Moulton's — two miles from Hope landing
Tuesday June 3d 1863
Dear Father

I wrote this morning to have you come then said wait and I would telegraph. This will go out in the morning and may get to you at the same time of the other and may one day later. This afternoon the young Doc came over and with him Doc Leone. I sent for Doc Leone by a sargent and he came. They had some talk, he thought young Doc was all right and told Newton to follow his directions, but changed the medicine by giving it in Rum and not so often. We must wash him all over once a day and young Doc sent a young man over to help me — which is a great rest — Doc Leone caled me out and said it would be at least two weeks before he could get out and said I might send for his wife which would comfort him *and if he should happen to worse twould be handy*. Now Newton has said all along dont write anything that will scare them — but said he would like to see you but could not afford to have you both. Now dont show this to Mary for it would make her feel bad, but she would want to come and she could not do much and there is not room here for both so keep this to yourself and do just as you think best. From what they came to the conclusion they do not think him so dangerous as many cases. One thing they all say that he is worring [wearing] himself out by freting. He frets becaus he cant get well in one or two or three days and Eld Crane told him that if he did not stop he would not live one week and that is a fact — now see how I am placed — if he gets well (which undoubtly he will) you would say all of you that you were sorry that you had come — if he went the other way you — mother and Mary would say, Oh, why didnt you write and always think me almost his murder — so you see how I am situated this will go in the morning. I will put in how things are one thing I honestly think and so they that his fever is broke that he has seen the worst — but a relaps once more would make short work, this is nothing but a relaps which he is now recovering from slowly and once more such a turn is good bye — this was brought on probably by eating he got a can of peaches of the sutler and it made me feal bad to see him eat them he was right smart and almost scolded me for teling him not to eat them then came the eggs. I told him that Doc Yade would no more let him eat them than so much so leather no mater if they were rais dou but down they went and down came him in les than no time. You know what Newton is when he is not well — this morning I told him I had sent for Leone he swore at me strong and when

I told him young Flood was intoxicated he ript awfaly — I told Crain that he was not old enough and I told him I deamed it my duty to tel him that Flood was in liquor. He said he never saw him so before but said that he smelt his breath last evening and said to that those fellows that wer with him wer drunk. Yet with that and his being so young and inexperianced he thought John Flood or Doc Flood Jr was all right, perfectly capable of sertainly nice young man — told me he was sorry that I wrote for you to come or hinted of your coming — sum it up — he is not over twenty — gets full often — has got on hand a silver case — and comes to see his patient so much under the influence of Liquor that the ladies notice and speak of it. I say I am right, I dont care who says contrary. I am looking out for Newton and I shall as long as I am here in spite of any one — When they all say get some one that knows something, when they all say he gets drunk once or twice a day and when I see it then i am going to do something my self — Just now Doctor Scheppel, Brigade Surgeon, came in to see Newton, a splendid man, I had a long talk with him. He used to attend the same institute that Doc Tesbele did, he is quite along in years. He staid and talked with Newton some time. He is a Free mason. I will tell you some time how he came to come here. He has more to say than Leone, that is more power — he told Newton that he was going to be sick a good while and proposed some new things — and he didnt care if Newton did not eat anything. If you are on the way all right if not all right —

Newton requested you to come and come alone last night, but do as you think best no fever this morning. When you come bring $7.00 and I will go home and see to things. Every thing looks like a desert on us or movement of oue Army [sic]

Good bye My love to mother Em Net all

Yours truly Henry[79]

Newton's father, then residing in Corning, N.Y., was advised that Newton was dangerously ill and to come at once. This he did, accompanied by Newton's wife Mary. They then moved Newton by ambulance to Acquia Bay and by steamer to Washington, D.C. He was taken by his father, who accompanied him to a boarding house on Pennsylvania Ave. Newton was carried up the stairs by persons who were passing by at the time, it being very early in the morning. His father reported his case to the Surgeon General's office and he was attended to by Surgeon General Barnes and another surgeon detailed from the Surgeon General's Office. He was treated at Washington from June 15 to July 7, 1863, and when partially recovered was then granted leave of absence for 30 days. He started home for Corning, N.Y., but was compelled to stop in Philadelphia a week while en route, being still too weak to endure the fatigue of travel.[80]

From the *Corning Journal*: "A paragraph stating that Lt. Col. Colby of the 107th Regiment was dangerously ill with typhoid fever, was mislaid last week. His wife and father were telegraphed to and went at once to the camp near Stafford Court House, Va. We are glad to learn that the fever has abated, and although very much prostrated there is good reason to believe that he is recovering."[81]

Washington June 19th 1863
Dear Mother

I can write you but a word or two, but know you are so anxious. I hardly know what to write about Newton, only he is no worse; neither can I say he is any better — He is so completely prostrated it seems as if nature will never help him rally. He has not sat up a minute yet, and cannot turn himself in bed yet, and he is a perfect skeleton. Father asked the Doct. this morning if it would do for him to go home, and he said no — not just yet — better wait till the Col improves a little more. Newton says he shall never get well, but his symptoms are good, only he is very weak. I hope when he does commence to pick up it will be fast enough to make up for this long time waiting. He has the best medical attendance — Dr Climer, medical director of the whole city has been to see him twice and it is something very rare for him to visit a patient. The Doct that comes twice a day understands his business. Col Baily was in to see him the other day. Col Crane has come and rejoins the Regt tonight. Maj Campbell was here yesterday — also Dr Hewilt. Since Van Etten gave him a call and is in persuit of Irvine — Thinks he will get a flag of truce to go to Richmond — But we guess he will slip up on it, although if brass will carry anyone through, he will get there. I am very anxious to get home, knowing the little ones must need me — but tell Mary to do the best she can and I will come at the very first moment when it will be safe to move Newton. Father says "tell mother I shall start for home monday, if Newton is no worse" and I wish he was coming too — I know the children must be ragged, but I cant help it. We have not had a line from any of you since we came here and if you write, direct to Washington. I feel anxious to hear from my little flock, and I shall not have to be away a very long time. Give my love to all who may inquire — The Doct says it is a wonder Newton lived through moving him from Stafford here, and says he never saw a person so completely run down — So if any of his good Corning friends think he has not been very sick, they have made a great mistake. He would surely have died if we had not been with him while he was moved and came near anyhow. But Newton says dont write any more and I must stop — write me soon.

In great haste, Mary[82]

"Lt. Col. Colby, of the 107th Regiment arrived in town [Corning] yesterday [July 15]. He had an attack of the typhoid fever about two months since, and for several weeks was in a very critical and is just now regaining his strength."[83]

September 5, 1863   Newton Colby was discharged due to illness.[84]

CHAPTER 15

The Veteran Reserve Corps

"As the government realized that the hope of a ninety day war was not reasonable, the need for continued manpower gave rise to the Invalid Corps. After a few failed attempts to use men that had been ill or wounded; on April 28, 1863, the adjutant general's office in General Order 105, authorized the formation of the Invalid Corps.

"The order originally had three catagories of men that could be included. The new corps was to have three battalions; the first was for those least disabled and still able to serve garrison duty. The second battalion was to include those who had lost an arm or hand or were severly injured enough to only be able to do duty as hospital guards or attendents. The severest and most hopeless cases of disability were to be in the third battalion. This third battalion was never realized, however, and those men were taken into the second battalion. By Oct. 31, 1863 the Invalid Corps had 16 regiments of 491 officers and almost 18,000 enlisted soldiers organized into 200 companies. The name Invalid Corps was also short lived as the men did not like being looked at as being inferior to the other men."[1]

Government Inspectors examined the condition of the belongings of the Government in the possession of an organization, and when in his opinion any property was unfit for further service it was declared condemned and marked with his official brand, I.C., meaning inspected and condemned. This I.C. became a by-word among the men, who made an amusing application of it on many occasions. This is supposed to be the reason that the Invalid Corps (I.C.) was changed to the Veteran Reserve Corps.[2]

March 18, 1864 General Order 111, renamed the Invalid Corps as the Veteran Reserve Corps.[3]

Washington D.C.
Sept 21, 1863
Dear Father

    I enclosed a note to Dr Graves—requesting his certificate as Surgeon of the board of enrollment to my disability and its probable duration. You know he prescribed for me and I want the strongest certificate he will give—in order to obtain the rank of Major in the Invalid Corps I also enclose a circular—in which you will notice what is required of the Surgeon.

    I am precious sick of staying here with nothing to do—and paying 10/—per day for board—and sometimes think I will come home and stay there but the bread and butter question renders necessary some employment and I hope I can get it in the Invalid Corps but it is doubtful—as there are not many officers needed of the rank of Major—which is the highest in the Corps.

    I still am obliged to visit the privy from 2 to 4 and 6 times a day and have little or no appetite and think I am stuck for a seige of Chronic Diarrhea—Dr Flodd voluntarily offered me a strong certificate of disability—but *his* will not do as the order requires that of the enrolling Surgeon.

    Tell the Doctor—that he must do the best he can for me in the certificate—as the case will bear him out in making it strong.

    Do not delay a day or an hour—for I am on expense and getting nothing. Direct to me—Care of Mrs Bishop's Boarding House No. 506 H St. Washington. I told you 504 before but that was a mistake No. 506 is correct.

    Why do I not hear from home? I have not received a single line or word from any of you since I left—and the order I wrote for has not come—(the order for my discharge I mean)

    Now hurry up and get Graves to give you the Certificate at once if he will. I shall anxiously wait it.

In haste yours as ever
Newton

    P.S. Have the Doctor sign as Surgeon of the enrolling board[4]

    Colby, due to a constitution enfeebled and broken by typhus fever in the field, took the oath of office before a magistrate Dec. 4, 1863, for the Veteran Reserve Corps.

December 5, 1863 Newton Colby was commissioned Lt. Col. in 18th Veteran Reserve Corps.
December 12, 1863 Colby was mustered into the regiment.
December 22, 1863 Lt. Col. Colby was to proceed to Cliffburne Barracks, Meridian Hill, and report to Lt. Col. Calvin H. Frederick.

Ordered by Provost Marshall General M.N. Wisewell[5]
No 506 H St. Washington
Sunday Dec 27 1863
Dear Father

As I have written twice to Mary since my arrival — I suppose you are posted in all that has occurred to me since leaving home — I wrote the last letter to her yesterday — and that I would employ my leisure to day in writing to you — I have not heard a word from home since I left and begin to *think* it time I should — Nothing has turned up yet and I think there is no immediate danger of being sent away — though I intend to use the letters of introduction to Harris and get him to get me on *detached* duty somewhere — Harris is now at home — the houses having adjourned — but will be back before long — The weather is mild and it is raining to day — so I do not attend service — I learn that Congress is going to do away with the 2d Battallion of the Invalid Corps (the 2d battallion is composed of cripples and men unfit for almost all kinds of duty) and put all who are capable of light duty in the 1st bat — and pension the balance — I live in "fear and trembling" lest they raise a row about something and upset me — but I must say that I have seen fifty officers who look better and stronger then I. I lead rather a lazy life just now — but am studying pretty hard to get posted in *everything*. I have learned that it was supposed to have been me who had been in the Old Capitol by some!!

When Harris gets back I intend to try him for assistance to get a detail. Tell Cale Clark he can get a place in the navy yard here without any doubt — as there are two or three Naval Officers of my acquaintance who have so assured me —

Give my love to mother and remember me kindly to Em and Nettie and believe me

Affectionately Yours
Newton[6]

No. 506 H St Washington
Sunday Eve Jany 31st 1864
Dear Father

    Very unaccountablly I have received but one letter from you since I left. I am still here — and am like to be for some time — if my information is correct — for I have been informed that I was to be detained here for special duty — such as being a member of boards and courts martial and c and c. They told me so at the I.C. Bureau — but I have been told by other officers — that little reliance could be placed on it — for they say there is a new shuffle of the cards every day — A few days ago (so one of the Clerks of the Department told me) an order was made for me to go to the City of Detroit and take command of a Regiment there — but for some reason a change was made and some one else sent. I am uneasy and shall be — until I am sent away — lest some mischance happens and I lose my place — I am doing literally nothing and have not had anything to do since I came here — only to eat and sleep and time hangs heavy on my hands. I very much wish to get my orders to join my Regiment at Indianapolis — as everything is much cheaper there than here — and I could do better every way. But I suppose I must be patient and wait the developments of time — There is very little new here — The weather for a week past — has been delightful — *too* warm — in fact — for comfort — but *now* it is cloudy and lowery and occasionally rainy — and colder. Expenses are enormous here — for everything — and I think there is not a city in the Union where you get so little for your money — Where the *necessaries* cost so much — the smallest outlay for comfort or amusements — seems like the "inch on a mans nose" — added to them — so I avoid them all I can — My position *requires* some expenses — beyond what would be necessary to a private citizen. Col Woodward (a son of the would be govenor of Pennsylvania — Copperhead candidate I mean) commands Cliffburne Barracks — and I am somewhat acquainted with him — He is great hearty looking young fellow — weighing about 200 and as robust looking an *Invalid* as you ever saw. How he got the place — except it was because his Father is a notorious Copperhead judge — who decided on the bench of the Pennsylvania Supreme Court — against the legality of drafting men to fight our battles — I am sure I cant immagine. Maj. L. Skinner (of Nunda) has been sent to Chicago to a regiment there — and went several days ago.

    Well I must close — as it is late. I have not been very well for a day or two — and suppose it is a result of the change in the weather — and hope it is nothing serious — Write very soon and tell me all the news. Give my love to Mother and Henry and Mary if she says she wants it and believe me

15. The Veteran Reserve Corps

Very Affectionately Yours
Newton[7]

Special Orders, War Department,
Adjutant General's Office,
No 36. Washington, February 17th, 1864

    Lieutenant-Colonel Newton T. Colby, Invalid Corps, is hereby relieved from further duty at Cliffburne Barracks, Washington, D.C., and will proceed to Indianapolis, Indiana, and report to colonel Charles F. Johnson, Commanding 18th Regiment Invalid Corps, for duty with that regiment.

By order of the Secretary of War:
E.D. Townsend,
Assistant Adjutant General[8]

CHAPTER 16

Camp Morton: Prison at Indianapolis

"In 1861 the Indianapolis Fairgrounds was a favorite spot for Methodist camp meetings. The park was located on 36 acres of the old Henderson farm. There was an excellent water supply from deep wells and a stream ran through one end of the property. An abundance of maple and walnut trees made the area one of the prettiest of the suburbs. With the coming of the Civil War, Governor Morton converted the Fairgrounds into a training facility for Indiana soldiers and the park was renamed Camp Morton. In 1862 the camp was changed into an internment center for Confederate prisoners-of-war and barracks were built to accommodate 3,000 men. The buildings were flimsily constructed from lumber that had been used for cattle sheds and designed on the theory that the war would soon be over."[1]

Newton T. Colby was assigned to Burnside Barracks on Feb. 17, 1864, to 18th Regiment Veteran reserve corps.[2]

Military Police Notice
Headquarters Provost Marshall's Office
Indianapolis, Ind., Feb. 17, 1864.

The following orders are published for the benefit of all concerned:
I. All soldiers whatsoever found in any part of the city in a state of intoxication, or creating any disturbance or making use of indecent language in public, will be arrested and sent to the General Guard House.
II. Soldiers or inferior officers belonging to any of the camps in the vicinity, must be protected by passes duly approved by the commanding

officer of their camp, otherwise they will be placed in arrest, or, in case of enlisted men, put under guard by the Provost Marshall and held until returned to their proper camps.

III. All soldiers of whatsoever command found lounging about drinking saloons or in any of the streets of the city after nine o'clock at night, will be taken in charge by the guards and patroles and confined in the guard house. And officers or men found at any time in houses of ill fame will be arrested by the patroles, and the names of all such officers, with the charges specified, will be sent up to Department Headquarters.

IV. Officers in command of or belonging to troops passing through or temporarily quartered in the city, will be held to account for any disorder in their commands.

V. Capt. Hugh Middleton, Co. D, 17th Regiment I.C., Provost Marshall for the city of Indianapolis, is charged with execution of these orders.

A.J. Warner, Col. 17th Regiment I.C.
Comd'g Military Forces in the City of Indianapolis.[3]

"We understand that orders have been given to the Provost Guards to arrest all officers in saloons, disreputable places, and lounging at hotels, & c., absent from and neglecting their men. These orders will be rigidly enforced, and will work a most salutary reform in a quarter where it is much needed."[4]

Generals Orders No. 2
Headquarters City Provost Marshall's Office,
Indianapolis, Indiana, Feb. 19, 1864.

1. All officers and men visiting the city on passes, or temporary quartered here are required to wear their uniforms. Recruits not yet supplied with uniforms are alone expected. [sic] The Provost Marshal will cause the arrest of all who neglect or disregard this order.

2. Citizens are prohibited by act of Congress from purchasing or obtaining any article of regulation clothing from soldiers, and any person found wearing any part of the United States uniform will be considered a soldier.

3. Soldiers, while in the city, unless they are on duty, will not be allowed hereafter to wear side arms. All such arms will be taken possession of by the Provost Marshall, and turned over to the Ordnance officer, unless called for by the soldier's company commander.

By order of A. J. Warner,
Colonel 17th Regiment Invalid Corps,

Comd'g Military forces of Indianapolis.
Official H. Middleton,
Capt. and City Provost Marshall.[5]

Special Order No. 16
Headquarters District of Indiana,
Indianapolis, Feb. 22d, 1864.

  III. Colonel A. J. Warner, 17th Regiment Invalid Corps, is hereby appointed Commandant of the Post of Indianapolis. His command will not include Camps Morton and Burnside, which will constitute a separate post, under the command of Colonel A.J. Stevens, of the 5th Regiment Invalid Corps. These officers will be obeyed and respected accordingly.

By command of J.S. Johnson,
Col. U.S.A. Com'ding Post.
H.S. Greenwalt, Lieut. and A.A.A.G.[6]

Indianapolis, Indiana
Feby 25th 1864
Dear Father

  To redeem the promise I made you upon leaving home — I sit down to inform you — at once — of my safe arrival at my destination. I made the trip without the occurrance of anything worthy of record getting here last night —(Wednesday night)— about 10 P.M. When I arrived at Cleveland I felt so free from fatigue — that I decided to go on and accordingly took a train waiting for us for Crestline — where we were again to change cars and where I was told — I could get a sleeping car — but upon arriving there — the train for Indianaplois had been gone ten minutes and there was no other train until about eleven o clock the next forenoon — and it was then about 11 at night — There being no help for it — I went to a hotel and stayed out the night —
  This morning I went to the barracks of my Regiment and found them about 1½ miles out of the city — or rather in the outskirts of the place — They are in board shanties or houses and are pleasantly located — I expect you are anxious to hear how I was pleased with the appearance of this city — but I will forbear trying to give you my impressions — both because I have seen so little of it — and because I could not now say that it has very greatly pleased me. In fact I am not at all ashamed to confess that I am a little homesick! Now laugh if you want to-while I — as Nettie would say "scratch where it itches" — I found two very official looking documents

awaiting me — one — an order to come here from the Secretary of War — and the other the Official report of the board who examined me — They say they found me "competent to hold my rank and effectively discharge all the duties pertaining to my position" so I think I have got along with that matter — for the present.

But I tell you I am in a tight place as regards money — for I am about out and have not enough to pay my bill at this hotel — I could not get quarters at the barracks till tomorrow.

Col Johnson of my Regt is rather a clever fellow I should judge — He has no idea that he failed to pass his examination and of course I have told him nothing. There are two or three field officers here who are cited to appear before the board to be examined and are dreading it badly — and were very anxious to find out what they were to expect —

My Regt and two others are employed in gaurding about 3000 rebel prisoners at Camp Morton — which joins our barracks — They (our regiment) have daily company and battalion drills — non commissioned officers drill and school for officers — so you see I shall be pretty busy — and shall have to get a horse before long — though I shall not hurry —

Well I have told you all the news and must close — as it is near bed time. Give my love to mother and all the folks — Write me as soon as you can and give me all the news.

Affectionately Yours
Newton[7]

March 1, 1864 "A soldier belonging to the 51st Indiana, inebriated and resisting arrest, was shot yesterday by Capt. Middleton, Provost Marshall. One ball struck his head and glanced; another inflicted a slight wound in one of his hands."[8]

March 2, 1864 "Every hotel in the city, yesterday, was crowded. The Palmer, the Bates, the Spencer, the Macy, the Oriental, and Little's, had throngs of guests. Every boarding house was full, and all the restaurants were liberally patronized. Ten thousand people, at least, counting the military, over and above the resident population, were in Indianapolis. This is a common occurrence, of late."[9]

March 2, 1864 "The patroles ordered by the Commandant of the Post are punctually and indefatigably upon their beats, and the result everywhere is seen in the general good order which obtains among the military."[10]

"During the month of February sixty-nine deaths occurred among the rebel prisoners confined in Camp Morton."[11]

"The Provost Guard arrested thirty-six men, including several officers, found at disreputable places, night before last."[12]

General Order No. 2
Headquarters Post Commander
Indianapolis, Ind. March 19th, 1864

Whereas, the unrestricted sale of intoxicating liquors to soldiers, while so many are in the city in an unorganized state, is producing unlimited drunkenness and disorder, tending greatly to the subversion of discipline and the demoralization of the troops at this Post, to the manifest detriment of the public service; giving rise, also to frequent riots and other excesses, extending in many cases to the destruction of property and loss of life, disturbing thereby the peace of the city to the annoyance and danger of citizens; which condition renders it absolutely necessary that more effectual measures of restraint be adopted by the military authorities, in the absence of civil power, than are at present in force: therefore,

From and after this date, and while the present exigency exists, the sale, or giving away, of intoxicating liquors, of any kind, to soldiers, or any soldier, within the limits of this command, by any party or parties whatever, is hereby strictly forbidden.

This order is positive and will be enforced by such means as may be found necessary.

By order of Col. A.J. Warner, Com'd Post
H. Middleton, Capt. and Provost Marshall[13]

"There are some 2,600 prisoners at Camp Morton, and we understand about 600 more are expected from various points in the South this week."[14]

Head Quarters Post
Burnside Barracks
Indiananpolis, Ind.

March 24th, 1864

Special Order No. 46: By request of colonel Conrad Baker A.A.P.M. Genl. for Ind.—Luit Colonel N.T. Colby of the 18th regiment V.R.C. is hereby temporily relieved from duty with said Regiment, and will report without delay for orders to J.S. Simonlow Col. U.S.A. Comdg. district of Indiana and Michigan at Indianapolis, Ind.

By orders of A.A. Stevens
Col. 3d Regt. V.R.C. Comdg. Post[15]

March 24, 1864 "At a saloon on Illinois Street, a day or two ago, several soldiers called and demanded something to imbibe. The proprietor told them that it was against military orders to sell to them. Words ensued, and the soldiers left, to return in a few minutes reinforced. The proprietor met them, pistol in hand, and signified to them that they had better leave the premises. He said that he was simply obeying the instructions of the military authorities, and that they had no business there. Thereupon the soldiers made a rush. The proprietor of the saloon fired. The first man fell, the ball striking him in the breast and glancing downward. He was conveyed to a hospital. His comrades pursuing the matter, the proprietor having retreated, were met upon the stairs of the house by his wife, who told them that she would shoot the first man who attempted to ascend.

"Things like these are certainly all wrong, and we must say that the military authorities here try to prevent them."[16]

"The patrols at Camp Morton occasionally get into squabbles with the rebels. Night before last a reb threw a large stone at a patrol, which struck his cartridge box and made him 'about face.' As yet nothing more serious than this has occurred.

"Tunneling by the rebels in the camp continues, and over a dozen holes have been discovered within a few weeks. They do not accomplish much, but would soon dig out if not closley watched."[17]

The name of the Invalid Corps was, by order of the War Department, changed to that of Veteran Reserve Corps.[18]

"The Sutler's Stand in Camp Morton was burned yesterday afternoon about three o'clock. Nearly all the goods were saved. Nearly a thousand men of the 'Veteran Reserve Corps,' were under arms within minutes from the first alarm, and the goods were secured without trouble. The fire is supposed to have caught from a box of hot ashes in the building. Loss trifiling."[19]

Head Quarters Post Commander
Indianapolis, Ind., April 3d, 1864
My dear Neice

In conformity with the promise I made to your aunt a few days since I devote this quiet Sabboth Evening — to writing to you — "I am well — and hope these few lines will find you enjoying the same blessing" — and many others. I am very comfortably situated here — the city is pleasant — and my duties agreeable — but after all it is not home nor wife to me. Perhaps you will be interested to know what my duties are — and I will tell you. I am in command of the 17th Regt Veteran Corps and of all troops in this city — and also commandant of this post — Perhaps you will understand some of the necessary labor connected with this — but I fear not all of it. I have under me all Patrols and Gaurds stationed in different parts of the city to preserve order (which is no small task where there are several thousands of old troops on furlough all the time) — and liquor and gambling houses to suppress if they violate orders — and the general supervision of all troops in the city — I keep four or five clerks and the Adjutant of the Post busy — and have two or three orderlies to carry dispatches — So you see I have my hands pretty full.

To day I attended church with Col Sweet (President of the Board for the Examination Office) and afterward dined with him at the Bates House — Then I jumped into the saddle and rode down to Burnside Barracks to Dress Parade — and had the honor of an introduction to Capt Cavendish of the British Army — and his wife Mrs Cavendish — The celebrated actress and singer — and one of the very few respectable ladies who follow that profession — and curiously enough I caught myself thinking that her respectability might perhaps be due to her plainess of personal appearance — Well — I took tea with the Officers at the Barracks and just at dark galloped back to my quarters.

Give my warmest regards to your mother and father when you see them again —

This is rather a rambling letter but if you will answer it I will do better next time-

Affectionately your
Uncle Newton[20]

Head Quarters Post Commander
Indianapolis, Ind., April 5th, 1864
Dear Father

Your welcome letter of the 26th of March has just come to hand this morning — The delay in my receiving it is due to the fact that you simply directed it to Indianapolis — without the necessary addition of "Burnside Barracks" I got it by accidentally inquiring at the general delivery of the P.O. So please remember to direct hereafter to me at Burnside Barracks Indianapolis for it is very annoying to have letters miscarry. I expect that Mary has been doing the same for I have not heard from her in a long time. You will see by the heading of my letter that I am still im command of this Post and will understand that I am pretty busy — For instance — I have just returned from a long walk — taken for the purpose of investigating into the facts connected with the murder of one of the men last night in a house of ill fame — He was shot and instantlly killed by a person connected with the house — and as the city authorities here are not remarkable for a sound loyalty — and care not much for the death of a soldier — I have ordered a strict investigation by the Provost Marshal to ascertain if the poor fellow had fowl play. I am of the opinion that *at least*— he was needlessly killed — although he perhaps did enough to give color to the defense set up by his slayer that it was in self defense. This is the second or third instance since I have been here of soldiers meeting their death in these houses of prostitution — and I wish I could hit upon some plan to prevent both such things as the houses and these occurrences.

You remind me that I promised to give you a description of the place and its inhabitants — but it is a difficult task — though I will try. Indianapolis is situated on a very level tract of country — not a hill or even elevation on either side. This would naturally make it rather unhealthy owing to the lack of draining — were it not for the fact that soil which is a rich loam — and very productive — lies upon a very thick bed of gravel — instead of "hard pan" and which of course permits the superflous water to drain through it. The city is well laid out (in fact the level nature of the ground is such as to furnish no excuse for ill arrangements in laying it out) — the streets very long — wide but rather poorly cared for. The first thing that attracted my attention as I came in to the place — (it was after dark) was the great length of the rows of gas lights — giving a very fine effect. Washington Street is the principle business street and there are some quite nice blocks of buildings on it — but unlike our eastern cities — the blocks vary much — and are irregular both in size and height — The principal buildings are the State house — (a neglected looking affair now — but which was evidently *once quite* a fine building) the Assylum for the blind — which is a nice house and with a neat yard surrounding it — the Baptist female College — quite a flourishing institution — and quite a large number of private residences — There are no street cars here — but I am told will be very soon. Business of all kinds seems to be very good now but I imagine that a sudden termination to this war would have a disastrous effect on business here — as else where — Lots are quite high now — but still are freely bought and sold.

Gov Morton resides here — and seems very popular — in fact the pet of the Hoosiers. He has been absent ever since I have been here and I have not had the pleasure of meeting him. I have made but few acquaintances among the citizens — but the few I have met I am much pleased with. They seem to be gentlemen and are especially hospitable and generous hearted to an extreme. I am of the opinion that this would be as pleasant a place to live as any *inland western* town.

The names of the Officers of this Corps are soon to be sent to the senate for confirmation and I intend to write Senator Harris and ask him to see to it — that my name appears on the list — though I have no particular apprehension that it will be left out. Yet it is so easy for an enemy to injure me by leaving my name off the list, that I will do it for precaution. However say nothing about it.

Write often — Tell mother that I will write her the next time I get time to write and give her my love — and Henry and all the folks — Write and tell me everything and believe me

Very affectionately your son
Newton[21]

April 14, 1864 "The patrol guard yesterday had its usual duties redoubled, aided by detachments. About the principal business corners of the city squads were stationed, with muskets and bayonets, to clear the sidewalks of soldiers who had been in the habit of interrupting the free pedestrianism of citizens, and especially of modest ladies. At the Palmer House corner particularly was good work done by the patrol guard in this regard."[22]

April 15, 1864 "Col. Colby. Post commandant, promptly orders the closing of houses where liquor is sold to soldiers contrary to orders."[23]

April 15, 1864 "The Patrol guard of this city exert themselves to maintain order, all slanders against them to the contrary and notwithstanding. They have efficient officers and they are efficient men. They are of the Veteran Reserve Corps and have demonstrated their unflinching valor on bloody battle fields."[24]

"The sale of liquor to soldiers has not entirely ceased, notwithstanding the strict order of the Commandant forbidding it, some time since. Some of the saloon keepers are violating the order, and they may soon get themselves into trouble for so doing."[25]

Head Quarters Post Commander
Indianapolis, Ind., April 16, 1864
Dear Father

Your welcome letter came safely to hand last evening and I reply at once. I thought you would read with some interest the *little incidents* that happen to me in my new place of residence — The spring here is said to be rather backward — but the buds are started out finely and the swallows promise that summer *is really* on the way — April is the rainy month — it having rained almost every day so far — I am still the Post Commander and so far have been able to get along smoothly — that is — as smoothly as is possible for any one to do — The difficulties and annoyances are numerous — not the least of them being to enforce a standing order against the sale of intoxicating liquors to soldiers — I have a gaurd now over one liquor saloon — with orders to permit no soldiers to enter it — which I thought was a better way than to close it up — or to seize their goods — The liquor saloons are very numerous — and it is next to impossible to *entirely* stop their selling — in fact I do not try to stop it altogether — but rather to keep them within bounds — and to exercise a wholesome restraint over them — The city papers speak encouragingly of my efforts and the majority of the citizens — especially the better part of them also seem pleased with them. I have almost made up my mind to ask to be transferred to the Regt. I am now commanding viz the 17th — They have the finest lot of officers and they have unanimously asked me to get transferred — which I consider quite a compliment Maj Genl Heintzelman was here yesterday with Gov Brough of Ohio and Gov Morton of this state — Something important seems to be cooking up — and the Washington Authorities are ordering all of our corps East that can possibly be spared — I look for activity in the field before long and I think Grant will make a desperate push somewhere and one that will tell too. Perhaps we may get a chance in — somewhere and if so — I believe you will be astonished to see what discipline will do for troops — We are not second to any troops in the service in drill and discipline and our parades are the admiration of even Regular Officers and attract a great many visitors — I should really like to fight them somewhere and demonstrate that we are not *Invalids* — altogether. If I can get a copy of the Sentinal of yesterday (the copper sheet here) I will send it to you — as I am told there is a puff in it for me. Dont you think I am doing well — when such papers say a good word for me? — I am boarding at the Bates House — The regiment mess being broken up by the absence of the family who had charge of it — I have to pay $5 per week — for table board and I have my bed in my office —

How is mother's health now? I will write her the very next letter I write to you at home — Tell her that there are holes in all my stockings — and I presume she would say as I do — "darn 'em." I cant get anybody to fix em either. What *shall* I do — Give both Mother my love and warm regards. But I must close as it is dinner time. Write often and tell me all the news —

Yours with affection
Newton[26]

"Fast riding, by military men especially, is getting so common on the streets of late as to call for public censure. An officer of the Veteran Reserve Corps, while riding very rapidly up Washington Street, yesterday, as the 20th was marching to the cars, ran over a little boy about eight years of age, and knocked him down. Fortunately the boy was not injured, but the officer was culpable for galloping through a crowd, and should be dealt with by the authorities."[27]

Burnside Barracks
April 21, 1864.

"Ed. *Journal*: Seeing a notice in yours of the 20th instant, that an officer of the Veteran Reserve Corps rode over a child on Washington Street, I would wish to notify the public that he did not belong to these Barracks. No mounted officer of this command would, I am sure, so far forget his honor as to be guilty of such barbarism or unpardonable carelessness. Let the act fall only at the door of the doer.

Yours respectfully,
An Officer of the Corps."[28]

From the *Indianapolis Daily Journal*: "Sentinels have been placed over nine saloons in various parts of the city, for selling liquor to soldiers in violation of the orders of the Commandant forbidding it, and no soldier or officer is now allowed to enter them. This is perhaps a better arrangement than closing of the saloons by the military, and the proprietors should be thankful to the Provost Marshall for letting them off so easily. We are assured, however, that if the order forbidding the sale of liquor to soldiers continues to be violated, the establishments of the offending parties will be closed up. The Commandant has not men enough to spare to guard every little groggery in the city, and those who seek to evade his reasonable and just request may find their own doors locked against them. We are glad to know that a large majority of the liquor sellers yield a cheerful obedience to the order, which has had the effect to establish and maintain remarkably good order where before was frequent rows and knock-downs."[29]

"The Provost Guard, composed of troops of the Veteran Reserve Corps, are frequently censured by unreflecting persons for the strict manner in which they perform the duties assigned to them. A comparison of the order of the city now with what it was a few months ago demonstrates conclusively the general efficiency of the provost work, and much praise should be awarded them for their vigilance.— Since this corps has been on this duty, an unusual number of veteran soldiers, recruits, and troops from other states have been constantly in this city and passing through, rendering the work of the provost guard ardous and difficult, and the treatment they have received has been sometimes very aggravating. It is true, however, that the guard has, on several occasions, fired at soldiers who refused to halt when commanded to do so, and the whistling of bullets near persons on the streets has caused alarm and complaint; but we are informed by the Provost Marshall that such things will be guarded against as much as possible. His instructions are to let such an offense pass rather than endanger the lives of citizens by shooting. At the Union Depot there is greater necessity for surveillance than at any other point in the city. It is almost constantly filled with passing troops or soldiers awaiting transportation, and as usual with soldiers out of camp or away from their principal officers; they do not always observe a very strict behavior, and many of them take the occasion to drink and become intoxicated and rude. It is often extremely difficult to preserve order among them. They get aboard the trains and stand upon the platforms, ready to cheer their friends when the train moves. The railroad companies not being able to enforce their rules in regard to standing upon the platforms, have requested the guard to keep them clear. It sometimes happens that some soldiers are unable to find seats inside the cars, and not being allowed to stand upon the platforms are compelled to remain behind while their comrades go and leave them. This appears to them a hardship, not to be endured without a good deal of complaint, but the guard have only done their duty and are not responsible for it. A recent case of this kind was made the occasion for censuring the Provost Guard by one of our city contemporaries, but learning the facts it has since apologized. The conclusion of the whole matter is this: we are engaged in a war which has somewhat disjointed the machinery of society. Nearly one-third of our population is now military, and Provost Guards are an imperative necessity. They protect us and we should sustain them."[30]

"Changes.-Lieutenant Colonel Colby, of the 18th Regiment Veteran Reserve Corps, and Post Commandant, has been relieved of his command of the Post, with orders to report to Washington. Captain Craig, commandant at the Soldier's Home, takes Colonel Colby's place, and Captain William Burress, of the 84th Indiana, takes command at the Home."[31]

From Field and Staff Muster Roll: N.T. Colby transfered to 19 Regt V R C by order of Pro Mar Genl dated Washington D.C. May 5/64[32]

"Lt. Col. Colby of the Veteran Reserves (late known as the Invalid Corps) who has been for a while stationed at Indianapolis, was in town this week [Corning], on his way to Washington where he is ordered for service."[33]

CHAPTER 17

Old Capitol and Carroll Prisons — Washington, D.C.

Sherburne Barracks
Washington. Sunday June 5th 1864
Dear Father

    No doubt you have wondered why you have not heard from me before this—announcing the safe arrival of the family—but I have been so busy that I really could not. I am on the military commission from 10 A.M. till 3 P.M. every day and the rest of the day has been consumed in "choring" and doing the thousand necessary jobs to get to housekeeping—But to day I have plenty of time—although no *more* inclination than I have had ever since the folks got here—so I am here—I met Mary and children in Baltimore.

    I had my quarters in good shape and cook had dinner ready very shortly after we got here—the children were a little tired—but vastly pleased to get "home" nor has their satisfaction abated as yet. Fred is much exercised about the soldiers and is getting acquainted with them pretty fast—Kittie thinks it is too bad to make a poor man walk backward and forward all day in the hot sun and carry his gun—Mary seems to be much pleased with my quarters and the satisfaction of Camp. You will of course see by this letter that we are still here—although the orders have not been countermanded as yet—and I can not say that they will be—No one seems to know if we are really to go or not—There seems to be some trouble somewhere about passing the bill to legalize the V.R. Corps—and some say it will be disbanded unless this Congress passes the bill for its organization.

The Major who has part of the house we live in — messes with us — Eatables cost rather heavily — fresh meat from 20 to 40 cts per lb — Butter fifty cents. Eggs 35 cts and c and c — However I can get most of the necessaries of the commissary department at Govt prices and that is much less — for instance I get white loaf sugar for 12/14 cts per lb. Beef steak — for 16 cts — coffee 44 cts and first rate too — flour 8 75 per bbl — rice 9 cts good black and green tea for 1 25 and the best ham I ever ate for 16 cts and c and c.

I may go down to the Convention at Baltimore this week possibly for I should like to attend *one* Presidential convention and I may not have as good a chance again very soon. I am getting tired of this profession — with its constant changes and if I saw a good business chance that would be both Profitable and permanent — I would quit the service — Such chances are rare I suppose and do not often come to one who has no capital. But I am really tired of being hoisted about the world — It is not pleasant to feel that you may be obliged to tear up and leave where you may be pleasantly fixed — for some other place — at a moments notice.

Last evening Mary and I attended the Opera and as we came out met old Abe Lincoln — the President. We were directly behind him (Mary boasts that she stepped on Mrs Lincoln's dress more than once). The President was telling his companion (I think it was Sec Chase) one of his funny stories and we heard it all — We were lucky in seeing him for we might have attended a dozen levees — and receptions without seeing him as long — or having a chance to notice his characteristics when free from official care. The lines on his face are deeper and he looks much more careworn than when I saw him last — and I do not at all wonder at it. There is nothing especially new here — the army news you get as soon as we do — Grant seems to be doing well — but the capture of Richmond will leave us rather a small army — The killed and wounded number very heavily — but I suppose it better to suffer the loss at once and thereby end the war than to be years losing the same number by slower approaches —

Give my and Mary's love to Mother

Affectionately yours
Newton[1]

Sherburne Barracks
Washington D.C.
June 19th 1864
Dear Father

After a *great long time* your letter came to hand and I hasten to answer it.

Fred and Kittie went to the theatre one evening with us and of course were immensely astonished to see ghosts and devils appear and disappear through the floor. Fred associates with the men considerably — riding the team horses — and imbibing the pecular opinions of the men about their officers. He says that some of the privates are just as good as any officer and that some of the officers are brutal to oblige their men to walk backward and forward in the hot sun with a barrel over their heads — He went with me to the Navy Yard and allowed there were some pretty tall cannon there.

Mary and I had rather a narrow escape the other day — Maj Lee and his wife were going to ride in their carriage and invited us to go along — The Major having but one arm I drove — and as we were returning we met a squad of Cavalry racing their horses towards us — I reined out of the road as far as possible but one of them ran into us — breaking both thills and otherwise damaging our carriage — I succeeded in stopping our horse after a few furious bounds and we luckily escaped injury — but not so the cavalryman — He was thrown over thirty feet and struck on his face — breaking his jaw — Knocking out all his front teeth and cutting his face up badly — When I went to him — he was insensible and the first thing he heard when he recovered his senses was what I told him in no gentle tone that it served him right and it ought to have killed him — I wrote a note to the Col of his Regt and demanded that the Corporal of the squad be punished and have since called on him and found him a gentleman and that he had reduced Mr Corporal to the ranks — Our carriage was used up and we had to walk to the street cars and get home that way.

To day the funeral of those killed by the explosion at the arsenal took place and the procession was an emense one — There is some anxiety felt here about the possibility of an attack by the rebs — as Grant has most completely uncovered this city — However we have troops enough to hold them till Grant could get up at any rate. We all unite in sending love to all

Affectionately Yours
Newton[2]

Sherburne Barracks
Washington July 6th 1864
Dear Father

Your two last letters have both been received and I hasten to reply. I see by your letter that you have not seen the official notice of my being confirmed by the senate as Lieut Col — It (with a number of others) was published here several days since and I shall soon have a comission as a U.S. officer — bearing the signature of our Uncle Abraham — Quite a number were not confirmed among them — was Col Johnson of my former Regt (the 18th) We are all feeling proud of our confirmation and begin to look down on volunteer officers — as common trash!! The Rebs have once more got on a Raid and we are under orders to go after them and will probably leave very soon for Harpers Ferry or Maryland — In fact as I write we are in expectation every hour of an order to start. I shall of course be obliged to leave Mary and the little folks here — but there will be the Col's family and one or two others here — and one or two officers and a camp guard and she will be cared for and safe I think. We may not be gone long — but once in the field I fancy we will not get away very easy or soon. The other day an order came for the Field Officers of the Brigade to get by July 1st — a good horse and the Regulation horse equipments — After much figuring and study I bought only the Regulation Equipment and decided to trust to luck in borrowing a horse — I could not buy one for I hardly had money to buy the saddle and c — and so I am without a horse still — The saddle and equipment cost me the modest sum of $75. — And I got them at the lowest cash price — I have had my light blue coat colored blue and it looks almost as good as new which will enable me to get along without a new one for a while yet.

We had a grand Review on the 4th before the President and Sec of War and Genl Fry — I will close here — leaving a blank to be filled up before I leave — that is if I have a chance to write — We may go in the night and if so I will not be able to write more but if I am here in the morning will finish it. Mary and all the children send their love to you and mother and all the folks Write to Mary as often as you can . Very affectionately yours Newton[3]

Col. N.T. Colby, who had charge of the Capitol and Carroll Prisons at Washington during the close of the war, was in frequent conference with President Lincoln.

At one of these conferences a message was received from a general in the field. The general had facetiously begun his message, "Headquarters in the saddle." "Humph," remarked the President, "I could have understood him better had he said, "Hindquarters in the saddle."[4]

On July 9, General Early arrived at the Monacacy River near Fredricksburg and was met by a much smaller force led by Union Major General Lewis Wallace. Wallace was able to hold off the Confederates most of the day, delaying them long enough for Grant to send troops toward Washington for its defense. This small Battle of Monocacy probably saved Washington from being taken.

"On July 10th, Gen. Jubal Early's forces camped near Washington at Rockville, Maryland and were about to capture the capitol the next day. By noon on the 11th his forces had moved to near Fort Stevens just outside the city.[5]

"Gen. Jubal Early, on the 11th, coming within 4 miles of the White House, all that stood between them was the assortment of government clerks of the 18th Veteran reserve Corps and the VI Corps of the Army of the Potomac that was dispatched by Gen. Grant. The defense of Washington was accomplished with the VRC 18th Corps manning the perimiter. Some of the regiment actually charged after the Confederates and were involved in a sharp skirmish with them until night fall."[6]

President Lincoln and his wife were sightseeing the skirmishing from inside Fort Stevens at the time.

It is thought to be during this time period that a family story handed down took place. Newton's wife Mary, showed her patriotism and support for the troops as they marched past their house in Washington. She reportedly went out on the front porch and sang a popular war song, "We are Coming Father Abraham."

According to Lt. Col. Colby's following letter of July 16th the VRC regiment was engaged at Tennallytown.

Washington
July 16th 1864
Dear Father

Some time since I wrote you a letter which I enclose — I could not send it in consequence of the broken communication between here and the north and I kept it several days beside that — in order to obtain the Red Book. I shall not be able to send you *that* however untill a day or two — but you shall have it soon — as I have an order for one. I have sent you some other books which I trust you will receive in due time. We have had a small *scare* here and things really looked squeally for a time. Our Regt went to Tennally town and was engaged in all the skirmishes there losing a dozen or fifteen killed and wounded in all. I did not accompany them — having been ordered quite unexpectedly to take charge of the Military Prisons (Old Capitol and Carroll) I have about 700 prisoners — one half of them (nearly) have been taken during the last week at different places from the Raiding Rebs. I also have charge of the Gaurds at the Depot and c. I hope and expect to get commutation of quarters and Fuel — but can not tell certain — During one two day seige — prices went up terribly — butter $1.00 per lb and c and c. Doubtless you have been a little anxious about us — but we have been all safe and well. I made up my mind to take Mary and the children to the Sisters of Charity if the Rebs did get in and to put my prisoners on a Gun Boat and take them to Fortress Monroe — But they are all going towards Dixie now fast as possible.

Rebel prisoners state that their force was 25 to 30,000 — all of them tell the same story. Troops are still arriving here to help us — but *as usual* too late. How I ever came to be ordered here I can not immagine — I had my troops all packed and ready to march — when the Military Govenor drove to my quarters and ordered me into his carriage without telling me where we were going — and took me to the Old Capitol Prison and informed me that I must *at once* go on duty as Superintendant — However — our Regiment had all the field officers with it and could spare one better than any other here and that may explain it — I will write again soon. Give my love to Mother and Nettie Emma — How does Willie get along?

Affectionately Yours Newton[7]

From Field and Muster Roll — 19th Regt. V.R.C: Lt. Col. Newton T. Colby is in charge of military prisons, Washington D.C. since July 11, 1864[8]

Old Capitol Prison

"Early in the war military authorities leased the Old Capitol Building at NE corner of 1st and A Streets NE. At the time it was being used as a school and was turned into a military prison. It came to be used almost exclusively as a place of detention for the class known as state prisoners, while those charged with infractions of military discipline were confined in a building at the southeast corner of Pennsylvania Ave and 13th street, which was leased by the government. By the fall, and four months after the Old Capitol Prison was opened, only fifteen prisoners suspected of disloyalty had been sent there."[9] "Then the arrests became so numerous that two of the houses in the Carroll or Duff Green Row, on the square to the south, were secured by the provost guard. Military discipline, in the opening months of the year, was not sufficiently effective to keep soldiers out of the city. A pay day was followed by drunken and disorderly occurrences."[10]

"Carroll Prison was an annex to the better known Old Capitol Prison. During the war this entire complex had housed at various times rebel prisoners of war, smugglers, blockade runners, contraband southern Negros,

17. *Old Capitol & Carroll Prisons — Washington, D.C.*

Colby, while serving in the Veteran Reserve Corps. Colby family collection.

Sword believed to be the one in the picture of Colby taken while he served in the Veterans Reserve Corps.

court-martialed Union officers, spies and a mass of suspects of all kinds interred under the broad powers of the Lincoln administration. The Old Capitol section located just across First Street from the Capitol, was built in 1815 to house Congress temporarily following the destructive British raid in 1814. Later it became a boarding house. The adjoining Carroll annex was originally a closely packed row of residences named Duff Green Row. During the war, the Old Capitol alone could not handle the masses of assorted prisoners, and this row of homes was hastily converted into a wing of the main prison."[11]

Headquarters Provost Marshal's Office,
Washington, D.C., July 14, 1864
Col. N.T. Colby
Actg. Supt. O.C. Prison
Colonel:

    The discrepancy between your report for June and our record of Prisoners confined in Old Capitol Prison is as follows:
Present but not reported:
Cashart, J.F. Priv 53 N.C.I.
Jones, J.M. Priv 2 Va Cav.
Jones, Daniel Priv 42 Miss. I.
Smith, Wm. " Lucas Batty.

Stuart, Jos. H. Priv 1 Md. Inf.
Wooley. L.W. Priv Cobb's Leg.
Reported but not present: Milstead, A. (R.F. Milstead, Priv 2 Va. Cav — trans to Hosp May 23 '64)
Please give such information as will enable our records to be corrected.

Very Respectfully
Your Obt. Serv't
Geo. R. Walthidge capt—
Asst. Prov. Marshall[12]

The following account was written by Lt. Col. Newton Colby after the war about Old Capitol Prison: "That which is commonly known as the Old capitol Prison, and which figured so conspicuously in the history of the late war, consisted, really, of two separate and distinct edifices, locally known by the names of the Old Capitol and Carroll buildings, and were situated, the first, on the corner of Pennsylvania Avenue and East First Street, and the other on the corner of Maryland avenue and East First — a block apart, and both facing the Capitol building and East Capitol Park. The 'Old Capitol' was so named from having been the temporary meeting-place of both Houses, I believe, after the destruction of the capitol buildings by the English under Ross, in the War of 1812, and the other from its having been the property of the Carroll family, descendants of him of Carrollton — vide the signatures to the Declaration of Independence. Of course the use to which they were devoted in the late war was far enough from that for which they were originally constructed, and, in fact, in their earlier and better days, they earned, historically, a higher reputation than many more pretentious Washington edifices. The Old Capitol, especially, after its abandonment by Congress, was occupied as a fashionable boarding-house, and was largely patronized by the 'crem de la creme' of the Southern dwellers in Washington. The great original nullifier, Calhoun, boarded here, and from out its doors went gallant, but ill-fated, Commodore Decatur, the morning he met his enemy, Barron, at Bladensburg, in the duel that cost him his life. No brick walls, old or new, in the capitol, have shut in stranger episodes and vissitudes of life than these, and, I doubt not, each of its four stories could many a tale unfold worthy of special record of life at our National Capitol in those comparatively primitive days. At the breaking out of our civil war they were not occupied, having, for lack of care, fallen into that neglected, down at the heel, slipshod condition of many buildings in Washington then, and there existed in their appearance little evidence either of their past greatness or future notoriety. Both buildings were of a size to indicate that they were built either for very large families, with many servants (which is probable, inasmuch as they were erected in the days when slavery made servants plentiful), or for boarding-houses, and contained in all forty or fifty rooms each — many of them quite large. Their tenant-less condition, added to, their roominess and location, doubtless, recommended them to a government suddenly and unexpectedly called upon to provide a place of confinement for many prisoners, and little outlay was needed to fit them for the purpose, as they always depended more upon the vigilance and care of the guards for the safe keeping of prisoners than upon bolts and bars. To be sure, there were iron bars at some of the windows; but as they were only inserted in soft wood of the window frames it will be seen that they were only an apparent, and not real addition to security. Locks were attached to each door, and, with some addition to the cooking apparatus, the hotel was ready for its guests. A guard of about sixty men, under the command of a captain or lieutenant, was daily detailed from a neighboring infantry regiment, to each prison, doing regular guard duty, two hours on and four off, day and night.

"The character of the prisoners was a matter of wide variation, differing in this particular from any other place of confinement. Especially is this true of the Old Capitol, where were held the prisoners of State particularly, such as parties charged with active disloyalty at the North, bounty frauds, counterfeiters of United States notes and other issues, contractors who had swindled the government, and, I doubt not, men who were arrested by deceives upon trumped-up charges simply to blackmail them, and who were wholly innocent. In fact, it would be quite unfair to assume that because one had been a prisoner here, that he was, therefore, a criminal, for I met many gentlemen there, as prisoners, too, whose claims to regard as gentlemen and men of refinement and social standing is to-day widely honored. Per contra, there were a few, and but a few, who gravitated naturally to a prison. In saying this I refer strictly to the civil prisoners, as among the prisoners of war there was the usual variety of humanity — generally of the better class— as very few privates of the Southern army found their way here, except they were special cases, either awaiting trial by court-martial or under sentence, and temporarily held there for the convenience of the government. Thus it was the pleasure of the authorities to regard those captured from Mosby's following ('guerrillas') as special cases, and I had some twenty of them — rough, dirty, ill-looking customers they were — in a large room on the fourth floor of the Old Capitol, fronting on the street. They were a turbulent and unruly set, and often amused themselves by throwing bricks (taken from an old fireplace in their room) at the sentinels on the pavement underneath their window, and, in one or two cases, barely escaped killing them. All other means failing, and provoked at last, I notified them that I had given orders to the guard to fire on any one showing himself at the window, and that they were responsible for it, and for the result. I am happy to say no one was injured, although they tested both the obedience and correct aim of the sentinel by putting one of their old hats on a stick and pushing it up to the window and getting a ball through it — but the brick throwing ended.

"It is proper to say, in this connection, that there was no means of punishing a refractory prisoner — as there were no 'dungeons' in either prison — nor did I ever see a prisoner ironed beyond being handcuffed, and that only in very few cases and for a temporary purpose, and not once as a punishment. The food served was a soldier's full ration, cooked, and many purchased at neighboring restaurants (by written order) anything they wished, even wine and cigars; the privilege of so buying, however, being mostly confined to civilians, who often had plenty of money, which officers or soldiers rarely had. Of course, the money and valuables of each prisoner was taken from him on his entrance to the prison, and a receipt given him by the superintendent, but he was at liberty to draw it for legitimate uses as pleased him. Knives were also taken from the prisoners, and upon assuming the command of the prisons I receipted for, to my predecessor, among other valuables, something like a hundred thousand dollars in money and United States bonds and a full bushel of pocket-knives! I speak thus accurately of the measure as they were contained in two half-bushel measures, fairly level full, being those belonging to prisoners then in confinement, as well as to many hundreds who had been released or sent elsewhere and forgotten to ask for them. A noted English hotel thief, who was held by the authorities as a witness, gave up on his admission to the prison about five thousand dollars worth of jewelry, mostly diamonds, and naively answered my query as to where he got them by saying concisely, 'prigged 'em,' i.e., stole them. He was a gentlemanly-looking fellow, and seemed actually to believe his profession as matter of fact as any other, and frankly admitted it. A Jew was arrested and brought to prison charged with having come through the army lines from Dixie, and upon being searched, previous to assignment to quarters, was found to be wrapped in a long piece of muslin in which several hundred dollars in gold pieces were carefully sewed, and his misery in seeing them ripped ruthlessly from their hiding place was extreme, equaled only by the scorn which he regarded my receipt for the much-loved hoard. After a trial which restored him to freedom, however, he presented his scorned acknowledgement, and thought better of it when it returned to his possession his treasure. The war had made money plenty, and it often fell temporarily into strange and unaccustomed hands, and from prisoners charged with bounty frauds I received as high as twenty or thirty thousand dollars in notes and bonds—the results, doubtless, of their rascality. The jealosy of the authorities regarding the safe-keeping of this large amount of money is illustrated by the following incident: Standing in the prison yard upon one occasion while a detachment of prisoners were taking their daily airing, I was approached by one who begged a few minutes conversation, the substance of which, after a slight preface, was the offer of five hundred dollars (which he held my receipt for, having given it up on his admission) if I would allow him to write a letter and forward it to its destination unread. Telling him I would communicate with him in regard to the letter later, he went to his room, from which I summoned him within an hour by the corporal of the guard and confined him alone in a small room on the ground floor, without wondows, save in the door, and kept him there a week on strict bread and water diet, and a few days after he was released from prison upon an order from the War Department. Nor did I learn till long after that he was a Secret Service Agent and imprisoned specially to make me the offer he did, and that his report of his success was received with roars of laughter from his superior officers.

"The fidelity with which the prisons were guarded is attested by the few escapes that occured, only two that were successful taking place during my command of over a year. One from Carroll Prison of a Virginia colonel, who lowered himself from a third-story window with a rope made from his blanket; which rope, by the way proved too short, and came near proving fatal to both life and escape. The night selected for the attempt was dark and rainy, and he carefully descended hand over hand till he felt the end of the rope; to reascend was impossible, and there was nothing for it but to drop, which he did, coming down on the pavement with a crash within six feet of the sentinel with his loaded musket. Probably no sweeter sound ever fell on the ear of that colonel than the dull, unmeaning click of the gun, which (doubtless owing to the rain) missed fire when leveled at his breast, the muzzle scarce a yard away; and ere aid could come, he bounded off into the darkness and disappeared. The attempt was gallant enough to have proved a permanent success, but he was returned to me by General Lew Wallace, within a month, having been retaken in Baltimore.

"Attempted escapes were more numerous, however, some of them of such a nature as, I think, to much interest the reader. One, especially, borders on the marvelous, and yet I vouch for its entire acccuracy, and can

17. Old Capitol & Carroll Prisons — Washington, D.C.

substantiate it fully from documents now in my possession. It is as follows: A citizen of Maryland, whom, for the purpose of this narritive we will name Brown, was arrested and sent to the Old Capitol, charged with having killed a Union soldier in an affray during a drinking spree; and, as he was well known to be an ardent sympathizer with the Southern cause, it was inferred that he was influenced by that motive in the killing — but with this our story has nothing to do. He was an uneducated, ignorant, superstitious man — probably a sample of 'poor white trash' of the South — and, as the result shows, easily imposed upon. He was assigned to a room on the fourth floor, in which there was already an occupant, who seemed ill-pleased to share his bed and board with a newcomer, whose appearance he evidently did not admire. However, nolens volens, Brown was and must be his room-mate, as the crowded condition of the building made other disposition impossible, and thus was developed a plan to be rid of him, purely devilish, as follows: For a few days he manifested a friendly disposition toward Brown until he succeeded in winning his confidence. Then, one day, upon returning to the room after a visit to the prison yard, he informed Brown that he had overheard the colonel commanding the prisons giving orders preparatory to his (Brown's) execution by shooting, to take place the next morning. Believing this absurd tale, the effect on Brown was terrible, and so thoroughly was he frightened that he dashed about the room with wild cries of anguish and despair, and it was with much difficulty his companion could quiet him sufficiently to reveal a plan which he pretended he had safely arranged for his escape from the impending doom. Escape! It was heaven, and Brown listened with an eager ear to anything that promised half a chance, and with credulity marvelous, as the doom to him was frightful. Brown was then told that his room-mate had long followed the profession of an acrobat in a circus, and, consequently, could explain how it was possible to jump from any place, however for the distance, without injury, and it consisted, simply, in always starting from a spring board. All that was necessary was to get the board, jump into the yard beneath, scale the fence surrounding it, and he was free. And the half-crazed Brown agreed. Taking up one of the floor planks, about two o'clock that morning, they ran it noiselessly out of the window, securing one end firmly to the window-sill. The night was dark, but the gas-lights in the yard below flickered on the paved surface of the ground, which echoed to the measured tread of the sentinels as they paced the midnight rounds. Bidding his mate 'good-bye,' Brown slowly emerged from the window on his hands and knees, crawling toward the extreme end of the narrow plank — bending more and more with his weight over the dizzy height. Reaching, at length, the end, he carefully arose into a standing position, and, following his instructor's orders, he began to spring the board more and more rapidly, finally bounding upward as high as the impetous thus acquired would carry him, and then down, down through the yielding air to the stones beneath. With terrible swiftness, just missing the point of a sentinel's bayonet as he passed, he struck the pavement. The guard, amazed and frightened, fled the length of the yard, and Brown, unhurt, sprang to his feet and dashed in headlong flight toward a pair of steps leading to the top of a shed, upon which, however, was located another sentinel, who successfully stopped his further efforts. Not a bone was broken, and he sustained no visable injury worthy of mention. Yet the leap could not have been less than forty or fifty feet, and the landing place a stone paved yard. His brain, however, was affected by the shock, and not long after he was shot and killed by one of the guards while attempting another escape — an attempt like the one above narrated, which no sane person would have dared, and the poor fellow met the very same fate he so madly strove to escape.

"Of the secret agents or spies in the service of the rebel government, there were some who achieved notoriety at least, and they were well represented at the Old Capitol, both male and female. Among the latter was Belle Boyd, who left the impression with those with whom she came in contact of a woman governed more by romance and love of notoriety than actual regard for the Southern cause. Undeniably good-looking, with a fine figure, and merry disposition, she could have been dangerous had she possessed equal good sense and good judgement. I believe the extent of the damage she inflicted on the Northern cause was in tempting from his loyalty a subordinate officer of the navy, whom it was affirmed she married. He also found his way to the prison, from which he dictated a challange to the editor of the Washington Star, for some rather scornful allusions to himself and wife. They were both 'light weights' in the profession.

"Mrs. Baxley was a woman of far different character — educated, remarkably intelligent and cultivated, and with a steady courage any man might envy. She was a shrewd plotter of mischief to the North, and utterly fearless in its execution. Her intense hatred of a Yankee, with her whole-souled devotion to the Southern cause, often impelled her beyond the line of propriety and discretion, even to the verge of the ridiculous — never, however, to the peril of the cause she loved. The first time my attention was called to her case was by a note handed me by one of the guards, directed to the colonel commanding the prisoners, asking me to bring her an arm full of wood! Of course, it meant defiance and insult, but provoked only a smile; and the next 'break out' of her irrepressible hatred to

Yankeedom had a tinge of tragedy rather than comedy. It was thus: Going once to the window of her room (which was located on the second story of the building), she began a scathing and contemptous criticism of the sentinel underneath, until, goaded by her tongue, he threatened to fire at her if she did not desist and leave the window. 'Fire, then, you Yankee scoundrel! You were hired to murder women, and here is an opportunity to exercise your trade,' was the reply. Stung by the words, and thinking to frighten her, he raised his piece, but aimed above her head, and fired the ball crashing through the window over her. Not a muscle stirred as she still cooly faced the window as before, saying, contemptuously: 'A shot worthy a Yankee; load and try another.' She was arrested while within our army lines searching for her son, who had been wounded and captured in one of the great battles. He was sent to the prison where his mother was, and she had the privilege of seeing him often and of standing by his bedside when he died. He was buried from the prison and lies in the Congressional Cemetery, his mother being allowed to accompany his remains to their last resting place. She was accompanied to the cemetery in the same carriage by Mrs. Surratt (who was afterward hanged for complicity with President Lincoln's assassination), and a couple of guards detailed for the purpose. Mrs. Surratt was a large fleshy woman, and when first sent to the prison was not supposed to be guilty of anything very serious, or that could involve a risk to her life. Her daughter was her frequent visitor, and always was permitted to see her. At her trial she was removed from the Old Capitol, to which she never returned, having been tried, condemned, and executed at the Old Armory."[13]

Supts. Office Old Capitol
Washington July 25th 1864 [Sunday]
Dear Father

I have not heard from you in a very long time and have written you twice — and set down to write you again. As I wrote you before I am detached from my Regt and have the charge of Carroll and Old Capitol Prisons and the R.R. Depot. The order detailing me — makes me commutation of quarters and fuel — which amounts to about eighty-five dollars per month addition to my pay — now and in October and the ensuing months — when the allowance of fuel is greater — will amount to over $100 additional pay. You will admit that with this addition my pay is very fair — being in all about $260 per month. I would advise however that you do not mention it as I have no anxiety to provoke farther envy or jealousy among the fierce population of the City of Corning. I sent about 700 Rebs to Elmira last Friday — and have a few left — about 3 or 400. I intend to come up with a squad of them by and by — and can run up to Corning and make a short visit and it will cost me nothing.

Mary's health is not very good just now — she is suffering with an attack of dysentery.

Of course you saw by the papers that we were "besieged" for a day or two — and I assure you it looked a little blue at one time — We could hear the firing quite plainly and the Rebs in the prison boasted that they would soon be released. I instructed the Lieut of the Gaurd to intimate to them that I had powder under the prison and would blow them all to thunder on the first intimation of their being mutinous or any prospect of being released. It had a soothing effect I assure you — I sent to Fort Delaware sixty Officers (Rebs) from the rank of Colonel to fourth Lieutenent.

Give my best love to mother and regards to Em and Nettie and all friends

Affectionately yours
Newton[14]

Sherburne Barracks
Washington Aug 2, 1864
Dear Father,

I received your last letter a few days since but business and sickness have prevented my replying before. Mary has been quite ill with the dysentery — but is much better — but Minnie is very low with it. I have been very anxious about her — and I do not think she is much better and fear the worst. She has suffered everything — The attack seeming to be worms and dysentery together. The severe pain has left her almost entirely but she is so weak and stupid like — that I have great fears that she can not get well. We have been able to give her good care and excellent treatment — but the weather is terribly hot and dry and the disease prevails here exstensively and seems to be severe most always. If she is worse I will telegraph you — Mary is far from being well and is poorer than you ever saw her — but she manages to keep up — My own health is as good as it has been any time this year and Fred and Kittie are well —

I had the distinguished honor of receiving a call at my office from that lying scoundrel Simon Van Etten. He is here with a man by the name of Smith from P Post [Painted Post near Corning] to get substitutes for the Corning gentlemen — Smith seems to be a decent kind of fellow — but is in poor company. He takes to Corning a Colored man I have had in my service as house servent by the name of Charles Burns—He (Smith) offered to pay me if I would let him go with him but I informed him that I could not take any money and that he might make any bargins he could with Charley. Charley is a first rate fellow and I think a great deal of him and hope he will do well and get full pay. He agreed to pay Charley $300 and his expenses to Corning and let Steve Hoyt have him as his substitute—I think that Steve ought to make me a present of a new uniform at least—for substitutes will be worth more than $300 when the Draft comes on and I told Charley so—but he says he is satisfied with that. He would stay with me however if I should say so and I only let him go to help out on the quota at home and oblige Steve.

Write me at once when you get this—I hope I may be able to write soon that little Minnie is getting better—The weather here is terrible being hotter than ever I knew it and very unhealthy. Will write you again soon-

In haste affectionately yours
Newton[15]

Washington Aug 7th 1864
Dear Father

I have written you once or twice and up to this time have received no reply—so I am left to *imagine* how you all are. Minnie is no better than when I wrote last—In fact there is but little change in her condition either way—Except that she is necessarily much weaker—She has had a *very* severe attack and you would not recognize her she is so poor—mere skin and bones. I have but slight hope of her recovery—Mary's health is quite poor too and she has no chance to improve—as she has to take care of Minnie night and day—and except the little help I am she has it all to do alone. If Minnie were well enough I should have her and Mary go out into the country—for the Dr's tell me that change of air would be better than medicine for both. Minnie has good medical attendance and everything in the way of delicacies that is to be had. In fact she is better off than she would be at home—The Sisters of Charity have a hospital close by and they are very kind in sending jellies and c-

I have just received from Missouri the whole gang of greenback counterfeiters and the officer who brot them says their money can not be distinguished from the genuine and that there is millions in circulation!! I presume you have seen accounts of their capture in the papers. Eleven Rebs tried to escape a few nights since by cutting through the floor and walls and nearly effected it too—but luckily were discovered and I had them all handcuffed and have put them on bread and water for thirty days—to teach them to be quiet. Tell me all the news when you write—which I trust will be soon—Have the Corning people begun to throw up earthworks yet to defend the town against Rebel raiders? If not I think they had better begin for they seem to go where they please and may call on you

 Give my love to Mother and Henry. *Write soon*

Affectionately Yours
Newton[16]

 Monday Aug 8 I received your letter to day and was very glad to hear from you—Minnie is about the same—but Mary is not so well and is very sick. I would like to have them both change the climate by going home and the Dr's all advise it strongly and if they get able I will try and bring them up during the balance of hot weather. Write again very soon.

In haste your
Newton[17]

Sherburne Barracks
Aug 10th 1864
Dear Father

 I sit down for a very few minutes to write to you—for I suppose you are quite anxious to hear from me about the sick. I am sorry to have to write that both Mary and Minnie are no better and I am alarmed about both. They suffer frightful pain and nothing seems to relieve them. Minnie is screaming with pain as I write—altho I have given her opium to quiet it temporarily—but it seems to fail. Her rectum comes out every time she has an asseration—Mary too is too weak to raise herself and I assure you I have a sick household. The weather continues fearfully hot and dry. I have not had my clothes off for three nights and am sleepy and tired—How will it all end? I have only had one letter from you and have written several—Nothing would give me more pleasure than to see you—Can you come I hardly dare ask it for I have poor accomodations and you would have to sleep on the floor—and risk your own health in this hot climate. If you can leave and are not afraid I will pay your expenses here and back again.

 Write soon—Give my love to mother and Henry. If you come—come at once if possible.

17. Old Capitol & Carroll Prisons — Washington, D.C.

In haste Yours affectionately
Newton[18]

"Opium was a common medication for diarrhea patients. It had a side effect of slowing down the action of the digestive tract, and would give some relief from diarrhea. Patients were given about one-quarter of a grain of opium, as opposed to a grain as a painkiller."[19]

Washington Aug 12th
Friday-
Dear Father

I write you again to let you know that Mary and Minnie are no better and much weaker — Minnie can not live more than a day or two at farthest Mary is worse I think and is very low — and I am discouraged about her — Nothing seems to relieve her — I had Dr Johnson called to consult with our Surgeon yesterday. He is the best Physician in this city — and he gave me small hope for either — He said Mary was in no immidiate danger but was a very sick person — and as to Minnie he seemed to be very doubtful of her recovery — though he did not say it was impossible. I feel sick at heart and depressed and can see no comfort any where — can you come to me in my trouble? It rained hard last night — but is just about as hot as ever now — What can I do?

Write or come — I have written to Almira to come at once

In haste yours as ever
Newton[20]

August 15, 1864 Mary Colby, wife of Newton Colby, died in Washington, D.C., on August 15, 1864. No known record has been found as to Little Minnie's fate, but she apparently passed away about this same time.

From Field and Staff Muster Roll, 19th VRC. Lt. Col. Colby — on leave of absence of thirty[30] days since Aug 14, 1864 per authority of the Military Governor.[21]

Newton accompanied Mary's body to her burial site in Oakwood Cemetery, Nunda, N.Y.

Old Capitol Prison
Washington Sept 15th 1864
Dear Father

    I suppose you are anxious to hear from me and learn how I get along and how I am situated. I arrived here in good season Tuesday and went up to the Barracks after depositing my luggage at Dyer — I am at present stopping at Dyers and paying at the rate of fifty dollars per month for board — room and c — but think I shall only stay until I can find a *good* boarding house — The most lonely place I ever saw is Sherburne Barracks — I could not hardly make up my mind to go there — and shall not again in a hurry I assure you — Cousin John Colby was here a few days since with some prisoners — taking them to the front — but I did not see him.

    How do the children get along? Tell them that Papa is very lonesome and already desires to see them — They must be good children and I shall not forget them-

    Give my love to Mother and Henry and Emma and write soon

Affectionately yours
Newton

    Mr Wood the Superintendant just came in to my office and said he was going to be gone for some time again and had asked to have me put in charge again — so I am to be here for some time.[22]

    Cousin John was Capt John Peck Colby, Uncle Luke's son, who was a member of the 58th New York National Guard for two years. This unit served the Union Army for 100 days August to December 1864. They served in Elmira, New York at the prison camp. It was not a glamorous assignment in that they rounded up escapees, draft dodgers and such.[23]

Old Capitol Prison
Washington Sept 20th 1864
Dear Father

    There is some fine shooting in the neighborhood and I think I will try it. Have the grease all wiped off and if possible a woolen case made and put over it — Mother can make one good enough of some pieces of woolen cloth about the house. Send me my *copper* powder flask and the lever shot pouch — put in them all the powder and shot you can find. I think you will find some in the upper part of my desk up stairs—Send me also the *wad cutter* which is there too and a box of cut wads with it—*Dont forget any of these things.*—Irvine has sent for his gun and we shall go shooting occasionally together. Politics run very high here and political meetings—flag raising and c abound. I heard old Abe make a short speech from the steps of the White House—in response to a call from a crowd who went up to call him out. Have Lower reminded of the matter at the lodge and forward me the demit as soon as you can.

Give my love to all my little motherless children and Mother and all the folks

Hastily Yours
Newton[24]

Headquarters Military District of Washington,
Provost Marshall's Office
Washington, D.C., Sept. 22, 1864
Lt. Col. Colby
Ach'g Sup't Old Capitol Prison
Col.

The Provost Marshall directs me to acknowledge the receipt of your communication of this date and also to state for your information that there is a strict Order of the War Department prohibiting the enlistment of Rebel Deserters in the United States Army, and if the Naval authorities refuses to receive the men referred to in your communication, they must be held until further orders from this office. A great mistake has been made in enlisting McFarland in the Army as the order from these Hd Qrs for the enlistment of these men stated that they were to be enlisted in the Navy and gave no authority for their enlistment in the Army. You will therefore hold the other four men, Gardner, Roberts, Owens and Rasser until further decision of the War Department can be obtained.

I have the honor to be Col.

Very Respectfully
Your Obt Servt.
Hiram S. Hunt
Lieut and Adj't[25]

Supts. Office O.C. Prison
Washington Sept 25, 1864

Dear Sister [in law]

Your very welcome letter was forwarded from Corning and reached me here a day or two since. I need not say to *you* that I was much pleased to hear from you—for I believe you wrote me because you *knew* it would be a comfort and pleasure to me—You can never know the trouble that I have experienced and the grief that is still such a heavy weight upon my heart—for *you*—nor *none* can ever be situated as I was in all respects. Mary was my wife—my darling from such an early age that our tastes had become alike in everything and so constituted were we both that I think enjoyment of life resulted to us from much less cause than to many others—and she was taken from me when it seemed I could do the best for her that my fortune has ever permitted—If I did well in anything her loving words were the best prized reward—and if by labor or calculation I succeeded in acquiring—the success was valuable to me only in connection with the idea that *she* would share it with me—Trouble and care and the petty annoyances of life I could shut out when I closed the door of my home—and came into the presence of my wife—my darling wife—Alas the words linger and yet when written stare me in the face and tell me of my loss—My wife! My own darling—I have so often looked into the blue sky and tried to imagine her happy far beyond the fleecy clouds—but cannot—for I seem to think of her as alone and wanting me—Is it true think you? Can she now look down and see me?—does her spirit quietly follow me here then in this world—troubled when I do wrong and made happy by every good deed? I have pondered till my very brain ached upon this subject—and looking forward to the future life after having shaken off this *mortal*—I ask what and how we assume the immortal? Ought I to be ashamed because I can not comprehend a body purely spiritual and happiness eternal with this new existence? I say it in all reverence—but feel it too—that if I could join my lost darling tomorrow and be permitted to enjoy her society as she was before death claimed her it would be to me fit heaven—Some earthly loss might be well refined away—in assuming the immortal—but I confess I fail to understand a greater happiness than *our* earthly love when not annoyed by care and pain and life's petty annoyances—

But I weary you with speculation I am here having charge of the O.C. Prison, Carroll Prison and c—I have been *obliged* once to visit our old quarters—and for days I did not get over it—It is terrible to go where we were once so happy—and where every object has a separate story with which to wring my heart.

Have you heard from Levi since Mary's death? What does he say about it? She was his favorite I think and he must suffer heavily—

Give my love to Mother and Elmira — and also to Julia and Kissie and believe me

Affectionately yours
Newton[26]

The previous letter is thought to be to the late Mary Colby's sister, Sarah.

Supts Office Oct 3d 1864
Father

After waiting a considerable time to hear from you I grow impatient and seat myself to write to *you*. I am still at the O.C. Prison and time hangs rather heavy on my hands—I received the gun and equipment all right — and have been out once after a new species of game — new to me — at least. They call it "ortolaw"—or Rail birds—It is a small bird about the size of a snipe — which it resembles except the long bill — The Rail has a short peaked bill — with long legs — and a short tail which sticks straight up behind — It can only be shot at high tide — when the water flows in among the reeds and flags—The manner of shooting them is as follows—You take a small light boat — and provided with a man to propel it — which he does by pushing it along over and through the reeds with a pole — while you stand up in the bow with your gun and shoot them as they fly up before your boat. It is pretty good sport and the chances of getting a ducking are quite fair inasmuch as it is not everybody who can stand erect and shoot in a narrow boat — which is propelled by pushing. I killed twenty the other day and had them for my dinner — and they were nice — I intend to kill some quail and ducks before long.

How do they get along with the draft in Corning? Is the quota filled yet? What bounty are they paying now? There is no especial news here.

I have repeatedly been asked if I would like to go to New York or Boston with prisoners—but have always declined — lacking the necessary energy — and not feeling able to stand the exposure — although Govt paid the fare.

Give love to mother and all the children

Affectionately Yours
Newton[27]

Headquarters Military District of Washington

Provost Marshall's Office
Washington, D.C., Oct 18, 1864
Lieut. Col. Colby
Acting Supt. Old Capitol Prison
Washington, D.C.
Colonel

    I have the honor to forward you herewith an Official Copy of a order from Com. General Posmirs ordering Rebel officers in your control also enlisted men to be transferred to Fort Delaware and Elmira, N.Y. respectively.

    You will please cause rolls to be prepared and forwarded to this office without unnecessary delay, exhibiting the names of the prisoners to be transferred according to the within office copy of orders from Col. Hoffman.
Very Respectfully
Your Obediant Serv't
Geo. R. Walthidge
Capt. and Asst. P.M.[28]

Headquarters Military District of Washington
Provost Marshall's Office
Washington, D.C. October 19th, 1864
Act. Supt. N.T. Colby
"Old Capitol Prison"
Sir:

    I have the honor to forward to you under guard the following named prisoners under sentence of General Court Martial who you will please hold until further orders.

    Thomas White 3d N.Y. Art.
    James Shields alias Benj. Riley C "H" 118th Pa. Vols.
    Augustus T Cushman C "J" 114th Pa. Vols.
    William Bonemaster Co "K" 107th Pa. Vols.
    Oscar Davidson 31st Iowa Vols
    Robert Rae Substitute
    George Ritter C. "C" 1st D.C. Vols.
    Joseph Baroford 3rd N.J. Cav.
    Willian H. Searans 1st D.C. Vols.
    James B Pine C "A" 21st V.R.C.
    Lewis Hankerson 59th N.Y. Vols.

Emil Fader 3d Batt N.Y. H'y Artillery
Charles W. Monroe C "E" 1st N.J. Cav.

By Order of
Col. T. Ingraham
Provost Marshall
C.N. Cross
Capt and Asst to Pro. Mar.[29]

Supts Office Capitol Prisons
Washington Oct 21st 1864
Dear Father

    I sent you a short letter a few days since written in too much of a hurry to make it a *reply* to your last. I am still at Dyers— but am thinking that I shall remove to a private family when the month is out. Charley Thompson is here — on behalf of the N.Y. Union Committee — attending to the soldier vote. W.W. Hoyt is also here — being Colonel of the 189th N.Y.Vols and is on his way to City Point.

    Election matters look well and I think there is little doubt of Lincoln's election — Grant they say is able to take Richmond whenever he shall decide to make the attempt and Sheridan has just given Longstreet a drubbing in the valley— so everything looks bright for the loyal side.

    I am very sorry to hear that mother's health is poor and that she finds it hard to work to look after my little ones— If necessary she must have another servent

    Write soon — Give my love to Mother and all friends

Affectionately Yours
Newton[30]

    The reference to Gen. Sheridan in reality was about the battle at Cedar Creek. Sheridan soundly defeated Gen. Early there and only Kershaw's Division of Longstreet was there.

Headquarters Military District of Washington
Provost Marshall's Office
Washington, D.C. October 22d 1864
Supt. Colby
"Old Capitol Prison" Sir:

You will receive and confine in the prison under your charge until further orders the following named prisoners under sentence of G.C.M.:

Private John Foster 20th N.Y.S. Militia; Private Milo Greenfield 17th Michigan; Private John McKeever 15th N.Y. Engrs.; Private Peter Riley 10th N.Y. Vols.; Private Wm.H. Portland 31st U.S. Cal. Troops; Private Francis X Eberle 15th Pa. Vols.; Private Jos. W. Sparkes 3d Del.; Private James Fettenberger 190th Pa. Vols.; Private Jos. a. Donaldson 8th Md.; Private Sam'l O'Brien 12th U.S. Inf.; Private Jno.T. Sebert 4th N.Y.H'y Art.

By order of Col. T. Ingrahm Provost Marshall
C.N. Cross
Capt and Asst Pro Mar[31]

Dyers Hotel Sunday Eve
Washington Nov 13, 1864
Dear Father

I have just reached this dismal place once more — and having nothing to do this evening I thought I would drop you a few lines — I had a pleasant trip to Baltimore — arriving there however too late for the morning train to this place — and I was therefore obliged to wait until 3.30 P.M. Happening to meet my friend Mr Hamilton Easter — he insisted on driving me about the city — You know I told you he was wealthy — and after driving all over town and through the splendid City park — he took me to his house which is about 3 miles out of town and then pressed me to stay over night which I did — He has everything that money can buy — horses — dogs — Guns (some of which I mean the *guns*—cost him three and four hundred dollars *each* and *all of them imported from London*) splendid furniture — Books — Graphics — Hot houses and c and c "ad infinitium" He has gas works on his place — soley to light his house alone — Perhaps you will be surprised to learn that he is a member of the Presbyterian Church and I believe a sincere christian — His wife is from Brooklyn and is a *quakeress* — I had the honor of accompanying her to the quaker meeting today — by special invitation — her husband going to the Presbyterian Church with his children — Dont immagine her to wear those horrible bonnets and c — oh no — though she drapes plainly yet richly and wears a diamond ring that would be a fortune to a poor man. She has lived a long time in France and of course is very refined and intelligent and yet not affected or pompous in the least. On parting from them this afternoon Mr Easter presented me with 500 cigars which he bought for me especially and for which he paid $50. I could have preferred some thing else of equal value — but of course

17. Old Capitol & Carroll Prisons— Washington, D.C.

I had nothing to say and confess that he is a very liberal generous man — Well I am here again in this miserable hole — and have no very inviting future before me. The little "Hotel Dyer" looks lonely and gloomy enough and *is in fact* a poor home — Whether I ever have a better one or not is in the vast future and the gulf between poverty and riches looks wide and deep to one who would essay to cross.

I forgot my velvet breeches and wish you would send them the very first chance you get of some one coming down— *dont forget*—I have not yet been up to the Old Capitol — Write me a little oftener than you have done-

Give my love to mother and all the little ones and believe me

Affectionately Yours
Newton[32]

Carroll Prison
Washington Nov 26th 1864
Dear Father

I received your note enclosed with the boys letters. I was glad to hear from you all.

There is no news here. I have just been greatly disappointed. It happened thus. I received orders from the Secy of War to be ready for a secret expedition — the result of which was to be the capture of Mosby and some of his Officers and for which I should have *certainly* been *promoted*— but there came a change and the Secretary gave it to one of his Favorites— a Colonel in the Regular Army. You will no doubt see an account of it in the papers before long —*if they succeed* — but if they fail — not — I almost hope they will —for their meaness in taking away my chance — I will write again before long. Give my love to Mother.

Yours as ever
Newton[33]

Washington D.C.
Jany 1st 1865
Dear Father

I sit down at my desk to write you — this News Years morning — and to wish you a "happy new year — with very many happy returns" — To me this new year comes under circumstances so different from my reasonable anticipations and hopes of the last new years day — That I will own to its being a sad one — and lonely — I have passed the period of time — when for some reason it was appointed to me to endure affliction and trouble — and look back to it with intervening months — with the self same sinking feeling at my heart — Time — by all the experience of others ought to bring — its sleepy draught to memory — and effaces some sadness — I am standing today by the cradle of the new born year — and trying to push my mortal vision into the future — trying to image its coming events aided only by experience — and lacking the usual stimulant of ambition and hope — and is it strange if I look to have the fruit I may pluck by life's path — fair and beautiful though it be in appearance — turn to ashes — like Dead sea fruit — when I would eat? — But I would fain believe the time worn saying — that "whatever *is* — is good" and wait with what patience I may for the revelations of time.

Your letter was duly received and pleased me very much — and I was glad to learn that my little ones were pleased with their presents. I went to Baltimore and bought most of them there.

I expected fully — when Col Wisewell was relieved — that being on his staff — I would also be relieved — but owing to the partiality of Mr Wood — who requested the Sec of War — to have me retained here — I am still here and feel that I have done my duty well or it would not be so — for I was the only one of Col Wisewell staff who was retained. There has been no order affecting commutation of Vet Res Corps Officers — Except one that applies to all Officers serving on *Boards* and *Court Martials*. The reason of its being issued I am told is that a Court Martial in this city was in session (or pretended to be) about ten months and only tried *Two* or *three* cases and were spreeing about town nearly all the time. It does not interfere with me at all and I get my commutation regularly.

Go to the Presidents reception tomorrow (Monday) with all the officers on duty in town — in full uniform sword and sash — I wish you could be here to go — for it is a splended sight — Generals — Foreign ambassadors covered with gold lace and wearing Cocked hats — Navy Officers and c and c — ad infinitium —

Give my love to Mother — Remember me to all my little ones with much love and affection. Write soon.

Yours Very Truly
Newton

I shall probably get my pay tomorrow and will remit you at once[34]

17. Old Capitol & Carroll Prisons — Washington, D.C.

Carroll Prison
Washington Jany 7th 1865
Dear Father

There is nothing especially new. The friends of our corps fear that it is destined to a short life. Present appearances look bad — I must confess — By the way do not direct your letters to me as "Supt of O.C. Prison" as that is a civil office — direct to me as Lt Col Comdg Post O.C. Prison — I received the letters from the children and was greatly pleased with them. They will hear from me very soon. I went to the Presidents reception on Monday and to Secy Stantons — Genl Fry's — the Mayor's and many other places too numerous to mention and what is better was quite sober all day —

Give my love to Mother and Henry and all my little ones — *Write soon*

Yours Affectionately
Newton[35]

Carroll Prison, Washington D.C.
Feby 4, 1865
Dear Father

I received your very kind and welcome letter.

I presume you have before this received the hasty note I wrote you from the Astor House in New York a few days since — and perhaps wondered why I was there. I will explain. Very suddenly and unexpectedly I received orders from the Secy of War — to go to Baltimore and arrest a certain person and convey him to the Albany Penitentiary. My instructions were from the War Dept — and marked "Confidential" — and I was required to make the arrest and "spirit" off the person without its becoming known. I had the advantage of knowing the person and went to his house alone and called him to the door after dark and quietly made the arrest. When I tell you it was my friend Chas E Waters you will understand that my duty was a very painful one — but of course my orders must be obeyed. The next morning I started with him to New York and Albany. I need not tell you that I treated him with all courtesy and kindness. We had a pleasant trip and reached New York Tuesday evening where I found I could not get my transportation before the next day. Waters being well known at the Astor House we went there — where he was welcomed with greatest cordiality by Mr Stetson and others — who I was at once introduced to — but who of course never suspected that Waters was a prisoner. You know that Waters is one of the heavyest Hardware dealers in Baltimore and has a large establishment in Cliff St N.Y. also—and is very wealthy and is son in law to my friend Mr Easter of Baltimore. He is a very young man—about 28 or 30 years of age and one of the most perfect gentleman I ever met. He goes to England every year to purchase goods and c. Well—after tea—or rather dinner—(at which the servants—who all recognised him—tried to overwhelm us with attentions) I left the Astor and went down Broadway—for a stroll leaving Waters there—I had his word of honor—and he would sooner have died than broken it—and I knew it very well and had no fears. I returned to the Astor about ten or half past when the clerk handed me a telegram—advising me that orders had been sent to Genl Dix to have me return with Waters at once to Washington! Well you believe I was glad and Waters too was of course greatly relieved. The next morning an A.D.C. of Genl Dix's Staff brought me an order from his Excellincy the President to return to Washington with my prisoner—and I accordingly did so that evening—reaching Washington Thursday morning. I submitted a written report and asked furthur instructions and was ordered to take Waters to the Old Capitol where he now is *I obeyed my orders*—but did all in my power to make Waters comfortable and carry out my instructions.

Well I am still in the miserable city of Washington and dislike it as much as ever. I have not made any outside speculations *yet*—though I shall try my luck in one pretty soon as I have got what I beleive to be a good chance—When it is a little more matured I will post you on it.

With regard to the children—I will write you in full before long. I can not decide as to their going to a boarding school—until I see more of some matters connected with my own future prospects.

Advise me at once of the receipt of the enclosed dft.

Give my love to mother and Henry and believe me

As Ever Affectionately Yours
Newton[36]

Old Capitol Prison
Washington D.C. Feby 19, 1865
Dear Father

I had the pleasure of receiving your last letter several days since—but having nothing of interest to tell you I have delayed answering it.

I came very near getting into a scrape over the arrest of my dear friend Waters—as the Department insinuated that I was *too friendly* towards him—They were mistakened about it however—for not only is it true that I would sooner lose an arm than disobey an order but it is also true that

17. Old Capitol & Carroll Prisons — Washington, D.C.

he (Waters) *would not ask me to do so*. He is the soul of honor and values his word more than his life — I would have been relieved — however — except for Mr Wood the Superintendant of the Prison — who informed Secy of War that it must not be allowed — and he has influence enough to carry any point he undertakes. Waters was yesterday released by order of the President from this prison and went home to Baltimore — He is my fast friend for life — and I love him as I never before loved a man — He is very wealthy and finely educated — but modest and unassuming and generous and frank.

I wish you would look about and find a *good No 1* school for Fred and Frank where they can be kept as they ought in all resepcts and write me — I intend to send them this summer and for that reason wish them to get ahead now as fast as possible — Are the children doing well or not? Tell me frankly — above all try and have my dear little daughter so educated as to become a *true* woman — without the trickery and affection they so often learn. Give my love to Mother — tell her I wish much to see her — and I sincerely hope she is well and happy as possible — Tell the children to write more often and believe me

Affectionately Your Son
Newton[37]

March 4, 1865 Lincoln was inaugurated for a second term.

3/9/1865
Dear Father

I had rather anticipated seeing you at the Inaugeration-but suppose your absence was due soley to what has so often compelled you to practice self denial — viz lack of money. There was an immense crowd-although the weather was very unpromising and every thing went off finely — I had the honor of receiving a complimentary ticket to the Ball on Monday night (the 6th inst) and attended it — with the daughter of Mr. King (firm of King and Burchell and very wealthy) and really enjoyed it. The crowd was immense and everything connected with the management superb. I had the honor of dancing several setts — and the supper was tasteful and expensive. One cake alone cost $575! I only reached my hotel at 5½ A.M.

Give my warm love and respect to Mother and the children.

As Ever Affectionately Your Son
Newton[38]

Carroll Prison
Washington, D.C.
March 29th 1865

    General Orders No. 5: I Until further orders—permission is hereby given to the officers commanding guards at Carroll and Old Capitol Prisons to allow each relief—immediately on being relieved from post—two hours recreation in the East Capitol Park. The men must be instructed that this privelege depends for its continuance—upon their good conduct—and that any neglect of soldiery appearance or conduct will be severely punished. Each relief will be accompanied by the Corporal who will be required to report any ill conduct on the part of the men to the Officer commanding the Guard—who will report to the undersigned.

    II The attention of Officers commanding the guard is called to the unsolderlike habit of the men lounging in front of the prison—and they will instruct them that they must rise and assume the position of a *Soldier* on the approach of an officer—before offering to salute him.

By order of
N.T. Colby
Lt. Col. and Mil. Comdt. Prisons[39]

Headquarters Department of Washington
Office Provost Marshall General,
Defences North of Potomac,
Washington, D.C. April 14th 1865
Lt. Col. Colby
Act. Supt. O.C. Prison
Washington, D.C.
Colonel

    You will please forward to this office Rolls of all "Rebel Officers" now confined in O.C.P. that they may be sent to Johnsons Island, Ohio.
    By order of

Col. T. Ingraham
Pro. Mar. Genr., N. of Potc.
Geo.R.Walthidge
Capt. and Asst.[40]

CHAPTER 18

The Lincoln Assassination

"A Crime Without a Name"

"Philadelphia, Pa., April 15, 1865.—A crime was perpetrated in Washington last night that will startle not only the people of the United States but the whole civilized world. The president of the United States, sitting with his wife in a box in one of the Washington theatres, was shot by an assassin, who, by the only exclamation he appears to have uttered, must be one of the Virginians whom the President has been most earnestly endeavoring to protect from the just retribution due to them for their agency in their wicked rebellion. During a pause in one of the scenes the assassin shot the President in the head, making a mortal wound, and then flourishing a drawn dagger he exclaimed 'Sic semper tyrannis,' (the motto of the State of Virginia,) rushed out the back of the theatre, mounting a horse in waiting and escaped. The crime appears not to have been the only one of the night, for a further dispatch announces that an attempt was also made to assassinate the Secretary of State. At the hour when this is written, there are few particulars of the latter of these bloody and brutal deeds. At first blush, this murderous business would appear to be the work of a madman, but the particulars of the fearful outrage perpetrated on the President, and the simultaneous attack on Mr. Seward, show it to have been a carefully planned conspiracy, in which a number of murderous confederates must have been concerned.

"This will be startling and terrible news to the country, now in the midst of its rejoicings over the near prospect of peace, and ranging itself under the lead of Mr. Lincoln upon the side of mercy, forbearance and pardon towards those whose murderous partisans have struck him his death-blow. Nothing short of interposition of Providence working upon the hearts of the people will be able to avert in instinctive impulse of the nation to punish this crime without a name, by some signal act of retribution that it sickens the heart to contemplate.

"It is impossible to give a rational motive of the villains concerned in the murderous plot. Of all men in the United States, the traitors and rebels who have been in arms for four years in their effort to destroy the Rebublic, owe most to the kindness of heart, the concientious endeavor to be just, and the resolute purpose to restore the fraternal relations of the people of the two sections of the country which actuated Mr. Lincoln from the day of his inauguration to his dying hour. In every stage of the war which they brought on by their unhallowed plots, he has been their powerful friend, protecting them at all times from those men in his own party who recommended from the start, that they should be dealt with accordingly to the severest dictates of stern and relentless justice. At any time since 1861, had almost any other Republican than Abraham Lincoln been invested with his power and beset with the appeals that were made to him for retributive justice upon the men who have wantonly and wickedly drenched the land in blood, many a traitor now living as securely as if his great crime had never been meditated would have swung from the gallows which has no office if not made for such as they. Even at the hour when his death-blow was struck, he was standing like a minister of mercy appealing to the country to sustain him in the universal pardon and oblivion in which he desired to sink their crimes, and yet the fiends he was guarding from punishment struck him down! What depth of damnation is there deep enough for devils such as these?

"We do not pause at this late hour to enlarge upon the terrible calamity to the nation, involved in Mr. Lincoln's death, in the crisis through which the country is now passing. We lose as sincere a patriot and as upright a magistrate as ever blessed the land. Even those who have been his bitterest foes will now admit this, for they have lost a friend who has stood by them in their direct need. He has borne himself "clear in his great office," and may Heaven send us one who will guide the country through its terrible trials as safely and as conscientiously as he made it the object of his life to do."[1]

Washington D.C.
April 15th 1865
Dear Father

Although I know very well that you will receive the terrible news of

18. The Lincoln Assassination

the murder of our President long before this reaches you — yet I can not forebear writing — It is so unexpected — so awful that really I feel unable to realize it. There is no doubt whatever but that it is the result of premeditation and conspiracy — and what is *worse* — it is in my opinion — not a conspiracy on the part of the *rebels of the south* — but of scoundrelly sympathizers this side of the Potomac — Nay more it is disowned and discountenanced by Rebel officers almost unanimously — who are in my charge — I have over 500 Rebel officers — ranking from Colonel down — They sent for me to day and asked permission to get up a paper signifying their utter detestation of the crime — and avowing their non connection and sympathy in it. I granted it of course and shall publish it if it is signed by them as numerously as they say it will be. On the evening of the assination — after it became known — the city was fairly wild with excitement. Crowds filled the main Avenue and loud threats were made to burn down the old capitol prison and kill the rebels confined there. I went up to the prison — placed the guards under arms at once and ordered the streets to be guarded — not allowing any one to pass — I was reinforced too by a Regiment of Infantry and part of a regiment of Cavalry. I remained up all night — but happily no demonstration was made. I am now writing at near midnight — at the prison — where I remain again all night to be on hand if trouble comes. The city has seemed all day like Sunday — stores and places of business all closed and nearly every building on the Avenue draped in mourning — Every face you meet bears the impression of gloom and even loud talk or laughter is not heard on the street — though the streets are crowded. I will send you the Washington papers containing the sad details — The President died at 7 A.M. to day — not having uttered a word after being shot. As I write I learn that Secy Seward will — it is hoped confidentially — get along — but his son Frederick is given up — his skull being badly fractured. Thus you see that this wicked rebellion began with murder and ends with it too. It is currently reported that Boothe the Murderer has been taken — but I do not know how reliable the rumor is — I sincerely hope so and that he will suffer tortures of the most cruel kind as a partial punishment for the crime he has committed — No man was ever more humane and forgiving than Abraham Lincoln and no one ever deserved a cruel fate less than him.

Sunday afternoon

There is no farther news to day except that the Funeral of the President is set for Thursday next. No doubt there will be one of the grandest spectacles ever known in this city or perhaps any other. Mr Seward is slowly improving but his son Fred is evidently hopeless or at least very critical.

Boothe *has not* been captured — The best detectives from New York and elsewhere are here and very busy. He *will* be taken without doubt. Col Ingraham assured me to day that they knew the *whole plot and all who were concerned in it.* You may look for some astounding revelations some future day. The body of the President now lies in state at the White House. I send you to days Chronicle with some interesting details— Write me very soon. Love to Mother and Henry and the children

Affectionately Yours
Newton[2]

Newton Colby later wrote the following: "The murder of the President brought many unexpected guests to the prison, among whom I remember Junius Brutus Booth, a brother of Wilkes Booth; John S. Clarke, the renowned comedian; Mr. Ford, of Baltimore, owner of Ford's Theatre, in Washington, where Lincoln was shot; Dr. Mudd, who set the broken limb of the flying assassin, and who repented therefor in the Dry Tortugas; Spangler, the stage carpenter, who held a ready saddled horse at the back door of the theatre for Booth's escape, and many others supposed to have possible connection with, or knowledge of the death of the assassination. I gave Junius Brutus Booth the knowledge of the death of his brother Wilkes, and the circumstances attending it, to which he sadly and sorrowfully answered, 'Poor, misguided boy.'

"On the night of the murder of Lincoln there were eight hundred rebel officers in Carroll Prison, and I need hardly say it was crowded to its utmost capacity. Every grade of rank, from a second lieutenant to a major general, had its representative, and, as a rule, they were an intelligent, gentlemanly set of men, and, as I thought, worthy a better cause. I announced to them myself the news that fell so like a thunderbolt on the country of the cowardly murder of the president; and to their honor, I record it, that with two exceptions they united in condeming the act, and regretting its occurrence most heartily.

"While Carroll Prison was thus crowded, it was attacked by a mob, and came near furnishing a bloody sequel to the death of Lincoln. It was when daily expectation of the announcement of the capture of his murderer was awaited with intense interest, that a sergeant and two privates were sent in charge of two prisoners, civilians, from the headquarters of the Provost Marshall, Colonel Ingraham, to deliver them at Carroll Prison, and it was surmised and believed that the prisoners were Booth and an accomplice. Instantly, they were followed by a crowd that rapidly increased in numbers and fierceness, till it seemed that the death of the entire party was inevitable. A mounted orderly, by another street, brought notice of their coming, and a warning to be prepared. But thirty men were to be spared, and they at once drawn up before the entrance, and the orderly dispatched for more troops. Presently, the mob came in sight — a dense mass, numbering thousands-while just before them, driven like chaff before a gale, was the sergeant and his men, running, but bravely keeping their trust, always surrounding and defending the prisoners— now struck down by some missle, but instantly up again, making straight to the shelter of the prison, which at last they reached, bloody and bruised — all of them, especially the prisoners, half dead with blows and fright. Then the mob, cheated of its prey, crowded the street with fierce yells, and began hurling stones at the windows, and, finally, at the little force still guarding the front doors, till the ominous clicking of the gun-locks began to intimate that, with or without the orders of their officers, they would fire in self-defense. Anxiously they looked for the coming of assistance; but, compelled at last to either give up their trust or to attack, they suddenly deployed as skirmishers, and, with leveled bayonets, sprang forward at the word of command upon the rioters, who, dismayed and surprised, fled down the streets and alleys-not one being killed, and but few wounded with the bayonet. The prisoners, I need not add, were not Booth, or connected in any way with his crime, but they barely escaped with life."[3]

Lt. Col. Newton T. Colby participated in the huge funeral procession in Washington. For years, after the war, his sword hung in the house of his daughter Jeanette Colby Tomlinson in Vineland, New Jersey. It has been described by family members as still having black material attached to it at that time.

CHAPTER 19

Old Capitol Prison — After Lincoln's Death

Headquarters Department of Washington
Washington, May 11, 1865
Lt. Col. Colby
Mil. Superintendant of the Old Capitol Prison:

    You will immediately deliver to accomp'g Guard the persons of thirty-six[36] Rebel Officers (more or less) prisoners of war whose names appear upon enclosed rolls now in your custody for the purpose of being transfered to Johnsons Island Ohio

C.C. Augur
Major Genl. Comdj.[1]

Old Capitol Prison
May 11th 1865

    Rec'd[34] thirty-four Rebel Officers.
M.A. Bower 2d Lt.
Co. "G" 24th Reg't V.R.C.
Comdg Guard[2]

Headquarters Department of Washington
Washington, May 11, 1865
Lt. Col. Colby

296

19. Old Capitol Prison—After Lincoln's Death

Mil. Superintendant of the Old Capitol Prison:

You will immediately deliver to accomp'g Guard the persons of Eighty-two[82] Rebel Officers (more or less) prisoners of war whose names appear upon enclosed rolls now in your custody for the purpose of being transfered to Elmira N.Y.

C.C. Augur
Major Genl. Comdj.[3]

Old Capitol Prison
May 11, 1865

Received[79] seventy-nine Rebel Officers

J R Stone
Capt. 24th VRC[4]

"Gov. Vance of North Carolina was taken from his home in Statesville on May 13, 1965. He was to be taken under close guard to Washington. He was however, treated leniently and even given a day of grace to take care of his affairs. The railroad being ripped up, and horses scarce, and the 35 year old being to heavy to make a long trip on horse required another method of transportation. A wealthy Jewish hat manufacturer of Charlotte came with a wagon and drove Vance to Salisbury. The ride began about 9 A.M. on May 14 with the buggy surrounded with troopers riding all around. Vance was then taken to Raleigh and thence by train to Washington, where on May 20 he was placed in the most famous of jails, Old Capitol Prison. The prison, at this time, seems to have been about as public as Pennsylvania Ave., with persons coming and going in sufficient numbers that a small crowd would gather around Vance's cell to pass comments with him."

"Mrs. Vance became seriously ill and had care of 4 young boys. Gov. Vance petitioned for a pardon on June 3 and it was finally granted on July 6, 1865."[5]

"On May 4, a telegram from General Grant ordered Gov. Letcher and all other particularly obnoxious political leaders in Virginia be arrested. May 17, a detachment of Union Cavalry left Winchester for Lexington. On May 20, before dawn, the cavalry men entered Lexington and quietly surrounded Gov. Letcher's house. The 52 year old Letcher was arrested and they took him by wagon towards Winchester stopping at Staunton that night. Letcher arrived at Winchester on the morning of May 23 and left the next morning for Washington. Arriving in Washington after midnight, he was kept in an army arsenal overnight. The next morning [May 25] he was taken to Carroll Prison, his home for the next 47 days. Letcher was treated well during his imprisonment. Responsible army officers and prison officials showed him every possible consideration. After a month in a private cell, Letcher was transferred to a larger cell with ex-Gov. Vance of North Carolina, ex-Gov. Brown of Georgia, banker Gazeway B Lamar of Savanah, General Edward Johnson of Chesterfield County, Va., and a Doctor Stewart of Va. A close comradeship developed between these political prisoners and Letcher and Vance forgot their wartime clashes and became particularly close friends.

"The withering heat of summertime Washington forced the prisoners to strip down to their under clothes, but prison life was not unbearable. Many hours were spent playing cards and conversing on every imaginable subject....

"Occasionally the prisoners could watch outside events from their windows, such as the gigantic Fourth of July celebration staged less than three months after the Union had overcome it's greatest menace.... Good food from nearby restaurants and large supplies of whisky and brandy were available as long as the prisoners had money [most received money from their families]. Letcher and his fellow prisoners were not maltreated by the government they had fought for four years. July 10 Letcher successfully applied and received a parole. He had a half hour interview with President Johnson before leaving for home."[6]

Maj. General Edward Johnson, CSA, was captured at the Battle of Gettysburg, but subsequently exchanged. He was again captured at the Battle of Nashville, [Dec. '64] and was imprisoned at Old Capitol until July 1865.

Lt. Col. Colby continues to write after the war: "The number of prisoners in 'Carroll Prison,' as I said before, at this time, was the most serious test of its capacity, and was the result of some difficulty in obtaining speedy transportation for them to the prison depots further North and West. Many friends of the Southern officers confined here came to see them, and, in all cases, so far as my knowledge goes, were permitted to see them, and provide them with much-needed comforts; and, more than that, I allowed, in one case at least, a young major, who met here for the first time in four years his lady love and intended wife, to accompany her home to tea, only asking his word of honor that he would return at a given hour, which he punctually did. His name has escaped my memory; but if the few hours of pleasure he enjoyed upon that occasion be not yet greatfully

19. Old Capitol Prison — After Lincoln's Death

remembered, then is he an ungreatful man. I recall, also, with pleasure now, that I, in testifying before a House committee, appointed to consider the propriety of retaliating the treatment our poor fellows received at Andersonville and other Southern prisons, condemned it as unworthy the name of any Christian people. When at last the order came to send away nearly all eight hundred, I stood near the door as they marched out, and, with hardly one exception, they shook me by the hand, in saying their 'goodbye,' and expressed their sense of the kind treatment they had received.

"Governor Vance, of North Carolina, Governor Letcher, of Virginia, and Governor Brown, of Georgia, were, for a few months recipients of the hospitalities of the Old Capitol, and endured the tedium of prison life with the patient courage of true-hearted men. Before the breaking out of the war, and while the propriety of secession was being discussed in North Carolina, Governor Vance came out strong against it, stumping nearly the whole State in favor of 'The Union as it was.' Finding it in vain, and called upon to decide between 'the devil and the deep blue sea,' or in other words, whether he would be politically and socially ostracized by his friends, who had always stood staunchly by him in the State where he was born, reared, and educated, or go in with them in an undertaking which he forsaw would fail, like many other good men in the South he chose to live or fall among friends. Who could blame him? He saw the failure and scorned to evade the result by changing to a Unionest, as many far less worthy did, feeling that he had deliberately incurred the risk, and willing, deliberately, to expiate it. Possessing a keen perception of the humorous, cheerful, ready witted, with a vigorous intellect, a story-teller par excellence — surpassing even Senator Nye — and, really, the best extempore speaker for any and all occasions, with or without notice, carrying always his audience like a whirlwind — such was Governor Zebulon B. Vance, the pet and pride of the old North State.

"I cannot refrain from an anecdote of himself, illustrative of the commencement of his political life and his popularity with all classes in his native State, as he himself related it. It was after his first election to a seat in the House of Representatives in Washington, and at about the age of thirty-eight years. He had attended the full session, and on his journey home had arrived at the end of railway travel, and was obliged to finish the journey by stagging across the country. Full of the pride of being a member of Congress, and to see and be seen, he mounted a seat outside the coach with the driver of the vehicle, and away they rolled behind four sorry-looking steeds. The Jehu was evidently of the earth earthy, of the stable odorous, a ragged, seedy specimen of his order, and in strong contrast to our friend, the Governor, who sat by his side, dressed in the more decorous results of a fashionable Washington tailor — and no doubt happy in so being. Pride, however, was destined to the usual fall, the author of which humiliation being close at hand. A tall, cadaverous, lank, pale specimen of the race known as 'clay banks,' was sleepily leaning against a fence as they passed. He was shirtless and ragged, and his remnent of broad-brimmed hat sank ungracefully over and about his long hair, the only laudable use for which was to cover his dirty neck and face. Gravely he saluted the driver, with 'Good-morning, Mr. Jobson,' and then lifting lazily his eyes on Vance, he became suddenly galvanized with the unexpected recognition, to which he gave vent with a 'Hell's blazes, Zeb Vance, is that yeow?' The Governor avers he did the rest of that journey as an inside passenger.

"Governor Letcher was a fine specimen of a Virginian, frank, dignified, courteous, and generous, firm and unchangeable in his deliberate and matured purpose, and of inflexible integrity and honor.

"General Edward Johnson occupied the same room with the above-mentioned Governors, and also a gentleman from Savannah named Lamar, and they exhausted thoroughly every means in their power to avert the tedium of confinement. Governor Vance, once looking from his window into the East Capitol Park, said, with a sigh, 'How I would like to stretch my limbs with a brisk walk over there.' I replied by saying, 'Put on your hat, then,' and suiting the action to the word, he did so, and I led him down stairs and past the guard, and away he went and enjoyed his stroll hugely, returning in a few hours safe to his hotel.

"One evening there arrived from the War Department an order to prepare for the reception of (as near as I can recollect) one hundred and fifty prisoners, who were coming from Baltimore, nearly all of whom were placed in solitary confinement and not allowed to communicate with each other. Now, every room in both prisons was occupied, and to carry out the command was simply impossible, and I did not attempt it. Their arrival was a fresh surprise, for the prisoners were some of the principal business men of Baltimore, with their employees-such gentlemen as Messrs. Johnson, Sutton & Co., Hamilton Easter & Co., Weesenfelt & Co., Charles E. Waters & Co., and many more. They were arrested by a leading detective for alleged selling of goods to be run through the blockade. I believe there was not a guilty man in the number, and that it was a put up job by the astute detectives, who knew that, being gentlemen of wealth, they could extort money from them by sufficient squeezing. Their coming brought a good influence in many ways, and many a poor devil then confined, with neither friends or money, could testify to their liberality and generosity, and benefited by the ill wind that blew these gentlemen into durance vile."[7]

Washington D.C.
May 26th 1865
Dear Father

    I received your letter. There is not much news here — Rumor says that there will soon be important changes in the cabinet — that Blair will succeed Stanton and that Adams will succeed Seward — I am not a little amused to hear *you* — a *military man* — talk about the expense of keeping a team here — I supposed you *knew* that Govt paid that — Of course I have the knowledge of keeping horses — and can draw forage for *three* even if I have the horses. I do not pay anything for stable rent as I put up a shanty stable at very small expense myself in the back yard. I keep a man to take care of them — but keep one if I have horses or not.

    I am in a little trouble just now and may be relieved from city duty here and sent to my Regiment — I will not explain it now — only will say that if I have justice done me I shall be all right — I have done nothing wrong in any form — and have the personal appearance of the Asst Secy of War — that I need fear nothing — so do not worry about me. Some one else is being whipped over my shoulders that is all.

    The 107th Regt is here and I have seen a number of my old comrades who are all glad to see me as I am them. The city is full of soldiers and officers and there is a good deal of drunkenness and c — Every one will feel relieved when the Army is paid off and disbanded — and the men go to their homes — It is generally understood that our Corps are to remain in the service — but there is as yet no offical announcement of it. Give my love to Mother and Henry. Tell my dear little ones that I think of them very often and trust that they are learning *very* fast — as I want them before long with me and I do not want to feel ashamed because they are not educated and intelligent. Write soon — oftener than you have and believe me as ever very affectionately

Your Son
Newton[8]

    As the war ended and the news of what had happened at Andersonville reached the North, retribution was quick in coming. The commandant, Capt. Wirz, was arrested in May and sent to Old Capitol Prison. He was the only soldier tried and convicted for war crimes during the war. He was hanged in Washington on November 10, 1865.

Washington D.C.
June 6, 1865
Dear Father

 I wrote you something more than a week ago and sent the pictures I had promised Mother — by express — I do not hear a word from you and this notwithstanding I specially asked you to write at once and tell me how Kittie was. You must be either awful busy or quite ill or you would not have left me so long in ignorance of everything at home. Now I warn you that I shall transfer my correspondance to some one more prompt — unless you write oftener. I have not yet received the expenses for May — although I have very often asked you to send them promptly at the end of the month —

 I wrote you the last time — that I was in a little trouble but did not explain — I will do so now. You saw in the papers that I was appointed to take full charge and control of both prisons — This was a surprise to me — as I had no intimation of it till one morning I was summoned before Genl Auger — who informed me that he was about appointing me — He did so in a special order — Making it necessary for all releases and commitments to go through my hands and every thing else the same way. This of course placed me over Mr Wood — who has been superintendant for over three years — Well just after being appointed and before the books and papers were turned over to me — it became necessary for our oil company to go to New York and dispose of our claim at some price as some of the owners were going out of service and I was selected — and to save expense — an order was made out — directing me to go and take a prisoner and deliver him to Genl Dix in New York. The order was by order of Maj Genl Auger comdg Dept of Washington and was made by Capt Walbridge — one of his staff (and an equal partner in the Oil Company too) who always writes such orders and is authorised to sign by order of Genl Auger. I went and had only been there about 12 hours when I was telegraphed to come home — did so at once — and was together with Capt Walbridge placed in arrest by order of the Secy of War — as soon as I returned. Well I was anxious of course to know *what* I was charged with and after a few days a friend of mine went to the Secy and asked what I had done? The Secy informed him that I had wrongfully used Govt tranportation in going to N.Y. on private business — Now if I had not have gone — some other officer would — and it cost Govt no more for me than any other and there it is of common occurrence to give such orders to any officer who has friends or business — and has been repeatedly done without censure or notice. Next and most important — the Secy said "I had gone off and neglected a very important trust just confided to my care" — Now when I went — Mr Wood who had been trusted with this important care for 3 years — agreed to see that everything went right in my absence and not then had the books and c turned over to me. While I was in arrest and of course not at the prisons at all — Wood went away *by order of the Secy of War and was gone longer than I was leaving no one in charge* — I was not much alarmed at being arrested — for I felt certain that Mr Stanton had acted upon false information and that his sense of justice would eventually set me right — It is very evident that some one who is hostile to me — reported me to the Secy. However I am released from arrest and returned to duty in the Old Capitol which shows that I did nothing intentionally or seriously wrong — The weather has been oppresively hot and sultry for the last few days —

I wish you were where you could ride with me occasionally behind my ponies — I have a stylish top carriage and enjoy a ride nearly every day — I believe it would do you ever so much good. The ponies are very fast and can go a mile *together* in less than three minutes and one of them has gone in 2.25. Write soon and tell me all the news.

Love to Mother and Henry and the Children *Write Soon*

Affectionatelly Your Son
Newton[9]

The above letter shows once again how times were. Jealousies drove many people to behave unscrupulously toward others in hopes of advancement in these unsettled times.

Capitol Prison
Washington, D.C.
June 17th 1865

General Orders No 11: I General Order No 10 is hereby revoked and Officers commanding Guards will enforce the following orders in its place.

II At Guard Mounting each morning a Non-Commissioned Officer and two superinumeraries will be specially detailed to have charge of the Guard room, Hall and c and he will be held responsible to the officer for its cleanliness and good order — The pieces at half cock will be neatly arranged in the racks — the haversacks hung only on the pegs and no boards will be taken out of the bunks — or permitted to lie about the room.

III Officers of the Guard will be held responsible for the instruction of the men in Guard duty and the regulations must be strictly carried out in all the details — Sitting down on post or lounging will not be permitted by any sentinel on duty at the Prisons. Officers will see that their men are thoroughly instructed in all their duties after which any neglect on the part of the men must receive prompt correction.

By order of

N.T. Colby
Lt. Col. Comd'g

This order will be transferred by each Officer to the one who succeeds him.[10]

Washington D.C.
July 2, 1865
Dear Father

I have allowed several days to pass before I answered your last letter — but have not forgotten that I owe you one. I am leading a *very* lazy life here — owing to the fact that there are but very few prisoners here — I am in daily expectation that the authorities will close one or both of the Prisons very soon — and if so my occupation will be gone and I shall doubtless be sent to my Regiment. There is considerable uncertainty yet — as to what is to be done with our corps — and opinions are about equally divided — I am greatly in hopes that we will be retained — for I have acquired a liking for the service — and beside I shall be terribly unfit to apply myself to *labor* — both physically and mentally. Yesterday I had the pleasure of meeting Lt Col Ely Parker of Genl Grants Staff — for the first time. I only heard a few days since that he was here — You will remember he was an Indian — and was in the Engineer Office of the G.V. [Genesee Valley] Canal at Nunda — He is much thicker set and larger than when there —

Enclosed I send you some confederate money — endorsed by Gov Vance of North Carolina — Gov Letcher of Virginia and Maj Genl Edward Johnson C.S.A. They are prisoners here and gave me the notes as keepsakes — Endorsing them at my request. The two Govenors are two very clever Gentlemen and do not hesitate to admit their defeat — and in fact seem to care very little for it. Gov Vance is not an ordinary man and will yet be prominent as a politican — He is well educated very intelligent and clear headed — as well as energetic and decided — and no better union man lives now in North Carolina in my opinion.

I have my team and carriage yet and generally ride every evening — Last evening I was driving on 14th St — and going rather fast — when lo — I was arrested by a Police officer and taken to the Station House and there fined $3 by the dispensor of justice — Just as I drove up I saw a friend — Maj Nickerson of the Marine Corps—coming out — who also had fallen into the hands of the law — I went into the office and inquired as follows— "Where is the amiable dispenser of justice?" The officer pointed him out and I said "My gentle friend — what amount of circulating medium do you require to satisfy the outraged majesty of the law?"— Everybody began to laugh —"No levity sir in the court" said his honor — "Most certainly not" said I —"but have the kindness to name the amount of Government stamps you want"— By Chapter 7 Section 12 of the Corporation Laws—"D_d your chapters and sections— said I —*how much* is it?" "Three dollars is the fine sir" said his honor and I paid it — remarking that in case he should at any time feel ashamed of playing such a dirty trick on a Gentleman and wish to return the money — he could send it to that address— handing him my card — I then jumped into my wagon and drove off faster than I had driven before — getting three cheers from a mob of soldiers and others who overheard the interview with "his honor"— The probabilities *now* are that our corps will cease to exist before long — and I am not a little puzzled to know what I can do. I contemplate with great dread — the necessity of again learning business habits and confining myself to them — But it must be I suppose —

Give my love to Mother and Henry and all my little folks—Write as soon as you receive this and acknowledge the receipt of enclosed ck.

Sincerely and Affectionately
Your Son
Newton[11]

Lt. Col. Ely S. Parker was secretary to General Grant. Parker was with Grant and Lee on April 9 and 10, 1865, and wrote out the various orders related to the surrender. Parker was the last Grand Sachem of the Iroquois Nation.[12] At some time before the war, Col. Parker lived in Nunda, New York, for about two years.

Balt. July 8, [1865]
My Dear Governor [Vance]

I regret to say "Good bye" on paper — rather than to shake your hand — but "fate abstant." Remember your *promises* and believe me

Sincerely Yours
N.T. Colby[13]

Washington D.C.
July 12, 1865
Dear Father

    Your very kind letter of the 5th came duly to hand and in reply would say that I have been quite busy — and have really hardly had time to write a letter — *Now* however I have plenty of leisure and I improve it at once in getting even with you. I have nothing especial to communicate — except that it is pretty certain that our corps will be mustered out of service soon and I left with nothing to do.

    I shall doubtless be out within a month and perhaps sooner and in the meantime I may be ordered to join my Regt at Elmira — as an order recently issued orders officers detached from their Regts to join them at once — if they are serving out of the departments where their Regts are. Carroll Prision is not now used as a military Prision — I moved all the prisoners down to the Old Capitol where I now am. I have but few left — but shall receive about 100 more from the Central Gaurd House soon. I am in sole command and have things my own way.

    I do not intend to live in Corning and if no better opening offers I shall go to Mexico — where I can have a Colonelcy in the service of the liberal party in fighting against the "Frog-Eaters" — and get a large premium in gold — in advance — I can not confine myself to "small potatoes" again — and a pea nut stand is decidedly distasteful to my feelings —

    In conversation with my friend Mr Hamilton Easter of Balt — a day or two since he advised me to get a coal agency and settle in Balt — I had not time to discuss the matter with him then — but will write and learn more about it. If my Balt friends will help me as they are abundantly able to do I can get a fine business and can soon get ahead-

    Give my love to all my dear little folks and to Mother and Henry.

    Should you come please write me before you start.

Affectionately Your Son
Newton[14]

Washington D.C.
July 17, 1865
Dear Father

    If you have decided to come and see me and make the trip we have talked of — come at once — I have asked to be relieved from duty at the Old Capitol and also for twenty days leave — which I think will be granted.

19. Old Capitol Prison — After Lincoln's Death

In haste Yours
Newton[15]

[to Statesville, N.C.]
Washington, D. C.
July 19, 1865
My Dear Governor [Vance]

Your very kind and very welcome letter came to hand to day and I hasten to reply. I was much pleased to learn of your safe arrival home but greatly regretted to hear that Mrs Vance was so ill. No doubt it was a surprise to you — and a very sad one too— to find her thus— but there is comfort in your assurance that she is improving — and I trust will soon regain her health.

Since your departure from Washington — "hotel De Carroll" has been abandoned — and the prisoners removed to the "Old Capitol." Gov Letcher has been released upon the same conditions you were. He went home about a week since. Mr Lamar — your other "companion du voyage" was also released yesterday and departed for his home. Genl [Edward] Johnson is still here and is like Sir John Moore — "left alone in his glory." He — however is in daily expectation of being permitted to once more place his "foot on his native heath." I very often go into his room and while away the time by playing euchu — *without* however — being allowed to take the left bones with the ace.

I read your account of the condition of things in your country — with much sympathy for the distress that exists there — and I must say I can hardly see any solution of the questions that present themselves. With poor prospects for the coming crops — with no circulating medium — and lacking in the necessary means and productions to draw capital to you — I can only see certain if our Northern people could once appreciate your exact condition and see for themselves the ruin in the South — that the bitterness evoked by the recent struggle would give way to sympathy — and become twice blessed — in being merciful. I desire you to feel at perfect liberty to ask anything within the limited scope of my ability to accomplish. I have applied to be relieved from duty here — but wherever I am I shall always feel obliged to you if you will let me know how I can serve you. I wish very much to correspond with you and if I leave Washington I will apprise you of my address. I have no doubt whatever — that you are entirely correct in surmising that any ill treatment experienced by your family is not due to instructions from Government as I believe they are actuated by motives far superior to those which would dictate the annoyance of families in the persons of ladies and children.

Gov Letcher left here before the arrival of your letter. I could not of course deliver your message to him — I have not heard from him since his departure but am in daily expectation of doing so. Although I have not received the tobacco you so kindly sent me — yet you will please accept my thanks and those of Wilson for the very acceptable present. I shall in smoking it ruminate pleasantly upon the pleasure I have enjoyed with you — while suffering durance vile — another instance (to me at least) of how good cometh out of evil. I trust you have not forgotten the promise you gave me to endeavor to interest in my favor a certain lady — of *rebellious* proclivities. I am anxious to place before her some Union arguments which if they are productive of no other good result will be an outlet for me of my Zealous Patriotism and — who knows — I may be the humble means of turning her from the error of her ways—*selah*.

Wilson Chambers and all unite in sending their kindest regards and good wishes. I desire (may I?) to have you present my regards to Mrs Vance and to express the hope that she may very soon enjoy perfect health. It will give me great pleasure to receive a line from her. Let me hear from you again as soon as the demands upon your time will admit — And now my dear Gov — if there is anything you need and can not obtain there do not hesitate to send to me and I will get and forward it with pleasure. In writing please direct to me at Dyers Hotel, Washington, D.C. and should I have changed my quarters it will be forwarded. I shall anxiously look for your next and believe me to be

Sincerely and Respectfully Yours
N.T. Colby
Lt. Col. and Mil. Supt.[16]

This is the first indication that Newton Colby was interested in finding a new wife, as shown by his interest in a Southern friend of Gov. Vance.

Deyer Hotel
Washington D.C.
July 25, 1865
Dear Father

I have waited several days since the receipt of your last letter in the hope that I could come instead of being obliged to write to you — Since I

19. Old Capitol Prison — After Lincoln's Death

wrote you — matters have taken a very different complexion with regard to my being able to come home — and I am very sorry to say that I do not think I shall be able to get away. When I wrote you last — I had been up to Genl Auger and asked to be relieved from duty at the Old Capitol and applied for 20 days leave — and he *promised* both — Now however he says he can not spare me! However I may be home soon with a longer leave — as there is a prospect of mustering out our corps or of consolidating it — which last — will render supernumerary a number of officers. Some officers of our Corps have already been sent home on half pay with orders to report to the Adjt General every thirty days by letter. No one seems to know anything *certain* about what will be done with us — I hardly dare go away for fear I shall be mustered out because I am absent. As soon as anything definite is known I will try again to come. I am still at Dyers Hotel — I go out very little except to ride — which I do every evening.

I desire to come home very much — and see you all — but it is hard telling with any certainty when I can come — unless I am mustered out soon. I have my horses and carriage yet although I have been offered an advance on their cost — I think I will sell them before long — however — though I would greatly like to keep them — they are so *fast* and *kind*. I drove them a mile on the race track here in 2 minutes and forty seconds — Pretty fair going eh? The trackmaster held the watch and said with training they would go *double* in less than 2-30. They are young — one 5 and the other six — sound and gentle — and are acknowledged to be the fastest double team in the city.

How are my little folks getting on? Do not let them entirely forget that they have a father — I often think of them and desire very greatly to see them.

Give my love to Mother and Henry — By the way what is Henry at now and how is he doing? I hope he is trying to do well and have no doubt he is.

Affectionately Your Son
Newton[17]

Field and Muster Roll, 19th Regt. VRC, July-Aug '65, lists Lt. Col. Newton T. Colby under remarks — "Commanding Regiment."[18]

Washington D.C.
Aug 3d 1865
Dear Father

I received your very welcome letter last evening and in accordance with your request I hasten to reply.

My position in the service is so uncertain that I can not tell what I had better do.

No decision has yet been promulgated in reference to our corps—but *it is said* that one will be given very soon either to retain or disband us. There is some talk of our being placed under Maj Genl Howard who commands the Freedmans Bureau and then we should be scattered all over the South. *No one knows certain however.*

I still keep my horse and carriage—but intend to sell as soon as I am offered what I consider them worth—though if we are to live near Balt. I would greatly like to keep them. I would like you to see and ride behind them—They are the best and fastest team in the City—I enclose draft for $50 for July acct.

Write as soon as you receive it.

Give my love to mother and the children and Henry.

Tell mother I send her by express the porait of another distinguished man—she will no doubt recognize it-

Affectionately Your Son
Newton[19]

This picture is thought to be the one showing Newton in full dress uniform.

[to Statesville, N.C.]
Old Capital Prison
Washington, D.C. 1865
Corning, Steuben Co. N.Y.
Aug 22d 1865
My Dear Governor [Vance]

Your very welcome and interesting letter reached me—not alas—by the fair hand by which you sent it—but through the mail. My evil fortune had decreed that I should be absent from Washington...

My unfortunate absence is a source of keen regret for I really wished to meet Miss Calloway very much indeed and nothing could be more unfortunate for me. She mailed your letter at Richmond and it was forwarded to me here and I received it last evening. I *deserve* and *feel sure* of your sympathy in this disappointment and desire you to explain to her the reason of my absence. You say she has gone to New York and if I knew her address I would certainly call upon her *there* but I fear I have by my absence from Washington lost a golden opportunity of forming her acquaintance.

I have been relieved from duty at "Old Capitol" and am under orders to rejoin my Regiment—but do not know where it is at present. Upon being relieved I was granted twenty days leave and I have been vagabondizing about this state since the 8th inst.

Could you not come North and bring Mrs Vance and thereby benefit her health as well as enjoy yourself for a time? It would afford me much pleasure to meet you—and show you the green pastures and pleasant places of our cooler clime. We could kill trout—visit places of interest here and there—moralise on the rise and fall of republics—discuss Negro suffrage with the "unterrified"—but pictures of Horace Greely and Wendall Phillips—originate new ideas upon re-construction—develop plans to elevate and refine our African brothers and c and c ad infinitum "how singular"—

I have received notice from the express agent at Washington of the arrival of the tobacco and have ordered it sent to me here—It will therefore probably reach me in a day or two.

It is impossible to say where I may be and therefore please address me here for the present and letters will be forwarded to me. It is not impossible that I shall be assigned to duty somewhere in your state—in which case I may have the pleasure of meeting you again before long—although "mon Pere" is endeavoring to persuade me to abandon the profession of arms and become "civil."

Do not fail to send me Miss Calloway's address if you have it and I may yet "conquer" a "*rebile*" and do the state some service. I wish to see her and thus satisfy myself—if it is possible for one of such dangerous proclivities to be fair and lovely and at the same time try to convince her that a northern birth place does not *always* or necessarily indicate a vagabond and loafer. When you see her again express to her my deep regret and mortification at being unable to have met her—and if in your opinion proper give her my regards.

I shall look anxiously for your reply.

I am Sincerely Yours
N.T. Colby[20]

"New Commander—Lieut. Col. Colby, who was serenaded at the Brainard House on Wednesday evening, has reported here [Elmira] to take command of his regiment, the 19th V.R.C. He has already established a favorable reputation in this part of the State as a Lieutenant in the 23rd

N.Y.V., and a Captain and Major [and Lieut. Col.] in the 107th N.Y.V. He has been assigned to the charge of the Old Capitol prison in Washington during the past year, from which he has been relieved by the recent breaking up of that institution. The regiment, in the meantime, has been well drilled and disciplined under the command of Major J.H. Donovan, who has earned an enviable praise as a rigid tactician, and the military efficiency of that regiment is owing to his careful and strict supervision."[21]

[to Statesville, N.C.]
Elmira Chemung Co N.Y.
Nov. 27, 1865
Dear Governor [Vance]

    Some time has unavoidably elapsed since receiving your last very welcome letter — and although I detest apologies *in letter* — yet I feel compelled to explain the reason of my delay in writing — and it consists in the fact of my having purchased a country residence near Philadelphia and removed my "houshold panates" thither. Your letter reached me in the midst of the turmoil and discomfort of packing furniture and c — hence my inability to immediately reply.

    I have eagerly watched the papers to find some trace of you but thus far in vain. To night as I read in the Herald the names of the prominent candidates for Senator from your state. I almost expected to see your name — although I knew you were yet an "unpardoned rebile" and therefore — of course it could not be.

    Try therefore to curb the desire of your heart to kill (and eat — no doubt some believe) the peacable and loyal dwellers of the North — put away from you the inclination to raise insurrections and rebellions—cease to advocate the burning and scalping of your talented but oppressed colored brethren — divorce yourself from the wicked pride that prevents your acknowledging the superiority or *equality* at least of the descendants of Ham — with whom you are surrounded — do not allow the handles of huge bowie knives and the butts of revolvers to peer from your boot legs and coat pockets— and I assure you — you will soon be allowed to come in out of the cold. This also is not official — selah

    I have not yet experienced the happiness of meeting Miss Calloway and by faith — I nearly despair. Often have I been tempted to write to her — but feared she with her unregenerated heart (you said she was a rebel) might from some unexpected redoubt fire shotted — angry guns upon me — or — by keeping within her works— overwhelm me with contempt — as an impudent Yankee. I fail to get encouragement from your letter too—because you say I will get "all sorts of receptions" if I wantonly invade her presence-and truly I would sooner face a battery charged with grape—than get a cool wicked fearfully keen and cutting reception. I believe—entro nous—that my visit would be an infliction upon her—but I would give a small sum to meet her somewhere by accident.

I am thinking seriously of leaving the service and retiring to more quiet life. If I only had a wife to make my home cheerful—I would not hesitate a moment. I know this want is one that might be quickly satisfied—but alas I fear I am to particular—hence I am "doomed to walk" alone.

Write as soon as you receive this and I faithfully promise to answer hereafter *promptly*.

Ask Miss Calloway if I might write her. Trusting to hear from you soon and wishing you health happiness, I am as ever,

Sincerely Yours
N.T. Colby[22]

[to Statesville, N.C.]
Hammonton, Atlantic Co. N.J.
Dec 25th, 1865
My Dear Governor [Vance]

To day is Christmas and looking, as usual from my boyhood for "goodies" and presents—lo your raiding letter came—a warmly welcome present. The Elmira P.M. kindly re directed it to me here—and notwithstanding its circuitous route—it reached me with commendable speed. If I *must* plead "guilty" to the stupidity of omitting to give you my present address in my last—I will try and do so as gracefully as possible and throw myself upon the mercy of the court—with the simple statement that it was quite an unusual occurrence of "absent-mindedness"—though the fact that I am a resident of *New Jersey now* —it may occur to you that I was ashamed to acknowledge it—which I solemnly deny. Believe me I am heartily glad to hear that you will soon receive even the limited boon of an extended parole and sincerely trust that your full release from all conditions of "durance vile" will very soon follow—Would that our worthy President would permit me to advise him in the matter and be governed by it—for I would "Emancipate" you "to once" and restore you again to your primitive condition.

My new residence is located 30 miles south east of Philadelphia—on the Camden and Atlantic R.R. It is just about an hours ride either to Phil or the coast. Atlantic City—the coast terminus of the R.R. is a fashionable watering place next to Cape May—which is about 50 miles from me. The place (Hammonton) is a rural settlement—mostly devoted to fruit farming—I bought about 25 acres with moderately good improvements and have been tearing down—adding to and building ever since and have an ambition to make it a pleasant home in time.

I can appreciate your objection to accepting any nomination to Office just *now*—but have not lost my confidence in your future—and I here beg to notify you that your promise to make me your Secretary is still remembered and looked forward to.

One of the most pleasant things in your agreeable letter—was the information of Mrs V's greatly improved health—upon which I congratulate both her and yourself and desire to Thank her for the kind rememberances of me and to return my most respectful regards and the Compliments of the season. Observing how your Christian example of returning good for evil has stimulated me—I pray you continue in well doing and weary not—and grant me the pleasure of another letter right early-

Sincerely Yours
N.T. Colby[23]

[envelope addressed:
Miss M. Virginia Calloway
Wilksboro, N.C.
Enclosed in envelope addressed:
Gov. Z.B. Vance
Statesville, N.C.]
Hammonton, Atlantic Co.
New Jersey
Dec. 27, 1865
Miss M. Virginia Calloway

Although I can hardly divest myself of the idea that I am taking an unwarranted and perhaps an unpardonable liberty in addressing you—yet I have yielded to the temptation—and must trust to your kindness to be forgiven. I may also urge in extenuation—my great disappointment in failing to have made your acquaintance during your recent visit North—a pleasure promised by my friend Gov Vance—and denied me by some freak of evil fortune. May I then avail myself of this means to seek your acquaintance and will you permit a correspondence?

You will decree this a bold request no doubt — but it is made with the deepest respect and referring you to Gov Vance as to the propriety of so far confiding in your unknown petitioner.

Seperated — perhaps by more than the leagues between us— why may not an interchange of thoughts and ideas prove agreeable?

I assure you it will be so to me and your compliance with my petition will afford me much gratification and happiness.

Very Respectfully and Sincerely
N.T. Colby[24]

CHAPTER 20

The Postwar Years

From Field and Muster Roll for 19th Regt. VRC September through October. Remarks for Lt. Col. Newton T. Colby, Comanding Regiment: Regt return Nov. 18, '65, shows him mustered out June 30, 1866, per A.O. No. 317, A.G.O. July 3, 1866. No subs rolls F+S on file.[1]

June 30, 1866   Newton was Honorably Discharged from Volunteer Reserve.

The future of the Veteran Reserve Corps officers in the re-organization of the postwar army was uncertain. Many of them were told to return home and to check in every 30 days. It appears that Lt. Col. Colby's last duty was the closing of Old Capitol Prison as a military prison in July 1865, and yet his name appears on the rolls until June 30, 1866. After leaving Washington for home in 1865, Newton and his father purchased a fruit farm near Hammonton, New Jersey. On January 26, 1866, a fruit farm at Hammonton, New Jersey was officially deeded to the Colby family. It was listed in the names of Merrill and Dolly Colby, Newton's father and mother. They held this property until September 9, 1868. Col. Colby had read an advertisement about how healthful the climate was in that area and thought it would be a good place to live and do business. However, it wasn't long before it became apparent that farm work was too difficult for Newton, due to his weakened constitution as a result of his bout with typhoid fever during the war.

In early 1866, Newton tried to obtain a position in the reorganized postwar army because he felt that he was as qualified as anyone and was in need of employment.

General Head Quarters State New York
Adjutant General's Office
Albany, March 20th 1866
To His Excellency,
Andrew Johnson
Sir

    I have the honor to respectfully recommend for appointment in the reorganization of the Army, Newton T. Colby, late Lieut. Colonel 19th Regiment V.R.C. Colonel Colby is a thorough soldier practically and entirely competent as an executive officer. Was in the volunteer service from the beginning of the war, until from temporary physical disability he was transferred with the rank he held in the volunteer service, into the Veteran Reserve Corps and was until his muster out, always designated for responsible duty for his excellent business capacity and thorough soldiering qualities.

I am Sir
Very Respectfully
Your Obedient Servant
Wm Irvine
Adjutant General[2]

State of New York
Executive Department
Albany, 6th April 1866
Hon. Edwin M. Stanton
Secretary of War
Sir:

    I have the honor to mention favorably Lieut. Col. N.T. Colby of the 19th V.R.C. for an appointment in the regular army. I am assured his record in the field is very creditable, and that he is a competent officer.

Very Respectfully
R E Fenten[3]

Baltimore 11, 1866
Hon. E.M. Stanton
Secty of War
Sir,

I write on behalf of Col. N.T. Colby of the Veteran Reserve Corps to add my own appeal to that of so many others in his application for a Lieut. Coloncy in the Regular Service.

Col. C. has actively & ably served throughout the war and has won for himself a reputation for soldierly conduct that is worthy as before of the highest form of government.

Hoping sincerely that he may be successful in his application.

I remain, as ever your obedient servent
Wm P Smith[4]

Hammonton Atlantic Co N.J.
His Excellency July 31st 1866
Andrew Johnson
President U.S.A.
Sir,

I respectfully ask to be appointed a Lieutenant Colonel in one of the four Regiments of Vet. Res. Corps. troops—recently authorized. At the interview you kindly granted me a week since—I had the honor of presenting a commendatory letter from the Hon Revered Johnson and others—asking my appointment as Captain in the Regular Army. The army bill now authorizes Vet. Res. Corps troops which permits me to ask your excellency for a restoration to my former rank in the corps-

Trusting my application may receive your favorable consideration.

I have the honor to be
Very Respectfully, Your Obt Servt
N.T. Colby[5]

[to Charlotte, N.C.]
Hammonton, Atlantic Co, N.J.
Sept. 9, 1866
My Dear Governor [Vance]

I came very near meeting you in Washington as I arrived there the day you left—but some unkind fate kept me from the pleasure of taking your hand again. I *did* meet our old friend Lamar and from him learned that you had been there and gone. I had been summoned to Washington and expected to be assigned to duty—but finding that I must go into the Freedmens Bureau—I respectfully declined and preferred to be mustered out of service — though I was not authorized by my pecuniary matters to throw away a good situation. I have applied for a reappointment in the army and have the Presidents *promise but* — well — there's no telling — and c and c.

I wish very much to see you again and should you make another visit to Washington if you will notify me before hand I will try and meet you there. *It is* strange that you have not yet received a pardon for your sins of Rebellion — possibly however you will not need one — as there may be a general remission ere long. Do not get into another rebellion — or allow your neighbors to do so — as it really creates trouble and there is enough now on hand to make the very liveliest kind of a political campaign if nothing worse comes of it.

Sincerely Yours
N.T. Colby[6]

Lt. Col. Colby and Victoria Whitcomb Wood were married in Nunda, New York, on November 25, 1867. Victoria's first husband, Capt. John Pulaski Wood, had served first as a Lieut., Adjt., and Aid de Camp to General King, 1st Army Corps, March — May '62. He was then requested to join the field staff of General Gibbon whom he served as Capt. & A.A.G in the 3rd corps through Sept. '62, the 1st corps through April '63 and the 2nd corps until his death due to illness at Stevensburg, Virginia on March 4, 1864.[7]

In mid–1867, Newton T. Colby moved to Haddonfield, New Jersey, about six miles from Philadelphia, where he lived until early 1875. He was a merchant, at 248 N Delaware Avenue, Philadelphia, until illness caused him to lose all that he had. It was hard to keep a business going in Philadelphia while being frequently sick and away from the business as well as having a rather long commute each day. He then tried insurance, and was listed in the 1870 census as a General Insurance Agent. He then took a job at the Commercial National Bank of Philadelphia as a Dividend and Discount clerk. Newton lived, until about 1872, at what is today 229 Kings Highway East in what was known as the John Clement House on the Historical Register. The Colbys were listed as members of Grace Episcopal Church in Haddonfield, New Jersey, from Feb. 1868 to 1874. A family listing, dated Feb 1, 1868, lists family members as: Newton T. Colby, Fannie W. Wood, Victoria W. Colby, Kitty Colby, Fred Colby, Carrie D. Wood, Frank Colby, Walter Colby, William B. Colby, Robert Vance Colby.[8]

On October 16, 1868, Newton officially adopted Victoria's two daughters, Fannie and Carrie Wood. His own family did not stay with him very long. His sons did not get along very well with the new wife and stepmother Victoria. Frank, Fred, William and Walter left to go out on their own as soon as they could.

A deed dated September 5, 1872, shows the sale of a piece of land on the corner of Grove Street and Thomas Evans Alley in Haddonfield on which he built a new house that stands today at 21-23 Grove Street. Newton continued to work for the Commercial National Bank of Pennsylvania in Philadelphia. He sold his house in Haddonfield and moved to the city to be closer to his work.

In 1879, at age 47, Newton T Colby was living at 314 Chestnut St., Philadelphia in 1879. He was described at this time to be 5'7" tall, with grey hair and blue eyes.[9]

He finally realized that he qualified for a pension for his army service and applied for it.

Invalid Claim No 276420 1879
State of Pennsylvania
County of Philadelphia

I Newton T Colby residing in the city and state aforesaid do certify as follows—That for five years preceeding the war of 1861—I was a resident of Corning Steuben County New York—That my occupation for that time was a merchant and after in the employment of the Buffalo N.Y. and Erie Rail Road—That when I first entered the Army I was to the best of my knowledge—in sound health—and had never had Typhoid Fever—and was not diseased in my liver or kidneys—and that my hearing was not impaired. That to the best of my recollection—I was never seriously ill or treated for disease while in the army until March or April 1863—That I am unable to fix accurately the date of the first attack—in as much as all my papers and memoranda—were carried away—when the regiment left me—sick and delirious at or near Stafford Court House Va—and I never saw them after—but that I truly believe it was some time in March or April—because the regiment went on the Chancellorville Campaign not long thereafter—That at or near the time referred to I remember that the Surgeon Dr Flood said to me "you are looking badly—if you are not careful—you will be down with this fever"—and that he then prescribed for me—that the Regiment was then located at Hope Landing on Acquia Bay—by the side of an extensive marsh—and that Typhoid fever greatly prevailed in the Regiment—and that very many deaths occurred from it there—That I firmly believe that I contracted the disease while there—and that I was not well from that time until after the Battle of Chancellorsville

20. The Postwar Years

and when the Regiment reached Stafford Court House — though I endeavored to keep up — and did not take to bed until reaching said location — where I was very ill — during which illness the Regiment moved away — leaving me there too sick to be moved — That I was treated by the Regimental Surgeon — That my father residing then in Corning N.Y. was written to that I was dangerously ill and advised him to come there immediately — which he did — accompanied by my wife — That I was afterward taken to Acquia bay and conveyed by steamer to Washington D.C. and taken by my father to a Boarding House on Pennsylvania Avenue — that I distinctly remember being carried up the stairs of said house — by persons who were passing by at the time — it being early morning — That my father reported my case at the Surgeon General Office — and a Surgeon whose name I do not remember was detailed to attend me — and the Surgeon General himself — also visited me — as I was informed afterward That I have never recovered from the effects of said disease — as I have suffered ever since from frequent attacks of malarious disease and have as I am informed and believe a chronic impairment of the liver and kidneys — and that my hearing has been unperfect ever since. And that I suffer from prostration and weakness thus induced and have never since been able to perform manual labor or endure fatigue — and that I am prevented by said disability to a great extent from earning a living. That I removed from Corning N.Y. to Hammonton Atlantic Co New Jersey — late in the year 1865 — as said place was largely advertised and commended as being a very healthy location — That I there purchased a small Fruit farm — in the hope that the caring for it would improve my health — That I found I could not endure the necessary labor — and about the middle of 1867 as near as I can recollect — I removed to Haddonfield Camden County N.J. distant about six miles from Philadelphia where I engaged in my former avocation as a merchant at no 248 North Delaware Avenue — and was again compelled to give up business — with a loss of all I had owing mainly I fully believe to absence compelled by sickness — That I there went into the Insurance business — and finally obtained light employment in the Commercial National Bank. That I furthur declare that to the best of my recollection I have suffered from no attacks of acute disease — save recurrances of malarial difficulties since leaving the service in 1866 — and that my illness and disability has always been — as I am informed and believe — that resulting from Malaria and exposer in the Army — trouble with the liver and kidneys and general prostration and weakness I furthur certify that my family Physican in Corning was Dr N M Herrington — and in Hammonton N.J. Dr N B Bowles and while a resident of Haddonfield N.J. Dr N B Jennings was my physican and upon removing to Philadelphia I employed first Dr A L Alstead — who removed to Harrisburg Pa afterwards — then Dr A R Thomas and I furthur certify that I should have applied for a pension upon leaving the service — except that I was informed and believed that the acceptance of a commission in the Veteran Reserve Corps barred my claim — and that I did not know to the contrary until about a year ago.

Newton T Colby[10]

Part of a letter from Newton to his daughter Jeanette:
Philadelphia, June 4, 1879
My Dear Daughter

My own health is not good — nor do I think it will be permanently — for I have no doubt but that my service in the late war has broken down my constitution — I have applied for a pension — feeling I am entitled to it and deserving of it — and if I am fortunate enough to convince the Govt authorities of that fact I shall feel better as to my future.[11]

Colby, although situated in a good position, continued to seek something better in Washington. He moved to 2141 Bainbridge St. Philadelphia, at this time. While he was working at the bank in Philadelphia, he continued to explore the possibility of receiving a government position. He sought an appointment through his good friend Senator Zeb Vance from North Carolina. Vance had been a prisoner of Newton's as the Governor of North Carolina and became very close to him at the close of the war. When Newton and Victoria named their son Robert, his middle name was Vance.

The Commerical National Bank of Penna.
Philadelphia, April 20 1882
Dear Father

I got back again night before last. Had an hours interview with President Arthur who said very kindly he would do something for me — took my name and address and I expect to hear daily — What it will be I can not definitely say — I asked for the consulship at Toronto — He said he would have to consult the Sec of State — Asked me if I would like a place in the Custom House *here* — I have little doubt of getting *something* — but do not know if it will be worth accepting. Senator Vance went with me and we had an appointment by letter with the President and saw him alone

20. The Postwar Years

After the war, Colby, in his early 50s, worked as a banker in Philadelphia. Colby family collection.

in his private Library—He is a fine man and the Republican party have got in him a much better President than they expected. His administration will be strong and I believe better than Garfields would have been—He was very kind to me and promised to provide for me.

Most affectionly
Your Son
Newton[12]

The Commercial National Bank of Penna.
Philadelphia, May 6, 1882
Dear Father

I have time to say a word only—I just returned from Washington last night and have very little news—The president did just as he promised—and directed the Secy of State to select me a nice snug counsulship which was done and then some other man with large influence antagonized it and kept the President from sending my name to the Senate—Genl [President] Arthur however sent me word to go to the Secty of the Interior and accept a place—saying he would take care of me and do better soon—I went and was offered a 1600 dollar clerkship which I peremptorily declined and came home last evening—The Secty said he would write me about a better place—first of the week—so it goes—I believe I shall get something sometime as I rely confidantly on the Presidents promise.

Please sign enclosed note and return at once—Will write soon—

Love to Mother and Kitty
Hastily Yours Newton[13]

The Commercial National Bank of Penna.
Philadelphia, May 15th 1882
Hon H Teller

Secretary of the Interior
Washington D.C.
Dr Sir

    I beg to acknowledge the receipt of your favor of the 10th inst — notifying me of my appointment to a fourth class clerkship in the Pension Office.

    In reply would say that I will accept and enter upon my duties by or before June 1st next.

I have the honor to be
Very Respectfully Yours
N.T. Colby[14]

Washington D.C.
May 31st 1882
Hon William W Dudley
Commissioner of Pensions
Sir

    My full name is Newton T Colby — born in Rochester N.Y. and living in the City of Philadelphia, Pa when appointed — which is my present legal voting residence — in the 1st Cong Dist. For the past 12 or 15 years I have been the Dividend and Discount clerk of "The Commercial Nat. Bank of Penna." and received an academic education — was a soldier in the late war — commencing as 1st Lieu of the 23rd N.Y. Vols in 1861 — and afterwards Captain — Major and Lt. Col. of the 107th N.Y. Vols and Lt. Col. of the 18th V.R.C. Was disabled by disease and now suffer there from the result of Typhoid Fever. I am married — my family consisting of a wife and three children. Do not know that I have any relations in the Government service — and to the best of my belief an qualified to become an examiner — My address is 1304 Connecticut Avenue.

I have the honor to be
Very Respectfully Yours
Newton T Colby[15]

    Upon attaining a position in the Pension Office, Newton moved his family to Washington once again.

Of course I have seen Senator Vance — but only for a moment — he is specially kind and has a heart of gold.

Affectionatly
Newton[16]

1304 Conn Av
Washington D.C.
Dear Father

I had supposed that I would receive a promotion to $2000 the first of July and have been here long enough to see that I can not get along on less — but I am told it will not be — as there are no places at that figure except on the reviewing board — for which no new comer is able — You will smile I guess in reading this and say as you often do I could get along on 1800 — May be — Before I had been in the office *a week* I received notice from the Republican Committee that I was expected to pay $36 as my proper assesment for party purposes! By jove I had not then earned it!

All kinds of influence is brought to bear to get office — and there are at least 10 disappointed ones to one that succeeds — Senator Laphan of N.Y. has a nephew in my office at $1200 — in fact the lowest places are eagerly snapped up — I carry you in mind always — although as yet — my own case has been uppermost — and I could not well ask for too much at once lest I lose all by being too greedy — My health has been poor ever since I landed here — Had to consult a Dr last week and go at the old dose, blue mass and quinine — I cannot get — nor have I had one nights steady sleep — and I dread Aug and Sept — May be I can get a leave for a few weeks and if so will pull out for cooler climates. Will send you a little money this week and some more next week — love to Mother and Kittie and Jo —

Write me how you get along as ever —
Affectionatly Yours as ever Newton[17]

---

to Merrill Colby
Cross Keys, N.J.
1113 17th St Washington D.C.
Aug 6th 1882
Dear Father

There's a rather curious state of affairs in the Interior Dept. You will recollect I told you that Sect Teller was from Nunda? Well a new Asst Sect has just been appointed — who comes from some western state — but who used to be a partner on Dave Swains at the mill in Nunda — and a brother of Doctor Jocelyn. Do you remember him? He knew you — and Walter Whitcomb well. Is it not curious? Teller — the Secretary Jocelyn — the Asst Sect and Lockwood the Chief Clerk — all from one town our old *Nunda*! I hoped that I could benefit by it — but alas the Asst Sect can not make an appointment more than he could fly — and in fact the Secretary himself has to be governed by members of the House or Senate — Each Senator and Member — by a recent arrangement has the appointments divided pro rata among them and no one can interfere — except the President — whose wishes of course are law-

My good friend Senator Vance left here today and the Congress will adjourn next Monday-

You will be a little surprised to know that I have *declined* a promotion to $2000 per year — yet it's true — I found to take such a place — was to accept a situation on a Review Board comprised of a dozen or fifteen men — who have been in the business from 5 to 10 years each and of course posted — and to accept it — would be to make my inexperience glaring — besides making about 200 personal enemies — and concluded that $2000 per year would not pay for all that — I am promised it however in a short time — when I shall have got a little more wise.

I have not been overwhelmed by abilities of the average Office Holder so far — as they are generally appointed for the political influence they happen to possess.

Affectionatly Yours Newton[18]

Washington D.C.
Nov 9th 1882
Dear Father

I returned yesterday from Phila where I had been to vote — By the time I write you will have learned of the overwhelming defeat the Party has sustained everywhere — While it was anticipated — the *extent* of the disaster was a surprise to most every one — and scarcely any of our more prominent men have sufficiently recovered from the shock — to venture an opinion as to what will be the result — It is a blow strait from the shoulder of the people — and it admonishes party leaders to show clear records or prepare to step down and out — That great injustice has been done the President Mr Arthur — I positively know — He has been charged with every rascality that has come to light in the party — with setting up the numerous political tricks — and with being after some devilment — Every time he went to the water closet — Two weeks ago he said to a member of his cabinet — who repeated it to me — That New York would go 50 to 100,000 Democratic — "That he had not and should not interfere — as, if the People wanted Democratic rule they were welcome to it — He could stand it — and they *must* and he thought it would hurt him as little as any one" A great howl was raised over political assessments — I had but just come and had been to a large expense in moving and to pay 36 dollars out of 4 months salary was a stumper — and I let it go till the last month — and then took the advice of those better posted and was told that while there was no compulsion — and no fear of losing my place if I did not pay it — yet those who expected to be promoted — could show their friendship to the party in no way so acceptable — and I felt myself that the people who are directly benefited by Party Supremacy — [sic] by my consideration of fairness ought to contribute to election expenses — Well — acting on my own convictions I borrowed part and raised part myself and paid it — $36 — On top of that I was told that every vote counted and that I ought to go home and vote and did so — about $12 more — I got a five day leave — intending to come to Phil — Friday or Saturday.

You ask if I have been promoted — of course not — or I should not be figuring as I have to — I only get the same as when I came here — but I am hopeful that now elections are over that some changes will occur to benefit me — and possibly you — At least no fair chance shall slip through my hands to do you a good turn — The overwhelming nature of the Elections however makes everything at sea for a while — and no body seems to know whether heads are to come off — where ever they have not been loyal — or not — but I incline to the idea that the President will take it as an indication that the People strongly desire democratic supremacy and he will not fight it — He has two years yet and may be able to reunite the party and come out ahead in 84.

My visit to N.Y. State was with the hope of getting Wadsworth nominated for Governor and had that been done there would have been different results — *you bet* — Write me at once —

Love to Mother — Will write you as soon as I hear from you or before

Affectionatly Newton[19]

During November of 1883, Newton was appointed to Supervisor of Examiners of Pensions in New York City. "It is considered a compliment — although it adds but little to actual pay — the expenses being so large."

Washington D.C.
6/14 "84" Hon H.M. Teller:
Dear Sir;

    Can you not do something towards increasing the pay a little of my friend and protege, N.T. Colby — of the N.Y. branch of the Examiners Dept. His health is poor, his expenses in N.Y. are very great and he informs me that his per diem ceases whenever he takes a little jaunt for his health. He is a very worthy man and I am sure you have found out by this time is a very faithful and efficient officer — Help him if you can-

Very Truly
Z B Vance[20]

    It is known that Newton Colby was still in the employment of the Department of the interior as late as 1893 in New York, and that Zeb Vance still supported him with his endorsements for positions.[6]

    It is not known exactly when Newton left the service of the Department of the Interior.

    The following letter to Newton returns to him a letter of reference similar in nature to the previous endorsement:

Department of the Interior
Washington
December 7, 1895
Mr. Newton T. Colby
2141 Bainbridge St,
Philadelphia, Pa.
Sir:

    The enclosed letter in your behalf, by the late Senator Z.B. Vance, is sent herewith as you may wish to preserve it, instead of allowing it to remain in the files.

Colby, approximately 60 years of age, was also employed by the Department of the Interior Pension Office. Colby family collection.

Very respectfully,
J. W. Holbrooke[21]

The afore mentioned follows:

United States Senate
Washington D.C.
Mch 31th 1893
Hon. Hoke Smith
Secretary Interior Dear Sir:

Col. N.T. Colby is very anxious to retain his position as special Examiner of Pensions located in New York City. He is the gentleman about whom I spoke to you as having been so kind to me while I was here in prison, and if not inconsistent with your ideas I would be much gratified if you would continue him in the service.

Very Respectfully Yours,
Z.B. Vance[22]

CHAPTER 21

Looking Back

Lt. Col. Colby is not known to have been active in veteran organizations such as the GAR or MOLLUS after the war. His old regiment did have at least one reunion; however, it appears that Newton did not attend.

Sept 16, 1885 Elmira, NY: "The 19th annual reunion of the 107th, N.Y. Vols. was ordered to be held on the battle field of Antietam on the twenty-third anniversary of the regiment's first engagement. The comrades assembled at the Erie depot in Elmira, sept. 16th, 1885, and took cars of the N.C.R.R., which had been provided with every care for their comfort by the officials of that road. The following members were present: Gen. A.S. Diven, Gen. N.M. Crane, Lieut. Cols. G.L. Smith, W.F. Fox and A.N. Sill, Major C.J. Fox, Adjutant Hull Fanton, Surgeon P.H. Flood, Captains Bachman, Clawson, Goodrich and Fitch, G.M. Sergt, Bray D. Hall, and the following non-commissioned officers and men; L.W. Babcock, W.A. Bagley, E.H. Riggs, and T.R. Osborne, of Co. A; Jas. W. Williams, of Co. B; Thos. Horner, F. Felie and T.R. Osborne of Co. C; S.R. Reniff, D.B. Vosburgh, E.N. Malette, John Lovell, M.S. Harrington, and J.M. Francis, of Co. D., Benj. J. Tracy, of Co. E., T.G. Smith, Robert Short, and R. Stevens, of Co. F., H. Stevens, S.D. LeGro, Jerry Hall, and F. Pooley, of Co. G. Sylvester Dunham and J.C. Wood, of Co. H, H.S. Goff and D.H. Brownell, of Co. K.

"A delightful ride of eleven hours brought the excursionists to Sharpsburg station, Md. Here they were met by the mayor of the town, and a multitude of citizens and comrades of the local Grand Army post. September 16, 1885. A handful of the veteran survivors are again approaching that historic field. The scene is changed, the youthful faces, the elastic step, the flush of youth no longer appear. They are men, bearded and thoughtful, gray-haired and grizzly, many of them. As night falls, the train arrives at the station of Sharpsburg. A throng of friendly faces meet them. Brightly glowing camp fires illuminate the night. There are friendly cheers and cordial words of welcome. They disembark and stand once more on the border of their first battle field. Conflicting emotions of joy and sadness fill their minds. A comrade asks to have his face turned in the direction of the battle field, a resident complies with his request, and he stands in company with others silently gazing into the gloom that envelops the field. It is no time for words; a troop of thoughts come unbidden to the mind, and they are all of the far-distant past.

"The formal welcome ended, the comrades gather about the camp fires and recite again experiences of that night twenty-three years ago. The murmur of their voices is heard far into the night. No 'tatoo' or 'taps' bid them be quiet. Far down the road leading to the town is heard the drum beats of the welcoming comrades, and at intervals comes echoing back the strains of the old army songs, high above all the rest, comrade Bruce Van Gorder's 'Tiding of Comfort and Joy.' At two o'clock A.M., quiet reigns, and the dreams are all of peace, and no dread of the morrow disturbs them.

"The morning of the 17th dawned warm and cloudless, like that other morning twenty-three years ago. The comrades and visitors were early astir proceeding through town to the National Cemetery, where the party was cordially received by Capt. W.A. Donaldson, the officer in charge. The cemetery occupied the exact centre of Lee's army during the battle. From the tower above the keeper's lodge every part of the field can be seen. The South Mountains, through which our forces debouched into the valley of the Antietam, the hillside where McClellan established his signal station, the house where he made headquarters, the woods to the east of the clearing where Hooker began the day's fighting, the field where the contending armies swept alternately back and forward, the Dunker church, around which surged the fiercest waves of the conflict, to the right the Burnside bridge, and at one's very feet the town itself, with Lee's headquarters in plain view. A fringe of vapor marked the courses of the Antietam, and the Potomac, showing the boundries of the scene of conflict. The national cemetery lay spread out, beautiful with foliage and well kept lawns, with the red, white and blue of the nation's flag floating gracefully in the morning breeze. It was a grand and beautiful panorama of the most interesting field. After all that had taken this view, the comrades separated, proceeding in little groups, some afoot, others in vehicles, to visit the field in detail.

"The old Dunker church was the objective point of many — this reached — a lane was discovered running back toward the position the

107th occupied. Along this lane the comrades hurried to a point that the right wing advanced to on the morning of the battle. The situation was at once recognized. We hurried down the lane to the spot where our companies lay. The next thing done was to locate the position where the regiment lay when ordered to support batteries in the cleared field in front of the woods. The secretary remembered a big stone pile in front company B, the right company, and thought he discovered the same with a clump of trees and bushed around it. Thus the right of the regiment was clearly fixed. One of the men found a stump with a bullit half imbedded in the wood, which was quickly removed and preserved as a momento of the field. Comrade Frost picked up a rusty and battered canteen which had lain undisturbed since the battle. Pieces of bone and parts of a skull were also picked up. A portion of the party now went back a mile to the Line farm, where the regiment bivouacked the night of the 16th, from thence advancing toward the field. The course of the advance on the morning of the 17th was easily traced. It was here that Gen. Mansfield rode out in front and was mortally wounded.

"Having traversed the field pretty completely, the comrades returned to the town and rested from their somewhat fatiguing tramp. A portion of them visited Bloody Lane and Burnside Bridge. Some strolled the cemetery and laid down upon the grass in the shade of the overhanging trees and talked over again the scenes of the battle day. By 9:00 P.M. all were gathered again in the train cars to travel to visit Gettysburg the next day. A telegram of greeting was sent during the day to the 27th Indiana Vols., who were also attached to Gordon's brigade, and who were holding a reunion the same day at Gosport, Ind."[1]

In about 1900 Newton T. Colby and Victoria were living at 92 High St, New Bedford, Mass., with daughter Caroline and son Robert.[2] Newton was a part of Sanford and Kelley's financial organization.

He is known to have worn a special commemorative medal to the 107th N.Y.S. Vols., on May 30, 1903, and may indicate some participation in veteran activities in New Bedford.

General A.S. Williams, Newton's commander at Antietam, wrote in 1862 to his daughters the following about kindness: "I am glad you are doing something for the comfort of the sick and wounded soldiers. You can hardly imagine how these little matters comfort the sick and discomforted; how they are remembered in after years. The smallest attentions- a simple kind word falls often with wonderful influence upon their hearts and will be repeated to you years hence, if you should chance to meet."[3]

These words had already come true with the many references about Newton and his kindness towards Gov. Zeb Vance along with others during

21. Looking Back

Colby, age 70–75. Colby family collection.

the war. The following experience echoes General Williams thoughts in reality.

From *The Evening Standard*—New Bedford, Mass.

July 21, 1903. Old Foes Meet As Friends
Confederate Prisoner and Union Keeper Renew Acquaintance.
Colonel Colby of This City and Dr. Gober of Atlanta Reunited.
Interesting and Romantic Incident in Sanford & Kelley's Office Recently.

"A bit of romance crept into the severely commercial atmosphere of Sanford & Kelley's office a few days ago, and has since furnished enough food for discussion to replace the cotton yarn gossip, which a few days ago held the boards entirely. And daily the incident has been the means of renewing an acquaintance which had been almost forgotten for forty years.

"Colonel Newton T. Colby of this city is one of the regular financial family of the establishment and seldom a day passes without finding the colonel holding down one of the comfortable arm chairs in front of the quotation board. A few days ago a stranger arrived on the scene, and as he became acquainted with the habitues of the place introduced himself as Dr. N.N. Gober of Atlanta, Ga., visiting friends in New Bedford. He noticed the gray old soldier among the rest and was informed that he was Colonel Colby, an honored veteran of the Civil War, with an enviable war record.

"The visitor promptly astonished the man with whom he was talking by declaring that he thought so, and had for several days. Then he approached the colonel and handed out his card, with the fact written on the back that in the Civil War he was captain of company F., 3d Georgia battalion, C.S.A. Extending his hand he greeted Colonel Colby as an old friend, but the colonel failed to recall him till Dr. Gober explained that in '65 he was a prisoner of Colonel Colby in the military prison at Washington. And then the two old soldiers sat down and spun yarns and swapped experiences enough to delight the heart of any one interested in 'soldier' tales.

"It turned out that the two men had been in many battles on the opposing sides, and each related many incidents which were well remembered by the other. Probably the most striking recollection, though, was with regard to the time Dr. Gober was Colonel Colby's prisoner. It seems that during the latter part of the war the colonel was superintendent of military prisons in the District of Columbia, and had under him some 800 southern officers in '65. One of them, though he could not remember the individual, was Dr. Gober, and the doctor related incident after incident which gladdened the heart of his old keeper. Two things in particular the

21. Looking Back

A rubbing of a stone at Hope Landing that reads, "New York Reg, 107, At place rest, Disturb us not! We are at peace with All." Location of stone — Chatham House, Fredericksburg, VA.

Georgian mentioned, that just after the assassination of Lincoln a sergeant and his guard brought in two prisoners who, it was rumored, were the assassins. Immediately the prison was surrounded by a mob of 5,000 howling populace. The prison guard was turned out and a rough scrap ensued at the prison gate. Incidental to it Colonel Colby, in a personal encounter with a Negro, drew his sword and gave the Negro a terrific slash on the head, which narrowly missed killing the man. [from a family account may have taken his ear off] But it ended the mob, and as the Colonel returned inside the gates, his prisoners admiringly applauded his bravery. Dr. Gober also recalled feeling how, when the 800 prisoners were discharged, they all passed out and shook the hand of their late keeper in recognition of the courteous and kind treatment he had accorded them during their incarceration. And now the Confederate was glad to shake the same hand again and repeat his happiness at the acquaintance.

"Ever since that first meeting few days have passed without the two old soldiers spending a while in swapping stories of the old days, and they seldom lack an eager and interested audience."[4]

Dr. Gober, a promising young doctor before the war, was Capt. Newton N. Gober, Co. F., 3 Battalion Georgia Sharp Shooters. Capt. Gober was from Anderson, South Carolina and mustered in March 15, 1862 at Marietta, Ga. and became Captain on June 5, 1863 Wofford's Brigade, Kershaw's Division, Longstreet's First Corps, Army Northern Virginia. He was captured at Harper's Farm/Sailor's Creek, Va. on April 6, 1865 and sent to Johnson's Island April 17, 1865 and to Washington, D.C. April 19, 1865 and released on June 18, 1865.[5] After the war, Dr. Gober returned to his home to take up the threads of life again. Once more he was called by his state, and answering he took part in the famous reconstruction struggle, when Georgia was dominated by the carpet baggers and ruled by former slaves. He was a member of the legislature which finally rid the state of them and was the author of one of the resolutions which expelled them from the state house. Dr. Gober died May 15, 1912 and was buried in Marietta, Ga.[6]

Newton Colby died August 8, 1905, in New Bedford and is believed to be buried in Oakwood cemetery in Nunda, New York, with his first wife, Mary.

Victoria Wood Colby applied for a widow's pension on December 19, 1905, and was living at 43 Foster St., New Bedford, Mass. She died April 24, 1906, in New Bedford and is buried in Nunda with her first husband Capt. John P. Wood.

Chapter Notes

1. The Development of the Militia in Corning

1. National Archives, Washington, D.C., Military records of Ephraim Colby.
2. *Corning Journal*, Corning, New York, April, 1854.
3. *Corning Journal*, August 18, 1854.
4. Uri Mulford, *Pioneer Days and Later Times in Corning and Vicinity, 1789–1920*, p. 201.
5. *Ibid.*, p. 201.
6. *Ibid.*, p. 203.
7. *Ibid.*, p. 204.
8. Colby Collection, held by various descendants of Lt. Col. Newton T. Colby.
9. *Ibid.*
10. Bowman, John S., ed., *The Civil War Almanac* (New York: World Almanac Publications, 1983), p.40.
11. Ida M. Tarbell, *The Life of Abraham Lincoln* (New York: Lincoln History Society, 1895) Vol. II, p. 161.
12. Mulford, p. 214.
13. Bowman, p. 42–47.
14. Colby Collection.
15. *Corning Journal*, April 18, 1861.
16. Tanner, Robert G., *Stonewall in the Valley* (Garden City, N.Y.: Doubleday 1976), p. 30.
17. *Corning Journal*, April 18, 1861.
18. Bowman, p. 52.
19. *Corning Journal*, April 18, 1861.
20. *Ibid.* May 9, 1861.
21. *Ibid.*
22. *Ibid.*
23. *Ibid.*
24. Bowman, p. 53.
25. *Corning Journal*, May 9, 1861.
26. *Ibid.*
27. *Ibid.*
28. Mulford, p. 211.
29. Bowman, p. 54.
30. *Corning Journal*, May 5, 1861.
31. *Ibid.*, May 23, 1861.
32. *Ibid.*, May 30, 1861.

2. The 23rd New York Volunteer Regiment

1. Sterling, Pound, *Camp Fires of the Twenty-Third* (New York: Davis & Kent Printers, 1863), p. vi.
2. Tarbell, vol. III, p. 52–53.
3. Harry Hansen, *The Civil War: A History* (New York: Penguin Books, 1961), p. 59
4. David A. Norris, "War's 'Wonder' Drugs," *America's Civil War*, May 1994, p. 42.
5. Hansen, p. 61.
6. Paul M. Angle, *The Lincoln Reader* (Rutgers University Press, 1947), p. 368.
7. Frederick Phister, *New York in the War of the Rebellion* (Albany: J.B. Lyons Company, State Printers, 1912), vol. III, p. 1994.

8. National Archives, Military records of Newton Colby.
9. Colby Collection.
10. *Corning Journal*, July 11, 1861.
11. Sterling, p. 12.
12. *Ibid.*, p. 14–15.
13. *Ibid.*, p. 13–14.
14. *Corning Journal*, July 11, 1861
15. Sterling, p. 14–25.
16. Colby Collection.
17. Tarbell, vol 3, p. 49.
18. *Corning Journal*, August 25, 1861.
19. Bell I. Wiley. "The Boys of '61," in William C. Davis, ed., *Shadows of the Storm*, Volume 1 of *The Image of War, 1861–1865* (Garden City, N.Y.: Doubleday, 1981), p. 128–131. This excerpt appears with the permisson of the current copyright holder, Primedia, Inc.
20. *Corning Journal*, July 18, 1861.
21. Tarbell, vol. 3, p. 50.
22. Colby Collection.
23. *Corning Journal*, July 18, 1861.
24. Bowman, p. 56.
25. *Corning Journal*, July 18, 1861.
26. Colby Collection.
27. Colby Collection.
28. Mordeci Lewis Collection, Private collection of Lewis Family, Vineland, New Jersey.
29. *Corning Journal*, August 8, 1861.
30. Bowman, p. 61.
31. Colby Collection.
32. Colby Collection.
33. National Archives, military records.
34. Colby Collection.

3. The 23rd New York Regiment at Arlington Heights

1. National Archives, Regimental records.
2. Colby Collection.
3. *Elmira Weekly Advertiser* and *Chemung County Republican*, Elmira, New York, August 24, 1861.
4. *Ibid.*
5. Colby Collection.
6. *Elmira Weekly Advertiser* and *Chemung County Republican*, August 31, 1861.
7. *Ibid.*

8. Colby Collection.
9. *Ibid.*
10. *Corning Journal*, August 27, 1861.
11. *Ibid.*, August 29, 1861.
12. *Elmira Weekly Advertiser* and *Chemung County Republican*, September 7, 1861.

4. Ball's Cross Roads Skirmish

1. *New York Times*, August 30, 1861
2. *Corning Journal*, September 5, 1861.
3. Sterling, p. 22–23.
4. *Elmira Weekly Advertiser* and *Chemung County Republican*, September 14, 1861.
5. *Ibid.*, September 7, 1861.
6. Colby Collection.
7. *Ibid.*, September 12, 1861.

5. Munson's Hill

1. Memorandum, The Historical Commission of the City of Falls Church, January 24, 1997.
2. *Philadelphia Ledger* and *Daily Transcript*, August 30, 1861.
3. Sterling, p. 25.
4. *Elmira Weekly Advertiser* and *Chemung County Republican*, September 14, 1861.
5. *Ibid.*
6. *Ibid.*
7. *Camden Democrat*, Sept. 7, 1861.
8. *Philadelphia Ledger* and *Daily Transcript*, September 4, 1861.
9. *Ibid.*
10. Colby Collection.
11. *Corning Journal*, September 19, 1861.
12. Colby Collection.
13. *Corning Journal*, September 12, 1861.
14. Mulford, p. 212.
15. Colby Collection.
16. *Ibid.*
17. Hansen, p. 172.
18. Sterling, p. 25.
19. Colby Collection.
20. *Ibid.*

6. Upton's Hill

1. Sterling, p. 34.
2. Colby Collection.

3. *Ibid.*
4. *Ibid.*
5. *Ibid.*
6. *Frank Leslie's Illustrated Newspaper*, December 14, 1861.
7. Mulford, p. 213.
8. A.S. Williams Letters, Detroit Public Library.
9. Colby Collection.
10. *Ibid.*
11. *Corning Journal*, January 16, 1862.
12. Colby Collection.
13. *Ibid.*
14. Sterling, p. 31.
15. Colby Collection.
16. *Ibid.*
17. National Archives, Military records and Department of the Interior employment records.
18. Colby Collection.
19. *Ibid.*

7. Bailey's Cross Roads

1. Sterling, p. 32.
2. *Ibid.*
3. *Ibid.*, p. 37.
4. Bowman, p. 90.
5. Colby Collection.
6. Sterling, p. 38.
7. Colby Collection.
8. *Corning Journal*, March 27, 1862.
9. *Ibid.*
10. Colby Collection.
11. Philip Van Doren, *Soldier Life in the Union and Confederate Armies* (Bloomington: Indiana University Press, 1861), p. 182.
12. Colby Collection.
13. *Ibid.*
14. *Corning Journal*, March 27, 1862.
15. *Ibid*, April 3, 1862.
16. Colby Collection.
17. *Ibid.*
18. Bowman, p. 93.
19. National Archives, Regimental records.
20. Sterling, p. 42.
21. Colby Collection.
22. Sterling, p. 44.
23. National Archives, Regimental records.

8. The Occupation of Fredricksburg

1. National Archives, Regimental records.
2. *Corning Journal*, May 8, 1862.
3. *Ibid.*, May 8, 1862.
4. *Ibid.*, November 13, 1862.
5. Colby Collection
6. *Corning Journal*, May 8, 1862.
7. *Philadelphia Ledger* and *Daily Transcript*, May 2, 1862.
8. *Ibid.*, May 6, 1862.
9. Colby Collection.
10. Sterling, p. 44–45.
11. *Ibid.*, p. 46–47.
12. Bowman, p. 97.
13. *Corning Journal*, May 22, 1862.
14. Colby Collection.
15. *Ibid.*
16. *Ibid.*
17. *Ibid.*

9. The 107th New York Volunteer Regiment

1. *Corning Democrat*, July 31, 1862.
2. *Corning Journal*, June 5, 1862.
3. Mulford, p. 215.
4. *Corning Journal*, July 24, 1862
5. *Ibid.*, August 7, 1862.
6. *Ibid.*
7. Mulford, p. 215.
8. National Archives, Military records.
9. *Corning Journal*, August 15, 1862.
10. *Ibid.*, August 21, 1862.
11. National Archives, Regimental records.
12. U.S. Department of the Interior, National Park Service, Antietam Battfield, Sharpsburg, Maryland.
13. Frederick H. Dyer, *A Compendium of the Rebellion* (1903; reprinted, New York: Thomas Yoseloff, 1959), p. 1447.
14. National Archives, Regimental records.
15. Jeffry P. Wert. "General James Longstreet." *Civil War Times*, December 1993, p. 59.
16. National Archives, Regimental records.

17. *Corning Journal*, August 8, 1862.
18. Colby Collection.
19. Wert, p. 60.
20. National Archives, Regimental records.
21. *Ibid.*
22. *Ibid.*
23. Jay Luvass and Harold W. Nelson, *The U.S. Army War College Guide to the Battle of Antietam* (New York: Harper & Row, 1987), p. 5.
24. National Archives, Regimental records.
25. Luvass, p. 6.
26. Capt. Arthur S. Fitch of the 107th NYV, "Revisiting the Scene of Conflict," a transcription by Samuel Calvin Mumma from *The Mail*, Hagerstown, Maryland, September 1885, of an account in the *Sunday Tidings*, of Elmira, New York, October 4, 1885.
27. C & O Canal National Historical Park.
28. Allen Pinkerton, *Spy of the Rebellion* (Lincoln: University of Nebraska Press, 1883), p. 565.
29. National Archives, Regimental records.
30. A.S. Williams Letters.
31. Luvass, p. xii.
32. National Archives, Regimental records.
33. A.S. Williams Letters.
34. National Archives, Regimental records.
35. A.S. Williams Letters.
36. "War of the Rebellion; A Compilation of the Official Records of the Union and Confederate Armies" (Washington, D.C.: U.S. Government Printing Office, 1887), vol. XXV, p. 176.
37. Pinkerton, p. 567.
38. A.S. Williams Letters.
39. *Ibid.*
40. National Archives, Regimental records.
41. National Archives, Regimental records.
42. Colby Collection.

10. The 107th New York Regiment at Antietam

1. *Harper's Weekly*, no. 301, p. 626, October 4, 1862.
2. Luvaas, p. xii.
3. *Corning Journal*, September 25, 1862.
4. Pinkerton, p. 569.
5. John Cannan. *The Antietam Campaign.* New York: Gallery Books, 1990, p. 113.
6. *Corning Journal*, September 25, 1862.
7. Cannan, p. 113.
8. John Michael Priest, *Antietam the Soldier's Battle* (White Mane Publishing Co., 1989), p. 25.
9. Cannan, p. 113.
10. A.S. Williams Letters.
11. Priest, p. 26.
12. A.S. Williams Letters.
13. Fitch.
14. Cannan, p. 113.
15. *Ibid.*, p. 114.
16. *Ibid.*, p. 124.
17. A.S. Williams Letters.
18. Cannan, p. 127.
19. *Ibid.*, p. 148.
20. Priest, p. 71–72.
21. Cannan, p. 127.
22. Priest, p. 72.
23. Cannan, p. 148.
24. Priest, p. 74.
25. Cannan, p. 148.
26. Priest, p. 74.
27. Cannan, p. 128.
28. Priest, p. 75.
29. Cannan, p. 128.
30. Priest, p. 75.
31. Cannan, p. 128.
32. Priest, p. 76.
33. Robert Underwood Johnson and Clarence Clough Buel, eds., *Battles and Leaders of the Civil War*, vol. II, Part 2, Grant-Lee Edition (New York: Century, 1988), p. 641.
34. Stephen W. Sears and James V. Murfin, "History and Tour Guide of the Antietam Battlefield," *Blue & Gray Magazine* 1995, p. 133.
35. Cannan, p. 128.
36. A.S. Williams Letters.
37. Cannan, p. 128.
38. *Ibid.*, p. 137.
39. Priest, p. 93–94.
40. *Ibid.*, p. 101–103.
41. A.S. Williams Letters.
42. Priest, p. 103.
43. A.S. Williams Letters.
44. Robert C. Cheeks, "Blood Poured Like Water," *America's Civil War*, March 1994, p. 56.
45. Cannan, p. 138.
46. A.S. Williams Letters.

47. Colby Collection.
48. *Corning Journal*, September 25, 1862.
49. William F. Fox, *New York at Gettysburg*, vol. II. (Albany: J.B. Lyons Co., Printers, 1900), p. 762.
50. Fitch.
51. National Archives, Regimental records.
52. Bushrod Washington James, *Echoes of Battle* (Philadelphia: Henry T. Coates and Co. 1895), p. 65–70.
53. Offical Records, XIX, p. 474–478.
54. *Ibid.*, p. 482.
55. *Ibid.*, p. 494–498.
56. *Ibid.*, p. 502–503.
57. *Ibid.*, p. 482–483.
58. A.S. Williams Letters.
59. *Corning Journal*, October 16, 1862.
60. Wilmer M. Mumma, *Antietam: The Aftermath*, 1993, p. 37.
61. National Archives, Military records.
62. *Corning Journal*, October 2, 1862.
63. A.S. Williams Letters.
64. *Corning Journal*, September 25, 1862.
65. National Archives, Regimental records.
66. *Corning Journal*, October 23, 1862.
67. A.S. Williams Letters.
68. *Harper's Weekly*, no. 302, October 11, 1862, p. 655.
69. *Corning Journal*, October 2, 1862.
70. A.S. Williams Letters.

11. The 107th New York Regiment at Harper's Ferry

1. A.S. Williams Letters.
2. Colby Collection.
3. *Ibid.*
4. National Archives, Regimental records.
5 Willard M. Wallace, *Soul of the Lion* (Gettysburg, Pa.: Stan Clark Military Books, 1960), p. 43.
6. Colby Collection.
7. *Ibid.*
8. Colby Collection.
9. A.S. Williams Letters.
10. *Corning Journal*, October 23, 1862.
11. Colby Collection.
12. A.S. Williams Letters.
13. *Corning Journal*, November 6, 1862.
14. *Ibid.*, October 30, 1862.

12. Antietam Ford

1. National Archives, Regimental records.
2. Wallace, p. 43–47.
3. National Archives, Regimental records.
4. Frances B. Smith, "My Army Experience," *Chemung Historical Journal* (Elmira, N.Y.), June 1995, p. 4440.
5. Colby Collection.
6. A.S. Williams Letters.
7. Bowman, p. 118.
8. National Archives, Regimental records.
9. Colby Collection.
10. C & O National Park.
11. Smith, p. 4440.
12. Colby Collection.
13. *Corning Journal*, November 13, 1862.
14. *Ibid.*
15. *Ibid.*, November 20, 1862.
16. William Walton, ed., *A Civil War Courtship: The Letters of Edwin Weller from Antietam to Atlanta* (Garden City, N.Y.: Doubleday, 1980), p. 14.
17. National Archives, Regimental records.
18. *Corning Journal*, November 27, 1862.
19. National Archives, Regimental records.
20. Colby Collection.
21. *Corning Journal*, December 11, 1862.
22. Colby Collection.
23. *Ibid.*
24. *Corning Journal*, December 18, 1862.

13. Near Fairfax Station and on to Chancellorsville

1. National Archives, Regimental records.
2. A.S. Williams Letters.
3. National Archives, Regimental records.
4. A.S. Williams Letters.
5. Colby Collection.
6. National Archives, Regimental records.
7. A.S. Williams Letters.
8. National Archives, Regimental records.

9. Colby Collection.
10. National Archives, Military records.
11. *Corning Journal*, January 8, 1863.
12. *Ibid.*
13. *Ibid.*, Januaray 15, 1863.
14. *Ibid.*
15. Colby Collection.
16. National Archives, Regimental records.
17. A.S. Williams Letters.
18. National Archives, Regimental records.
19. A.S. Williams Letters.
20. National Archives, Regimental records.
21. A.S. Williams Letters.
22. *Ibid.*
23. Colby Collection.
24. National Archives, Regimental records.
25. A.S. Williams Letters.
26. National Archives, Regimental records.
27. Colby Collection.
28. Bowman, p. 128.
29. National Archives, Regimental records.
30. *Ibid.*
31. O'Shea, Richard; David Greenspan and Robert Kirk, *Battle Maps of the Civil War* (Tulsa, Okla.: Council Oak Books, 1992).
32. Colby Collection.
33. National Archives, Regimental records.
34. *Ibid.*
35. *Ibid.*
36. *Corning Journal*, February 12, 1863.
37. A.S. Williams Letters.
38. National Archives, Regimental records.
39. A.S. Williams Letters.
40. National Archives, Regimental records.
41. *Corning Journal*, March 12, 1863.
42. A.S. Williams Letters.
43. *Corning Journal*, March 26, 1863.
44. *Ibid.*, May 7, 1863.
45. National Archives, military records.
46. A.S. Williams Letters.
47. *Corning Journal*, April 9, 1863.
48. "Day One at Chancellorsville," Al Hemmingway, *America's Civil War*, March 1996, p. 44.
49. A.S. Williams Letters.
50. *Ibid.*
51. *Corning Journal*, April 9, 1863.
52. *Ibid.*, April 16, 1863.

14. The Chancellorsville Campaign

1. National Archives, Regimental records.
2. A.S. Williams Letters.
3. National Archives, Regimental records.
4. A.S. Williams Letters.
5. Roger Hicks and Frances Schultz, *Battlefields of the Civil War* (Topsfield, Mass.: Salem House Publishers, 1989).
6. A.S. Williams Letters.
7. Official Records, XXXVII, p. 677.
8. Colby Collection.
9. A.S. Williams Letters.
10. Official Records, XXXVII, p. 677.
11. A.S. Williams Letters.
12. Official Records, XXXVII, p. 677.
13. A.S. Williams Letters.
14. O'Shea, p. 85.
15. Official Records, XXXVII, p. 677.
16. A.S. Williams Letters.
17. National Archives, Regimental records.
18. O'Shea, p. 85.
19. A.S. Williams Letters.
20. *Ibid.*
21. *Ibid.*
22. Official Records, XXXVII, p. 677.
23. *Ibid.*, p. 717.
24. Henry Commager, *The Blue and Gray* (New York: Fairfax Press, 1950) p. 252.
25. A.S. Williams Letters.
26. *Ibid.*
27. *Ibid.*
28. Official Records, XXXVII, p. 677.
29. O'Shea, p. 89.
30. Official Records, XXXVII, p. 708.
31. *Ibid.*, p. 717.
32. *Addison Advertiser*, May 20, 1863.
33. Official Records, XXXVII, p. 708.
34. *Ibid.*, p. 720.
35. *Ibid.*, XXXVII, p. 628.
36. A.S. Williams Letters.
37. *Ibid.*
38. *Ibid.*
39. Hansen, p. 306–307.

40. A.S. Williams Letters.
41. Commager, p. 254.
42. O'Shea, p. 87.
43. Hansen, p. 315.
44. Hicks, p. 124.
45. A.S. Williams Letters.
46. Official records, XXXVII, p. 718.
47. O'Shea, p. 87.
48. A.S. Williams Letters.
49. Official Records, XXXVII, p. 718.
50. Hicks, p. 125.
51. Official records, XXXVII, p. 679.
52. A.S. Williams Letters.
53. Official Records, XXXVII, p. 680.
54. Hansen, p. 315.
55. *Addison Advertiser*, May 20, 1863.
56. Hicks, p. 126.
57. *Ibid.*
58. A.S. Williams Letters.
59. Hicks, p. 127.
60. A.S. Williams Letters.
61. *Addison Advertiser*, May 20, 1863.
62. A.S. Williams Letters.
63. *Addison Advertiser*, May 20, 1863.
64. A.S. Williams Letters.
65. *Ibid.*
66. *Addison Advertiser*, May 20, 1863.
67. A.S. Williams Letters.
68. Official Records, XXXVII, p. 681.
69. *Addison Advertiser*, May 20, 1863.
70. Official Records, XXXVII, p. 681.
71. *Ibid.*, p. 177.
72. *Ibid.*, p. 178.
73. *Corning Journal*, May 5, 1863.
74. Hicks, p. 129.
75. National Archives, Regimental records.
76. *Corning Journal*, May 14, 1863.
77. *Ibid.*
78. National Archives, Pension records.
79. Colby Collection.
80. National Archives, Pension records.
81. *Corning Journal*, June 18, 1863.
82. Colby Collection.
83. *Corning Journal*, July 16, 1863.
84. National Archives, military records.

15. The Veteran Reserve Corps

1. Fred Pelka, "Commands," *America's Civil War*, September 1994.
2. Van Doren, p. 49.
3. Pelka, p. 82.
4. Colby Collection.
5. National Archives, military records.
6. Colby Collection.
7. *Ibid.*
8. National Archives, Military records.

16. Camp Morton—Prison at Indianapolis

1. McGrady, p. 43.
2. National Archives, Military records.
3. *Indianapolis Daily Journal*, February 18, 1864.
4. *Ibid.*, February 20, 1864.
5. *Ibid.*, February 22, 1864.
6. *Ibid.*, February 23, 1864.
7. Colby Collection.
8. *Daily Sentinel*, Indianapolis, Indiana, March 1, 1864.
9. *Ibid.*, March 2, 1864.
10. *Ibid.*
11. *Indianapolis Daily Journal*, March 8, 1864.
12. *Ibid.*, March 11, 1864.
13. *State Sentinel*, March 19, 1864.
14. *Indianapolis Daily Journal*, March 21, 1864.
15. National Archives, Military records.
16. Daily Sentinel, March 24, 1864.
17. *Indianapolis Daily Journal*, March 28, 1864.
18. *Ibid.*
19. *Ibid.*
20. Colby Collection.
21. *Ibid.*
22. *Daily Sentinel*, April 20, 1864.
23. *Ibid.*, April 15, 1864.
24. *Ibid.*
25. *Indianapolis Daily Journal*, April 16, 1864.
26. Colby Collection.
27. *Indianapolis Daily Journal*, April 20, 1864.
28. *Ibid.*, April 22, 1864.
29. *Ibid.*, April 23, 1864.
30. *Ibid.*, April 25, 1864.
31. *Ibid.*, May 2, 1864.
32. National Archives, Military records.
33. *Corning Journal*, May 5, 1864.

17. Old Capitol and Carroll Prisons — Washington, D.C.

1. Colby Collection.
2. *Ibid.*
3. *Ibid.*
4. *Ibid.*
5. Eric J. Wittenberg, "Roadblock en Route to Washington," *America's Civil War Magazine*. November 1993, p. 82.
6. Pelka, p. 84.
7. Colby Collection.
8. National Archives, Military records.
9. Official Records, Series II, Vol. II, p. 223.
10. Wilhemus Bogart Bryan, *A History of the National Capitol, Vol. II, 1815–1878* (New York: Macmillan, 1916), p. 481.
11. F.N. Boney, *John Letcher of Virginia: The Story of Virginia's Civil War Governor* (University: University of Alabama Press, 1966), p. 218–219.
12. National Archives, Military records.
13. Col. Newton T. Colby, "The 'Old Capitol' Prison," *Annuals of the Civil War* (New York: Da Capo Press, 1994), p. 502–509.
14. Colby Collection.
15. *Ibid.*
16. *Ibid.*
17. *Ibid.*
18. *Ibid.*
19. Norris, p. 54.
20. Colby Collection.
21. National Archives, Military collection.
22. Colby Collection.
23. Sally Hall, Village Historian, Nunda, New York.
24. Colby Collection.
25. National Archives, Records of Old Capitol and Carroll Prison.
26. Colby Collection.
27. *Ibid.*
28. National Archives, Records of Old Capitol and Carroll Prison.
29. *Ibid.*
30. Colby Collection.
31. National Archives, Records of Old Capitol and Carroll Prison.
32. Colby Collection.
33. *Ibid.*
34. *Ibid.*
35. *Ibid.*
36. *Ibid.*
37. *Ibid.*
38. *Ibid.*
39. National Archives, Records of Old Capitol and Carroll Prison.
40. *Ibid.*

18. The Lincoln Assassination

1. *Philadelphia Ledger and Daily Transcript*, April 15, 1865.
2. Colby Collection.
3. Colby, p. 509–510.

19. Old Capitol Prison — After Lincoln's Death

1. National Archives, Records of Old Capitol and Carroll Prison.
2. *Ibid.*
3. *Ibid.*
4. *Ibid.*
5. Glenn Tucker, *Zeb Vance: Champion for Personal Freedom* (New York: Bobbs-Merrill, 1965), p. 411–429.
6. Boney, p. 217–219.
7. Colby, p. 510–512.
8. Colby Collection.
9. *Ibid.*
10. National Archives, Records of Old Capitol and Carroll Prison.
11. Colby Collection.
12. David Woodbury, "An Iroquois at Appomattox," Ely S. Parker, *Civil War: The Magazine of the Civil War Society*, Vol. X, No. 5, Sept-Oct 1992, p. 19.
13. Z.B. Vance Papers, Private Collections, State Archives, Office of Archives and History, Raleigh, North Carolina. Vol. VIII, 1865, p.c. 15.8, page 964.
14. Colby Collection.
15. *Ibid.*
16. Z.B Vance Papers, N.C. Archives, Vol. VIII, 1865, p.c. 15.8, page 973.
17. Colby Collection.
18. National archives, Military records.
19. Colby Collection.
20. Z.B. Vance Papers, Vol. VIII, 1865, p.c. 15.8, page 1000.
21. *Elmira Advertiser*, Sept. 1865.

22. Z.B. Vance Papers, Vol. VIII, 1865, p.c. 15.8, page 1067.
23. *Ibid*, page 1083.
24. *Ibid*, page 1084.

20. The Postwar Years

1. National Archives, Military records.
2. National Archives, Name reference file microfilm.
3. *Ibid*.
4. *Ibid*.
5. *Ibid*.
6. Z.B. Vance Papers, Vol. IX, 1866–1877, p,c, 19.9, page 1161.
7. *Ibid*.
8. Grace Episcopal Church Records, Haddonfield, New Jersey.
9. National Archives, Pension records.
10. *Ibid*.
11. Colby Collection.
12. *Ibid*.
13. *Ibid*.
14. National Archives, Department of the Interior, Pension Office.
15. Colby Collection.
16. *Ibid*.
17. *Ibid*.
18. *Ibid*.
19. *Ibid*.
20. *Ibid*.
21. National Archives, Department of the Interior, Pension Office.
22. *Ibid*.

21. Looking Back

1. Fitch.
2. Census records, New Bedford, Massachusetts. 1900.
3. A.S. Williams Letters.
4. *The Evening Standard*, New Bedford, Massachusetts, July 21, 1903.
5. National Archives, Military records.
6. *Marietta Journal*, Marietta, Georgia, May 31, 1912.

Bibliography

Angle, Paul M., editor. *The Lincoln Reader*. Piscataway, N.J.: Rutgers University Press, 1947.
Boney, F.N. *John Letcher of Virginia: The Story of Virginia's Civil War Governor*. University: University of Alabama Press, 1966.
Bowman, John S., editor. *The Civil War Almanac*. New York: World Almanac Publications, 1983.
Bryan, Wilhemus Bogart. *A History of the National Capitol, Vol II, 1815–1878*. New York: Macmillan, 1916
Buchanan, Richard S. Private photo collection.
Camden County Deeds Records. City Hall, Camden, New Jersey.
Cannan, John. *The Antietam Campaign*. New York: Gallery Books, 1990.
Cheeks, Robert C. "Blood Poured Like Water." *America's Civil War*. March 1994.
Colby, Col. N.T., "The 'Old Capitol' Prison," as printed in *The Annals of the Civil War*, a collection of articles reprinted from the *Philadelphia Weekly Times*, 1878.
Colby Family Collection of files and newsletters.
Commager, Henry Steele. *The Blue and Gray*. New York: Fairfax Press, 1982.
Corning Democrat, Corning, New York.
Corning Journal, Corning, New York.
Daily Sentinel, Indianapolis, Indiana.
Dyer, Frederick. *Compendium of the War of the Rebellion*, 1903.
Elmira Weekly Advertiser and *Chemung County Republican*, Elmira, New York.
Evening Standard, New Bedford, Massachusetts.
Fitch, Capt. Arthur S. "Revisiting the Scene of Conflict," transcription by Samuel Calvin Mumma from *The Mail*, Hagerstown, Maryland, September 1885, of an account in the *Sunday Tidings*, of Elmira, New York, of October 4, 1885, found in 107th NYV file at U.S. Department of the Interior, National Park Service, Antietam N.B.P.
Fox, William F. *New York at Gettysburg*, 3 vols. Albany: J.B. Lyons and Co., Printers, 1900.
Frank Leslie's Illustrated Newspaper, New York.
Hansen, Harry. *The Civil War: A History*. New York: Penguin Books, 1961.

Hemmingway, Al. "Day One at Chancellorsville." *America's Civil War*, March 1996, p. 44.
Hicks, Roger, and Frances Schultz. *Battlefields of the Civil War*. Topsfield, Mass.: Salem House Publishers, 1989.
Indianapolis Daily Journal, Indianapolis, Indiana.
James, Bushrod Washington. *Echoes of Battle*. Philadelphia: Henry T. Coates and Co., 1895.
Johnson, Robert Underwood, and Clarence Clough Buel, eds. *Battles and Leaders of the Civil War*, vol. II, Part 2, Grant-Lee Edition. New York: Century Company, 1888.
Luvaas, Jay, and Harold W. Nelson. *The U.S. Army War College Guide to the Battle of Antietam*. New York: Harper and Row, 1987.
Marietta Journal, Marietta, Georgia, May 31, 1912.
Mulford, Uri. *Pioneer Days and Later Times in Corning and Vicinity, 1789–1920*.
Mumma, Wilmer. *Antietam: The Aftermath*, 1993.
New Bedford, Mass., 1900 census
New York Times, New York.
Norris, David A. "War's 'Wonder' Drugs," *America's Civil War*, May 1994.
O'Shea, Richard, David Greenspan, and Robert Kirk. *Battle Maps of the Civil War* (American Heritage). Tulsa, Okla.: Council Oak Books, 1992.
Pelka, Fred. "Commands." *America's Civil War*, Sept. 1994.
Philadelphia Ledger and Daily Transcript.
Phister, Frederick. *New York in the War of the Rebellion*. Albany, N.Y.: J.B. Lyon Company, State Printers, 1912, Vol. III.
Pinkerton, Allan. *Spy of the Rebellion*. Lincoln: University of Nebraska Press, 1883.
Priest, John Michael. *Antietam: The Soldier's Battle*. Shippensburg: White Mane Publishing Co., 1989.
Sears, Stephen W., and James Murfin. "History and Tour Guide of the Antietam Battlefield." *Blue & Gray*, 1995.
Smith, Frances B. "My Army Experience." *The Chemung Historical Journal*, vol. 40, No. 4. Elmira, New York, June 1995.
Sterling, Pound. *Camp Fires of the Twenty-Third*. New York: Davies & Kent, Printers, 1863.
Tarbell, Ida M. *The Life of Abraham Lincoln*. New York: Lincoln History Society, 1895.
Tucker, Glenn. *Zeb Vance: Champion for Personal Freedom*. New York: Bobbs-Merrill, 1965.
Vance, Zebulon Baird. Papers of Zebulon Baird Vance, Private Collections, State Archives, Office of Archives and History, Raleigh, North Carolina.
_____. Papers of Zebulon Baird Vance, Southern Historical Collection, #3952, Wilson Library, University of North Carolina at Chapel Hill.
Van Doren, Philip. *Soldier Life in the Union and Confederate Armies*. Bloomington: Indiana University Press, 1961.
Wallace, Willard M. *Soul of the Lion*. Gettysburg, Pa.: Stan Clark Military Books, 1960.
Walton, William, editor. *A Civil War Courtship: The Letters of Edwin Weller from Antietam to Atlanta*. Garden City, N.Y.: Doubleday, 1980.
War of the Rebellion, Official Records of Union and Confederate Armies, Operations in Va., W.Va., Md., and Pa.
Wert, Jeffry D. "General James Longstreet." *Civil War Times Illustrated*, Dec. 1993.

Bibliography

Wiley, Bell I. "The Boys of '61," in William C. Davis, ed., *Shadows of the Storm,* Volume 1 of *The Image of War, 1861–1865* Garden City, N.Y.: Doubleday, 1981.

Williams, Alpeus S. Letters of Alpeus S. Williams. Burton Historical Collection, Detroit Public Library.

Wittenberg, Eric J. "Roadblock en route to Washington." *America's Civil War,* Nov. 1993.

Woodbury, David. "An Iroquois at Appomattox," Ely S. Parker, *Civil War: The Magazine of the Civil War Society*, Vol X, No. 5, Sept.-Oct. 1992.

Index

Acquia Creek 87, 216, 217, 236
Albany, N.Y. 35, 133, 135, 136, 203, 287, 317
Alexandria, Va. 17, 28, 49, 58, 63, 66, 69, 84, 101, 105, 109, 111, 120, 124, 133, 137, 210
Antietam, Md. 142, 143, 147, 148, 149, 156, 160, 161, 165, 166, 167, 171, 179, 185, 188, 192, 193, 194, 195, 196, 197, 201, 202, 204, 205, 206, 208, 209, 210, 222, 332
Arlington, Va. 17, 34, 36, 39, 43, 46, 49, 50, 51, 54, 56, 59, 63, 69, 71, 73, 76, 84
Arthur, Chester 323, 327
Auger, Maj. Gen. 302, 309

Bailey's Cross Roads 67, 84, 101
Baldwin, Lathrop 14, 62, 132, 201, 203, 217, 222
Ball's Cross Roads 56, 58, 59, 63, 64, 66
Baltimore 9, 13, 20, 21, 24, 76, 259, 284, 286, 287, 289, 294, 300
Beauregard, Gen. P.G.T. 50, 71
Best, Capt. Clermont 160, 161, 230
Bristow, Va. 110, 111, 113
Brown (newspaper editor) 50, 101
Brown, F. 174
Brown, Gov. (Ga.) 298, 299
Bronw, Sgt. Johnny 154, 155, 174, 222
Bull Run 33, 63, 87, 104, 106

Cameron, Gen. 7
Camp Morton 246, 249, 250, 251
Carman, Col Ezra A. 139, 164
Catlett Station 112
Centreville, Va. 93, 98, 100, 104, 106
Chamberlain, Lt. Col. 179, 192
Chancellorsville, Va. 224, 225, 226, 227, 228, 229, 230, 232, 234, 235, 236, 321
Chase, Mary 4; *see also* Colby family members
Chase, Salmon P. 28, 260
Chemung County 46, 131, 200, 202, 203
Colby family members 1, 2, 3, 4, 5, 6, 8, 10, 19, 41, 42, 48, 54, 77, 82, 94, 95, 96, 102, 108, 113, 117, 121, 125, 126, 127, 128, 129, 130, 131, 132, 141, 155, 161, 166, 167, 168, 171, 188, 189, 190, 196, 200, 201, 202, 207, 211, 212, 214, 216, 219, 220, 222, 223, 224, 233, 234, 235, 236, 239, 240, 242, 243, 245, 250, 254, 257, 258, 262, 263, 264, 265, 266, 267, 277, 278, 279, 282, 283, 290, 294, 295, 296, 298, 304, 305, 308, 309, 311, 313, 314, 315, 316, 317, 318, 319, 320, 322, 323, 324, 325, 328, 329, 333, 334, 336
Colgrove, Col. Silas 139, 162, 164
Corning, N.Y. 4, 5, 6, 8, 10, 12, 14, 19, 25, 35, 73, 75, 76, 79, 80, 82, 87, 104, 111, 128, 129, 130, 132, 135, 186, 200, 202, 204, 213, 235, 238, 239, 240, 273, 274, 276, 280

Corning Journal 7, 9, 21, 23, 33, 51, 54, 63, 71, 74, 89, 101, 117, 123, 142, 155, 167, 172, 185, 206, 212, 235, 239
Cothran, Capt. 154, 160, 161, 163, 165, 166, 170
Crane, N.M. 14, 52, 54, 57, 59, 63, 64, 72, 93, 99, 101, 110, 132, 135, 207, 210, 212, 219, 221, 226, 237, 240, 330

Dickenson, Bray 7, 177, 221
Dingleday, Capt. William W. 39, 42, 44, 55, 56, 58, 63
Diven, Col. A.S. 18, 23, 27, 30, 33, 129, 165, 169, 176, 180, 185, 187, 188, 195, 197, 198, 200, 202, 203, 205, 209, 210, 213, 215, 217, 219, 222, 228, 229, 233, 235, 236
Dunker Church 147, 148, 149, 151, 152, 153, 156, 168
Dyers Hotel 278, 284, 308, 309

Early, Gen. Jubal 263
Ellsworth, Col. Elmer 17, 18, 28, 29, 30, 31
Elmira, N.Y. 9, 10, 12, 13, 14, 17, 18, 19, 20, 22, 24, 27, 28, 29, 43, 46, 52, 54, 58, 59, 63, 73, 76, 87, 110, 111, 116, 124, 130, 131, 132, 133, 141, 168, 169, 174, 176, 178, 180, 184, 187, 189, 193, 200, 201, 203, 212, 219, 221, 233, 235, 236, 274, 278, 282, 297, 306, 311, 312

Fairfax, Va. 33, 43, 47, 78, 84, 87, 100, 208, 210, 213, 214
Falls Church, Va. 39, 41, 45, 46, 54, 67, 72, 81, 84
Falmouth, Va. 112, 116, 119, 121, 123
Fitch, Cpl. Arthur S. 144, 155
Flood, Dr. P.H. 130, 131, 150, 153, 169, 189, 236, 238
Frederick, Md. 136, 139, 222, 293
Fredericksburg, Va. 112, 113, 115, 116, 117, 118, 119, 120, 121, 123, 125, 126, 127, 133, 208, 209, 214, 225, 226, 229, 232

Gober, Dr. N.N. 334, 336
Gordon, Gen. George H. 138, 139, 145, 146, 147, 148, 149, 150, 151, 157, 158, 159, 160, 161, 165, 166, 170, 187, 192, 203, 207, 208

Greene, George S. 146, 147, 149, 157, 158, 159, 161, 162, 164, 166
Gregg, Maj. W.H. 14, 29, 101, 108

Hagerstown, Md. 143, 151, 157, 173
Hampton, Capt. 160, 161
Harpers Ferry, Va. 9, 155, 175, 176, 177, 195, 214, 262
Hoffman, Col. H.C. 13, 14, 20, 23, 27, 30, 45, 54, 58, 62, 71, 94, 98, 99, 100, 122, 123, 126, 135, 144, 282
Hooker, Gen. Joseph 143, 144, 145, 146, 150, 152, 157, 161, 162, 216, 221, 222, 225, 226, 228, 229, 232, 234
Hope Landing 216, 218, 219, 220, 224, 237
Hunter, Col. 18, 68

Indianapolis 244, 245, 246, 247, 248, 250, 251, 252, 253, 258
Invalid Corps 241, 242, 243, 245, 247, 248, 251, 258

Jackson, Gen. Thomas Jonathan "Stonewall" 142, 152, 232, 233
Johnson 78, 81, 186
Johnson, A. 174
Johnson, Andrew 317, 318
Johnson, Dr. 277
Johnson, Maj. Gen. Edward 298, 300, 304, 307
Johnson, Col. J.S. 248, 249, 262
Johnson, Judge T.A. 62, 112, 117, 128
Jones, Alfred 14
Jones, Ens. 22, 74, 91, 99
Jones, Pvt. J.M. 266
Jones, 2nd Lieut. William H. 10, 41

Knap, Capt. 160, 161

Lamar, Gazeway B. 298, 300, 307
Lee, Gen. Robert E. 9, 37, 40, 51, 136, 141, 226, 232, 234, 261, 305
Lee's Mills 115
Letcher, Gov. John 297, 298, 299, 300, 304, 307, 308
Lincoln, Abraham 6, 9, 13, 17, 18, 23, 27, 28, 86, 138, 142, 179, 222, 260, 262, 273, 289, 291, 292, 293, 294
Lowe, Prof. 56, 68, 69, 74

Madill, Dr. William X. 14, 29, 47, 48
Maine 3, 22, 96, 146, 160, 179, 192
Manassas 30, 32, 33, 81, 93, 98, 100, 101, 104, 105, 106, 107, 108, 111, 142
Mansfield, Maj. Gen. Joseph K.F. 138, 139, 142, 143, 144, 145, 146, 150, 152, 156, 157, 160, 161, 162, 169
Maryland Heights 165, 174, 175, 176, 179, 182, 183, 185, 192
Massachusetts 9, 20, 25, 86, 139, 151, 162, 163, 164, 229, 233
McClellan, Gen. George B. 34, 41, 46, 72, 82, 83, 84, 85, 86, 100, 102, 106, 110, 111, 123, 134, 135, 136, 137, 138, 143, 144, 179, 194, 197
McDowell, Gen. Irvin 18, 30, 34, 57, 62, 66, 81, 83, 85, 86, 87, 89, 91, 93, 96, 98, 100, 116, 119, 127
Meade, Gen. George G. 86, 145, 151, 216, 225, 228, 235
Miles, Capt. 156, 181, 218, 222
Miles, Col. 141, 174

New Bedford, Mass. 334, 335
New Jersey 139, 146, 158, 162, 163, 164, 230, 295, 314, 318, 321, 322
North Carolina 102, 103, 214, 297, 298, 299, 304
Nunda, N.Y. 3, 4, 19, 22, 141, 183, 244, 277, 304

Old Capitol 259, 263, 266, 267, 268, 269, 271, 272, 273, 278, 279, 280, 281, 282, 283, 288, 289, 296, 297, 299, 301, 303, 307, 309, 310, 311, 312
107th N.Y. Volunteer Regiment 128, 130, 131, 136, 137, 138, 141, 142, 144, 145, 146, 147, 148, 149, 150, 151, 152, 153, 155, 157, 161, 162, 163, 164, 165, 166, 167, 168, 169, 171, 172, 173, 174, 175, 177, 179, 153, 155, 157, 161, 162, 163, 164, 165, 166, 167, 168, 169, 171, 172, 173, 174, 175, 177, 179, 182, 183, 185, 188, 189, 190, 191, 192, 193, 194, 195, 197, 200, 201, 202, 204, 205, 206, 207, 208, 210, 211, 212, 213, 215, 216, 218, 219, 220, 221, 222, 224, 225, 226, 227, 228, 229, 231, 234, 235, 236, 239, 240, 301, 312, 332, 335

Patrick, Brig. Gen. M.B. 18, 107, 108, 109, 111, 112, 113, 115, 123, 125, 126, 194
Pinkerton, Maj. Allan 143
Pope, Gen. John 134, 136, 138, 172
Potomac River 18, 25, 29, 33, 46, 56, 75, 83, 85, 90, 100, 134, 136, 138, 157, 161, 172, 175, 183, 192, 194, 195, 197, 201, 208, 216, 217, 263, 290, 293

Rapidan River 225, 226
Rappahannock River 113, 115, 117, 118, 119, 120, 124, 134, 142, 207, 225, 226, 234, 235, 236
Richmond, Va. 62, 87, 96, 101, 109, 110, 111, 113, 119, 120, 123, 134, 209, 226, 240, 260, 283, 310
Rockville, Md. 136, 137, 138, 140, 263
Ruger, Col. Thomas H. 139, 162, 164, 221, 225, 226, 227, 229, 230, 233, 234
Rutter, 2nd Lt. Natheniel E. 59, 133, 141, 153, 155, 178, 181, 187, 203, 209, 230, 233, 235

Saylor, 2nd Lt. Lewis O. 201
Scott 91
Scott, Col. 86, 230
Scott, Capt. H.B. 167, 233
Scott, Gen. Winfield 28, 32, 82
Sedgwick, Gen. John 18, 86, 159, 216
Seward, William H. 18, 28, 133, 135, 136, 291, 293, 301
Sharpsburg 139, 141, 142, 143, 156, 157, 173, 179, 192, 193
60th Regiment N.Y.S.M. 4
Smith, Gen. 85, 86
Smith, Lt. Col. Gabriel L. 129, 131, 192, 197, 201, 205, 210, 212, 217, 330
Smith, Henry P. 185
Smith, Theodore 156
Smith, Pvt. William 266
Southern Tier 14, 17, 18, 20, 25, 29, 50, 59, 123, 128
Stafford Court House, Va. 215, 221, 224, 235, 236, 239
Steuben County, N.Y. 6, 78, 129, 131, 141, 184, 189, 203, 218, 310
Sumner, Gen. Edwin V. 86, 139, 152, 162, 167, 175

Todd, Capt. Luzern 4, 10, 13, 14, 22, 34, 41, 42, 59, 61, 63, 64, 71, 72, 73,

74, 75, 76, 78, 83, 84, 87, 88, 91, 97, 98, 99, 109, 116, 122, 125
Twelfth Corps 136, 138, 157, 161, 165, 224, 225, 226, 232, 233, 234
Twenty-Third New York Regiment 17, 18, 20, 21, 23, 27, 33, 37, 39, 46, 51, 54, 58, 63, 71, 75, 79, 82, 89, 91, 94, 108, 112, 113, 115, 117, 123, 125, 126, 127

Van Valkenburgh, Col. R.B. 4, 23, 109, 133, 184, 193, 198
Vance, Gov. Zebulon B. 297, 298, 299, 300, 304, 307, 308, 310, 312, 313, 314, 315, 318, 322, 325, 326, 328, 329
Veteran Reserve Corps 241, 242, 263, 277, 296, 297, 309, 317, 318
Virginia 15, 17, 22, 28, 32, 33, 35, 53, 66, 71, 72, 81, 85, 86, 117, 124, 125, 138, 140, 161, 197, 202, 215, 224, 236, 270, 291, 297, 299, 300, 304, 314

Wadsworth, Brig. Gen. James 18, 37, 50, 57, 62, 69, 71, 74, 77, 78, 80, 82, 84, 86, 100, 108, 178
Washington, D.C. 6, 7, 9, 17, 18, 21, 22, 23, 25, 29, 30, 32, 33, 34, 40, 43, 51, 63, 66, 67, 68, 70, 74, 75, 77, 78, 85, 87, 92, 96, 106, 107, 111, 124, 125, 127, 133, 134, 137, 138, 139, 155, 172, 176, 178, 180, 185, 188, 200, 203, 204, 205, 210, 213, 215, 217, 220, 226, 238, 239, 242, 243, 245, 253, 255, 256, 257, 258, 259, 260, 261, 262, 263, 266, 272, 273, 274, 275, 277, 278, 279, 282, 283, 284, 285, 287, 288, 290, 291, 292, 294, 296, 300, 301, 302, 303, 304, 306, 307, 308, 309, 310, 311
Williams, Gen. A.S. 136, 137, 138, 139, 143, 144, 145, 151, 152, 157, 160, 161, 162, 163, 165, 167, 171, 172, 174, 175, 188, 194, 209, 210, 220, 221, 222, 224, 225, 226, 228, 229, 232, 233, 234, 235
Wirz, Capt. 301
Wisconson 139, 192, 230

Zouave Cadets 18, 28, 47

www.ingramcontent.com/pod-product-compliance
Ingram Content Group UK Ltd.
Pitfield, Milton Keynes, MK11 3LW, UK
UKHW041922140426
5217IPUK00014B/268